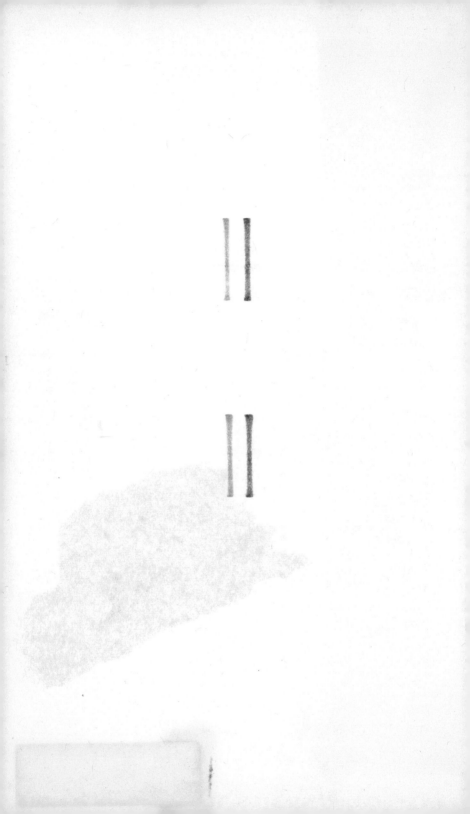

George Sand

Nohant during George Sand's lifetime,
by her son Maurice Sand

RUTH JORDAN

George Sand

A Biographical Portrait

Taplinger Publishing Company

New York

First published in the United States in 1976 by
TAPLINGER PUBLISHING CO., INC.
New York, N.Y. 10003
Copyright © 1976 by Ruth Jordan
All rights reserved
Printed in Great Britain

Library of Congress Catalog Card Number: 76–5190
ISBN 0–8008–3199–3

Acknowledgments

This book owes a debt of gratitude to all past and present *Sandistes* whose works are listed in the bibliography. I am particularly indebted to Professor Georges Lubin, editor of the unrivalled *Correspondance de George Sand*, for his interest and courtesy, and to his publishers, Garnier Frères, for permission to base many of my translations of George Sand's letters on their text. My thanks are also due to the staff of the British Library Reading Room and the Bibliothèque Nationale for their help, to M. J. L. Bourget and Mme Micheline Syed for their kindness, and above all to Mr Lance Thirkell for going over the final draft. Last but not least, *mille merci* to the curators of the Bibliothèque Nationale, the Musée Carnavalet, the Musée historique de la Ville de Paris and the Musée George Sand at La Châtre for providing the requested illustrations and giving their kind permission to reproduce them.

Contents

Contents

Illustrations

ix

Illustrations

George Sand

Introduction

I never asked myself why I wanted this or that.
The inner me always proudly answered: Because
I want it. That said everything.[1]*

George Sand

George Sand (1804–1876) is perhaps best known to those who
have not read any of her novels for her love affair with Chopin
and her short-lived practice of wearing trousers and a top-hat at
a time when such accoutrements were considered unbecoming in
a lady. She is also broadly labelled as the first champion of
women's emancipation in France and even credited with having
lived generations ahead of her time.

Far from having lived generations ahead of her time, she was
very much a child of her age and environment, with a strong mind
of her own. She was certainly no champion of women's emancipation in the sense that Mrs Pankhurst and the Suffragettes were
in Britain. She was essentially a self-centred woman who wanted
to have her own way and who had the courage, as well as the
means, to ignore conventions which interfered with her personal
desires. Complaints about women's inequality had been voiced in
France for some time when *Indiana* burst on the literary scene in
1832. Its impact was in no small degree due to the fact that it said
with eloquence and panache what had hitherto been argued with
more emotion than skill. In *Lélia* and many of her following
novels George Sand popularised the notion that women had a
moral right to move away from a social contract which gave the
husband all the privileges. While airing a personal grievance she
gave readers to understand that her plight was symptomatic of a
social structure.

At the same time she had no political aspirations for herself,
and therefore none for women in general. Moreover, she strongly

* References are given on p. 341.

xiii

disapproved of women who wanted to take an active part in parliamentary life. 'Politics,' she wrote in a letter to the press after the 1848 Revolution, 'are not proper for my sex.'[2] She cherished the notion that equality would be the result of a moral evolution.

In forty-five years of gregarious living she wrote over a hundred novels and plays, not to mention thousands of letters. Not all her novels had a controversial social message; many were romantic love stories with a highly idealised moral. Some of her work was considered outstanding; some, even in her own lifetime, was pronounced mediocre. 'She was a victim of her own facile pen,'[3] wrote her friend the critic Gustave Planche. Indeed she wrote with extraordinary facility. The pages flowed from under her pen with hardly a correction or an erasion and were often sent straight to the publisher. In her younger days she took her facility for granted. In her old age she conceded that it might well have led to shoddiness, but by that time she was no longer seeking the heights. 'I write as others might do the gardening,'[4] she used to say towards the end of her life.

Her research was perfunctory. She often relied on others to fill in the gaps she had left and correct her inconsistencies. 'Concerning the age of majority,' she once wrote to Musset about her novel *André*, 'you might check for me at what age a son can marry without parental consent and then make my three or four references to it agree. I seem to remember that once or twice I gave it as twenty, then later as twenty-five.'[5] When she had completed *Les Maîtres Mosaïstes* she thanked Planche for having put his erudition at her disposal. 'Thanks to him,' she told her friends, 'it will have a veneer of scholarship.'[6]

Perhaps more than most novelists she drew on personal experience as subject matter for her writing. Her heroes were so recognisably modelled on friends and acquaintances that when she once asked her platonic lover Aurélien de Sèze to return her old love letters, he deferentially asked permission to destroy them instead. 'I am afraid,' he said, having read several of her novels, 'that if you read them again some memory of them would escape in the future into one of your books.'[7] Indeed her writing so much reflected the intimate details of her tumultuous existence that a study of her life helps towards a greater enjoyment of her work. There was a consistent correlation between her personal experiences and her books. They were all there, her husband, her friends, her children, her social prophets, her servants, and above all her lovers. 'She is like the Tower of Nesle,' wrote a friend who had watched her career for nearly forty years. 'She devours her lovers but instead of afterwards vomiting them into the Seine she lays them in her novels.'[8]

Professionally she had her ups and downs, but mostly her ups. Few of her contemporaries, if any, had her financial success. Every single one of her books, except *Indiana*, was written on commission. Within ten years of her literary début she was already extensively translated into English as well as into other languages. The sheer volume of her work, quite apart from its intrinsic merit, kept her constantly in the public eye, as did her unconventional thinking and mode of life. In her later years she became a revered old lady, exerting much influence on younger readers not so much by the quality of her writing but by the magnetism of her personality. Even before she died she had become a cult.

Today, when the romanticism of nineteenth-century literature is not readily acceptable to contemporary readers, there are still six or seven George Sand evergreens which come out in new editions in France every few years. Moreover, there is a continuous literary activity round anything which she has ever produced. Scholars study her books, her voluminous correspondence, her minutest scribblings, comparing, analysing, disputing, suggesting new readings of mutilated texts. She seems to inspire as much adulation or hate as if she were still alive. In fact she is very much alive to anyone who has read even part of her vast correspondence, to this day not fully retrieved and published. It is in her letters that she is revealed as a person of many facets, ambitious as well as self-deprecating, generous as well as mean, selfless as well as selfish, idealistic as well as practical.

At various stages during her lifetime and after her death critics tried to classify her genius as either masculine or feminine. Oddly enough it was the literary gossip Arsène Houssaye who rose above such distinctions. 'Genius has no sex,' he wrote of her a few years after she died. 'There are women who write just as there are men who write. George Sand was part of a contemporary Olympus whose fire and flames guided a whole generation.'[9]

This book makes no claim to assess George Sand's literary merit. At the same time it seeks no excuse for inviting contemporary attention to a remarkable life which fresh data have rendered all the more probeworthy. Each generation has its own criteria and pronounces its own judgment. Ours, it is hoped, may well feel that George Sand deserves to be remembered with wonderment and admiration, not least because she was that rare product of nature, an elemental woman.

Chapter 1

Aurore

In November 1804 a young French officer sent his aristocratic mother in the country an eye-witness account of Napoleon's coronation which had just taken place in Paris:

'I saw one, two, three, four, five regiments: hussars, cuirassiers, dragoons, carbineers and mamelukes; one, two, three, four, five, six, seven, eight, nine, ten, eleven, twelve, thirteen, fourteen carriages full of courtiers, drawn by six horses each; a carriage with ten glass windows full of princesses; the Chancellor's carriage and finally the Emperor's, eight cream-coloured horses, beautiful creatures, caparisoned and decked with pompoms as high as the first storey of the houses on either side of the processional route. The ten-window carriage, elegant and well-finished rather than magnificent; its top covered with a sort of cloth representing the eagles of the crown; thirty pages in front and thirty behind. The Emperor inside the carriage on the right, the Empress on the left, Prince Joseph and Prince Louis facing them. The Field-Marshals Moncey, Soult, Murat and Davoust riding on either side of the carriage, their horses covered with dazzling gold cloth, each with two reins of silk and gold, led by two mamelukes on foot, equally magnificently dressed. The Pope's carriage, drawn by eight white horses wearing plumes on their heads. The Pope on the inside seat by himself, two cardinals opposite him. . . .

'Inside Notre Dame, the throne set up near the inner door, made to look like a huge triumphal arch whose Greek style looked out of place against the Gothic architecture of the cathedral. The Empress seated somewhat lower than her consort, the

Princes two steps lower. . . . After Mass the Emperor and Empress descended the throne, followed by the Princes and Princesses. They crossed the cathedral slowly and solemnly until they reached the altar. The Pope put some oil on the forehead and hands of the Emperor and Empress; then Bonaparte rose to his feet, took the crown from the altar, placed it on his head with his own hands and pronounced in a loud voice the oath to keep the rights of the people and maintain their liberty. Then he walked back to the throne and the *Te Deum* was sung. During the return of the procession there were magnificent illuminations, dances, fireworks etc. It was all very beautiful, very impressive, the play well directed, the main parts well acted. Goodbye to the Republic. Neither you nor I, dear mother, will miss it for what it was but for what it should have been, for what it used to be in my childhood dreams. . . .

'Now read on in a low voice:

'My Aurore is wonderfully well. She is beautiful and everybody admires her. I am delighted you take an interest in her.'[1]

The writer of that letter was called Maurice Dupin. His mother was Madame Dupin de Francueil, châtelaine of Nohant and grand-daughter to a king of Poland. The beautiful Aurore mentioned at the end of the letter was Maurice Dupin's five-month-old baby daughter who, twenty-eight years later, changed her name to George Sand. Born in the last year of the Republic and the first of the Empire, she was to see the political pendulum swing backwards and forwards several times during her life, creating that turbulent social climate which encouraged her to defy conventions and seek personal freedom within the national struggle for liberty and equality.

She was born in Paris on 1 July 1804 and baptised the following day Amantine Aurore Lucile, the legitimate daughter, though only just, of Captain Maurice François Dupin and his wife Antoinette Sophie Victoire Delaborde. The father was twenty-six, the mother thirty-one. They had married, by a civil ceremony, less than four weeks before the baby was due.

It was an easy childbirth. At a family party in honour of the forthcoming wedding of Sophie Victoire's sister, Maurice was playing the violin and his pregnant wife dancing the quadrille when she felt the first pangs of labour. Discreetly retiring to a back room, without as much as taking off her pink party dress, she gave birth to a healthy baby girl. It was only when her prolonged absence made her sister follow her into the back room that the news broke out. Maurice, violin in hand, was deeply moved by the sight of the baby although neither he nor his pretty wife for that matter were novices to parenthood. Maurice had a five-year-old illegitimate son by a servant-girl at his mother's château, while Sophie Victoire had a five-year-old daughter by a former lover.

They had married secretly, without notifying Mme Dupin de Francueil who had shown fierce opposition to the project. The old lady considered her son's choice a stain on the family name, choosing to forget that her own illustrious forebears had also entered into questionable liaisons. In fact many of them had been born out of wedlock, as was she.

The family tradition of illegitimacy began a century earlier, when Augustus the Strong, Elector of Saxony and later King of Poland, took the beautiful Swedish Countess Aurora Koenigsmarck for a mistress. The liaison lasted long enough for Aurora to give birth to a son whom Augustus, reputedly the father of three hundred and fifty-four children, allowed to bear his name. That son, Maurice of Saxony, better known as Maurice de Saxe and Field-Marshal in the French army, followed in his father's footsteps. With an amiable opera singer he sired Aurore the Second, to whom a High Court of Justice later accorded the father's proud name.

At eighteen Aurore de Saxe was married to a captain of infantry and some eight or nine months later was left a widow. For the next ten years she led a virtuous and cultured life, meeting the most intellectual people of Paris through her still popular mother. At twenty-nine she accepted the hand of an old family friend, M. Dupin de Francueil, who was wealthy, respectable and sixty-two. They had one son, whom they named Maurice. Ten years later M. Dupin de Francueil died leaving his widow to experience, and escape, the horrors of the Revolution. By her own standards she was hard up; but she had salvaged enough money to buy, in 1793, the country estate of Nohant, in the region of Berry, about a hundred and fifty miles south of Paris, which she ran with the help of a royalist friend, some said a defrocked priest, called Deschartres.

By contrast with her ancestors Aurore the Second, now widowed for the second time, had been strictly virtuous all her life. Aristocratic and gifted like her grandmother Countess Aurora, she brought up her son Maurice to appreciate culture and intellectual freedom. His obvious gift was for music; not only did he play the violin but he also composed pleasant pieces which, as he naïvely informed his mother, were deemed worthy of Haydn, still alive and widely acclaimed. His ambition however was to make a name for himself on the battlefield, like his grandfather the Maréchal de Saxe, after whom he was called. He joined the army and it was in 1800 in Milan, while serving under Napoleon's brother-in-law Murat, that he met the young woman whom he later married.

When he first met Sophie Victoire she was the mistress of an ageing general who could afford to keep her in comfort. The impecunious Maurice, resplendent in his officer's uniform with a yellow plume and a gold-fringed sash, swept the young woman off her feet. He made no secret of his liaison and wrote to his mother about his luck in love. Mme Dupin de Francueil, already saddled with an illegitimate grandson, was prepared to tolerate one mistress as well as another; but when Maurice started talking about marrying his new mistress in order to give his name to another child on the way, the old lady lost her equanimity. Sophie Victoire's father had kept a billiards hall and sold canaries and goldfinches on the streets. His daughter grew up on the pavements, sang, danced and gave her youth and beauty to well-to-do patrons. Mme Dupin de Francueil was appalled when she realised that her son was seriously proposing to give her a guttersnipe for a daughter-in-law.

The marriage was therefore kept a secret until after the birth of the baby, whom the young couple named Aurore, the Third, to placate the grandmother and commemorate the foundress of the line. Far from being placated the great lady drove the hundred and fifty miles from Nohant to Paris, more than ten days' distance in the heavy family coach, in order to have the marriage annulled. She repented when the pretty baby was put in her arms and Sophie Victoire had the satisfaction of undergoing a second marriage ceremony, this time a religious one. The ideas of the Revolution about civil marriages were basically alien to the guttersnipe. Hers had to conform to the demands of the Church.

Once the situation was regularised, Maurice returned to his regiment to play his part in the Napoleonic wars in Europe. Sophie Victoire and the baby were left in Paris. Young Mme Dupin became a model mother. She made frocks, knitted bonnets, cleaned, cooked, sang lullabies and took her baby for walks in the public gardens. For a time she had her eldest, illegitimate, daughter Caroline living with them; then she had her boarded out. She lived entirely for the baby and for the infrequent occasions when Maurice came home on leave.

Napoleon loomed large in the life of the family. Maurice was fighting for him abroad; little Aurore was re-enacting his wars with the children of the suburb. She was about three or four when she caught her first sight of the Emperor. Her mother had taken her for a stroll near the Place de la Madeleine where a military parade was being held. Someone gave the little girl a pickaback. It so happened that Napoleon, who was scrutinising the crowd with his eyes, allowed them to rest on her for a split second, long enough for Sophie Victoire to shout excitedly: 'He has looked at you, this will bring you luck.'[2] Napoleon rewarded mother and child with a smile. Forty years later George Sand could still recall how the smile softened the austere face of the already weary Emperor.

Sophie Victoire was a woman of the people, simple, superstitious, semi-literate. But she had native wit and charm, she was clever with her hands and she was imaginative. Her bedtime stories created for little Aurore a world far beyond that of her immediate surrounding. She had a sweet singing voice and in

later years George Sand recalled with nostalgia a favourite
nursery rhyme her mother used to sing to her:

> Let us go to the barn
> To see the white hen
> Who lays a beautiful silver egg
> For my sweet little child.[3]

Young Mme Dupin missed her husband. On one occasion she
left her baby with relatives in order to rejoin him in Italy; mostly
she had to content herself with his brief visits to Paris. After three
years of infrequent home leaves she began to fret. Maurice had
been writing regularly and tenderly; but instead of swearing
eternal love he assured his wife that she had no reason to fear
infidelity on his part because he was not likely to meet anybody
except men in the foreseeable future. Sophie Victoire sensed
danger. In the spring of 1808, seven months pregnant but spurred
on by jealousy, she decided to join her husband at his headquarters in Madrid. By that time Maurice Dupin was Field-
Marshal Murat's aide-de-camp with the rank of Colonel.

The journey across France and French-occupied Spain was no
mean undertaking. Sophie Victoire and her daughter had to brave
riots, brigands, wolves. On their arrival in Madrid they were
installed in a wing of the palace occupied by Murat and his court.
The three-and-a-half-year-old Aurore was presented and learnt
to address him as *Mon Prince*.[4] To make her presence at military
headquarters less conspicuous, she was made to wear a soldier's
uniform: a jacket trimmed with fur and embroidered with eagles,
tight-fitting breeches, boots, belt and sword. In her maturity
George Sand remembered the uniform chiefly for its discomfort.

Sophie Victoire's baby was born blind. She was convinced that
the Spanish doctor who delivered it wilfully blinded it to avenge
himself on the hated French. By that time Maurice was due for
home leave. His mother agreeably surprised him by inviting him
with his wife and children to spend it with her at Nohant.

The journey back was even more hazardous than the journey
out. The coach drove through burnt villages, hurtled against

corpses strewn on the road, was often stopped by desperate fugitives demanding transport. The horses could not be replaced, the passengers had to go without food, the children were taken ill. The plight of a war-stricken country imprinted itself indelibly on Aurore's mind. On arrival at Nohant the baby died. Sophie Victoire went into hysterics, insisted that he had been buried alive, forced her husband to dig him out in the middle of the night and put him in her lap to nurse. Only thirty-six hours later did she allow herself to part with him and see him re-buried, this time under a tree in the garden. A few days later she was woken from her sleep to be told that her husband was dead, killed in a riding accident. After four years of marriage she found herself dependent on the charity of a mother-in-law who had never approved of her.

But Mme Dupin de Francueil was prepared to tolerate Sophie Victoire for the sake of Aurore, to whom she transferred all the love she could no longer give her dead son. She treated the child like her own, sometimes lapsing into calling her Maurice. She entrusted her education to old Deschartres, Maurice's own tutor, who was still living at Nohant and running the estate. Deschartres was a man of learning with unusual ideas about education, believing in offering the same curriculum to a girl as to a boy. He taught Aurore along the same lines he had taught her father twenty years earlier, making no concession to the convention that a girl was destined to grace a salon rather than hold her own among intellectuals. His influence played an important part in moulding Aurore's character. He taught her botany and the medicinal use of herbs, which she enjoyed; mathematics, which she tolerated; and Latin, which she intensely disliked, as she did Greek. Her resistance to classical languages once drove the exasperated Deschartres to aim a Latin dictionary at her, which she avoided by judicious ducking. The incident was not reported to the grandmother, but it put an end to Aurore's classical education. Deschartres however must have been able to give her a solid grounding, for at seventeen she was reading Tacitus in Latin for pleasure.

Religious instruction did not play much part in her curriculum.

The grandmother and the tutor held progressive ideas and allowed their charge to read about the miracles of Christianity, Judaism and the pagan world without prejudicing her in any direction. The Sunday visit to the rural church was eagerly awaited chiefly because it offered a chance of a ride inside the donkey side-basket, counterbalanced by a playmate on the other side.

On the whole the accent was on rural activities. Aurore associated freely with the peasant children from the cottages outside the château, was allowed to drive pigs with the swineherd, make hay, tend the sheep and climb trees for birds' nests. She was growing up like a peasant-girl. Her speech became uncouth, her bearing ungracious, her face tanned, her hands rough. Mme Dupin de Francueil who, as an admirer of Rousseau, at first encouraged this return to nature, was forced to admit that her grand-daughter was acquiring ways most unsuitable to a future heiress of Nohant. Sophie Victoire on the other hand could see nothing amiss. She approved her daughter's innocent rustic pleasures, tried to instil in her a simple religious faith, passed on some of her own unsophisticated tastes. Old Mme Dupin de Francueil often clashed with the woman she persisted in regarding as the bird-vendor's daughter. The two women were extreme opposites. Young Mme Dupin was uneducated, timid in society, quick-tempered when crossed, unreasonable, passionate; while the elder Mme Dupin was well read, of a philosophical turn of mind, dignified, condescendingly kind. Mother-in-law and daughter-in-law were constantly at loggerheads, with little Aurore unconsciously adding fuel to the fire by an early manifestation of stubbornness, disrespect for formalities and a tendency to day-dreaming. It soon became evident that Nohant was not large enough to hold the two Mmes Dupin. Sophie Victoire decided to return to Paris and leave Aurore to the grandmother, bearing in mind not only her own need to live more unrestrainedly, but her daughter's chances of inheriting Nohant. Her decision was facilitated by Mme Dupin de Francueil's offer of a regular allowance and a standing invitation to come down to Nohant every summer.

In all the family rows between the two women, Aurore unfailingly took her mother's side. Sophie Victoire might well lose her temper with her daughter, scold her and even hit her, but Aurore's love never faltered. A letter she wrote after her mother's departure showed that although far from unhappy, she lived for the summer reunion:

> Nohant, 24 February 1815
> Yes, dear *Maman*, I kiss you, I am waiting for you, I want you and I am dying of impatience to see you here. God, how you worry about me! Set your mind at rest, dear *Maman*, I am very well, I am making the most of the fine weather, I go for walks, run, come and go, play games, eat well, sleep even better and think of you again. Goodbye, dear *Maman*, you must not worry. I kiss you with all my heart.[5]

Aurore was four months short of eleven when she wrote that letter. Her constant companion in those days was her half-brother Hippolyte Chatiron, officially acknowledged but surnamed after the servant-girl who had brought him into the world. Old Mme Dupin de Francueil brought him up like a gentleman. He too was tutored by Deschartres and vainly envied Aurore her dispensation from Latin. Growing up with an illegitimate half-brother, Aurore could not understand why she was forbidden the company of her illegitimate half-sister, born to *Maman* before she met *Papa*. She soon discovered that aristocracy had its own rules. Caroline belonged to the bird-vendor's side, while Hippolyte had the blood of the Maréchal de Saxe and Augustus the Strong running in his veins. Aurore rebelled.

She found more cause for rebellion when Mme Dupin de Francueil, who from time to time took her to spend a few months in Paris, forbade her to see her mother except on Sundays. The old lady had her reasons. Sophie Victoire had been a widow for some time, and was still attractive. She had resumed her former way of life, depending on wealthy protectors to supplement her allowance; or so Mme Dupin de Francueil chose to believe. Back at Nohant the rebellious Aurore made childish plans to run away, share a garret with her mother and help her earn a living with her needlework. To wean her once and for all of her childish dream

Mme Dupin de Francueil told Aurore that her mother was 'a fallen woman'.[6] The child retired to her bedroom pale and tight-lipped to emerge the following morning more determined than ever to prefer her mother to her grandmother. There was nothing for it but to send the unreasonable girl to a convent school in Paris where she would be taught some sense.

❦❦❦❦❦

Chapter 2

Heiress of Nohant

The *Couvent des Anglaises,* which Mme Dupin de Francueil chose for her grand-daughter's education, had been established in Paris in the seventeenth century by English catholics fleeing from Cromwell's protestantism. During her first widowhood and after her mother's death, she took up lodgings there as was the custom among ladies of quality. In 1793–94, already widowed for the second time, she was imprisoned in it by the Republican authorities as a suspect aristocrat. Somehow the *Couvent* survived the Revolution and the anti-clericalism which devastated other religious foundations and after a brief phase as a state prison was allowed to resume its religious and educational activities.

In 1817, when the thirteen-year-old Aurore was accepted as a boarder, the convent school was patronised by daughters of the aristocracy and the well-to-do bourgeoisie. It retained its English character to such an extent that once a girl crossed its threshold, she felt as if she had crossed the Channel, as George Sand later recalled. The nuns were English, Scottish or Irish, as were two-thirds of the girls. The classrooms were hung with portraits of English prelates and princes, and a portrait of Mary Stuart was given pride of place in the Mother Superior's study. At certain times of the day French was forbidden and only English was spoken. English textbooks were used for spiritual edification as well as for language tuition. The nuns were addressed by their English designations, Sister or Mother Superior, and took tea in the afternoon.

It soon became apparent that the grand-daughter brought in by Mme Dupin de Francueil was very different from the other girls at school. Aurore's wide reading had given her an intellectual stimulus far in advance of her contemporaries, yet her informal education had left such gaps in her general knowledge that in spite of her age she was put in the bottom class. Her unconventional religious upbringing caused another setback. When she innocently crossed herself from right to left, as taught by a maid at Nohant, the shocked nuns called her a sinner and a pagan. Instinctively Aurore joined a group of girls who were constantly in disgrace for their naughtiness and brought such dash and inventiveness into their timid acts of indiscipline that she soon became their leader. Once, at midnight, she enticed them out of their cells in search of a skeleton of a man alleged to have been buried alive in the masonry of the convent at some unspecified date in the past. The sisters were distressed. They explained to Aurore in English that her behaviour was '*mischievous*'; and when she persisted in her high-spirited pranks, they branded her a '*madcap*'.

Like the other boarders, Aurore had her own tiny cell. It was so small that the bed filled most of the space between the wall and the window opposite. There was also a harp, a wicker chair and a chest-of-drawers over which she had to hop every time she wanted to reach the door. The ceiling was so low that she could not get out of bed without banging her head against the timber-work. The window looked over rooftops and chimneys, hungry sparrows and courting cats. The faded wallpaper had been scribbled on by previous inmates with proverbs, verses and adolescent reflections, to which she added some of her own. One wall was decorated with a flag, captured with her own hands during one of the frequent battles waged between the French girls and the English girls of the school.

Most girls were allowed to be taken out by their mothers on their afternoons off. Aurore was not. Her grandmother had left specific instructions forbidding Sophie Victoire to take her daughter out without special dispensation. Aurore accepted the ruling without regret. She needed a respite from the constant antagonism between the grandmother whom she had learnt to respect and to like, and the mother whom she still loved with the unquestioning instinct of a child. She was content to immure herself in the convent, for the first time in her life freed from the pull of two conflicting loyalties.

By the end of her first year she began to be bored with the innocent pranks of the naughty clique and fell to brooding. Her active mind, nurtured by Deschartres's unorthodox teaching methods at Nohant, needed a more stimulating outlet. 'You are low-spirited today,' her classmates would say to her in English; or, to one another, still in the prescribed language: 'She is in her low spirits, in her spiritual absences.'[1] She took to frequenting the convent chapel, spent long hours in contemplation and discovered an affinity with St Augustin, the convent's patron, who achieved sainthood after repenting his youthful sins. Her own repentance was a logical conclusion. She shunned all company, whether naughty or recommended, confessed as often as possible, attended communion and eventually informed Mother Superior that she wanted to become a nun. Mother Superior was a sensible Englishwoman who could tell the difference between a true vocation and an adolescent phase. She enlisted the help of the convent confessor, who instructed Aurore to abandon her brooding and serve God with joy.

Again the transformation was uncompromising. Aurore, in her sixteenth year, threw herself body and soul into school life. She accepted the discipline, took part in organised entertainments, excelled in her work. She re-wrote, from memory, Molière's *Le Bourgeois Gentilhomme* which she had read at Nohant, and directed the much-altered play in honour of Mother Superior's birthday. The sisters were so pleased to see her channel her energies into a good cause that they credited her with the sole authorship of the piece. The elder girls admired her artistic direction just as much as two years earlier they had admired her mischievous verve. The younger ones looked up to her as a model of good sense and piety. She enjoyed the privileged position of a head girl. But just as she was beginning to hope that she had overcome Mother Superior's objection to her project of becoming a nun, the well-informed Mme Dupin de Francueil ordered her back to Nohant, this time for good. In the old lady's rational scheme of things there was no more room for a religious infatuation than for an emotional one.

In the spring of 1820 the blue family coach stopped again by the gates of the *Couvent des Anglaises* to collect the girl deposited there three years earlier. To make the unexpected recall more of a homecoming than a fall from grace, Mme Dupin de Francueil had Aurore's old room papered in lilac, with a new rug flung over the bed. The young girl examined with fresh interest the portrait on one of the bedroom walls, representing her ancestress Aurora Koenigsmarck, whose looks she was said to have inherited: thick black hair, dark eyes, voluptuous white breasts. It was spring. The view from the bedroom window contrasted pleasantly with the dreary rooftops she used to see from her convent cell. The trees were in bud, the shrubs were beginning to bloom. The countryside called. But when Aurore rushed out to embrace her childhood peasant friends, they hung back and called her *Mademoiselle*.

A great sadness descended over her. At the convent she used to give vent to her feelings by scribbling on the walls. At home, perhaps in deference to the fresh wallpaper, she scribbled on the window, revealing that remarkable combination of romanticism and practicality which characterised her actions throughout her life. Later she copied the text into a pocket diary, noting meticulously: 'Written at Nohant, upon my window, at setting of sun [*sic*], 1820.' She wrote in English, succumbing to the notion that thoughts expressed in a foreign language gained a quality denied to a mother-tongue:

Go, fading sun! Hide thy pale beams behind the distant trees. Nightly Vesperus is coming to announce the close of day. Evening descends to being melancholy on the landscape. With thy return, beautiful light, Nature will find again mirth and beauty, but joy will never comfort my soul. Thy absence, radiant orb, may not increase the sorrows of my heart: they cannot be softened by thy return.[2]

Joy did comfort her soul. There was a great deal at Nohant to distract a robust young lady who loved the countryside. Her half-brother Hippolyte, twenty-two and an officer in the Hussars, came home on leave and undertook to give her riding lessons. His instruction consisted of one simple rule: mount and hang on. Fortunately Colette, the mare assigned to Aurore, was docile and steady. Rider and beast became inseparable. When Hippolyte returned to his duty, old Deschartres became Aurore's riding companion. It was he who, unorthodox and practical, advised her to put on man's clothes for her riding expeditions, so as not to be hampered by long skirts when jumping over ditches. Aurore took to her masculine outfit with tomboyish enthusiasm. In a letter to a convent friend she described herself astride Colette wearing breeches, a man's shirt and cap, a rifle slung over her shoulder, riding after hares. She was indefatigable. She thought nothing of riding six hours to visit a cave, then ride straight back, partly in drenching rain. Deschartres could not keep up with her. Nor could her young groom André, who was made to ride with her at a furious gallop that left the countryfolk gaping and the aristocratic matrons at their Berry châteaux shaking their heads with disapproval.

With her inexhaustible physical energy Aurore combined an insatiable thirst for intellectual activity. At sixteen she became an avid reader. She read as furiously as she rode. Her grandmother's library was well stocked, and the young girl took in literature, philosophy and poetry, consuming Chateaubriand, Constant, Mably, Montesquieu, Bossuet, Pascal, Montaigne, Locke, Bacon, Shakespeare, Dante, Virgil, Aristotle, Tacitus and Leibnitz. Mme Dupin de Francueil guided and encouraged. She only drew the line at Voltaire, whom she made Aurore promise not to read until she was thirty; a promise that was apparently kept. As the days were full, the girl disciplined herself to sit up at night to work and take notes.

Since her return to Nohant her grandmother had been looking for a suitable husband for Aurore, but candidates were not easy to find, for the girl was not considered a good match. Aurore once overheard a remark which she later contemptuously described as the conventional attitude of old countesses. It suggested that although Mlle Dupin was an heiress, she could not expect to be well married because her mother had a street pedlar for a father and an illegitimate elder daughter to boot. Her only chance, the gossips suggested, was to be accepted by someone who had good reasons of his own to overlook the stain on the family honour: a forty-year-old widower, a fifty-year-old general. A lady friend of Mme Dupin de Francueil, who served as a go-between for one of the likely candidates, described Aurore's assets at the time:

> She is dark, well-made, with a pleasant face. She has wit and much learning, she is musical, sings, plays the harp and piano, paints, dances well, rides and hunts; all with good grace. Her fortune is estimated at between eighteen to twenty thousand *livres* in revenue which she may be in a position to enjoy at any moment.[3]

Aurore herself was not concerned about her matrimonial prospects. Deep down she had not yet given up the idea of becoming a nun; and in the meantime she was enjoying an independence most unusual for a well-born young lady of the time. She continued her riding explorations of the Berry region and made the acquaintance of at least two young men in a most unorthodox way.

One young man saw her surreptitiously picking some dahlias which grew on his parents' property and sent her a quantity of rare bulbs. Another, also on a riding expedition, made way for her on a narrow path. The first was Jules Néraud, son of a respectable Berry family and a budding botanist; the other was Stéphane de Grandsagne, son of an aristocratic Berry house, already a promising scientist and a classical scholar. The friendship with Jules Néraud took some time to mature, but the impact on Stéphane de Grandsagne was immediate. He was charmed to discover a lively mind behind a girl's exterior, which the unconventional riding-habit did not altogether conceal. It was exhilarating to try to satisfy an intellectual curiosity which was all the more attractive for being combined with dark dreamy eyes, a mass of black curls and a complete lack of self-consciousness.

Stéphane de Grandsagne, who was studying to be a doctor, volunteered to teach Aurore biology and presented her with a skeleton which she kept in her bedroom. His frequent calls to Nohant set the old countesses of Berry speculating about the nature of his visits. The gossip reached Sophie Victoire in Paris and Aurore's local priest at La Châtre, who both demanded an explanation. She refused to let public opinion interfere with her freedom.

Her chief companion however was still the elderly Deschartres who, with Mme Dupin de Francueil's approval, continued to teach her subjects more suitable for a young man about to embark on a professional career than for a young lady with expectations of an early marriage. He supervised her botany and biology, taught her how to manage the estate and passed on to her his practical knowledge of medicine. She accompanied him on his visits to the village sick and assisted him with his treatment which sometimes included surgery, learning to overcome her squeamishness at the sight of blood. She also kept up her music for which she had an inherent talent. She sang and played at sight, and although modest about her performance, had both technique and discrimination. Only her spoken English was getting rusty for lack of practice.

Eighteen months of busy independence passed quickly. In 1821 life at Nohant took on a sad, if not altogether unexpected, turn. Mme Dupin de Francueil had a stroke, and although she rallied once or twice, she became partly paralysed and was not always lucid. She could no longer tell the difference between day and night and expected Aurore to be at her beside at any time. Aurore nursed her, read to her, never left her bedroom for a rest, tried to make do with an occasional nap in an armchair. One day Mme Dupin de Francueil summoned a step-grandson, René de Villeneuve, to her bedside and appointed him Aurore's guardian. She lingered on for ten months, dying on Christmas Day of the same year. Deschartres took charge of the funeral arrangements. The old lady was to be buried in her own garden, beside her beloved son Maurice. While the grave was being prepared, Deschartres had an inspiration. He dug out Maurice's skeleton, and when he found that the skull had become detached from the neck, lifted it up to the waiting Aurore for a reverent kiss. Neither regarded the ritual as macabre. It was in keeping with the romantic spirit of the age.

Sophie Victoire came down for the reading of the will. Aurore's feelings for her had undergone an unavoidable change. She was no longer the adoring little child who passionately longed to be reunited with her mother. She was seventeen, independent and critical. During the years she was allowed to see her mother only at intervals, she acquired the tastes of her grandmother, if not the conventional outlook of her milieu. She now knew Sophie Victoire to be an uneducated woman of the people, with her own prejudices and limitations. She had kept up a regular correspondence with her, but the unquestioning love had turned into tolerant affection. Seeing her at Nohant, where Sophie Victoire had not set foot for several years, made Aurore appreciate more acutely the abyss that separated the Dupins from the Delabordes.

Mme Dupin de Francueil had named Aurore her sole heiress, leaving her Nohant and an investment house in Paris. She had also left a legacy to Hippolyte and settled a life pension on Sophie Victoire. But when the latter learnt that she had been denied the guardianship of her daughter she gave vent to a spurt of language the like of which had never been heard in the salon of Nohant. The Villeneuves looked at one another knowingly and made no attempt to conceal their contempt. Aurore was stung to the quick. If her mother was vulgar, her grandmother's relatives were prigs. Impetuously she turned to Sophie Victoire and announced that she would go and live with her in Paris. The Villeneuves washed their hands of any further responsibility. They confirmed Deschartres as steward of Nohant until such time as he should wish to retire.

Life in a Paris apartment cluttered up with nicknacks, ribbons, half made-up bonnets and wigs was very different from the stimulating freedom of Nohant. Aurore realised she had left behind not only her mare, her books and her skeleton, but her independence. The days in Paris were filled with boredom enhanced by futile occupations. Sophie Victoire was arbitrary, emotional, coquettish and restless. There were endless quarrels and reconciliations. Aurore was mature enough to appreciate that at the same time her mother was also honest, generous and without pretensions. She learnt not to judge her for having lived according to a pattern set and abused by the same aristocratic society that outwardly condemned it. She treated her with gentleness and forbearance, but she began to realise that the only way to escape her was through marriage. Unfortunately the candidates favoured by Sophie Victoire were totally unacceptable.

A welcome change from the dull routine came when Sophie Victoire accepted an invitation for herself and daughter to spend a few days with M. and Mme Duplessis, old friends of Maurice Dupin, in their comfortable country house at Melun, near Fontainebleau. Within a few days Sophie Victoire had enough of the country and returned to Paris, but Aurore was allowed to stay on for several months. The Duplessis, who had five young children of their own, treated her like a daughter. Aurore called them mother and father, played with the children and was impressed with her first view of a happy marriage. It was through the Duplessis, while out with the children for a treat at a fashionable Paris café renowned for its ice-cream, that she met Casimir Dudevant.

Casimir was the illegitimate son of Baron Dudevant, a retired colonel who lived with his childless wife on his estate in Gascony. When it became obvious that the baroness was not likely to produce children, the baron recognised Casimir and made him heir to his estate and title. The baroness supported the legitimisation and welcomed the little boy as her own. In due course Casimir was sent to the military academy of Saint-Cyr and graduated with the rank of second-lieutenant. When he met Aurore he was about to resign his commission in the army and take up law. He was a pleasant-looking young man of twenty-six, affable, without airs. He was no intellectual; his tastes ran to hunting and shooting. But he pleased Aurore, when invited down to Melun, by falling in with the childish games she had organised for the younger Duplessis. He was attentive without being amorous. Aurore felt they shared a love for the outdoor life and had little doubt that a student of law could also be made to appreciate the sophisticated joys of reading. She was happy when he asked for her hand in marriage and looked forward to a life she imagined as an everlasting idyll.

Unexpectedly, Sophie Victoire raised objections. Casimir was not good-looking enough to be her son-in-law; his nose was the wrong shape; he was no son of a baron but a former waiter in a Paris café. The Duplessis listened patiently and served as a go-between with the Dudevants. Then Sophie Victoire became practical. She insisted on a marriage contract which would register her daughter's property separately and guarantee her a personal allowance of three thousand francs a year from the revenue of the estate. After many delays and setbacks the wedding took place on 10 September 1822. Aurore was just over eighteen, Casimir twenty-seven. They had decided to make Nohant their home and shortly after the wedding drove down to the château, where the loyal Deschartres had prepared for them Mme Dupin de Francueil's old bedroom with its fourposter shaped like a hearse. In June of the following year, nine and a half months after the wedding, Aurore gave birth to her son Maurice.

Chapter 3

৽৽৵৵৽৵৵৽

Madame Dudevant

In middle age George Sand wrote a revealing letter of advice to her brother Hippolyte, who was about to marry off his daughter:

> See that your son-in-law does not use your daughter brutally on their wedding-night, for a woman with a delicate system may sustain internal injuries which result in difficult childbirth. Men are not sufficiently aware that their pleasure is our martyrdom. Tell him to control his desire and wait until he can gradually bring his wife to understand and respond. Nothing is more terrible than the fright, the pain and the revulsion felt by a poor child who knows nothing and sees herself raped by a brute. We bring them up like saints, then hand them over like fillies.[1]

The letter, written twenty-one years after her own wedding-night, may well have been a retrospective view of Aurore's own experience. Casimir need not have been particularly unkind on that occasion; by the standards of the day he may well have been more considerate than most. But he had not been brought up, as few young men of his age had, to 'control his desire' and wait until he could 'gradually bring his wife to understand and respond'. If, in the course of their married life, he accused Aurore of frigidity, it was no doubt due to his initial failure to handle her in the way she later prescribed for her niece's future husband.

But the fault was not Casimir's alone. The bride's disenchantment on her wedding-night was partly due to her own romantic expectations of it. Aurore had not been brought up like a saint, or like her own idea of one. She had spent a great part of her childhood and adolescence in the country, was used to farmyard animals copulating in full view, familiar with the human anatomy as demonstrated with the aid of a skeleton. She had heard enough about illegitimacy within the family and about her mother's past to know what intercourse meant. But the knowledge was unrelated to reality, grasped through the mind rather than the senses. Her conception of love, and at that time it meant only married love, was fundamentally romantic. The soul had to be captivated by a scintillating intellect or a poetic nature before the flesh could be roused. Casimir was neither scintillating nor poetic; Aurore was bound to be unresponsive. Casimir, in his simplicity, never grasped that fundamental trait in his wife's character; Aurore, at that stage, only dimly. When she did, several years later, it was impractical to admit that it was her own unattainable ideal of sublime love rather than her husband's ordinariness that brought about the breakdown of their marriage.

At eighteen Aurore took to maternity with the same intensity as she had once taken to religion. She, who had never held a needle in her hand, began to sew, embroider, prepare a layette. Casimir could not do enough for her. He sent to Bordeaux for a special brand of sweets, to Paris for songs by Béranger; he pandered to her every whim. Deschartres fussed over her and made her take to bed for six weeks. Shortly before the baby was due the Dudevants moved to Paris and it was there, on 30 June 1823, that Maurice was born. Aurore experienced maternal love at first sight:

> The most beautiful moment of my life was when, after an hour of heavy sleep which followed the terrible pains of labour, I woke up to see this little creature asleep on my pillow. I had dreamed of him so much, and I was so weak, that I was not sure whether I was not still dreaming. I feared that if I moved the vision would vanish as it had done so often before.[2]

She decided to nurse the baby herself, which won her Sophie Victoire's approval. At four months she bragged of his first two teeth; at seven, of four more. By that time the young family had returned to Nohant. Aurore's letters to her mother in Paris were full of little Maurice:

> He is superbly plump and vigorous; he has a healthy colour, a resolute air and a character to match. He still has only six teeth, but he makes full use of them to eat bread, eggs, crisp pastry, meat, everything he can lay his hands on. When his hair is being combed he snaps like a little puppy at the hands which interfere with him.[3]

In the autumn, after their return to Nohant, Deschartres retired and Casimir took over the management of the estate. He cut down trees, re-made paths, got rid of old horses and mangy dogs. Nohant began to look much tidier, but Aurore felt like a stranger. It was no longer the home she had known. Deschartres's departure for Paris added to her feeling of uprootedness. He did not keep in touch and it was only accidentally that she learnt of his death five years later. He had badly invested his life savings and died poor, alone, too proud to call for help.

Aurore was becoming moody. The experience of womanhood, closely followed by pregnancy and motherhood, had not allowed her time to think. Now, for the first time since her marriage, she had a chance to look back and take stock. Married life had not come up to her romantic expectations. Casimir was a tolerable companion, but he could not stir her soul. He hunted with his neighbours, brought them home for food and drink, talked horses, meets, beats and local politics. Aurore found his conversation uninspiring. When, after dinner on their own, she tried to tell him about the essays of Montaigne she had been re-reading, he was bored; when she pushed books of her choice into his hands, he dozed off; when she offered to play the piano, he hurriedly left the room. In a letter to a convent friend Aurore admitted that her husband's tastes were alien to her. What she did not admit, not even to herself, was that she was frustrated. She became ill. Casimir diagnosed her illness as feminine self-indulgence. All the same he was worried and suggested a change of air. They decided to go and stay with their old friends the Duplessis.

At Plessis Aurore went from one extreme to another. She was exuberant, played rough games with the Duplessis children, became a tomboy all over again. Casimir was ashamed of his wife, a mother and a future baroness, behaving like an urchin. Once, when she had repeatedly thrown sand at him and his hosts, some of which landed in M. Duplessis's coffee, he lost his temper and slapped her as he might a naughty child. In 1832 George Sand reproduced the incident with great effect in *Indiana* and in 1836, when she was trying to get a judicial separation from her husband, she claimed that the slap marked the beginning of the estrangement between her and Casimir.

Her letters to him at the time of the incident and after it showed no such estrangement. The plain fact of the matter was that in 1824 she was as fond of her husband as any young wife might be; he was often dull and irritating, but he was after all the man of her choice. When he left her and Maurice at Plessis and returned on his own to Nohant to attend to the estate, she felt lost. He had only been gone two days when she wrote to him:

> 22 June 1824
> I spent all yesterday and today like a soul in anguish, everything is wrong, everything irritates me, I feel as if I am alone in the world and that a hundred years have passed since you left. And there are at least 8 long days to go. Oh my dear, please come back on Sunday, I am so unhappy without you. . . .[4]

She wrote of Maurice, of the day's events at Plessis, of the chilly nights in bed without him, and concluded:

> Goodbye, my angel, my dear love, my good friend, I kiss you, I kiss you a thousand times and hold you tight against my heart. How I am going to kiss you on your return! How impatient I am for that day! I shall not feel alive until you come back. Goodbye, I adore you, you know that, you cannot

have any doubts about that. Love me too, dear angel, think of me and do not forget me, because it will hurt me.[5]

She wrote many more letters in that vein, for Casimir had to make two more trips to Nohant during their stay with the Duplessis. He too disliked the unaccompanied trips and wrote to his wife with longing and love:

Oh my dear sweet little angel, how hard and painful it is to live alone. I have never realised how precious you were to me until I went away two months ago. I shall not want to go away a third time, I have had enough. Let Nohant and the whole countryside perish if I am ever tempted to return here on my own. Oh my good angel, I do not want to offend you, but I fear you do not believe enough in my love for you. I must stop or I shall make a fool of myself, but I love you so much that it should be enough reason to forgive me. My dear little love, my good angel, I adore you. Goodbye.[6]

It was easier to be tender from a distance than to maintain a highly romantic attitude in their day-to-day routine. At home Casimir continued to exasperate his wife by resisting her attempts to further his literary education. She turned away from him and immersed herself in motherhood. In her state of mind it was only natural that her over-preoccupation with the baby should increase her tension rather than disperse it. She was constantly beset by fears and premonitions. One evening, when Casimir and she were dining with friends at nearby La Châtre, Aurore had a sudden vision of Nohant on fire and the baby being burnt to death. Without saying a word to her husband she made her excuses, mounted her horse and galloped the three miles back to Nohant to find it as quiet and peaceful as she had left it. Yet the vision was so vivid in her imagination that for a long time she refused to believe the evidence of her eyes.

It was a state of mind that time did not cure. Maurice was already a sturdy boy of three-and-a-half when Casimir walked into a room where she was talking to a woman-friend and sombrely said: 'He is dead.' It never occurred to Aurore that Casimir was referring to his father, Baron Dudevant, who had been ailing for some time. She could only think that her child had died and crumbled down in a swoon. Fortunately the friend realised the misunderstanding and revived her by shouting that it was only the old baron who was dead. Aurore could not suppress what she later described as a 'wild manifestation of joy'.[7] She never recorded what Casimir's reaction was to the way she received the news of his father's death.

As the years went by her maternal anxiety developed into possessiveness. She entwined herself round Maurice and had the satisfaction of seeing him grow up docile and adoring. She encouraged his emotional dependence and whenever she was away exhorted him in her letters to love her as much as she loved him.

In the spring of 1825 Casimir suggested a family holiday in the Pyrenees, together with little Maurice and his nurse. The party first stopped in Bordeaux, where Casimir had numerous relatives, then went on to Cauterets to take the waters. It was at Cauterets that Aurore fell in love with Aurélien de Sèze.

Aurélien was a promising young barrister of twenty-six who came from a distinguished Bordeaux family. He was a man of culture and fretted about the evils of the world; he was 'tormented by things divine',[8] to use George Sand's own definition of people whose moral and intellectual searching appealed to her. Aurélien was engaged to be married and when his fiancée's parents took her to Cauterets, he took time off to join them.

The company at Cauterets consisted of the usual assortment to be found at a fashionable resort. There were the elderly countesses discussing their ailments, the bourgeois mothers keeping an eye on their marriageable daughters, the docile husbands escorting wives and aunts to their various engagements. Aurore was annoyed to see her own husband pursuing pleasures she had no taste for. He left her bedside at two o'clock in the morning to hunt chamois and shoot eagles, returning late at night only to start again a few hours later. Sometimes he did not return at all.

She was bored and not a little hurt. In her diary – she had been keeping a diary, irregularly, ever since her convent days – she wrote:

> In one's dream of perfect love the husband does not continually invent compelling reasons to be away. . . . An absence passionately sought by one spouse is an object lesson in humility for the other. A beautiful lesson no doubt, but rather chilling.[9]

And chilled she was. She was left to pass the days with old convent friends and Bordeaux acquaintances who had come to Cauterets with their parents. But the girls were conventional, unadventurous and mostly concerned with their prospects of marriage. Aurore, who had brought along not only a nurse for Maurice but a groom for the horses, organised riding expeditions which her friends were invited to join. She and Aurélien rode together, admired the beauty of the Pyrenees, talked endlessly and discovered that they shared the same lofty tastes and ideas. Aurore was exhilarated. For the first time since her adolescent friendship with Stéphane de Grandsange she met her intellectual match in an attractive and attentive young man. Aurélien was the embodiment of her romantic ideal, while for him she represented something unique in his experience of young womanhood: physical charm heightened by a forceful personality. In comparison his fiancée looked insipid and dull. It was not long before he declared his love.

Aurore reacted in accordance with the code of honour she had been brought up to believe in. She reminded Aurélien that she was a married woman and sent him back to his neglected fiancée. Once he went away her torment started. She had to admit to herself that she no longer loved her husband. In her diary she wrote:

> The supreme object of love is marriage. When there is no love, or no love left, only sacrifice remains. . . . Sacrifice has its own compensations which the average person may well appreciate. It gains the approval of society, offers the mild pleasures of a

sensible daily routine, gives some peace and affection without exhilaration; sometimes money, trinkets, clothes, luxuries, what have you – a thousand little things which help you forget that you are deprived of happiness.[10]

That was as far as she could go at that stage without violating her own notions of honesty. Aurore's unusual upbringing at Nohant had made her indifferent to public opinion; her only guide was her conscience. And her conscience told her that although she was in love with Aurélien, there was no question of deceiving her husband. Deceit would debase the love it was meant to serve. The only honourable course open to her was renunciation.

That was precisely what she could not, and would not, bring herself to accept. When Casimir took her to spend the rest of the summer at his father's château at Guillery, in Gascony, Aurore established a clandestine correspondence with Aurélien; and when she returned with her husband to Bordeaux, she invited Aurélien to call on them at their hotel. Aurélien arrived full of loving anticipation; Aurore received him with a sense of guilt. As soon as Casimir left the room she informed Aurélien that they would have to give one another up. She was so overwhelmed with her own sacrifice that Aurélien had to support her in his arms. At that moment Casimir returned. Aurore threw herself at his feet and asked for his forgiveness. There was no more question of a voluntary renunciation but of an imposed separation. The conflict took on a different complexion.

She spent the rest of that day pouring out her heart to Zoé Leroy, a young girl from Bordeaux with whom she had struck up a friendship at Cauterets, and who became a confidante and a go-between. With her aid Aurore contrived to meet Aurélien again and offered him spiritual friendship instead of adulterous love. Aurélien, another romantic with a high sense of honour, accepted with enthusiasm. They were both intoxicated with the nobility of their sacrifice and visualised long years of sublime spiritual communion. But Casimir was not aware of their understanding. He took his wife and son back to Guillery, then returned alone to Nohant to see to the estate. He was disturbed, but not mistrustful. The correspondence between him and his wife remained affectionate; somewhat strained and apprehensive on his part, jolly and solicitous on hers. At the same time Aurore continued her correspondence with Aurélien, and she also kept a sentimental diary, which she later sent to him so that he should know and appreciate her innermost feelings.

By the end of the autumn she had come to terms with herself. She had undergone an emotional conflict from which she emerged largely as the world was destined to know her in her years of fame: a woman who could justify to herself any of her actions which gave her what she craved for at the moment; who could be eloquent, persuasive, persistent, casuistic and passionate when she wanted to get her own way; who, without ever being consciously dishonest, could mould her conscience to suit her desire.

Her desire at that moment was to keep her love without tarnishing the chastity of her marriage. She was no longer in doubt about the propriety of the course she was proposing to take. In November 1825 she sent Casimir a long letter which she called her confession. She analysed her feelings for him ever since their first meeting in the ice-cream café, described the pure nature of her love for Aurélien, and suggested that a wife's spiritual friendship with another man was not only tolerable, but something a husband could honourably share for his own enjoyment of the finer things of life. She wrote with fire in her pen, pleading with her husband to grant her the rarefied love he could never inspire himself:

Casimir, my friend, my indulgent judge, at this point in my confession please cease to be my master, be my father, let me open my heart to you and shed my tears and my repentance on your shoulder. Let us forget vain prejudices, false principles of honour which turn a husband into a detestable tyrant. Your indulgence, your magnanimous goodness of heart, will make me repent my error more than any threats of revenge. It is when you show yourself big and generous as you always have been that you reaffirm your rights over my heart.[11]

To reassure her husband of her blameless intentions she told him of the pact she had made with Aurélien:

We agreed to renounce forthwith, and without relapse, any expression of passionate love. Not only would we never seek to be alone with one another, but we would deliberately avoid any such opportunities that might arise. In any case we would not need to seek one another out as we would have no secrets to tell one another. Never again would Aurélien allow himself the slightest touch; we would never write to one another. We would not become strangers or indifferent to each other – that will never be possible – but we would be such good friends, so pure, so disinterested, that you should be able to see everything we do, follow our footsteps, listen to all our conversations without feeling that your presence is superfluous or embarrassing. On the contrary, we would welcome it and would always want you to take part in our amusements and discussions.[12]

The letter ran to more than twelve thousand words, at the end of which Aurore set out the conditions which she had worked out for the success of the tripartite existence she envisaged for the future. There were eight of them, clearly set out like items in a legal document. Roughly speaking, they fell into two headings: those concerning her future relationship with Aurélien, and those outlining the new pattern of her life with Casimir. Under the first she undertook not to write to Aurélien more than once a month and submit her letters to Casimir for inspection; and not to visit Bordeaux, where she would be able to meet Aurélien socially, unless escorted by Casimir, in his own good time. Under the second heading she instructed her husband, in case he decided they should spend the winter in Paris, to take up a foreign language and read to her from select books while she would be painting; or, in case he decided they would live permanently at Nohant, to study her favourite authors available in her grandmother's library, report regularly on his progress and discuss ideas emanating from the reading. In return she promised not to play the piano unless she was sure that Casimir was out of ear-shot. It was the very expensive piano that he had bought her, at her own repeated request, after Maurice's birth.

Aurore felt that she was being scrupulously fair, but Casimir was out of his depth. He was proud when he heard Bordeaux friends praise his wife for her brilliance and erudition, but the more she was praised, the more he became conscious of his own inadequacy. He was torn between a sincere desire to give her what she lacked and the fear of being ridiculed. He felt responsible for her. Had she not put herself entirely in his hands when she wrote: 'Remember, my dear, that if you refuse my request, I shall abide by your decision, but all happiness will go out of my life for ever'?[13] When he consulted Hippolyte, the latter told him not to be a fool and put his wife in her place. Instead, Casimir wrote to Aurore about his chat with her brother and added:

. . . my wounds have reopened, my eyes fill with tears. To-morrow I shall visit the graves of your father and grandmother, it will comfort me. They are in Heaven, they have the reward of the just, it is given to them to see into people's hearts. I shall swear on their grave to make you happy. A secret voice tells me I shall find peace there. Goodbye, my good angel, my dear love. I do love you, I adore you.[14]

After which he valiantly attacked Pascal's *Pensées* and informed Aurore that he found them elevating. Aurore, for her part, wrote a scathing, two-thousand-five-hundred-word-long letter to her brother, telling him off for having criticised her to her husband.

The year 1826 began auspiciously. Aurore had her husband's permission to sublimate extra-marital love into friendship and was thrilled with the prospect of an everlasting spiritual communion. There were frequent communications between Nohant and Bordeaux, a pleasing exchange of ideas and presents. Aurore crocheted a purse, embroidered a pair of braces; Aurélien sent back a basque beret, a book, some chocolate for Maurice. In his letters he sometimes called Aurore *Madame et chère amie*, sometimes, a little less formally, *Ma chère amie*. For Aurore he was the 'absent being'[15] that kept her company day and night. Aurélien often concluded by sending his regards to Casimir; and Casimir sometimes obliged by taking his wife's replies to Bordeaux, where he went, as yet, without her. The letters contained lengthy expositions on books, education, politics. Aurore wrote frequently, far exceeding her self-imposed ration of a letter a month, charmed with the chance of expressing her thoughts to a kindred spirit; Aurélien, immersed in his legal career and inhibited by the need to control his feelings, less so. There followed reproaches and counter-reproaches. The spiritual love, which was not allowed to call itself by any other name than friendship, began to languish. The friends' first reunion, sanctioned by Casimir only after a long separation, was not what they had visualised. Reality had taken its toll of romance. At Nohant Aurore renewed contacts with childhood playmates who had grown up into fine young men and gave free rein to her natural coquetry; while Aurélien began to look for pleasures that were not forbidden to him according to the terms of the friendship pact, or so George Sand later suggested in her autobiography.

In September 1828, not having seen Aurore for a long time, Aurélien arrived unexpectedly at Nohant and was flabbergasted to learn that his soul-mate was expecting a baby any day. He stayed long enough to congratulate the Dudevants on the birth of their daughter Solange, then returned to Bordeaux in a state of agitation. Perhaps he had overheard some disturbing rumours about Solange's paternity. The correspondence stopped abruptly, then picked up for a while only to die a natural death, without explanations or recriminations.

Several years passed in silence. In 1833, when Aurore had already made a name for herself as George Sand, she heard that Aurélien de Sèze had got married. She immediately wrote to congratulate him, to which he replied:

1 December 1833

For some time past, my dear George, I have been meaning to inform you of the event which chance had brought to your notice. I do not know what a multitude of conflicting emotions prevented me from doing so every time I picked up my pen. It would take too long and be more than useless to tell you what a series of misfortunes had led to a point in my life when all my past career, whatever it was, came to pieces, never to be put together again. These misfortunes cannot be told, only felt. He who was Aurélien thanks you from the bottom of his heart for the good wishes you expressed, for he knows you are sincere. Oh how I wish your own happiness would be the reward for the kind wishes you sent me; but we both know what that word means. . . . Goodbye. My heart will carry the memory of you until it is extinguished.[16]

There was no further communication until 1836, when Aurore decided to obtain a judicial separation from her husband and was advised to base her claim on his proven infidelities as opposed to her own chastity. She then wrote to Aurélien and asked him to send her back the innocent diary of her youth. Zoé Leroy, her one-time confidante, was also contacted after several years' silence. There followed a spate of letters between confidante and Aurore, confidante and friend, friend and Aurore. Aurélien was prevailed upon to forward the diary, excerpts from which were in fact read out in court. He was well aware by then, like all George Sand's acquaintances, that she had had several love affairs since she had written that diary, last but not least with the lawyer who was representing her case against her husband. But the realities of life did not turn him into a cynic. Deep down he was convinced that none of his successors was loved as purely and sublimely as he had been.

Towards the end of 1836, when still involved in the three-cornered correspondence concerning the forwarding of the diary, he wrote to her:

I have perhaps committed an indiscretion tonight when I opened a letter not addressed to me. I could not help glancing through it before putting it back into the envelope, not sure whether I was allowed to read it or not. It always seems to me that this handwriting is for me. May you be blessed, a thousand times blessed, for having written it. You have kept an ever-lasting friendship for me. I knew it. In my heart of hearts I was sure of it, but I needed to see it written before I dared say it to myself. Yes, may you be blessed a thousand times, you and all those who love you now. God, you have done me much good when you wrote that your friendship for me is everlasting. Oh I know this is so. Farewell, farewell.[17]

That was his last letter to her. In spite of his setbacks he lived to achieve a distinguished career and had nine children. Aurore, or George Sand as she was by then, never wrote to him either after 1836. He had gone right out of her life.

Chapter 4

A chance to make a living

In her middle-age George Sand claimed that for six whole years she lived with an invisible Aurélien always at her side. That was a deliberate misrepresentation. With all her romantic puritanism the young Aurore was too earthy to find contentment in a relationship that had condemned itself to extinction by the very terms of its acceptance. As the letters languished life made fresh claims.

She and Casimir tried to have more people around them. Friends and their families came to stay. The young châtelaine took to visiting the village sick, looked after the welfare of the servants, shared in the management of the estate and once, when her husband was away on business, was responsible for the entire harvest. She began to show the practical side of her nature and developed the knack of getting people to run errands for her. Casimir, on a trip to Limoges, was instructed to bring back a quantity of hand-basins and chamber-pots for the guest-rooms at Nohant. On another occasion he was asked to bring back a small canary – male, non-crested and a good singer – as her old one had been eaten. A family friend living in Paris was asked to buy and send a hat, a fur hood, some sheet music, a length of flesh-coloured silk, an ell of black material for an apron, three or four boxes of tooth-powder. He was also asked to subscribe in her name to a fashion magazine. Once he was instructed to collect a guitar which had been sent to Paris for repair and pass it on to Aurélien who would be calling on him and arranging to have it dispatched from Bordeaux to Nohant. She developed an unerring instinct for singling out the right person for the right job. Her letters in those days were lavish with expressions of thanks, followed by renewed errands with detailed specifications.

When old Baron Dudevant died in 1826 at Guillery, Casimir came into the title though not into the estate, which the widow was entitled to hold on to until her death. The following winter Casimir and Aurore, now Baron and Baroness Dudevant, threw themselves into public life. Casimir had been taking an active interest in politics and in 1827 canvassed for a local republican candidate to the Paris Chamber of Deputies. To make his services more readily available he rented a house at nearby La Châtre, where *Madame la Baronne* gave dinners, receptions and balls for potential supporters. In no time she became the centre of attraction. Her zest for life was such that nobody who met her could help being swept by it.

Her new friends were mostly childhood playmates. As a little girl Aurore had been taken to neighbouring châteaux to play with the children of the Duvernets, the Fleurys, the Papets. These children, mostly boys, were younger than her and on her return from convent were away at their boarding-schools. Now some of them were back, young strapping lads, whom Casimir first viewed with mistrust, then with tolerance, as they shared his own republican views. Aurore was delighted to see the change in them. Little Alphonse Fleury had grown into a giant of a man with a beard to match; fair-haired Charles Duvernet had become a dreamer with a melancholy disposition; and Jules Néraud, encountered during adolescence, had been to Madagascar and returned with an explorer's aura. These three were joined by Alexis Dutheil, a lawyer whose pock-marked face was redeemed by his brilliant conversation.

The young men, two of them already married, formed with Aurore a mad, carefree gang. Late at night, perhaps after a serious political meeting at the Dudevants' rented house, they would burst into the moonlit town, chase one another noisily along the quiet streets, gate-crash a labourers' dance. The men were exhilarated by *Madame la Baronne*'s unconventional ways. They found irresistible the combination of an insatiable thirst for learning with a tomboyish spirit of adventure. They vied with one another in teaching her history, botany, mineralogy, and from masters turned into their pupil's captives.

After the successful outcome of their canvassing at La Châtre the Dudevants returned to Nohant, but Aurore kept up her innocent escapades with the help of her brother Hippolyte. Hippolyte had used his share of Mme Dupin de Francueil's legacy to leave the army and marry a Villeneuve relative. He got on well with Casimir, with whom he shared a love for the bottle, and accepted his invitation to live permanently at Nohant. While Mme Chatiron and Baron Dudevant were fast asleep in their respective beds, brother and sister would mount their horses and gallop to La Châtre to sing loudly under Dutheil's windows. Sometimes Aurore would ride out at the crack of dawn to collect plants and insects with Jules Néraud. Mmes Dutheil and Néraud resented her magnetism, and the latter went as far as to accuse her of hypocrisy, of which Aurore was innocent, and coquetry, of which she had more than her fair share. She enjoyed her hold over her companions and consciously sought to strengthen it. To her husband, when he was away, she wrote of her conquests with guileless astonishment. She was intoxicated with her power, remaining emotionally untouched.

But a high-spirited young woman, no longer in love with her husband and obediently separated from her romantic idol, could not long remain in an emotional vacuum. In the autumn of 1826 fate brought back into her life Stéphane Ajasson de Grandsagne, whose gift of a skeleton and frequent visits to Nohant a few years earlier had given rise to agitated gossip. Since those early days of adolescent courtship he had been living in Paris, only occasionally coming down to Berry to see his parents, the Count and Countess de Grandsagne, and his nine brothers and sisters.

At twenty-four, only two years older than Aurore, he was already beginning to lose his youthful looks. He was thin and bent, with hollow cheeks, febrile eyes and an ominous cough. In him the future George Sand met for the first time a combination which was destined to attract her all her life: an intellect she could look up to in a body that needed nursing like a child. 'A woman's love is usually very maternal,' she was to write many years later.

'This sentiment has governed my life more than I would have wished it to.'[1]

But to Stéphane de Grandsagne a young woman's maternal love could only mean interference with personal freedom. He wanted to go his own way and was not prepared to allow anybody, not even the seductive Aurore, to tell him what was good for him. After the autumn visit he returned to Paris to pursue his academic career and his bouts of drinking, refusing to mind his health or his finances. Aurore found him utterly unmanageable. When she offered solicitous advice about his health he took no notice; when she reproved him for his extravagance he became ungracious or ignored her letters. The more he resisted the more she wanted to save him. Distance put her at a disadvantage. She therefore tried to reach him through her brother who from time to time went up to Paris to stay in the house his wife had brought him as a dowry. A letter of Aurore's to Hippolyte, disguised as an ordinary neighbourly concern, ill concealed the hurt caused by Stéphane's refusal to be reformed:

Nohant, April 1827

What you tell me of Stény makes me very sad; he will neither look after his health and his affairs nor will he spare himself and his purse. What is worse, he loses his temper when he is offered good advice, treats his real friends like doctors and answers back in a way that silences them. I have known all this even before you told me and I too have been fed a lot of false excuses. I have never taken offence because I know this is the way he is, and being his friend I see no reason to withdraw my friendship in spite of his faults, particularly now that he is on the way down. . . .

I would like to be able to stop being concerned about him, because it hurts me to see him go to his ruin with his eyes deliberately shut. But I must love my friends to the very end, whatever they do, and I will not withdraw a friendship once given. I can foresee that with all his talents St. will never get anywhere. I have known it for a long time. . . . Sten will always be dear to me, however unfortunate he is. He is in a bad way, and the more he is the less people will care; this is how it is in this world. But I at least will always try to soothe his unhappiness as much as I can. I shall always be there when all his other friends will have turned their backs on him. Even if he sinks lower than his brother I shall still love him out of compassion if no longer out of respect.[2]

Some months later Stéphane came down again to Berry to see his family and accepted an invitation to spend a few days at Nohant. Casimir was away. On his return Aurore informed him that she was unwell and hastily left for Paris, where Stéphane had preceded her, to consult some eminent physicians. They found nothing wrong with her. All the same she stayed on and wrote to her husband that she had been seeing a great deal of her mother and had accidentally run into Stéphane and his brother Jules. After a two-week stay she returned to Nohant.

In the absence of any documentary evidence, what actually took place during that fortnight in December 1827 is a matter for conjecture. Stéphane was no puritan. He was a professed atheist and extended his intellectual freedom into the field of conventional morality. Aurore must have realised by then that sublimated love ran contrary to nature. In February of the following year, already knowing herself pregnant, she wrote to her confidante Zoé Leroy in an unusual vein: 'I no longer expect you to love me as you used to. I no longer deserve anybody's friendship.'[3] On 13 September 1828, exactly nine months after the visit to Paris, she gave birth to a baby daughter who was named Solange.

In her autobiography George Sand took great care to stress that Solange was a premature baby, thus firmly fixing her paternity on Casimir, with whom no intercourse could have taken place until after the return from Paris. The gossips of Berry had no hesitation in attributing Solange to Stéphane and La Châtre friends openly joked about it. The hints could not have escaped Aurélien de Sèze who was staying at Nohant at the time of Solange's birth and may well have been the reason for his agitated return to Bordeaux and his distraught state of mind which lasted a long time.

Whatever the gossip, Casimir preferred to shut his eyes and go his own way. That he was complacent rather than fooled became evident several years later when, in his lawsuit against his wife, he claimed that her 1827 visit to Paris specialists was only a pretext to meet her lover. For the time being however he left things as they were. He had long given up the attempt to reach the spiritual heights which his wife had prescribed for him and returned to the simpler pleasures of a gentleman farmer. He hunted, drank and took mistresses. In her autobiography George Sand claimed that she gave up marital intercourse because of the discovery, made only a few hours after the birth of her daughter, that Casimir was having an affair with a servant-girl. In view of the circumstantial evidence it was probably only a timely excuse to put an end to a physical relationship which had long become odious and which had been tolerated only for the sake of covering up Stéphane's traces.

For the time being however husband and wife continued to treat each other with friendliness. Whenever one of them was away from home, they exchanged cordial and affectionate letters. Aurore wrote in a jolly wifely tone, discussing domestic news and giving her husband more errands to carry out. Casimir's replies were matter-of-fact and conventionally affectionate. But since there was no need to keep up pretences any longer, Aurore left the conjugal bedroom and moved into a suite of rooms on her own. The children were installed in a nursery which offered the only access to her bedroom. She slept in a hammock and crammed her room with books, stones and butterflies. She even kept a herbarium in it. It became her sanctuary and her study. It was there she sought refuge from Casimir and his boon companions and it was there she wrote letters and later stories on a makeshift desk.

The birth of Solange did not interrupt her round of activities. Eight days after the confinement she was up and riding. She continued her unescorted visits to Paris but was unable to tie Stéphane down to any pattern of regularity. In the spring of 1830 she went again to Paris, leaving Solange behind but taking Maurice with her. Stéphane came to see her at once, spruced up and attentive, but by then she had learnt not to expect permanence. 'We shall see how long this honeymoon will last,'[4] she wrote to Casimir with disarming frankness, pretending to no more than a civil reunion of old compatriots. Obviously the honeymoon did not last long. After no more than a fortnight Aurore suddenly left for Bordeaux in a state of utter dejection. She looked up Aurélien whom she had not seen for a long time and whom she found, not surprisingly, 'much altered, greatly aged and very sad'.[5] When she returned to Nohant, sometime in the summer of that year, she must have realised that her relationship with Stéphane, whatever it had been, could not give her what she wanted.

Stéphane continued to avoid any ties until, at the age of thirty-nine, he married a woman who a year earlier had borne him a son and who, after their marriage, gave him three more children in rapid succession. He died of consumption at the age of forty-three, a distinguished member of the Académie des Inscriptions and a Fellow of the Royal Academy. In her autobiography, written long after his death, George Sand dismissed him as a mere acquaintance of her adolescent days, who came to a bad end. But his eldest son, himself a distinguished scholar, later hinted at a correspondence which lasted until shortly before his father's death and which frequently alluded to Solange, among other 'peculiar'[6] subjects. He also claimed, on the evidence of the letters which he had seen, that George Sand owed her early literary success entirely to the beneficial influence of Stéphane de Grandsagne.

It is hardly possible to pinpoint the exact moment in an author's life at which he first started to write; nor, in the final analysis, is it of paramount importance. Many poems, plays and novels written during childhood or early adolescence are often no more than a phase of growing up, while mature achievement does not always owe its origins to early scribbling. It would be an over-simplification to suggest that George Sand was a natural writer because she started writing at an age when most children only begin to read. In fact it was only in her mid-twenties, after she had tried her hand at other forms of expression, that she came to regard writing as something more than a social or emotional outlet.

She had first put pen to paper at the age of five, when her uneducated mother introduced her to the alphabet. The child took to it as to an exciting new game and scribbled with enthusiasm. Her grandmother smiled at the spelling but was charmed with the contents. Aurore wrote with relish, perfecting her technique with experience, never tiring of describing her minutest actions, her thoughts, her emotions. These were all subjects for letters to her brother, her mother, a distant cousin.

She had always been imaginative. At the age of two or three she used to make up long involved stories to tell her mother. Sophie Victoire reproached the child with straying off the subject; 'a fault of which I have never been able to cure myself, or so I am told,'[7] George Sand wrote at the height of her fame. At the *Couvent des Anglaises* she started keeping a diary, noting down descriptions and observations of convent life. She also wrote two long stories and gave the hero of one the name Fitz-Gerald, reflecting the influence of her anglicised environment. Both stories were admired by girls who were allowed to read them, but the author judged them unworthy and consigned them to the fire.

Even at an early age it was already clear that writing for her was more than a passing phase. Although gregarious by nature, Aurore was tongue-tied in a large company; writing gave her a chance to express herself without restraint. She wrote as some people might speak, fluently, eloquently, confidently, and at great length. Her facility did not strike her as unusual. 'Women aged between twenty and thirty, who had little formal schooling, generally write better French than men of a similar age,' she observed many years later, airing her views on education in general and on Latin and Greek, her pet aversions, in particular. 'I submit that this is so because women do not waste eight or ten years of their early life on dead languages.'[8]

Her sources of inspiration were introspection and personal experience. The first dictated her letters and her self-analyses to Casimir and Aurélien; the second a semi-autobiographical essay based on a holiday spent with Casimir in the summer of 1827, which was posthumuously published under the title of *Voyage en Auvergne*. It was also the source of *Voyage en Espagne*, written in 1829 and describing her journey to Spain when she was four years old.

Eighteen twenty-nine, when Aurore was twenty-five, may perhaps be regarded as the year when writing became a task rather than an occasional delving. That year, when an old convent friend was sick, Aurore wrote a novel and sent it to her to cheer her up; and when Hippolyte's wife complained of boredom at Nohant, she did the same for her. *La Marraine* was published posthumously, as was *Le Voyage chez M. Blaise*. A novel called *Aimée* did not survive. None of these early works had great literary merit, but they all had some of the characteristics of the future George Sand: inventiveness, romanticism, a descriptive capacity and an inexhaustible fluency. Without realising it, George Sand was serving her apprenticeship.

There was still no conscious desire to become a writer. Writing, like painting or playing the piano, was an emotional outlet. In fact the young Aurore set more store by her painting than by her literary efforts. In 1825, when presenting her husband with her eight-point plan for domestic co-existence, she exhorted him to do his homework while she would be engaged on her painting. In December 1828, three months after the birth of a second child, she was already back at the easel, working with crayons and water-colours. In a letter to her mother she apologised for not sending her any more home-made jam, explaining that she had let it burn to a hard crust while working on a picture.

What eventually decided her to concentrate on writing was her failure to supplement her marital allowance by selling her artistic products. Although practical in everyday matters, she always spent more than she had; it was a characteristic which stayed with her all her life. The three thousand francs a year which Casimir allowed her for her personal needs were not enough to cover her charities to the village poor and the expenses incurred by her unescorted travels to Bordeaux, Périgueux or Paris. She tried to earn money by putting her various talents to a profitable use. She decorated snuff-boxes and fans and was thrilled when a Paris art-dealer actually bought some; but she soon realised that the demand for such goods was limited. She tried her hand at portrait painting but was forced to concede that her pictures had no marketable value. Translation work proved unprofitable and needlework unremunerative. It was only when her efforts to make money out of art had failed that she began to consider writing as a possible source of income. She looked back at her written output of the past year or two and came to the conclusion that she could write at least as well as some contemporary authors whose works she had been reading. Many years later she recalled how she assessed her literary chances in the years 1828–30:

> I realised that I wrote quickly, easily, for hours on end, without getting tired; that my ideas, sluggish inside my head, came to life and followed one another in a logical sequence once I held a pen; that during a life of contemplation I had observed a great deal and sufficiently understood the characters that chance had brought my way, and that consequently I knew human nature well enough to describe it; that finally, of all the small jobs I was capable of doing, literature was the one which offered me the best chance of professional success; not to mince words, which offered me a chance to make a living.[9]

It was precisely lack of observation with which Henri de Latouche, George Sand's first literary mentor, reproached her when in 1831 she asked for his opinion of *Aimée*: nor was it strictly true that her writing was solely motivated by her desire to make a living. Her amibition to live by the pen was bound up with an unavowed deisre to shake off the last vestiges of a dull domestic routine and find fulfilment in an environment of her own choice. But in 1829 such ideas were only half-formulated. The events which helped Aurore to crystallise her thinking had not yet taken place.

She continued to divide her life between the domestic realities of Nohant and the dream-world created in her small room. Nobody could detect the future writer of romantic novels in the practical Mme Dudevant who kept arguing with her husband about his handling of their finances, inundating her correspondents with requests and errands, supervising the upbringing of her children. When Maurice was six she engaged a resident tutor who was reputed to have performed miracles with a new method of teaching. Jules Boucoiran, the first of many tutors who were to fall in love with their enchanting employer, was only eighteen. After a term he returned to his former employer in Paris, possibly fearing a dangerous entanglement. Aurore persistently asked him to come back. Her letters pursued him wherever he was, disarmingly frank, cajoling, coquettishly maternal. She called him *cher enfant*, the first of many *chers enfants* to come. In July 1830 after her disillusioning visit to Stéphane de Grandsange in Paris, she wrote to him in her usual personal vein:

I have nothing interesting to report. You know how we live at Nohant: Tuesday is like Wednesday, Wednesday is like Thursday, and so on. Only the transition from winter to summer brings some movement into this state of stagnation. We get the feeling, the sensation if you like, of the cold and warm weather to tell us that time marches on and that life flows like water. It is a calm course I follow, and I have no desire to roll on more quickly.[10]

She was too resilient to follow such a course for any length of time. Before July was out she had met the young man who was instrumental in deciding her to make the break with Nohant and reach out for a new life. The chance meeting of Jules Sandeau and Baroness Dudevant heralded the birth of George Sand.

They met on 30 July 1830 during one of Aurore's unescorted visits to the Duvernets' château, where young Charles was entertaining some La Châtre friends. Jules Sandeau was then a shy young man of nineteen, frail, with a mop of golden hair that made him look like a cherub. He came from a poor family, had shown academic promise and was studying law in Paris. When Baroness Dudevant joined the party he discreetly retired with a book. Aurore followed him and claimed his attention. Before she left, already mounted, she invited the entire party to dine with her at Nohant the following evening. Sandeau became a frequent visitor.

He was more interested in literature than in law, but his chief attraction for Aurore was his diffidence. *Le petit Jules*, as she fondly called him, was awkward, deferential, in obvious need of mothering. He aroused her pity, which in her case nearly always resulted in a fierce desire to help. In her old age she recognised it as a recurrent pattern in her life:

> Kindness, which should be a clear-sighted and moderate virtue, was in my case a tumultuous, torrential emotion, which sought only to expand. As soon as someone roused my pity, he possessed me. I pounced on the chance to do good with a blindness which more often than not invited hurt.[11]

Little Jules, so different from the independent Stéphane, seemed to want to be done good to. Aurore knew herself in love and impetuously told Jules of her feelings for him. Jules adored her. Throughout the rest of the summer they met in a secluded pavilion on the grounds of Nohant and gave the old countesses of Berry further reason to disapprove of Baroness Dudevant. They had a pleasant time deciding which of four aspirants was the successful lover: Sandeau, Fleury, Duvernet, distant Boucoiran, or all four. Aurore took no notice and lived in a turmoil of excitement.

The summer passed all too quickly. In the autumn the young students returned to Paris to resume their studies. Baroness Dudevant was left behind to yearn for the capital which held her little Jules and which she imagined as the centre of that magic world of the spirit she had been seeking ever since her adolescence.

Casimir was out one day when, for no explicit reason, she went through his desk and found an envelope addressed to her in his hand, to be opened only after his death. 'I did not have the patience to wait until I should become a widow,' she wrote to Boucoiran on 3 December. 'Besides, with my kind of health I had no reason to expect to survive him.'[12] She opened the envelope there and then and was flabbergasted to discover it contained a document stating Casimir's opinion of her marital conduct over the past few years. She smarted under his uncouth expressions.

Writing to Boucoiran of Dudevant's unwarranted manifestation of hate, she warned him to send his reply poste restante to La Châtre, as her brute of a husband was not above going through her mail.

As soon as Casimir returned home she faced him with her find and announced that in the circumstances it would be best for her to go and live in Paris on her own. In vain did Casimir plead with her to change her mind. She was adamant. But when he resigned himself to her departure and suggested locking up the château, Aurore objected. She had had second thoughts. She explained that she was not leaving home; she was only going to divide her life between Paris and Nohant, in stretches of three months at a time. It would be necessary to keep a skeleton staff in the château.

The arrangement made it easier to solve the future of the children. Maurice was seven years old, Solange two. There was no question of their mother taking them to Paris and making herself housebound, although she did hint that later on she might want to have Solange with her. For the time being she needed to be unencumbered. Her plan to live away from her children three months out of six did not strike her as maternal negligence. She had always had maids to look after the children, and her role as a mother was emotional and supervisory rather than purely domestic. The proposed departure only emphasised the need to delegate responsibility.

Casimir suggested simplifying matters by sending Maurice to a boarding-school and allowing him to take a small house for himself and Solange. Aurore would not hear of it. She knew that if the children went on living in their familiar surroundings, with their father about as usual and their mother regularly back, they would not feel the disruption in the family pattern. It was only a question of finding a suitable person who would give the children the care and security they needed. Boucoiran was the obvious choice. Aurore renewed her appeal to him and used so much eloquence to press her need that he finally agreed to return to Nohant to become Maurice's tutor as well as little Solange's. What may well have decided him was an equivocal promise in Aurore's letter of appeal: 'My heart is not cold, you know that, and I feel it will not remain indifferent to its obligations towards you.'[13] Five days later, when Boucoiran had accepted the post and hopefully suggested meeting her alone in Nîmes, his home town, she replied that it would not do to rouse Casimir's suspicions against the future tutor of his children.

There only remained a few practical points to settle. Casimir promised to keep up his wife's personal allowance and she, for her part, undertook not to exceed it. Hippolyte tried to dissuade his sister from what he considered an impractical plan and warned her against the high cost of living in the capital. When she turned a deaf ear, he offered her the free use of his Paris house.

On 4 January 1831, four weeks after the discovery of Casimir's offensive letter, Aurore set out for Paris and was joyfully received by Jules Sandeau. Her luggage contained some fashionable, though impractical, dresses and the manuscript of her novel *Aimée*.

Stéphane Ajasson de Grandsagne, by Devéria

Early days in Paris: Aurore Dudevant with a friend, by Gavarni

Chapter 5

❦❦❦❦

Do not make books, make children

Long before her departure for Paris, the future George Sand had been taking a lively interest in the social and political upheavals which had been rocking France for many years. Without realising it she was absorbing material for yet unconceived works.

Aurore's background had made her politically aware though not, as yet, politically active. She was impressionable. Even as a child she could not help sharing the national sense of pride which Napoleon's victories brought to France. 'I regarded my nation as invincible and the imperial throne as that of God himself,' she recalled years later. 'At that time we imbibed the pride of victory with our mother's milk. The wild fancy of the aristocracy had expanded and communicated itself to the other classes. To be French was an honour, a title of nobility.'[1]

At the age of eight she was keenly aware of the impending Russian Campaign of 1812. Wherever her grandmother took her visiting they met officers who had come down to Berry to take leave of their families before joining the *Grande Armée*. That year she shared the general despondency after the disastrous retreat from Moscow, then the resurgence of hope when Napoleon won fresh victories in 1813 against the Prussians and Russians in Lutzen and Bautzen, the Austrians in Dresden. One day she met an unescorted prisoner-of-war, a hungry German soldier who passed by Nohant on his way to the town of Châteauroux, some fifty miles away. Soon he was followed by many others, all hungry, dispirited, humbled, driven towards Châteauroux by the force of events. With their grandmother's consent Aurore and Hippolyte posted themselves in a pavilion commanding the passage of the prisoners and handed out bread and wine. She never forgot their haggard, frightened faces.

In the spring of 1814 the Allies closed in on Paris, forced Napoleon to abdicate and pointed as successor to Louis Stanislas Xavier, brother to the guillotined Louis XVI. In April Napoleon left for Elba and in May the sixty-year-old Bourbon prince, who had spent in England the last seven of his twenty-three years of exile, arrived in Paris to become Louis XVIII. The following year Aurore, aged eleven, lived the excitement of the Hundred Days. Her grandmother, never a great admirer of Napoleon, feared he might take revenge on the entire Bourbon dynasty. Aurore could not make up her mind whether the returning emperor was a 'monster' or a genuine 'father of the people'.[2] She held long imaginary conversations with him which invariably ended with her putting her trust in him and touching him with a magic sword of fire to make him invincible.

With Napoleon's expulsion to St Helena and Louis XVIII's return to power, France gained a constitutional king. Louis issued a charter guaranteeing the people of France equality before the law, individual and religious liberties, and the freedom of the press. The government was to consist of two Chambers: the House of Peers, nominated by the king, and the Chamber of Deputies, elected by a franchise based on tax qualification.

The restoration of the monarchy brought about a sorely needed respite. Young men stayed at home and reared families instead of going to the wars, trade revived, intellectual life surged ahead. Poetry, philosophy, historiography, literary criticism, drama, all received a fresh impetus. The benefits of peace reached into every branch of life. When Louis XVIII died in 1824 his crown passed without ado to his sixty-six-year-old brother Charles Philippe, who ascended the throne of France as Charles X.

It was during the early years of Charles X's reign that Aurore began to take an adult interest in politics, possibly thanks to Casimir who was a keen liberal, or republican. When the king dissolved Parliament in 1827 and called for new elections to the Chamber of Deputies, Casimir firmly supported his local republican candidate Duris Dufresne. Baron Dudevant had the vote, as did the Fleurys, the Duvernets, the Papets, the Dutheils, for they were all wealthy enough to pay the qualifying three hundred francs a year in direct taxes. Aurore played her part in the campaign and took great pride in 'our Deputy'.[3]

Charles X's reign was not a smooth one. His policies did not go far enough for the new generation of liberty-conscious Frenchmen, and his hope of reasserting himself by dissolving Parliament in 1830 and ordering new elections were frustrated when the results showed a landslide for the republicans. The king dissolved the new Chamber even before it had a chance to convene, but the liberal press called on the people to fight for their liberties. On 27 July the shops of Paris remained closed, demonstrations were held, barricades were put up. The royal troops, instead of dispersing the insurgents, joined them. The people were intoxicated with the new revolution. Bourgeois, workmen, war veterans and students marched together in the streets of Paris, hoisting the Tricolor, chanting the *Marseillaise*. By the end of three glorious days, *les Trois Glorieuses*, Charles X abdicated in favour of his nephew, Louis Philippe of Orléans, who had been propagated by his own party as the best possible of all possible constitutional kings. Charles X went into exile and Louis Philippe, aged fifty-seven, became King of the French by the Will of the People. To the optimists it looked as if at long last France had a constitutional monarch with respect for republican ideas.

News from the stormy capital trickled to the country by post and by word of mouth. Baroness Dudevant had a first-hand account of the political upheaval through Boucoiran, who wrote from Paris on the second of the Three Glorious Days. She received his letter on 31 July, the very day that Jules Sandeau was brought to dinner at Nohant for the first time. She read it out to her guests. La Châtre voters were stolid republicans and the party was elated. Casimir was appointed officer of the local National Guard with a hundred and twenty men under him to resist the king's men should they attack; and Aurore wrote Boucoiran an ecstatic letter in praise of the brave new world, not forgetting to tell him to 'run'[4] to her mother's and aunt's, to see whether they had not been too badly shaken by the disturbances in the streets.

By the time she arrived in Paris, in January 1831, Louis Philippe had things firmly under control. The young Berry republicans, up for their studies, looked to him with hope. They included Jules Sandeau, Alphonse Fleury, Gabriel Planet, students of law; Gustave Papet, Emile Régnault, students of medicine. Aurore felt at ease with those students, all younger than her, who were serious and frivolous at the same time, hard up but carefree, eager to seize what the capital had to offer. She went with them to republican meetings, shared their cheap seats at the theatre and opera, took part in their rags. She explored Paris from one end to another, driven by her inexhaustible curiosity and energy.

The elegant outfits she had brought from Nohant could not withstand the strain she imposed on them. Her long skirts swept the muddy pavements and got frayed, her fashionably pointed shoes made her trip, her velvet hats lost their shape in the rain. She knew herself to be tatty. Balzac, whose acquaintance she made shortly after her arrival, used to say that to be elegant in Paris a woman needed an income of twenty-five thousand francs a year. Aurore's mother seemed to be well dressed on three thousand five hundred, but then she did not subject her wardrobe to such wear and tear as did her daughter. Aurore decided to forgo elegance for practicality.

Her long-established practice of wearing a man's shirt and gaiters for riding helped her towards a step which her Berry admirers, who had seen her thus dressed at home, did not consider unbecoming. The fashion of the day for men favoured ankle-length, army-type coats, with square shoulders and no belt. Aurore ordered one, of thick grey material, with trousers and a waistcoat to match. She added a cravat and a grey hat, and replaced her dainty shoes with hob-nailed boots. It was a sensible outfit for the winter and a convincing enough disguise to allow her into the cheap theatre pit instead of being directed to the expensive dress circle or boxes where ladies were expected to sit. The crowd in the pit was rough, but the Berry cavaliers formed a protective belt round their delicate colleague and shielded her from the jostling and bustling. To all intents and purposes she looked just like any other young student from the provinces. Père Pinson, the owner of a restaurant much patronised by hard-up students and literary people, was once astonished to hear one of his male clients address another as *Madame*. Aurore took him into her confidence and swore him to secrecy. The following day she came in wearing a dress. Père Pinson, true to his oath, addressed her as *Monsieur*. He could never get it right, for Aurore constantly changed from male to female attire, depending on the need of the moment.

What with the theatre, the opera, the restaurants and the new outfits, Aurore found that within two weeks she had run out of her entire quarterly allowance. 'It simply is not adequate for someone like me, who likes to give and dislikes calculating,'[5] she justified herself. Not daring to ask her husband directly, she tried to touch him through their son. 'Tell *Papa* to send me some more money,' she wrote to the seven-year-old Maurice less than three weeks after her arrival in Paris. 'As soon as I get it I shall buy you that National Guard uniform.'[6] She was not discouraged by the high cost of living in the capital, against which her brother had warned her. She was intoxicated with her independence and determined to keep it. Within days of her arrival in Paris, at the height of her uncensured love for Jules Sandeau, she was already looking for an opening that would enable her to turn her gift for writing into a source of income.

She set about it in her customarily practical way. Before leaving Nohant Baroness Dudevant had taken the precaution of obtaining a letter of introduction from Mme Duvernet, a neighbouring châtelaine and the mother of Charles Duvernet, to a cousin of hers in Paris. He was Henri de Latouche, a well-known author, playwright and literary critic, who had recently bought up a moribund journal called *Le Figaro*. Within a few months of his editorship the journal, which during its first five years had changed hands twice, once for the nominal sum of three hundred francs, became a paper to be reckoned with. Its political columns, often criticising Louis Philippe's policies, were read at court; its literary supplements were highly thought of. It became a hothouse for budding talent.

Latouche was forty-five when Aurore went to see him in mid-January in his apartment, which also served as the editorial office. He was a large man, with impeccable manners and a deliberate way of speaking that made him sound affected. He listened courteously as his visitor read out to him all of *Aimée*, then shook his head. Aurore described that meeting to Charles Duvernet, who later reproduced it in his memoirs:

'Have you any children, Madame ?' Latouche asked the author.

'Alas yes Monsieur, but I cannot have them with me, nor can I go back to them.'

'And you propose to stay in Paris and make a living by the pen ?'

'I must, definitely.'

'How tiresome, because I do not see here the elements of success. Take my advice, Madame. Arrange things so that you can return under the conjugal roof.'[7]

Under his daunting exterior Latouche was not an unkind man. He liked the young woman with the black curls and dark eyes who braved social conventions to live her own way. Besides, she was a native of Berry, as was he, and Berry people stood by one another. Before he saw Aurore out he had invited her to become a regular contributor to *Le Figaro*. In a letter to her husband Aurore said that it was not much of an offer and that she was not going to accept it. She changed her mind when Jules Sandeau and another law student from Berry told her of their own unsuccessful attempts to break into the literary world. In a letter to Charles Duvernet she wrote of Latouche's offer more realistically: 'I am told that his patronage is not easily come by. Without your mother's recommendation I might have sought it for a long time without success.'[8] She accepted.

It was a strange new world that she now entered. The journalists worked a nine-to-five day, seated behind small desks provided by the *patron* in his parlour cum office. Aurore, always

shivery, planted herself by the fireplace. Latouche directed opera-
tions. Every morning he handed out to his staff sheets of paper
on which he scribbled down topics for comment. The sheets
varied in size, each being only as large as Latouche thought the
article needed to be. Aurore was a novice to the art of brevity.
She wrote one draft after another, only to throw them all into the
fire; every time she thought she had made a good start, she was
told it was too long. The prescribed length was a straitjacket.
Journalists on *Le Figaro* were paid seven francs a column. By the
end of her first month Aurore had made only twelve francs and
fifty centimes. She aired her grievances against Latouche to
Boucoiran who was looking after her children at Nohant:

4 March 1831
We are not exactly free on *Le Figaro*. M. de Latouche, our
worthy chief (oh if you only knew that man) breathes down
our necks, makes cuts, chops without discrimination, imposes
his whims, his errors of judgment, his caprices. We have to
write as he tells us; it is his business after all. We are only
matter in his hands. A labourer-journalist, an errand-boy hack,
that is all I am at the moment.[9]

She came to regard writing for *Le Figaro* as 'the lowest of
jobs'.[10] She had a moment of near glory when at long last she
produced a suitably short article, on a political theme, which was
so much frowned upon by court circles that *Le Figaro* was
threatened with legal action. It was a storm in a teacup. Aurore
had to admit that she was not cut out to be a journalist and continued her efforts to penetrate the world of literature. 'Literature
has become a passion,' she wrote to Dutheil five weeks after her
arrival in Paris. 'The more obstacles I encounter, the more difficulties I perceive, the more I am determined to overcome them.'[11]
Through an old Berry friend, the Deputy Duris Dufresne for
whom she had once canvassed, she obtained an introduction to
a fellow Deputy who was a fashionable writer and a member of
the Académie Française, and went to see him.

The interview with M. de Kératry was disastrous from the

start. Aurore presented herself at his house at eight o'clock in the morning and immediately antagonised him when she mistook his young wife for his daughter. Kératry, with his silver hair and rotund figure, looked ancient to her. She tried to atone by telling him how much she had been moved by his recent novel but failed to sound convincing. Kératry took one look at the shivering woman in a plain woollen frock and muddy shoes, so unlike his elegant young wife, and decided to put her in her place. 'M. Duris Dufresne tells me that you want to write and I have promised to talk to you about it,' he began importantly. 'I need only a few words to tell you what I think about it, and I shall be quite frank with you. . . . Take my advice. Do not make books, make children.'[12]

The story later went round Paris that Aurore looked the old man straight in the face and said: 'You do, if you can,' then ran out of the house roaring with laughter. She herself coyly denied such wit. But the lesson of the interview had not been lost on her. She realised that she had to contend with something that her life within a close-knit circle of admirers had not prepared her for: male prejudice. Kératry had said that a woman writer was a contradiction in terms, and Aurore was sensible enough to appreciate that he was not alone in thinking so. He represented a school of thought. It was perhaps then that she first formed the idea of adopting a male pen-name instead of exposing her future work to pre-conceived judgment. She was clear about not writing under her married name when her mother-in-law, the widowed Baroness Dudevant, interrogated her on some disturbing rumours that had reached her while visiting Paris that winter:

'It is true that you are proposing to print books?'
'Why yes, Madame.'
'Really, what an idea!'
'Yes, Madame.'
'It is all very well, but I hope you will not put the name I bear on covers of printed books.'
'Of course not, Madame, no danger of that.'[13]

A few weeks on *Le Figaro* had made Aurore change her mind about Latouche. He had his idiosyncrasies, but his literary judgment was sound and he had helped many a young writer, including Honoré de Balzac. Besides, he did not share Kératry's prejudice against women writers. His main objection to *Aimée* was that it was abstract, not drawn from life. He advised Aurore to observe, get involved, gain experience. She threw *Aimée* into the fire and kept her eyes and ears open. In the meantime Jules Sandeau too gained a foothold on *Le Figaro*. The lovers embarked on a literary collaboration and in due course produced a short story which was accepted by the *Revue de Paris*. For the first time since they started writing professionally the authors were faced with the pleasant prospect of seeing their names in print. Articles in *Le Figaro* were usually unsigned, but a short story for the *Revue* was another matter. Latouche, far from being displeased with his protégés' success on another paper, was consulted about a joint pen-name and suggested Jules Sand. Aurore was disappointed that the story was not published immediately on acceptance, but she knew she had found her vocation. To Boucoiran she wrote:

I am more than ever determined to follow a literary career. In spite of difficulties which sometimes put me off, days of inactivity and weariness which interrupt my work, and a monotonous existence, I feel that my life has been fulfilled. I have an aim, a task, a passion if I may use the word. Writing is a violent passion, virtually indestructible. Once it has got hold of you it will never let go.[14]

In April 1831, faithful to her agreement with her husband, Aurore returned to Nohant. The homecoming was pleasant. The children looked well cared for, Boucoiran was in the process of seducing a maid, Casimir was as hearty as ever. Aurore kept herself feverishly busy. By day she rode, gardened, helped Maurice with his French and Latin; by night she sat up writing until daybreak. With her husband she established an admirable state of tolerance. He left her to herself and did not question her movements when she sometimes returned from a visit to La Châtre well after midnight. For her part she stopped criticising his management of the estate and turned a blind eye to his horseplay with the maids. To her mother she wrote that her husband's marital freedom justified hers. Her thoughts were in Paris, with Sandeau. She was looking forward to her next three months with him and instructed Emile Régnault, a medical student whom she knew to be more practical than little Jules, to find her a suitable apartment. Apparently Hippolyte had hinted that she could not use his Paris house indefinitely. In a letter to Régnault Aurore explained what sort of accommodation she had in mind:

> I would like it to have a back exit which would enable Jules to slip out unnoticed at any time. After all, one fine day at 4 o'clock in the morning my husband may drop in, if not out of the blue, at least out of the *diligence*, and as he may have nowhere suitable to lay his head, he might do me the honour of descending on me! Imagine what would happen if I heard him ring the bell and sensed his sweet presence behind the door.[15]

Régnault found her a three-roomed apartment in the garret of a large house on the quai Saint-Michel. She asked him to send her the measurements of the rooms so that she could decide what furniture to bring over from Nohant. In July she returned to Paris and found the garret delightful but the furniture scanty. She asked Casimir for extra money on top of her allowance in order to furnish it to her taste, and when he pleaded hardship she wrote back furiously that she had not expected her own husband, or her brother for that matter, to force her to borrow from strangers. After that she borrowed five hundred francs each from Latouche and Duris Dufresne, and two hundred francs from her mother. In August Hippolyte came to see her, was given a severe scolding, gave as good as he got and reduced his sister to tears. To Casimir he wrote that 'in spite of her confounded obstinacy it was impossible not to love her'.[16]

This time she did not stay the full three-month period but

returned to Nohant in September, for little Jules was due back home for the holidays. They flaunted their association all over La Châtre and Aurore went as far as to invite him to spend the night in her bedroom, while Casimir was camping out with the harvesters. It was a daring operation, which could not be achieved without an accomplice. Gustave Papet, also down for the holidays, volunteered to stand guard and alert the lovers in case of danger. The following morning Aurore wrote to thank him:

20 September 1831

Dear Gustave, how kind you are! How you love Jules and how my heart returns your sentiment. You have spent the night bivouacked in a ditch like a poor soldier, while we, selfish with happiness, could not tear ourselves apart. Oh it was not for lack of saying some thirty times: 'Let us stop, we must, Gustave is waiting, poor Gustave'. Jules can tell you, in the midst of our craziest raptures we blessed you, your name mingled with our kisses, all our thoughts were for you, you were in our hearts with our love. . . .[17]

The loyal Papet was nineteen at the time, Jules Sandeau twenty, Aurore twenty-seven. She was so ecstatic that she had to share her joy with Emile Régnault who had stayed in Paris:

Jules came last night under everybody's nose: Brave [the watchdog], my husband, my brother, the children, the maid and so on. I sleep right in the middle of all this company, but my good little room is lockable and sound proof, and it has an excellent cupboard. I have calculated everything, foreseen everything. . . . He was there, in my own room, in my arms, happy, groaning, crying, laughing, beaten, kissed, bitten. It was a storm of pleasure the like of which we have never experienced before. . . . I want him to come again tonight. Twice is not too much. After that it would be imprudent, my husband is bound to find out that Jules is in Berry within reach of his gun. But up to now he has suspected nothing. He is harvesting and sleeps like a pig. I am silly, I know. I am covered with bites and bruises. I can hardly hold myself up. I am frantic with excitement. If you were here I would bite you until I drew blood to make you share a little in our ecstasy.[18]

All that autumn Aurore and Sandeau collaborated on a novel commissioned by a Paris publisher after the publication of their first joint short story. When winter set in *Rose et Blanche* was finished. Jules took the manuscript back to Paris while Aurore stayed on at Nohant, quite content to be at home. The raptures were over. She returned to Paris only in November, when she heard that little Jules had been taken ill. She nursed him with that devotion which was to prove then as on future occasions a sub-conscious atonement for a passion in decline. In December *Rose et Blanche* was published under the joint pen-name of Jules Sand and was well received. Casimir came up to Paris and took his wife out in style, careful to find his own lodgings. The day after he left, a parcel was delivered to Aurore's garret, containing a beautiful dress he had bought for her. To show her gratitude she started making him a pair of embroidered carpet slippers.

This time she did not stay her full three-month quota either. She was unwell and Régnault, in his medical capacity, prescribed country air. On her return to Nohant she shut herself in her room and worked at her desk seven, eight, sometimes ten hours at a stretch, occasionally putting on a pair of blue-tinted glasses. She was still unwell, but she pressed on with that unremitting self-discipline that was to sustain her throughout the most difficult crises of her life. By the spring of 1832 she had written *Indiana*. Forgetting her aches and pains, her haggard cheeks and her sunken eyes, she rushed back to Paris to show Jules her own brain-child.

The Berry friends could hardly believe their eyes when they saw her descend from the *diligence* holding by the hand the three-and-a-half-year-old Solange. Aurore explained that the child was too young to notice anything irregular in the domestic arrangements of quai Saint-Michel. Jules himself stepped into the role of father with good grace. He took Solange for walks in the Jardin des Plantes and invented games for her when they were indoors.

Aurore became ill again; she imagined she had cholera, which had claimed several victims in Paris. Jules looked after mother and daughter, got up in the middle of the night to comfort Solange when she woke up crying, washed and dressed her in the morning. Love in the garret made way for domesticity.

Indiana impressed Sandeau and made him uncomfortable. He suggested that Aurore should publish it under her own name, as he had had no hand in it. The publisher did not want to lose the name Sand which thanks to *Rose et Blanche* had already achieved some popularity. Again Latouche was consulted; so were friends and well-wishers. Respecting the publisher's point of view, Latouche suggested altering the first name only and keeping the surname. The story went that nobody could agree on a choice of another first name, until somebody opened the calendar and pointed out it was the day of *Saint Georges*; and *Georges* it was. For some time after that Aurore signed herself *Georges* Sand, omitting the *s* only a year or two later. In her autobiography she explained that *George* had associations with Berry.

Getting a book set and printed was only a matter of a few weeks in those days. In May *Indiana* was out. Latouche accepted an autographed copy, glanced perfunctorily at a couple of pages and condemned it out of hand. Back at his comfortable apartment he sat up all night reading the book from beginning to end and in the morning sent Aurore a handsome note of apology, ending with the rare praise: 'Oh my child, I am so pleased with you.'[19] Balzac wrote a glowing review in *La Caricature*; and Gustave Planche, the dread critic of the *Revue des Deux Mondes* praised the book sky-high and declared its author superior to Mme de Staël. These reviewers knew the author's identity. Uninitiated ones, equally enthusiastic, were mystified by the half-familiar pen-name. They referred to the author of *Indiana* as *Monsieur* G. Sand, and took him to be a cousin of Jules Sand. They refused to credit the persistent rumour that George Sand was the pen-name of a woman writer, and suggested that the characters of the book could have been drawn only by a firm virile hand. On the other hand they conceded that the emotional delicacy of the writing might well have been due to a collaboration with a woman. Aurore read the reviews and congratulated herself on having pre-empted anti-feminine prejudice by hiding behind a man's name. All those fine connoisseurs of literature, she wrote many years later, 'had something of the Kératry about them'.[20]

The scene of *Indiana* was set partly in France and partly in Madagascar, which Aurore had come to know through the vivid accounts of her admirer, the explorer Jules Néraud. Indiana was a beautiful young Creole married to a much older French colonel. She was dreamy and romantic, while the colonel, without being uneducated, was devoid of sensibility. He never understood that the relationship between husband and wife should be based on a communion of souls. Their marriage was unhappy. Chance made Indiana meet a handsome young nobleman who seemed to combine good looks with a lofty mind. They fell in love and the husband, mistaking the pure nature of the friendship, slapped his wife round the face. When things eventually came to the crunch the young lover rejected Indiana for a rich heiress. She decided to commit suicide. At this juncture, as always in her moments of unhappiness, her cousin Ralph Brown turned up and informed her that her husband had died on his travels. She was still determined to die and Ralph offered to die with her. On the very edge of the precipice from which they were going to jump to their death they suddenly realised that they were in love with each other and stepped back into life and happiness.

Indiana was a book with a message. In it George Sand claimed for women unsuitably married the right to seek love outside marriage. It was not an attack on the institution of marriage as such. That came later. It was not a licence for adultery either. It required the death of an unloved husband to bring true love to its natural conclusion. For Indiana, as for Aurore Dudevant, the supreme object of love was marriage. A happy chance, or providential justice, had to intervene to give love respectability.

But the literary contrivance which diverted love from the course of adultery and guided it safely into a happy second marriage did not deceive the readers of the time. Whatever the solution, the basic message was revolutionary. Women were made to realise with clarity that their marital problems were not individual cases of incompatibility, but the result of a social structure invented and perpetrated by men. They began to question an order of things that made wives the chattel of their husbands and denied them freedom of choice. Men of letters were impressed. Sainte-Beuve called it a 'daring work';[21] Balzac, 'the reaction of truth against fantasy'.[22]

Overnight Aurore found herself famous. Leading literary journals competed for her future contributions; her publisher commissioned another novel; all offered handsome advances. In less than eighteen months she achieved her ambition of making a living by writing. She no longer needed to badger her husband, the prototype of *Indiana*'s Colonel Delmare, for extra money to buy furniture, a piano, presents for the children. She no longer needed to live in a garret. She could afford to take over the lease of the elegant apartment at quai Malaquais which Latouche had recently vacated. The thick white carpet which had so inhibited her when she was an apprentice journalist was now hers to drop as much snuff on as she pleased. She no longer needed to do the chores. She could afford to bring over a maid from Nohant to do the housework.

Yet she was depressed. Her literary success came when her emotional life was at a low ebb. She could no longer conceal from herself the fundamental incompatibility between herself and Sandeau. She was a disciplined worker; Jules believed in waiting for inspiration. Aurore could write in any surrounding; Jules was still a boy who could not settle down to write at will. She reproached him with laziness; he accused her of inhumanity. 'You want me to work,' he once wrote in self-defence. 'So do I. I just cannot. I was not born like you with a little steel spring inside the head, with a push-button which only needs touching in order to start the will-power going.'[23] But it was more than that. Aurore had exhausted her passion and now realised that little Jules did not possess the spiritual qualities which could make her soul soar. Her choice of a lover proved as misdirected as her choice of a husband.

In the summer she took Solange back to Nohant, while Jules joined his parents in the Loire Valley. Aurore immured herself in her room and tried to ignore the vacuum in her heart by working hard on her next novel, *Lélia*, in which she described the anguish of a woman no longer capable of believing in the existence of love. Jules was tormented. From the Loire he wrote unhappy letters to his old friend Gustave Papet and asked him to call at Nohant and tell Aurore that he loved her and could not live without her.

The autumn reunion in Paris brought a reconciliation sealed with an exchange of rings. It was no use. Aurore knew herself bored and Jules knew himself unloved. Under the pretext of work, she persuaded him to move out of quai Malaquais and take up lodgings on his own. Jules sought to dull the pain as best he could. The story went round that one day Aurore called unexpectedly and caught him making love to the washerwoman; the one in charge of fine linen, some people asserted knowledgeably. The break-up was complete and Sandeau, in his misery, took a dose of morphine which was just large enough to make him ill. Aurore too felt suicidal. To Emile Régnault she wrote on the day of the final separation:

My friend, go to Jules and look after his body. The spirit is broken. You will not be able to uplift it, so do not try. I am not calling you to my side yet, I do not need anything. Today I prefer to be alone. There is nothing left for me to live for. Jules will suffer badly for a long time, but then he is young. One day he will look back and will not be sorry to have lived. . . .

Do not try to repair the damage. This time it is irremediable. We do not blame each other for anything. We have fought this terrible necessity for a long time. We have suffered much pain. There is nothing left for us but to kill ourselves. But for the children we would have done it.[24]

In the spring of 1833 Sandeau left for Italy to seek forgetfulness. By that time Aurore felt less charitable towards a young man she was no longer interested in. She packed up the bits and pieces he had left in her cupboards and sent them to Régnault's lodgings with a request to pass them on to Jules on his return from his

Italian tour. 'He had lost everything, even my respect,'[25] she wrote to Régnault. She was referring to the incident of the washerwoman which, in view of some of her own friends' unfriendly reaction, she began to make much of, to justify her own cooling off. She concluded her note to Régnault with a firm declaration that she would never again allow Jules to see her.

In the increasingly crowded life which Aurore was beginning to lead, it was not difficult to avoid an undesirable meeting with a former lover. Three years passed before chance brought them together again, at Gustave Papet's Paris lodgings. By that time Aurore had had several love affairs. Without the least embarassment she made straight for Sandeau and mentioned the unpleasant rumours which were still circulating Paris about the manner of their separation. In her diary she noted that Sandeau was honest about his past guilt and enquired about little Solange. She made him promise not to cut her dead should chance make them meet again. When they did meet again, some twenty or twenty-five years later, in the waiting-room of the Minister of the Interior, neither recognised the other; or so the literary gossipmongers claimed.

Sandeau published many successful novels, notably one which was based on his love affair with Aurore, and in 1852 was elected to the Académie Française. Although he had other love affairs and finally made a happy marriage, he never recovered from his bitterness against Aurore. He was visiting the house of his friend François Buloz, editor of the *Revue des Deux Mondes*, when little Marie, Buloz's daughter, settled on his knees and asked him to name the illustrious people whose photographs filled her father's album. When George Sand's photograph came up Sandeau said with venom: 'Take a good look at this woman, little girl. Look at her. She is a graveyard. Do you understand? A graveyard.'[26] George Sand, for her part, came across a photograph of him at the Bulozes' house without even recognising him; he had long lost his golden curls and put on weight. When told it was Jules Sandeau she merely remarked that he had aged. His memory evoked no tenderness in her heart. In 1864 she wrote to her son Maurice that she had been to the Comédie Française to see a new play by Sandeau. 'It was very poor,'[27] she wrote curtly.

In his old age Sandeau cut a pathetic figure. He had lost his beloved son, a naval officer, and sank into apathy. Paris café gossips would whisper to one another that the unkempt old man, corpulent and bald, sitting alone before his glass of absinth, had once been George Sand's lover. He died in 1883, surviving her by seven years, leaving no more memorable a legacy to French literature than the first half of his surname.

Chapter 6

Sappho

At the beginning of 1833 Aurore wrote a fan-letter to the actress Marie Dorval whose performance at the theatre she had just seen. It led to a friendship which lasted until Dorval's death sixteen years later and which from its very beginning gave rise to suggestions of lesbianism.

In 1885, when both women had long been dead, the writer Arsène Houssaye commemorated in his *Confessions* what he imagined to have taken place fifty years earlier:

At that time Sappho lived again in Paris. . . . An eloquent woman flung her arms round a great actress who had given her life to passion. Every midnight, after the actress had kindled fire and passion in every heart, either at the Boulevard du Crime or at the Comédie Française, she returned to her small blue-upholstered room, to find that strange woman seated in front of a blazing fire with a boiling kettle ready for tea, a cigarette in her mouth, waiting for her prey. It was a most loving dialogue. The dark-haired woman ruffled the golden hair. The blonde woman ruffled the black hair, and the hair mingled with their kisses and bites. Never did Sappho speak so fair to handsome Phaon, never did Errine answer Sappho in a more caressing voice. The nocturnal hours were more radiant than the hours of day. Both women, burning with the fire of love, were incensed with the unexpected, insatiate for love. It was more than the licentiousness of the heart, it was the voluptuous indulgence of the orient, of India, Japan. The two

priestesses of love parted at daybreak, still drunk with fulfilment about to fade like a dream.[1]

The author of this posthumous description, who was only
seventeen when these love scenes were supposed to have taken
place and in no position to have had first-hand information about
them, added that 'Paris was not surprised to see these two shining
stars burn with the same fire under the literary firmament of the
romantics'.[2] He spoke for a Paris which could not conceive of a
passionate attachment between two artistic women without a
carnal element, and which was eager for good savoury gossip
from any source.

Whether the interpretation of the Sand–Dorval friendship was
deliberately malicious or just unperceptive, it was delightfully
intriguing. Literary and artistic Paris had discovered in the unconventional author of *Indiana* an inexhaustible source of spicy
gossip, and the comings and goings at quai Malaquais were
reported with many embellishments. George was credited with at
least three simultaneous affairs: one with Sandeau, unwanted but
still officiating, another with Latouche who had retired to the
country, and yet another with Gustave Planche, the unkempt,
uncombed, unwashed brilliant critic of the *Revue des Deux
Mondes*. Marie Dorval was the latest, most sensational addition
to a cohort of unproven lovers.

Six years older than George Sand, she was born illegitimately to
a touring actress. At four she had her first walk-on part; at fifteen
her first love affair. At twenty-two she was a widow with three
daughters, only two of whom had been born in wedlock. At
thirty-one she married Jean Merle, a writer and a Paris theatre
manager who espoused her career, her daughters and her lovers.
After years of frustration she became one of the most sought-
after actresses of the French stage and could dictate her own
terms to the toughest of theatre managers.

She was not an educated woman, but what she put into her
acting could not have been acquired by any amount of book-
learning. It was inspired, to judge by the reviews of the period.

Professionally she was hard-working and made tremendous demands on herself. Behind the scenes she was emotional, melodramatic, easily pleased, easily forgiving. With her husband she had established a state of tolerance which enabled her to have discreet love affairs without upsetting a pleasant domestic routine. Her proudest conquest was Alfred de Vigny. She loved to show that haughty aristocrat off to her friends and mortified him when she insisted on his attending her Sunday dinners which included her husband, her three daughters, some of her former lovers and several of her new friends. Vigny, squeamish and cautious, never invited his mistress and her husband to meet his English wife.

In January 1833, when Aurore wrote to Dorval, she was just beginning to be known as the author of *Indiana* and did not expect more than a courteous acknowledgment. She little dreamed that her letter would bring the famous actress panting into her own garret. This is how years later she recalled their first meeting:

My letter must have struck her by its sincerity. The very day she received it, just as I was telling Jules Sandeau about it, the door of my garret burst open and a breathless woman rushed in, flinging her arms round me and crying out: 'Here I am.'

I had never seen her before except on stage, but her voice was so familiar that I had no hesitation in recognising her. She was more than pretty; she was charming; and yet she was pretty, but with it so charming as to make prettiness superfluous. Her face was more than a face, it was an expression, a soul. She was still slim, and her figure was like a delicate reed, floating on a mysterious gust of air.[3]

The following Sunday Aurore and Sandeau dined with the Dorval ménage. Alfred de Vigny looked aghast at the young woman dressed in clinging breeches and knee-high boots. He found her unfeminine and unattractive. In his diary he noted:

She must be twenty-five or so. She reminds me of *Judith* in the museum [the apocryphal seductress and killer of Holofernes].

Her hair is dark and curly, falling freely over her collar, rather like a Raphael angel. She has large black eyes, shaped like the eyes of those mystics one sees in pictures, or in those magnificent Italian portraits. Her face is severe and inexpressive, the lower part unpleasant, the mouth ill-shaped. No grace of bearing, coarse in her speech. She is like a man in her manner of dress, her language, the sound of her voice and the audacity of her conversation.[4]

But Marie Dorval liked George, claiming to recognise in her a kindred spirit. Both women had a partly vulgar parentage, an artistic heritage and a creative urge. Both were taking liberties with conventions without actually breaking away from them. Both wanted careers and lovers together with the security of domesticity and children. The mutual attraction flattered them and uplifted them. George, feeling empty after the evaporation of her love for little Jules, suddenly felt alive again. Inviting herself to lunch a few days after the Sunday visit, she wrote to Marie Dorval:

Do you think you could tolerate me? You do not know yet, neither do I. I am so awkward, so stupid, slow and tongue-tied, particularly when I have so much on my heart. Do not judge me by appearances. Wait to find out whether you can have compassion and affection for me. For my part I feel I love you with a heart rejuvenated and made young by you. If it is a dream, like everything else I have wished for in life, do not rob me of it too quickly. It does me so much good.[5]

A routine was established. They saw each other as often as possible, meeting of necessity late at night after the performance of the day was over. They talked into the small hours, discussing themselves, their lovers, their children. Gustave Planche was much perturbed by the attachment between George Sand and Marie Dorval and, being in love with the first, suspected the latter of the worst. The two women had only known each other for a couple of weeks when Planche took it upon himself to warn

George against Marie's lesbianism. His warning fell on deaf ears and a few days later he repeated it in writing:

27 January 1833

My warning against Mme D. must have seemed incomprehensible, crazy. The vehement threats you made last Thursday during lunch indicated quite plainly what you felt about it. I had told Jules why I was so worried to see you embark on this dangerous friendship. I know it is an unforgivable presumption on my part, but what will you have me do? In spite of the voice of reason I would feel guilty if I did not reveal to you what I have learnt. . . . A friend of mine who is on intimate terms with J——te [Juliette Drouet, the actress] and who has every reason to trust her word, tells me that Mme D. had once had for J——te the same sort of passion that Sappho had for the ladies of Lesbos.[6]

Hoping to save George from Dorval's clutches, Planche made a last-minute attempt to reconcile her with Sandeau. When the inevitable break-up took place a few weeks later, it was to Marie that George turned for sympathy for her old friends openly sided with Sandeau. Balzac invited him to stay with him while Régnault accused George of coquetry. In her indignation she appealed to Marie:

Will you condemn me when I am to be pitied? I know you will not, women do justice to women because they understand one another. You will not condemn me in my hour of grief. Alas it was nobody's fault, it was fate.[7]

Vigny too frowned upon the growing attachment between his mistress and that overbearing woman whom he found utterly unfeminine. He tried to force Marie to give George up and Marie, not to antagonise him, pretended that George was pursuing her against her will. On the other hand she made scenes to her lover when, in company, he failed to show Mme Sand sufficient courtesy. At the same time the two women continued to meet as often as they could, and when they could not meet they exchanged letters and brief notes.

The most recurrent theme in their letters was the quest for complimentary tickets, either through Dorval's theatre managers or George Sand's literary contacts. Into these practical exchanges they poured expressions of love. 'The days I do not see you are days lost,' George wrote to Marie, 'but I am working like a horse. Be sorry for me and do not forget me.'[8] 'I love you,'[9] Marie ended one of her briefest notes. 'If you happen to pass by please call and let me embrace you,' George wrote on another occasion. 'I wished someone loved me much as I love you.'[10]

Such endearments as they addressed to each other were mostly the clichés of the age. 'Great and beautiful', George called Marie, 'the fairest of them all', 'dear soul'. Dorval, an inspired actress but a pedestrian writer, called George 'My dear beauty', 'Dear friend', or simply 'My dear George'. Marie sometimes added, 'I love you with all my soul'; George, with affectionate humour, 'I kiss your pretty paws'.[11] She often signed off with a thousand embraces, as she did to Boucoiran, to her children, even to her husband. A thousand embraces did not mean that she was consumed with desire any more than a thousand thanks meant that she was prostrate with gratitude. The general tone of the correspondence was chatty, confident and devoid of drama. There was no trace of that element of torment which nearly always accompanied George's letters to her lovers, or Dorval's to hers. It was many years before they began to address each other regularly as *tu*.

After *Indiana* George was commissioned by the same publisher to write another novel and embarked on *Valentine*, following it up with *La Marquise*, *Melchior* and some verse. She had left *Le Figaro* and accepted an offer from the *Revue des Deux Mondes* to submit thirty-two pages of copy every six weeks against an annual fee of four thousand francs. According to her own favourite description she was working like a convict.

Her fame was spreading fast. She no longer needed introductions to literary celebrities. Celebrities asked to be introduced to her. Apart from Balzac, whom she had met during her early days on *Le Figaro*, she had now met Saint-Beuve, Alfred de Vigny, Alexandre Dumas the Elder. She frequented the theatre, looked after Solange whom she kept with her in Paris, and kept up a busy correspondence with friends back home and her husband. Yet she was deflated. Life without the stimulus of love was vapid. She was consciously looking for someone to fill the vacuum when she was introduced to Prosper Mérimée, the greatest cynic in literary Paris.

When they met, at the beginning of 1833, Mérimée had already published several novels and was a contributor to the *Revue de Paris*. A year older than George, he was unattached and lived with his mother and a number of cats. He was finicky in his habits and would not work by a fire unless assured it had been lit by his mother's own hand. He made a fetish of his cats, kept them in his study when he was working and allowed them to sleep in his bedroom. He had some English blood in his veins and in December 1832 spent some time in London, commenting wittily on the general elections, Lord Palmerston's canvassing and the Whig victory.

Literary Paris watched with interest the progress of the friendship between Mérimée the cynic and George Sand the unconventional. Speculation began after he had been seen several times, aloof and unconcerned, carrying little Solange on his shoulders before depositing her in her mother's carriage. His courtship was direct and unromantic. The turning point came one day in April during a stroll along the embankment of the Seine. Disdaining the notion of romantic love as understood by George, Mérimée suggested that she should become his mistress for the sheer physical pleasure of it. He himself later commemorated the words of her capitulation:

'All right,' she said to me. 'I agree. Let it be as you wish, since it gives you so much pleasure. But as far as I am concerned I must tell you I am positive it gives me none.'[12]

They went back to quai Malaquais where George donned a costume which she considered seductive: a man's shirt over a yellow silk shift, a Spanish hair-net, bright red oriental slippers. They had a meal, then George began to undress with what Mérimée later described as a shocking lack of *pudeur*, mistaking for brazenness a determined effort to conceal absence of desire. The effect on him was petrifying, but honour demanded consummation. By the time it was achieved all thoughts of pleasure had been abandoned; there remained only squeamishness, disgust, frustration and brute force. Before he left Mérimée made some scathing remarks. George wept with humiliation.

In her anguish she rushed over to Marie Dorval and poured out her heart. Marie repeated the confession to Vigny who confided it to his diary, then to Dumas who confided it to the rest of Paris. Within days literary and artistic circles were enjoying the lurid details of the consummation and ascribing to George the brazen remark that she had had Mérimée for a night.

Three months after the episode was over George felt it necessary to explain herself to Sainte-Beuve to whom she had transferred the role of father confessor which Emile Régnault could no longer play. In a letter nearly three thousand words long she wrote among other things:

'Still young but already old, I wanted to have done with that frustrating struggle of yesterdays and tomorrows. I wanted to order my life for ever. Like everyone else I had days of serious determination and sane resignation, and like everyone else I also had days of anxiety, suffering, mortal anguish. On such days I was pitifully sombre and gloomy, so depressed that I wanted to drown myself, miserably asking Providence if there was no such thing on earth as happiness, solace, or even pleasure.

'You have not asked me to confide in you, but what I am about to tell you will not encumber you because I am not asking for your silence. I would be prepared to tell or publish all the facts of my life if I thought they could be of use to anybody. As I value your respect and need it, I feel I have the right to show myself to you as I am, even if you are put off by my confession. . . . . One day when I was troubled and despondent, I met a man who knew nothing of my turmoil, a quiet strong man who did not understand the first thing about me and made fun of my suffering. The strength of his spirit captivated me; for a week I thought that he possessed the secret of happiness, that he would reveal it to me, that his disdainful unconcern would cure me of my childish susceptibilities. I thought that he had suffered like me and that he had overcome his outward sensitivity. . . . I thought of myself as a woman without restraint, and she seemed sublime. Me, austere and a near-virgin, I was hideous in my egotism and isolation. I tried to overcome my nature, to forget the miscalculations of the past. That man who could love on one condition only and who knew how to make me desire his love, persuaded me that there could exist for me a love acceptable to the senses, intoxicating to the spirit. This was how I had understood love in the past and I told myself that perhaps I had not known enough spiritual love to tolerate the other kind. I was overcome by that romantic trouble, that dizziness of the spirit which drives you, after you have repudiated everything, to commit graver mistakes than ever. Having believed that after several years' intimacy with one person I could not get attached to another, I allowed the attraction of a few days to determine my existence. At thirty I behaved more stupidly than a girl of fifteen. I became the mistress of Prosper Mérimée.

'Be brave, the rest of the story is odious. But why should I mind being ridiculed when I was not to blame? The experience was a complete failure. I cried with anguish, disgust and despondency. Instead of finding sympathy and affection to make up for the past, I encountered only bitter and frivolous mockery. That was all, and people summed up the story in words I had not said, which Mme Dorval had neither betrayed nor made up, and which do little credit to M. Dumas.

'If Prosper Mérimée had understood me he might have loved me, and if he loved me he might have dominated me, and if I could be dominated by a man I might have been saved, for my independence is gnawing at me and killing me. But he did not know me well enough, and instead of giving him time to do so, I was immediately discouraged and rejected the only condition which could have attached him to me.

'Having made an ass of myself I was more distressed than ever, you saw me in a suicidal mood which was very genuine. But if there are days of frost and fever, there are also days of sunshine and hope. Gradually I have recovered and even that unhappy and ridiculous struggle made me take a big step towards a future of serenity and detachment which I promise myself on my good days. I feel that love does not become me any more than roses on the forehead of a sixty-year-old, and for the last three months (surely the first three months of my life) I have not felt the slightest temptation for it.'[13]

George never sought to see Mérimée again. As with Sandeau, the end of the affair meant another unvisited tomb in the graveyard of the soul. The pattern was becoming more defined: loves which ended in unforgiving estrangement, non-physical friendships which used the language of love and lasted unto death. In this case however the last word was Mérimée's. In 1848, fifteen years after the brief affair, he met George by chance. He described the occasion in a letter to the beautiful Countess de Montijo, in Madrid:

6 May 1848

A couple of days ago I was invited to dine with an English friend of mine whom you may have met in Madrid two years ago. He is a Mr Monkton-Milnes [later Lord Houghton], a man of culture and rather livelier and crazier than most Englishmen. He said it was going to be a small dinner party and I was not a little surprised to find myself at table with three ladies and half a dozen men, one of whom was Considérant, the follower of Fou ier [the philosopher and sociologist]. One of the women had very beautiful dark eyes which she kept lowering over her plate. She was seated opposite me and I thought her face was not unfamiliar. At last I asked my neighbour at dinner who she was: it was Mme Sand. I thought she was far more attractive than she used to be. We did not exchange a word, as you may well imagine, but we spent a great part of the evening eyeing each other through our *lorgnettes*.[14]

They never met again. In her sixties George Sand once spent a few weeks with friends who had a house on the French Riviera, where Mérimée was then living. George, who knew him to be a good friend of her hosts, asked them to ask him not to call during her stay. Mérimée obliged.

One of the more painful aspects of the Mérimée fiasco was the realisation that Marie Dorval had betrayed intimate details given in confidence. For some time there was coolness between the two women, increased by reports of what they were alleged to have said about one another. It was all very hurtful. At the beginning of the summer Dorval went on tour without taking leave of George. Suddenly George realised that she was about to lose her only intimate female friend and decided to overlook the breach of confidence. She sent the reluctant Planche to the Vigny residence to enquire about Dorval's provincial address, then wrote impetuously and eloquently:

18 July 1833

Where are you? What has become of you? I cannot get hold of any paper which has something about you, yet many papers must be writing about you. You must be a resounding success because you are beautiful and an angel and everybody who sees you admires you and worships you. But I do not know where you are. I have just dropped a line to M. de Vigny to find out where to address this letter. Why did you go away, naughty girl, without saying goodbye, without leaving me your itinerary so that I can run after you? Your leaving without saying goodbye hurt. I was in a bad mood. I imagined you did not love me. I cried like an ass. Since you left people have been saying all sorts of things in order to stop me loving you. Can you imagine that people actually take pleasure in making you suffer? People I hardly know and who do not know you at all tell me or write to me that you have betrayed me. Betrayed what? They can talk of nothing else, they are all like chattering jays. I took no notice and I do not remember a single word of what they said, their stupidity made me come to my senses. I told myself that you had not had time to come and see me before you left and that I ought to have come to see you. What sort of friendship is it which puts on airs and counts the number of visits? I am a fool. You must forgive me. There are tiresome sides to my character, but my heart is capable of loving you, I feel it. In vain do I look at others, not one is comparable to you. No other nature is so frank, true, strong, versatile, kind, generous, gentle, great, clownish, perfect, whole. I want to love you always, either to cry with you or laugh with you. I want to join you, spend a few days where you are. Where are you?

If you answer me quickly saying no more than 'come', I shall come, even if I had the cholera or a lover.

Always yours,
George.[15]

The posting of the letter was delayed, for M. de Vigny took several days to answer George's query. Even then he only sent word that Marie had recently been playing at Laon, about eighty miles north of Paris, and that Mme Sand could have looked it up in a provincial paper. George added a fulminating postscript against Vigny and sent it off to Marie. Marie, anxious to ward off her lover's jealousy, sent it on to Vigny in Paris to ask for guidance. Vigny scribbled angrily on the letter: 'I have forbidden Marie to reply to that Sappho who is annoying her.'[16]

George did not join Marie Dorval on that tour, or on any other tour, because within days of her writing that letter she embarked on what was to prove the most violent love affair of her life: she had met Alfred de Musset. But the friendship with Dorval was restored, though on a less frantic note. In 1835, having seen Marie create the part of *Kitty Bell* in Vigny's *Chatterton*, George wrote with her customary warm impetuosity:

My dear, I must tell you that I have never seen you so beautiful, so intelligent and so admirable as last night. Everyone must be telling you so, but you must know that I am one of those most moved and most grateful among those who bow before you. . . . The play is extremely moving, exquisite in its sentiments. I came out in tears. . . . Unlike you, I do not like M. de Vigny in the flesh (that's witty, isn't it?) but I assure you that as from one soul to another I think of him differently. Make him happy, my child, these men need it and deserve it. I embrace you, my dear, and am still devoted to you for ever.[17]

Still the rumours about the two women persisted. In 1836, when Casimir Dudevant was contesting his wife's demand for judicial separation and custody of the children, he asked a friend of his in Paris whether he could not lay his hands on some letters which Aurore had written to Mme Dorval and which 'badly compromise her as far as people say and as I have myself heard in Paris'.[18] No such letters were found.

In 1838, after seven years of ups and downs, Vigny broke up with Dorval. Her next lover was Jules Sandeau, who by that time had become an established writer. They had not seen each other for several years after his liaison with George, and on the face of it there was no reason for jealousy on the part of either woman. George however frowned at the attachment and warned Marie against Sandeau's duplicity. Marie took no notice and wrote Jules frantic love letters: 'Oh I am dying, I love you so, you are the apple of my eye, the enchantment of my soul, the ecstasy of my senses, the joy of my heart.'[19]

But jealousy, for Dorval, was the food of love, and she would not have been herself if she had not re-enacted in real life the parts she had played on the stage. About a year after the beginning of her liaison with Sandeau, the latter was asked to contribute to an anthology about famous French women. He chose to write about George Sand. Marie noticed the draft on his desk, glanced at it and cried out dramatically: 'Her again! Always her! That woman will be the death of me!'[20] Snatching a paper-knife she stabbed herself with a well-practised flourish and allowed a few drops of blood to smudge the sheet of paper. The scene was witnessed by young Arsène Houssaye who was then collaborating with Sandeau on a novel. He persuaded Sandeau to part with the blood-stained script and added it to his collection of original documents. After the death of both Dorval and Sandeau he reproduced it in his *Confessions.*

But Dorval's melodramatic outbursts were only skin deep; as Vigny had once observed, she felt the need to practise her art at all times. Her friendship with George remained unimpaired. In 1840, when the Théâtre Français, forerunner of the Comédie Française, accepted George Sand's first play *Cosima*, she obtained for Dorval the title role. The play was a failure and had to be taken off, but not before people noticed that the two women had been using the informal *tu* at rehearsals. The posters which billed the names Dorval and Sand also helped to revive old rumours, although at that time George was living with Chopin. Two years after *Cosima* Sandeau broke up with Dorval to get married. Marie accepted the inevitable with good grace but to George she wrote that she had been right all along about Sandeau's duplicity. Friendship was vindicated.

Marie's last years were unhappy. Two of her daughters made unsuitable marriages and one died of consumption. In Paris she had bad seasons and was forced to tour the provinces, no longer in the comfort of her own carriage, but using public transport. She had daughters, sons-in-law and grandchildren to support, and her health was failing. Her only comfort in her last years was her little grandson Georges, whom she took with her on tours. When he died, aged five, she lost the will to live. She spent days by his grave, bringing along her own folding-chair, her bible and her tapestry. To George Sand she wrote:

12 June 1848

You cannot possibly know the deep, irreparable grief in my heart. I do not know what to do, what to believe. I do not understand why God takes away from us such dear creatures. I want to pray but I feel only anger and rebellion. I spend my life on his little grave. Does he see me? Do you think he does? I do not know what to do with my life any more. . . . Forgive me for distressing you, my dear friend, but I come to you as to one I have loved so much, who has always been kind to me. . . . I come to you so that you may give me strength. Help me with my grief. I know where to find those beautiful words which come from your noble heart, your lofty mind. But they will comfort me more if they came from your heart straight to mine. Goodbye, my friend, my dear George, the name I hold so dear to my heart.[21]

Marie Dorval, by Léon Noël

Aurore and Casimir Dudevant, about 1835, by François Biard

George Sand's two children, Solange, aged 9 (*left*),
and Maurice, aged 14 (*right*), by Charpentier

George's answer was everything that Marie wished it to be. By that time she was living permanently at Nohant and did not witness Dorval's brilliant comeback in a play where she acted the part of a mother who had lost her child. But when the season was over Marie was out of work again, lonely, ailing and penniless. People like Victor Hugo, Alexandre Dumas, Alfred de Musset, Théophile Gautier and Jules Sandeau, though not Alfred de Vigny, signed a petition to the Minister of the Interior asking him to make Dorval a full, paid member of the Comédie Française. It was too late. At fifty-one she died poor, half-forgotten, with only a few people by her bedside. She was buried at Montparnasse, and the epitaph on her gravestone was the one that she herself had worded: Marie Dorval, died of grief.

George learnt of her death from one of Marie's daughters, who added in her letter that the very last book her mother had read was *La Petite Fadette*, only recently published. The friendship which George had felt for the mother was transferred to her family, and for many years to come Nohant was a holiday home for Dorval's daughters, sons-in-law, children and grandchildren. In her autobiography, written not long after Marie's death, George Sand devoted to her one of the most elegiac chapters in the book, giving her in death the praise that Dorval would have liked to hear in life: 'She was one of the greatest artists of the century, and the kindest of women.'[22]

Had the two women ever had a lesbian relationship in the physical sense implied by Vigny, Planche, Casimir Dudevant and Arsène Houssaye? Their extant correspondence does not suggest it and the durability of their relationship seems to rule out such an interpretation. George Sand had never been able to turn a love affair into friendship. Once it was over it was replaced by total estrangement. Only people who exhilarated her spiritually without rousing her desire retained her goodwill and brought out the loyal friend in her. Marie Dorval was surely one of them.

~~~~~~~~~~~~~~~

Chapter 7

Lélia

François Buloz, editor-in-chief of the *Revue des Deux Mondes*, had an unusual flair for writers of promise. When the publisher of *Indiana* announced another novel called *Valentine*, Buloz hastened to offer the rising young author an attractive annual fee for the right to publish her future output in his magazine prior to its publication in book form. From 1832 until her death in 1876, with the exception of a ten-year period of estrangement, most of George Sand's novels were first published in the *Revue*.

Buloz was a self-made man. The eighth child of unwealthy parents, he had to leave the *lycée* at seventeen to make a living as an unskilled hand in a provincial chemical factory. After a while he took himself to Paris and enrolled as a chemistry student at the Sorbonne, at the same time teaching himself English with the aid of a grammar book and a dictionary. He became a printer, a type-setter and a proof-reader, working twelve hours a day and supplementing his income by translating science books from English into French.

In 1831 his luck turned. A fellow-printer bought up the newly founded *Revue des Deux Mondes*, already in difficulties, and offered him the post of editor-in-chief. He was twenty-seven. He had little capital but a great many connections made during his proof-reading stage. He was utterly dedicated and succeeded in attracting the élite of French writers with more promises than pay. His contributors included Alfred de Vigny, Balzac, Alexandre Dumas and Théophile Gautier. Being a young man, Buloz encouraged young writers. He welcomed George Sand who was his own age, Alfred de Musset who was twenty-two, Gustave

Planche who was twenty-three. It was through her association with the *Revue des Deux Mondes* that George came to know these two budding writers who were to play such an important part in her literary and emotional development.

Gustave Planche, today perhaps one of the least remembered of the *Revue* galaxy of those years, was a reviewer who considered literary criticism holy gospel and himself the prophet chosen by God to spread it among the literate. He was convinced it was his sacred duty to tell authors what he thought of their work and wielded his pen like a scourge. Within months of his joining the *Revue des Deux Mondes* he became the most dreaded critic in Paris.

At twenty-three he was already an eccentric. His clothes were tatty, his hair dishevelled, his manner unprepossessing. Cleanliness was not one of his virtues and his colleagues often found his presence offensive. The story went round that when at long last he was persuaded to go into the public baths, he got side-tracked by a cheap dish of *sauerkraut* served on the premises and, after he had ordered and consumed it, left without remembering what he had come in for. From time to time Buloz treated him to a new set of clothes. For a day or two Planche would turn up clean and spruce, then pawn the elegant outfit to pay pressing debts and resume his comfortable rags. His tall hat became a byword. Buloz's little son once got hold of it during an editorial conference and filled it with warm water to serve as a toy bath. Planche clouted the boy and reinstated the hat.

It was Planche who first brought George Sand's merit to Buloz's notice. From an admirer of Sand the writer the young man turned into an admirer of Sand the woman. He became her escort, her errand-boy and her help-about-the-house. When Solange was ill he ran for the doctor, when Casimir came up to Paris he showed him the sights. At the same time he continued to be a relentless critic. George was annoyed with the sharpness of his remarks but often followed his advice. Soon Paris gave him to her for a lover.

Unwittingly Planche was one of the causes of her break-up with Latouche, her first editor and literary mentor. Latouche had left Paris and *Le Figaro* with a sense of grievance. At first George used to go to see him at his country retreat, shop for him, cook for him and talk with him late into the night, leaving Jules Sandeau to look after Solange. Soon gossip made Latouche another of her lovers.

When Planche published an uncharacteristic article in favour of the romantic writers of the day, whom Latouche had taken to task two or three years earlier, the latter took it as a personal affront, partly instigated by George. He accused her of being dazzled by success and using people as stepping-stones. She asked a mutual friend who lived near Latouche's country place to plead her innocence. The friend returned to Paris with a message saying that Mme Dudevant was a hypocrite and need not come down again. Other friends confirmed that Latouche was suffering from persecution mania and never kept any of his friends. George was grieved but decided to leave well alone, at least for the time being.

She had begun to court a literary man of her own age. At twenty-eight Charles-Augustin Sainte-Beuve had already published some verse and distinguished himself as a critic. After he had given *Indiana* a favourable review, George asked the ever-ready Planche to bring him to quai Malaquais. They arrived there together in early January of 1833. It was midday. 'I saw a young woman with beautiful eyes, a beautiful forehead and black hair cut somewhat short,' Sainte-Beuve recalled. 'She was wearing a sort of dressing-gown, sombre and very simple. She listened to us, said little and asked me to call again.'[1]

There the acquaintance might have ended but for George's persistence. She knew Sainte-Beuve to be a close friend of twenty-six-year-old Victor Hugo, or rather of Mme Adèle Hugo, and wrote to ask if he could get her two complimentary tickets for Hugo's *Lucrèce Borgia* which was having its first performance. When Sainte-Beuve obliged she wrote to thank him and again asked him to call. When he did she was out. She wrote again, insisting on another call. He came, curious, attracted, but on his guard.

The next few months saw her separation from Sandeau and the interlude with Mérimée. Her brief notes to Sainte-Beuve became more pressing. She asked him to renew his calls; he stayed away. She invited him to dinner; he indicated he was not hungry. George was not used to such resistance and wrote to ask if he was by any chance in love with a jealous woman who might consider her a rival. Then she added with a touch of her heavy sense of humour:

If that is what she fears could you not reassure her, tell her that I am three hundred years old, that I ceased to regard myself as a woman long before her own grandmother was born, that I do not care for men, that I am only interested in spiritual dissertations which do not attract men to me any more than they push me towards men?

She assured Sainte-Beuve that all she wanted was friendship and concluded:

After all, my dear, if I do not please you, you will keep your freedom. It will sadden me, but not offend me. If I am a nuisance, leave me. However great my grief would be at losing a friendship I hold most precious, I would rather have certainty than be kept in doubt.[2]

Sainte-Beuve did not keep her in doubt. He indicated that he respected her as a writer and thinker, but was emotionally unfree. She then made him her confessor and began by telling him about her misadventure with Mérimée, still groping towards an elusive intimacy. A regular correspondence was established. Sainte-Beuve set the tone, never allowing it to become unduly warm. Taking her cue from him, George hardly ever ended her letters with anything more effusive than 'Yours cordially' and mostly signed as George Sand, or even G. Sand. She wrote often and much, discussing many of her problems with him.

When they had both become famous a temporary cooling off put a stop to the correspondence, but after a while it was renewed and cordially continued until Sainte-Beuve's death in 1869, seven years before hers.

Contrary to what Latouche had said about her, the success of *Indiana* did not dazzle George. On the contrary, it made her realise how difficult it would be to live up to it. To Charles Duvernet in Berry she wrote: 'The success of *Indiana* frightens me. Until now I thought I was working without making an impact or gaining attention. Fate has ordained otherwise. I must justify the unmerited admiration of which I have become the object.'[3]

Whatever her emotional state, she was a disciplined worker. People who knew her well said that she could turn herself on like a tap. She worked most nights from about midnight to early morning, with a blazing fire to keep her warm. Now she could give free rein to her eloquence and expansiveness without fearing the blue pencil of a space-conscious editor. She thought out complicated plots, drew on her personal experience, modelled her characters on people she had met. The pages accumulated on her desk with hardly any erasions.

Her early works were all variations on a theme. *Valentine* was a noble-minded lady married to a mediocre husband, in love with a young peasant whose greatness of soul made up for his lowly birth. The *marquise*, virtuous and cultured like old Mme Dupin de Francueil, married to a boorish husband, was in love with an actor whose familiarity with classic roles had ennobled his mind. *Melchior* was the unfortunate husband of a madwoman, in love with an innocent girl. None of these extra-marital loves ever led to sin or breach of convention. When virtue was about to yield, death intervened to keep it intact. Yet the message was clear. Women, like men, had the right to seek love outside marriage, even outside their class, love being the most sublime and desirable of all human experiences.

In her later writings George Sand claimed that her books were not an attack on marriage but on 'married people'.[4] She declared that she had no quarrel with any existing social structure and no ambition to change the French constitution. Yet in presenting married women as victims of society, she condemned the laws which sanctioned their status. She interpreted her own marital dependence as symptomatic of a social order established by men for the perpetration of their privileges. Women readers recognised themselves in her stories and upheld her as the champion of their downtrodden rights.

She was not the first to speak up for her oppressed sex. The climate of the 1830s was conducive to social reform and women's emancipation was a logical development of the ideals of the July Revolution of 1830. In a critical essay published in *Le National* in September 1833, Sainte-Beuve discussed the bloodless revolution which was taking place in French homes:

Notice should be taken of the unusual moral and literary movement which is manifesting itself among the women of France and which has spread considerably over the past few years. True enough, there have always been women, mostly born into conditions of leisure which facilitated the cultivation of the spirit, who distinguished themselves throughout the ages by writing novels, poetry, books on education. Mme de Staël [1766–1817] combined imagination and sensibility with a comprehensive political and philosophical outlook. But Mme de Staël was unique among women, and since her even the most distinguished amongst them have confined themselves to pleasant little songs, delicate paintings, a subtle and tender analysis of emotions under the wing of Christianity.

For the last three years however, since the decline of the well-ordered *bon ton* and the moral veneer prescribed by the Restoration, socialism has brought forth a call for emancipation which has roused women in the same way as men. Many amongst them began to speak their mind and are now writing articles for the press, short stories and novels. They are revealing their suffering, claiming a more equal part in life, appealing against society. . . . Nowadays women from all walks of life have taken to writing. Each has her own secret grievance, her own love story, which she uses to support her plea for emancipation. It is not only the ladies of society or rank who give vent to their feelings in this way. In this field, as everywhere else, there is no more class distinction and democracy flows freely.[5]

Against this background of feminist awakening, Sainte-Beuve assessed George Sand's contribution and pronounced her, if not the first in time, most certainly the first in quality:

Of all women who have hurled themselves into the turmoil with a grievance to proclaim, there is none more eloquent, more audacious or more outstanding than the author of *Indiana*.[6]

Not everyone agreed with Sainte-Beuve's favourable opinion of George Sand. While progressive thinkers praised her calling attention to the unequal status of women in an enlightened society, conservatives accused her of moral subversion. Not only was she preaching free love, but she was trampling down time-honoured class barriers, allowing ladies of high birth to fall in love with actors and peasants. Admirers and detractors alike conceded that she had literary talent, and her publisher pressed for another full-length novel. By the end of 1832 she had conceived the idea of *Lélia*, and by the summer of 1833 she saw it published. She dedicated it to Latouche who was still sulking in the country.

Of all George Sand's novels, *Lélia* was perhaps the one which contributed most to her reputation. It was the story of a young woman, so disenchanted by her legitimate first taste of love, that she began to doubt its very existence. As Lélia herself defined it, it was a tale of 'an unhappy heart, lost in its own wealth of potential, blighted before it had a chance to live, worn out by hope and rendered impotent by too much potence'.[7] Initiated readers easily recognised George Sand in her.

The plot was complicated and fanciful. When the young poet Sténio fell in love with Lélia, she could not bring herself to love again. The only person who understood her inner doubts was Trenmor, a one-time convict who had expiated his crime and become a philosopher. Young Sténio could not understand the affinity between Lélia and Trenmor and accused her of coquetry and frigidity. In his despair he became the lover of her sister Pulchérie, an attractive creature of easy virtue. Debauchery failed to cure him of his love, and feeling that it had lost him Lélia for ever, he committed suicide. Lélia shunned the world and sought spiritual solace in religious seclusion. Even then she found no peace and died in Trenmor's arms, who buried her next to Sténio's grave.

Lélia was basically a novel of ideas. It was a vehicle to expound theories, criticise conventions and uphold woman's right to seek emotional and spiritual fulfilment. Ideas mattered so much more than physical details that Sténio was allowed black curls in an early chapter, golden locks falling over his shoulders in a later one. The characters however were modelled on recognisable living people. Lélia was a reincarnation of George in a state of abnegation, Pulchérie a somewhat depraved edition of Marie Dorval, and Trenmor a respectful version of François Rollinat, a young Châteauroux lawyer who over the past year or so had become what George described as her other self.

The Rollinats were a well-known Châteauroux family, several of whose members were lawyers by profession, republicans by faith. Casimir met some of them while canvassing for the local republican Deputy and in 1831 invited François to spend a few days at Nohant. The stay coincided with Mme Dudevant's return to the family home after her second three-month stay in Paris. François was twenty-five at the time, his hostess twenty-seven.

He fitted admirably into her cast of mind. He was a romantic, an idealist, a political dreamer and, as fate would so often have it in George Sand's life, younger and weaker than her. He could no more resist her engulfing strength than other young men could, Boucoiran, Sandeau, Gustave Papet, Emile Régnault. They held long conversations and discovered a spiritual affinity. When he left they took to writing. The letters flowed from Châteauroux to Nohant and Paris, from Nohant or Paris back to Châteauroux. George found him 'affectionate, gentle, simple, even-tempered, silent, sad and compassionate'.[8] Rollinat was moved by the agony of a soul in search of elusive perfection. 'How noble and beautiful your suffering is,'[9] he wrote to her.

As usual, George was forthright and effusive, professing her friendship in the language of love. 'I am so depressed,' she wrote one day from Nohant, urging him to come to stay. 'Only you can cure me. Love me, even if I do not deserve the friendship of someone like you. All the more reason why I need it.'[10] When he could take time off from his legal commitments at Châteauroux, George would take his arm after dinner and stroll with him in the Nohant grounds late at night, discussing the sorrows of her soul and the unhappy state of society. Not for him the personal confidences about her disenchantment with Sandeau or Mérimée; those could be made only to someone like Sainte-Beuve who held the potential ability to replace them. Rollinat neither stirred nor excited her, and George left him in no doubt about it:

> I have never felt for you either spiritual or physical love; but, from the very day I met you I have felt one of those rare affinities, deep and indestructible, which nothing can ever change because the more one delves into one's soul the more one knows oneself identical with the person who is the subject of such an affinity. I have not found you superior to me by nature; had you been I would have conceived for you that intoxication which leads to love. In you I found my equal, my parallel.[11]

Rollinat accepted the role of a spiritual double, resigned to being the reflection of a sweeping personality. He too allowed himself to use the language of love; but whereas George's loving expressions were effusive rather than profound, his were full of pathos: 'Yes, my dear, it is towards you, you, you alone that my thoughts always turn on good and bad days alike. You are the soul which agrees with mine, great, proud, bold, free, generous and tender, tried and purified by suffering.'[12] Sometimes his feelings ran away with him: 'I am writing these few lines only to tell you that I love you, I adore you, I revere you like my guardian angel. You know it already, but it does not matter, I shall never tire of saying it over and over again.'[13]

He had his other uses for the busy châtelaine that George was when living at Nohant. From time to time he received gay little notes asking him to order some beer for the Nohant cellar, choose a horse for Maurice, negotiate for the purchase of a new piano, buy a favourite perfume, send some sheet music by Berlioz. He devoutly obliged, seeing in these requests a sign of George's trust in him. Indeed he was to her, at the time of her disenchantment with love, a pillar of strength. Whatever the yearning in his heart, he did not burden her with it and gave her the undemanding, uncomplicated devotion she needed at that stage.

What Rollinat was to George, Trenmor was to Lélia. Both women had a secret craving for a man who would be totally committed without expecting an emotional involvement in return. Trenmor was the philosopher of the piece, and unlike Rollinat, more of an abstraction than a living human being. George considered his role in the novel so important that for a while she called it by that name. While working on *Lélia* she hardly wrote to Rollinat; instead she kept having imaginary conversations with him which helped to crystallise her ideas. When the book was finished she wrote a disarming letter of apology, acknowledging her debt:

Paris, 20–19 May 1833.

In a few days I shall send you a long letter; it is a book I have written since we last met. It is a continuous conversation between the two of us. We are the most serious characters in it. As for the others, you may interpret them as you like. This book will help you reach the very bottom of my soul, as well as yours. I do not consider these few lines as a letter. You are with me in my thoughts all the time. You will see what I mean when you read me.

Goodbye for now, Trenmor. Write to me, tell me about your family, about the greatness, beauty and sorrows of this life. . . . Believe me yours for ever,

Your friend,
George Sand.[14]

Lélia burst on the literary scene with unprecedented force. Readers either loved it or hated it; everybody discussed it. Some acknowledged it as the ultimate expression of the century's anguish and Chateaubriand hailed the author as 'the French Lord

Byron'.[15] Sainte-Beuve praised the conception but regretted the absence of a firm conclusion. In his review he wrote:

If I was asked what I thought of the moral of *Lélia*, in the only possible sense of the question, I would say that the anguish and despair of the situation having been so admirably put, the author did not lead either her heroes or her readers to a safe haven, and the violent crises encountered in the book do not culminate in a morally satisfactory solution.[16]

Sainte-Beuve concluded that *Lélia* was 'extraordinary rather than beautiful' and expressed the hope that the author, having given vent to 'a lyrical and philosophical work', would return to her earlier romantic *genre*. Other critics were less tolerant. *La France littéraire* accused *Lélia* of destroying current ideas without proposing any new ones instead. The man who took the greatest exception to *Lélia* was Capo de Feuillide, the literary critic of the short-lived *Europe littéraire*. He considered the book so dangerous that he devoted two articles to it, warning his readers against its amorality. Among other things he wrote:

The day you begin to read *Lélia*, lock yourself in your study. If you have a daughter, a tender flower you wish to protect from the breath of vice, whose soul you wish to keep virginal and innocent, send her away to play with her girl-friends in the country. If you have a young wife whose love is dear to you, allow her the fancy-dress of her choice so that she can take herself to a ball; if your daughter stays at home and picks up *Lélia* she runs a greater risk than if she is away from home, and as for your wife, no amount of flirtation at a ball will tarnish her purity as much as the corruptive pages of that book.[17]

The first of Feuillide's two articles appeared on 9 August 1833. On the 15th Planche published a reply. On the 22nd Feuillide published his second article. On the 25th Planche challenged him to a duel.

George was displeased; not so much because she felt that a duel was hardly the way to settle a literary argument, but because she had recently become the mistress of Alfred de Musset, and it suited neither her nor her lover to allow Planche to take up the defence of her honour. But Planche was adamant. Somehow he persuaded Buloz and Emile Régnault to act as his seconds, and the duel took place two days later in the Bois de Boulogne. Fortunately both critics were better at wielding a pen than a pistol. The shots misfired, nobody was hurt. The Paris press however got hold of the story and published it with every possible embellishment. Planche was made to look a fool, Musset a coward and George the mistress of two lovers. One day George found a burlesque poem pushed under her door, set to a well-known tune called *Le Maréchal de Saxe*, retelling the story of the duel in a way that made Planche look more ridiculous than ever. It had been written by Musset, surely in one of his off-moments, and ran to twenty-four verses here quoted in a freely translated, abridged version:

> De Feuillide the outrageous
> To Lélia was unkind.
> Monsieur Planche had a mind
> To prove himself courageous,
> And from midnight to three
> Penned a fierce repartee.
>
> He wrote a brave letter
> In French most correct,
> Raging that no respect
> Was paid to his patter;
> And full of indignation
> Pulled on his combination.
>
> Buloz in his chamber
> Slept the sleep of the just,
> Waking up as he must,
> Yawning with anger,
> When suddenly Planche came in
> Waving papers before him.

By way of consultation
Monsieur Régnault he brought along,
Who could see what was wrong
And gave an explanation,
While Planche leaned on his arm
To protect himself from harm.

The enemy kept them waiting
Until quarter past four,
A cad he all the more,
For Buloz was straining
Mme Dudevant to see
Over a cup of tea.

A carriage with a gelding
Behind a tree at last loomed,
Feuillide stepped down well groomed
As if for his own wedding.
His seconds stepped down too
With pistols for the two.

The combatants stood still,
Taking aim from four feet.
Planche's shot was a feat,
Straying over a hill.
Feuillide as quick as lightning
Hit a distant clearing.

After the detonation
The seconds nipped in the bud
The shedding of blood
So precious to the nation,
And Planche was proclaimed
Properly avenged.

Into the arms of the knave
Planche, who was wobbling,
Threw himself sobbing:
We are both so brave,

My mind has been eased,
You too should be pleased.

And so they adjourned,
And it was through this venue
That of George Sand the virtue
Was at last confirmed.
And from that day of disaster
They lived happily ever after.[18]

It was also from that day of disaster that the sales of *Lélia* went up beyond precedent. A second impression was immediately followed by a third. They appeared however without the original dedication to Latouche who had made it known he regarded it as an insult to his name, not least because it had been spelt Delatouche instead of de Latouche. With the third impression more than three thousand copies had been published, a high figure in the terms of the day. George became known all over France as the author of *Lélia*, or even, quite briefly, as Lélia. She had arrived. Alfred de Musset paid her the highest compliment she could have wished to hear:

Before *Lélia* you might have remained Mme So-and-So who writes books. Now you are George Sand.[19]

Chapter 8

꧁ৡৢ꧂ৡৢ꧂ৡৢ꧁

The love that launched a thousand books

Today it may be hard to understand why the love affair between George Sand and Alfred de Musset, which was intermittently conducted between 1833 and 1835, roused so many tempers and brought forth so many contradictory pronouncements. People like Sainte-Beuve, Buloz, Planche, Liszt and Delacroix were drawn in, made to sympathise, listen to endless unburdenings of love and grief, mediate. George went about Paris declaring that once she had written her memoirs to assure the financial future of her children, she would commit suicide; Musset fluctuated between periods of feverish pleasure-seeking and utter dejection. Both gave vent to their sorrows in eminently publishable forms. George's *Lettres d'un voyageur* bore witness to her unhappy state of mind; Musset's poems *Nuit de mai* and *Nuit de décembre* expressed his, as did his novel *La Confession d'un enfant du siècle*. These works, published during or immediately after the affair, caused a stir not only because of their intrinsic merit, but because of the identity of the writers. Anybody who knew Sand and Musset, or who had read anything by them in the *Revue des Deux Mondes*, was intrigued by the intimate revelations the two writers made about each other in the same literary journal. It was literature with a difference.

A quarter of a century after the end of the affair, when George was in her mid-fifties and Musset dead for a year, she brought out her novel *Elle et Lui*, which was taken to be her own version of the old love story. Today it is difficult to believe that at that stage in her life she felt impelled to whitewash herself of a guilt she never felt; it is more likely that, true to a lifetime habit, she delved into her romantic past to find a theme for a new work of fiction. Personal experience had always been an unfailing source of inspiration; it was her privilege as a writer to mould it and present it as the spirit moved her.

This time however she sparked off something she had not expected. Paul de Musset, the late poet's elder brother, treated her novel as pure autobiography, and as such full of malicious distortions. He struck back with a book of his own, *Lui et Elle*, in which he claimed to reveal the real truth about George's relationships with Musset. Again everybody felt impelled to read, accuse and defend, disregard poetic licence and seek in works of fiction concrete proof of moral callousness. The gossipmongers of twenty-five years earlier were joined by a new generation of impassioned truth-seekers. Every alleged detail of the Venice drama was minutely discussed. Did George, or did she not, take tea from the same cup as the doctor who was keeping watch with her over the delirious Musset? Did she, or did she not, become the doctor's mistress under Musset's feverish eyes? Did she, or did she not, try to persuade Musset that he was suffering from hallucinations and that he had only imagined an act of infidelity? The scandal was revived.

The passage of time did nothing to abate the ardour of learned researchers bent on exonerating or convicting. At the end of the nineteenth century a wave of scholarly curiosity led to the discovery of fresh documentary evidence. The novelists and gossipmongers were replaced by serious researchers like Paul Clouard, Paul Landau, Arvède Barine, Doctor Cabanès, Paul Mariéton and Spoelberch de Lovenjoul. The twentieth century produced further researchers like Charles Maurras, E. Feugère, A. Adam, and in the last decade or so, notably Annarosa Poli and Henri Guillemin. Countless articles were published analysing the factual, literary, psychological and social aspects of the case. Whatever the interpretation put on it, it remained undisputably the most extrovert of George Sand's love affairs, and one which continued to fertilise her work long after it had burnt itself to ashes.

They met in June 1833 at a dinner given by Buloz to the contributors of the *Revue des Deux Mondes* at a fashionable Paris restaurant. George, escorted by Gustave Planche, was seated next to Alfred de Musset who had joined the *Revue* only a month earlier.

At twenty-two he was a slim elegant youth, with golden curls falling over his shoulders and rosy cheeks. But his cherubic appearance was deceptive. He was a smoker of opium, a frequent visitor to lowly brothels, the spoilt child of society ladies. He was always strikingly dressed, affecting wide-brimmed hats, silk waistcoats, coloured cravats, flowing velvet cloaks. When a few weeks before the dinner Sainte-Beuve suggested introducing him to George, she declined saying that he was reputed to be a *dandy* – her own word – and that they were bound to have nothing in common.

It was therefore with some reluctance that she forced herself to talk to the young poet sitting next to her. She was never at her best in a large company. She had no small talk, could think of nothing witty to say, preferred to listen rather than contribute. Musset on the other hand was irrepressible, brimming over with wit and curiosity. He embarrassed George when he asked her why she was wearing a dagger in her belt, and laughed to her face when she explained that she travelled a great deal on her own and needed it for self-defence. He suggested that she would not know how to use it and she angrily retorted that it was up to him to have a practical demonstration. He laughed again, and to her astonishment she found herself laughing with him. The ice was broken. After they parted Musset read *Indiana* and wrote George a handsome letter, accompanied by a flattering poem entitled *On Reading Indiana*. She graciously invited him to call.

Musset became a frequent visitor to the quai Malaquais apartment. George, six years his senior, coquettishly maternal, received him in her plain dressing-gown, Spanish hair-net and oriental slippers, smoking endlessly, tempted to dominate and be dominated. Within a few weeks he wrote her a declaration of love. She still hesitated, wondering whether, like Lélia, she had lost the capacity for love. One summer morning towards the end of July or the beginning of August – scholars are still arguing about the precise date – he came to see her in her apartment, pleaded, cried like a child and was comforted like a man. In her compulsive need to be properly understood by those of her men friends who mattered emotionally, George broke the news to Sainte-Beuve. A few days later the lovers left Paris to spend a week at Fontainebleau.

George was indefatigable. By day she strode the woods in a man's outfit and sensible shoes, singing at the top of her voice, dragging the delicate Musset behind her. By night she changed into fashionable dresses and looked enchanting. On their return Musset left his mother's house – his father had died a year earlier – and to her consternation moved to quai Malaquais. George had a taste for orderly family life.

Intimates of the household like Papet, Régnault and above all Planche, frowned at the new arrival and prophesied doom. George and Musset proved them wrong. A humorous poem of his reflected the happy atmosphere which prevailed at quai Malaquais at that early stage. George was described as leaning against the pots of indoor plants she had inherited from Latouche, inspecting her guests through clouds of smoke; Solange sitting on the carpeted floor, gravely engaged on writing a novel like *Maman*; Buloz, also on the floor, telling *Maman* off for some minor literary offence; Boucoiran, back in Paris after Maurice had been sent to a boarding-school, looking disapprovingly at Musset sporting a bohemian outfit; Paul de Musset helping himself to a second cup of tea; Planche complaining of ear-ache to conceal hangover; Papet embarrassed by stomach-ache; all waiting for the cook to serve dinner.

Women were rarely, if ever, included in these social gatherings. George had a theory about them:

With very few exceptions I cannot stand women for long; not because I feel they are less intelligent than me; on the contrary, I take so little part in the business of everyday life that nearly everybody around me is cleverer than me. But women are usually nervous, anxious creatures who will confide to me, much against my will, their ceaseless worries. I listen much against my will, am won over by my natural curiosity, only to realise again that all those childish troubles I have been made to listen to are no more than a storm in a teacup. Some women become vain as soon as they begin to take an interest in serious things, and those who are not professional artists often become immeasurably conceited as soon as they leave behind the world of gossip and the exaggerated preoccupation with little things. This is the result of an incomplete education. But even if their education was less at fault, women would still retain their intrinsic mental agitation. I therefore prefer men to women and I say this without malice.[1]

Where men were concerned George was most tolerant. One evening she asked her colleagues on the *Revue des Deux Mondes* to have dinner with her at home. The guest of honour was Lerminier the philosopher, and there was also an English diplomat. It was whispered that he was *en route* for Austria on a secret state mission. In vain did Lerminier try to draw him out on Lord Peel, Stanley, the British political scene in general. The diplomat, chin firmly dug into his chest, hands behind his back, replied in monosyllables. Musset was late as usual from wherever he had gone to and the guests sat down to dinner without him. That evening the homely cook was replaced by a young country maid who had never served at table before. She kept dropping crockery, misunderstanding orders, bumping into chairs. George kept apologising for her and the guests forgave her because of her fresh complexion and flaxen hair.

In the middle of the third course the diplomat indicated that he was willing to speak about the state of Europe. An expectant hush fell over the assembly. The diplomat picked up an empty plate, spun it in the air, caught it on the tip of a knife, balanced it precariously for a few seconds, then pronounced: 'This is the state of Europe.' The guests roared with laughter and tried to do the same. The young maid, not to be outdone, emptied a flask of wine over Lerminier's head. Only then did George reveal to him – what most of the others had already guessed – that the diplomat was a disguised fellow-philosopher and the maid none other than pretty Alfred de Musset. George had a taste for practical jokes.

But even in the midst of her transports she had to have her eight hours of work a night, retiring to her study in the small hours while Musset continued to sleep. Soon she realised she had another truant child on her hands. But Musset, unlike Sandeau, dismissed her reproaches with a joke. 'I have been working all day,' he would say disarmingly in her presence. 'By the evening I had written ten lines and drunk a bottle of brandy. George had drunk a litre of milk and written half a volume.'[2] George found his humour irresistible. As soon as *Lélia* was out she gave him signed copies of the two volumes. In the first she wrote 'To my mischievous Alfred, George'; in the second, 'To Viscount Alfred de Musset, a respectful homage from his devoted servant George Sand'.[3] It was one of their in-jokes.

Planche, who had helped George form her ideas about *Lélia* and corrected her grammatical mistakes, was sent a copy only after he published an article in defence of the book. It was dryly inscribed 'To Gustave Planche, from his true friend George Sand'.[4] The devoted escort and general factotum had been ousted by the lover. That the lover was the dandified Musset made Planche smart all the more.

The animosity between the two young men had begun long before either had met George. Musset, the aristocrat, the handsome, the spoilt darling of Paris society, had the entrée of all the great houses; Planche, the provincial, the smelly, the poor, was only beginning to be grudgingly invited into the drawing-rooms of the enlightened aristocracy where he felt he had a right to be by virtue of his writings. Envy bred dislike. The climax came one night in 1830 at a masked ball to which both had been invited. Musset, resplendent in his fancy dress, had every chaperoned young lady eager to dance with him. Planche, unwanted as usual, tried to spoil Musset's fun by spreading some malicious gossip which was easily traced back to its source. The apology which was forced out of Planche there and then did not improve matters. A state of hostility was declared.

To please Musset George intimated to Planche that his assiduity was no longer welcome. When he failed to take the hint she invited him for a long talk and explained that they must never see each other again. 'We parted with a firm handshake,' she reported to Sainte-Beuve, 'loving from the very bottom of our hearts, promising each other everlasting respect.'[5] Planche did not give up and waited for a suitable occasion to prove his superiority over Musset. Feuillide's attack on *Lélia* was the suitable excuse and the duel to which Planche challenged him set Paris speculating on his right to vindicate Sand's honour. For George, it was necessary to sever all connections with him in order to prove that he had no place in her bed.

However, it was not convenient to lose him altogether. Planche was a scrupulous grammarian and had voluntarily gone over George's manuscripts with a toothcomb, correcting mistakes in style, syntax and even spelling. The humiliation of a definite dismissal was therefore palliated by assurances of goodwill. When her affair with Musset began to disintegrate, she asked Planche through an intermediary to go over the proofs of *Jacques* and correct her style as before. After that she sent him the proofs of *Spiridion*. While going over her scripts as meticulously as ever, Planche could not help spreading malicious gossip about Musset, whom he hated as much as ever. George was offended and dropped him again, this time without ceremony.

Several years later, when her love for Musset had long been a thing of the past, she sent Planche a conciliatory letter and invited him to call as of old. By that time he had been, oddly enough like Sandeau, in and out of love with Marie Dorval and was co-habiting with a mistress. Shortly after George's friendly overture he inherited a fortune and left for Italy, where he stayed for five years. On his return he re-joined the *Revue des Deux Mondes*, but there was no resumption of friendship between him and the already middle-aged George. When he died in 1857, the same year as Musset, she showed little regret and only recalled his acrid comments on her punctuation.

In the autumn of 1833 the lovers decided to realise a long-cherished dream and go to Italy. George set about it with her customary practicality. From Buloz she obtained a handsome advance against a written undertaking to send him the finished manuscript of a new novel by the following summer; to her husband she wrote that she was suffering from rheumatism and was going to Italy in search of a cure; to ten-year-old Maurice, languishing in a Paris boarding-school, she explained that she needed sunshine for her health; and five-year-old Solange was sent back to Nohant. The difficulty arose from an unforeseen quarter. Countess de Musset refused to allow a dependent son to go on a mad escapade with a notorious married woman. George was undaunted. She drove to the Mussets' residence, had herself announced, and with that eloquence which came to her naturally when she was bent on getting her own way, persuaded the countess to confide Alfred to Baroness Dudevant's maternal care.

They set out in mid-December. On the steamboat from Lyons they met Henri Beyle, the French consul in Civita Vecchia, who was returning to his post after two months' home leave. Better known to his younger contemporaries as Stendhal, the author of *Le Rouge et le noir*, he shocked them both with his cynicism. George was not sorry when he disembarked at Marseilles to continue his journey by land. She and Musset took the sea route. Betrousered again, she walked on deck smoking cigarettes while Musset was sea-sick below. As soon as they landed in Genoa the tables were turned. George was feverish, Musset impatient. In a fit of hankering after the old life he picked up a local dancer and went to bed with her, allowing George to hear about it. Her fever persisted. She looked listlessly at the sights, travelling indifferently through Livorno, Pisa, Florence. Musset continued to shun the company of an ailing woman and George, concealing the real reason for her disenchantment, wrote to her husband that Italy had not come up to her expectations. From Nohant, bitter under his apparent complaisance, Casimir wrote back:

Thank you, my dear, for your letter from Florence in which you inform me that you are only stopping over on your way to Venice. I am pleased your health does not deteriorate in a country where the sun is capable of curing both colds and fevers, but I am sorry to hear that you are disenchanted with the tour.

You seem to view coldly and dispassionately, objectively if you like, those monuments, sites and splendours which have made so many hearts beat faster, inspired so many minds, dictated so many pages of fire. That country bewitches with its brilliant history, and everybody can find in it some of his own past. You now walk the scenes of the military exploits of your father and the *Grande Armée*. You are familiar with your father's letters to your grandmother; you are bound to come across some battlefield where he had risked his life only to find death near La Châtre. This should be a moving chapter for you.[6]

But George was too ill and unhappy to find pleasure in sight-seeing. She and Musset travelled on and arrived in Venice with the New Year, not as the carefree lovers of Fontainebleau, but on the verge of an emotional crisis. They put up at the Danieli.

It was a former palace converted into a hotel only ten or twelve years previously. Situated at the entrance to the Grand Canal, it had a magnificent view from the windows, elegant gondolas waiting to serve the patrons, splendidly furnished suites, some with pianos, baths fitted with fresh and saltwater taps. In the midst of all that luxury George's sickness turned into dysentery. Musset, more disgusted than ever, explored Venice on his own and relapsed further into debauchery. Again there were women, orgies, brawls. For a while he and George kept the communicating door between their rooms closed. George shut herself in her room and sought consolation in work while Musset went out in pursuit of pleasure. Never again was she to forget those long nights, the sound of church bells marking the lonely wait, the calls of passing gondoliers filling her heart with hope succeeded by deeper despair.

One morning Musset returned from his nightly prowling covered with blood, then collapsed. His health had always been delicate and now he was seriously ill, running a high temperature and groaning with pain. At the sight of the sick boy all bitterness vanished. George sent an urgent note to a doctor who had attended her a few days earlier and gave him a detailed case history, putting the patient's condition before her wounded pride:

I would like to tell you in advance that I fear for his reason more than his life. Since he fell ill his mind has become feeble and he sometimes reasons like a child. And yet he is a man of energy and imagination. In France he is a much-admired poet. But the exaltation caused by the work of the mind, wine, orgies, women, the gaming table, have all taxed his strength and excited his nerves. He gets agitated by small things just as easily as by graver ones. . . . I do not know whether this is due to his temperamental make-up, an over-excitation of the nerves, or an element of madness. Perhaps a bleeding might help. I beg of you not to be put off by the difficult disposition of an undisciplined patient. He is the person I love most in this world and I am greatly distressed to see him in this condition.[7]

The letter, in imperfect Italian, was full of crossings and corrections. Even the doctor's name was wrongly spelt. Doctor Pagello arrived however without delay, already intrigued by the unusual Frenchwoman he had treated a few days earlier.

At twenty-six Pietro Pagello was a handsome young man at the beginning of his medical career. He came from a cultured Venetian family and took an interest in literature and the arts. After the premature death of his well-loved mother a year earlier, he left his father's house to live in bachelor lodgings where he could enjoy the favours of a mistress or two. In a small place like Venice it was impossible not to have noticed the French visitors at the Danieli, and Pagello was pleased when he was first sent for to attend to the lady, then to the gentleman.

George's one thought was to save the boy who had been entrusted to her care by his mother. For eight days she slept fully dressed on a couch in the patient's room, ready for his beck and call. She never left his side, paid for the expensive medicines from her own purse, wrote to Buloz for more money and warned him not to tell Mme Musset of the seriousness of her son's condition. She was all mother, dispensing that driving devotion which for her was easier to sustain than love. 'I need to nourish that maternal solicitude in me which is accustomed to watch over someone ill and tired,'[8] she later analysed herself.

The handsome young doctor kept her company during the long hours of the vigil. They discussed the patient, Venice, Italian art and literature, the patient. The shared responsibility and the intimacy of the vigil bred a mutual attraction. Pagello, fair-haired, virile, reassuring, was a mysterious Italian who excited curiosity; George, striking, independent, maternally anxious, was a temptation. Pagello devoured her with his eyes and once or twice supported her by the waist with more ardour than courtesy. On the whole he was too unsure of the set-up to take the first decisive step.

One evening when he asked her conversationally whether she intended to write a book about Italy, George turned her back on him and started writing. Pagello waited uncomfortably, not knowing whether to stay or take his leave. After a long time she handed him a sheet of paper and when he asked whom it was for, she put it in an envelope and wrote on it: 'For stupid Pagello'.[9] It turned out to be more of a self-analysis than a declaration of love. At thirty George was no longer the starry-eyed young wife who believed in spiritual love, nor the inexperienced adulteress who thought that freedom of choice was a guarantee for everlasting bliss. Driven by an irresistible need to love and be loved, she already knew that love held out no promise of happiness. She wrote to Pagello in French:

'Born under a different sky, we do not share the same thoughts or ideas; do we at least have the same heart? The warm foggy climate of my country has left me with sweet and melancholy impressions; what passions have you been endowed with by the generous sun which has tanned your forehead? I know how to love and suffer; and you, do you know how to love? The ardour of your glances, the powerful clasp of your arms, the audacity of your desire all tempt and frighten me. I cannot quell your passion nor can I share it. In my country we do not love like that. Next to you I am like a pale statue. I look at you with wonder, desire and anxiety.

'I do not know whether you really love me. Perhaps I shall never know. You hardly speak my language and I do not know yours well enough to ask you subtle questions. Perhaps I shall not be able to make myself understood even when I learn your language thoroughly.

'Because we have grown up in different countries and have been brought up by different people, we probably have ideas and emotions which are inexplicable to one another. My slow nature and your fiery temperament are bound to have produced dissimilar ideas. You do not know, or despise, the thousand little sorrows which I feel; perhaps you laugh at things which make me cry. Perhaps you do not know what tears are.

'Will you be my mainstay or my master? Will you console me for the pain I suffered before I met you? Will you understand why I am sad? Have you compassion, patience, friendship? Perhaps you have been brought up to believe that women have no soul. Do you know they have? Are you a Christian, a Moslem, a civilised person, a barbarian? Are you a man? What is there behind that virile chest, that lion's eye, that superb forehead? Do you think noble and pure thoughts, fraternal and pious? When you sleep, do you dream that you are flying towards Heaven? When people hurt you, do you hope to God?

'Will I be your companion or your slave? Do you want me or do you love me? When your desire is satisfied will you know how to thank me? When I make you happy will you know how to tell me? Do the pleasures of love leave you gasping and dazed or do they throw you into divine ecstasy? Does your soul survive your body when you leave the arms of your beloved? When I see you silent will I know whether you are deep in thought or just resting? When your eyes look languid will it be with tenderness or weariness?

'If you were a native of my country I would ask you questions and you would understand me. Perhaps I would be all the more unhappy, for you might not answer truthfully.

'But as you are you do not know the deceitful words of the

language. You will not make vain promises or swear false oaths. You will love me the way you know and the way you can. Perhaps I shall not find in you what I have vainly looked for in others, but at least I shall be able to imagine it in you. You will let me interpret those treacherous looks and gestures of love as I wish, you will not have words to lie with. I shall interpret your day-dreams and give eloquence to your silences. I shall attribute to your actions the meaning I would like them to have. When you look at me with tenderness, I shall tell myself that your soul is calling mine; when you look at the sky I shall imagine that your soul is soaring towards its source.

'Let us stay as we are. Do not learn my language and I shall not learn yours. I shall not seek to study those words which will reveal my doubts and fears. I do not wish to know what you make of your life and what part you play in the world. I wish I had not known your name. Keep your soul from me so that I can always imagine it beautiful.'[10]

Once in the privacy of his home Pagello read the letter three times over. In his diary he recorded that he felt like rushing back to the hotel and throwing himself at George's feet; yet how he already sensed that hers was basically a passing whim magnified by fantasy. He thought of professional etiquette and his duty to his patient. He looked at his dead mother's portrait and remembered her warning not to succumb to temptations which ran counter to his moral convictions. He spent the rest of the night composing a serenade in Italian. The following morning he called on Musset as usual. George appeared in an elegant town outfit and graciously asked the doctor to escort her on her shopping. Pagello later noted in his diary that the entire conversation during the three-hour walk consisted of the 'usual variations on the theme of *I love you*'.[11]

George was touched by Pagello's total involvement. 'Everything you think, everything you do is right and holy,' she wrote gratefully from the Danieli. 'Yes, I love you, I should have always loved you. Why have I not met you before? . . . I see nothing in you which does not wholly please me or satisfy me. It is the first time I love without feeling unhappy at the end of three days.'[12]

A few days later she wrote again: 'My Pierre, my Pierre, you are a man. I can love you and respect you. You are kind, sensible and generous. . . . I love you, I love you, I love you.'[13]

The patient was getting better and could not wait to get away from the combined solicitude of his doctor and his nurse. As soon as he could stand on his feet he left the sick-room and spent long evenings out; Pagello went round Venice looking for him and brought him back to George. Musset reluctantly admitted that Pagello was a man of honour. 'What a man Pagello is,' he said to George. 'What a heart, what strength of character. He virtually admitted to me that he is in love with you, yet he goes out to fetch me and takes me back to you when he could benefit by our quarrels. I forgive him. Next to you two I feel dwarfed. I am ashamed of myself. I feel I ought to put your hand in his and go away to cry over the happiness I did not know how to keep. Pagello should have been the man for you, my poor George; he would have treated you with respect.'[14]

By that time George and Musset had moved into two separate rooms in a modest hotel which Pagello had found for them. The Danieli was too expensive and money was short. Now that Musset was out of danger George was able to throw herself back into work and keep up her quota for Buloz. Hardly removed from the emotional scene of the past few weeks, she was already able to use some of its elements in a new novel. In February she wrote *Leone Leoni* in fourteen days and sent it off to Sainte-Beuve with a request to go through it before passing it on to Buloz for publication. Musset, still unwell, still idle and resenting Pagello's constant presence without tangible proof of deception, decided to return to Paris. George was thinking of accompanying him, then returning to Venice on her own. In a letter to Pagello she explained that the arrangement would prevent ill-feeling, but admitted that it would be difficult to go on dissimulating for another whole month.

The arrival of Tattet, a friend from Paris, changed the situation. Tattet was quick to diagnose the true nature of the brotherly triad and opened Musset's eyes. Musset was mad with jealousy and wanted to kill both George and Pagello; then turned his wrath on Pagello alone and challenged him to a duel. George was able to persuade him that he had no claim over her since they had ceased to be lovers before she ever met Pagello. She reminded Musset of her devotion during his sickness and after it, and assured him that she still loved him like a brother. It was she who was the brother: ever since she had taken on the name George she used all nouns and adjectives pertaining to herself in the masculine gender.

Jealousy having rekindled his dying love, Musset realised too late that he was no longer wanted. He decided to return to Paris on his own. George, always practical, found a young Venetian barber called Antonio to accompany him to France and look after him, and also undertook to raise the money for the journey. Musset was too tormented to wait. On an impulse he wrote a note of farewell and sent it to George by a gondolier, waiting in the gondola for the reply he knew was sure to come. He wrote:

Even if you are indifferent or hostile, and even if the parting kiss I gave you today is the last of my life, you must know that the moment I left the house with the knowledge that I had lost you, I felt that I deserved it. . . . He who did not know how to respect you when he possessed you, can still see clear through his tears and respect you in his heart, where your image shall never die. Goodbye, my child.[15]

George pencilled a hurried reply on the back of his letter and sent it back with the gondolier:

Don't go away like that. You are not well enough and Buloz has not yet sent the money for Antonio's fare. You must not leave on your own. Oh God, why quarrel? Am I not your brother George, your one-time friend?[16]

Tormented as he was by his resurgent love, Musset put off his departure by a day or two, allowing George to make the necessary arrangements. He was little comforted when she gave him a farewell present, a leather-bound diary, inscribed: 'To Alfred, her good comrade, brother and friend, from his mistress George.'[17] They promised to remain friends and write to each other. In March 1834, barely three months after their arrival in Italy George saw Musset off as far as the mainland, then returned to Venice with her heart split in two. Pagello was kind and understanding. He took her to see his father who disapproved of the liaison but was courteous to a lady and a writer; then set off with her on a week's walking tour at the foot of the Alps. They visited small villages, ruins and historic monuments, sometimes walking fifteen miles a day. George's spirits revived. One day she engraved her name and Pagello's on the wall of a cave. When they returned to Venice she was composed and ready for work. She moved into Pagello's little house which he shared with a younger brother and a half-sister, and adjusted to a life of domesticity and hard writing.

The four-month period which followed Musset's departure was one of the most prolific in George's career so far. She worked without interruption, sometimes as long as thirteen hours at a stretch. She drank endless cups of tea, smoked a pipe and described herself to her Paris friends as being ruthlessly driven by a niggardly editor. She sent him a series of articles entitled *Lettres d'un voyageur*, in which she described her walking tours in Italy with a grey-haired doctor of respectable age. Musset was alluded to in between the lines and George sent him the text first, authorising him to delete anything he thought fit before passing them on to Buloz. Musset thought they were beautiful; so did the readers of the *Revue des Deux Mondes* who liked their glimpses of Italian scenery spiced with hints about the emotional life of two literary celebrities. Buloz was pleased with the resumed flow and became more generous with payments on account.

In between her *Lettres*, each several thousand words long, George completed two novels. One was *André*, set in Berry and neglected during Musset's illness; the other was *Jacques*, her first undisguised attack on the institution of marriage. She had sounded the Italian book market and was planning a series of translations to be carried out by Pagello and herself. Musset was instructed to send copies of *Indiana*, *Valentine*, *Métella*, *La Marquise* and *Aldo le Rimeur*, as well as favourable press cuttings which he was to retrieve from a cupboard in quai Malaquais.

She was her old self again, reproaching friends for not writing often enough, expecting them to run errands for her. Her husband was instructed to keep Solange at Nohant instead of sending her to a *pension* as he had proposed; Boucoiran was told to go to Maurice's boarding-school and see why the boy had not been writing for two months; Buloz was asked to make 'the necessary corrections to my style and spelling';[18] and Planche, through Boucoiran, 'to chastise my style and correct my mistakes in French'.[19] Musset, in between professions of everlasting friendship, was asked to edit *André*, send a quantity of cigarette-paper so that she could roll her own, the score of two Beethoven symphonies and Weber's *Valse sentimentale*. The shopping lists were detailed and prosaic:

Send me a dozen pairs of glacé leather gloves, two pairs of black satin shoes and two pairs of black maroquin shoes from Michiels, on the corner of rue du Helde and the boulevard. Tell him to make them a little larger than my size, I have got swollen feet and the maroquin they have in Venice is as hard as a buffalo. Also a quarter of patchouli from Leblan, rue Sainte-Anne, opposite No. 50. Don't let them cheat you, it costs only 2 francs a quarter.[20]

She was economical with Pagello's money, generous with her own. She re-upholstered the furniture in her room with her own hands, embroidered, knitted, prepared dainty dishes. Pagello's younger brother Roberto did not think much of her cooking nor, for that matter, of her shape. Neither was solid enough for his taste. He described George as '*quella sardella*',[21] that sardine; she knitted him a pair of socks. Pagello's father continued to disapprove and tried to persuade Roberto to move out of that house of sin. Venice was not as tolerant as literary Paris of irregular attachments between people of good families. Some of Pagello's old friends, and several of his well-to-do patients, cut him dead when they passed him on the piazza San Marco with George on his arm. There were other unpleasantnesses. Pagello's neglected mistresses besieged him in the house and tried to reclaim him. One actually tore his waistcoat and pulled his hair and when George threw herself into the affray, she threatened to kill her. George threatened to call the police.

Gradually a routine was established. Friends would call, the half-sister would sing, George would accompany her on the piano. There was time to go to the theatre, attend concerts, visit churches, discover the intimate charm of Venice through the eyes of a native. It was all very pleasant, very tame, very therapeutic. It was also very dull. Within six weeks of this regime George was writing to Musset: 'For the first time in my life I love without passion.'[22] She was approaching the moment of truth. Passion, the intense agony of the soul, was for her the essence of love. She could not do without it.

Even before Musset had left Italian soil George already felt that their love was not dead, only dormant. Musset too sensed that the last chapter had not yet been written. The letters between Paris and Venice followed hard upon one another. George called Musset her child, her sweet angel, her brother; Musset called her his child, his little bird, his brother. He had gone back to his mother's house, but from time to time called at the old love nest at quai Malaquais, wandered among the familiar furniture covered with dust-sheets, smoked a cigarette rolled by George and left in a saucer, carried away a broken comb he had found in the bedroom. 'It is not my mistress I long for,' he deluded himself into writing. 'It is my comrade George I miss.'[23] His comrade, for her part, did her best to keep his longing alive. 'You are naughty, my little angel,' she wrote on 29 April. 'You arrived in Paris on the 12th and you did not write until the 19th. If I only had a couple of lines from Antonio to reassure me about your health.'[24]

From that distance however she was worried less about his health than about his physical susceptibilities. She could not forget that he had once accused her of frigidity; nor could she delude herself that she would ever be able to attain that passionate abandon that Musset seemed to arouse in his whores. Her only hope of keeping him was through the passion of the mind. He had hardly been gone two weeks when she wrote to him:

> I am glad that the pleasure I gave you was more austere and restrained than the pleasure you get with others. At least you will not be thinking of me when you are in another woman's arms. But when you are alone, when you need to pray and cry, then you will think of your George, your true comrade, your nurse, your friend.... Goodbye my Alfred, love your George.[25]

She was alarmed when he wrote that he proposed to seek oblivion in the pleasures of the flesh. It was the one thing she could not compete with. From eight hundred miles away she wrote to dissuade him, disguising fear as maternal solicitude:

> What worries me most is the thought that you are careless of your health. I beg of you on my knees, no drink yet, no women yet, it is too soon. Think of your body which is not so strong as your mind and which I saw nearly die in my arms. Do not abandon yourself to pleasure until nature imperiously commands you to seek it. Do not seek it as a cure for boredom or sadness. Pleasure turns out worst when it is not the best. You must take care of that life which I have perhaps saved through vigil and devotion. Does it not belong to me a little because of that?[26]

Like Aurélien de Sèze a few years earlier, Musset felt there was nothing more ennobling than a friendship born of renounced love. He wrote:

> It is not a dream then, my dear brother. This friendship which survives love, which people make fun of, which I myself used to make fun of, this friendship does exist. It does. You say so, and I believe in it. You love me.[27]

In the same letter, still in a noble mood, he announced a thousand words later:

I am going to write a novel. I would like it to be our story; I feel it might cure me and lift my heart. I would like to build you an altar even if I have to do it with my bones. But I shall wait for your formal permission.[28]

Her permission was given in terms which were bound to bring tears into his eyes:

Jacques is well in hand and is progressing in leaps and bounds. It is not about either of us. In my present state of mind I could not write a book about us. But you, my angel, you must write what you like, novels, sonnets, poems. Speak of me as you will, I deliver myself into your hands with my eyes bandaged.[29]

Musset continued to write in his new mood of euphoria. 'How I love you, Georgeot! What happiness to have this sweet and elevated happiness which has survived between us like the perfume of love.'[30] And on another occasion: 'O my child, the most beloved of women, my only beloved one! I swear to you on my father's grave that if the sacrifice of my life could give you a year's happiness, I would jump off a precipice with everlasting joy in my heart.'[31] And on 10 July, more practically: 'I have started that novel I had told you about. If by any chance you have kept the letters I have written to you since I left Venice, perhaps you would have the kindness to let me consult them.'[32] She had, and did.

There was however that awkward liaison with Pagello which George had to put into perspective in her correspondence with Musset. She wrote of him amicably, as a wife might after years of tolerable if dull marriage. She never failed to emphasise his devotion and kindness, but made it plain that he lacked that finer understanding so much needed in a man. Pagello would no more take notice of the ills of her soul than if she had a corn on her toe, she informed Musset. Musset wrote back that he was glad she had such an honest, reliable and loving person to look after her, and George replied that 'the doctor' was indeed the most generous, devoted and loyal of companions. Between them they demolished

Pagello with words of praise. Emotionally he had ceased to exist.

After four months with Pagello George felt ready to return to Paris. She wrote to her son that she would be back in time for prize-giving day and instructed Boucoiran to have her curtains laundered. Pagello was informed of her plan at the last possible moment and left to decide for himself what he wanted to do about it. He knew that his part in George's life had been played out. 'I suddenly realised that I would have to go to France with her and return without her,' he wrote in his diary. 'But I loved her so much that I was prepared to brave a thousand unpleasantnesses rather than allow her to go unaccompanied on a long hazardous journey.'[33] He suggested that when they reached Paris he would put up at a hotel, and George gratefully accepted. From that moment on, Pagello recorded, they ceased to be lovers.

They left Venice at the beginning of August 1834, George excited at the prospect of returning to French civilisation after eight months in Italy, Pagello unhappy but unable to tear himself away. To his father he wrote:

> So far I have not answered any of your letters reproaching me with living with a foreign woman, wasting my youth, ruining my career and publicly repudiating the Christian principles of morality which had been inculcated upon me by the best of mothers, because I had no words to justify my behaviour, yet did not wish to stoop to promises I knew I would not be able to keep. Today I am writing to you from Milan. I have reached the last stage of my folly, and I must go on with it with my eyes shut as I had done before. Tomorrow I am leaving for Paris where I shall part with La Sand and return to embrace you more worthy of you than I am now. I am young and should be able to start my career all over again. Do not cease to love me and write to me to Paris.[34]

In Paris they were met by Boucoiran, who drove George to quai Malaquais and Pagello to a cheap hotel. They never saw each other on their own after that. George had no thought for anybody but Musset who, like her, had been waiting to see if the tenderness of their recent correspondence could be rekindled into love.

For the next few weeks Pagello lived impecuniously on his own, gaining a foothold in a Paris hospital, rarely seeing George but following bitterly the latest gossip about the resumption of her relationship with his one-time patient. As often before, George tried to atone by being generous. She discreetly advanced him money on the expected sale of some pictures he had brought over from Venice, gave him an introduction to Buloz as a potential contributor, and even persuaded Casimir Dudevant to send him an invitation to come down to Nohant. But Pagello had had enough and decided to cut his losses. Two months after his arrival in Paris he asked Boucoiran to take him to quai Malaquais so that he could bid his farewell before returning home. George had nothing to say. They shook hands in silence and Pagello went out of the house and her life. In his diary he described that last meeting:

> My presence embarrassed her. He was tiresome, that Italian who, with his simple common-sense punctured that deceptive air of sublimity with which she used to envelop her weariness of her lovers. I had already let her see that I had fathomed her heart and found it full of excellent qualities marred by many failings. My perceptiveness annoyed her and that was why I cut my farewell visit as short as possible.[35]

Once in Venice Pagello picked up the old threads, became a well-respected doctor, married a plain woman and had many children and grandchildren. He died at ninety-one, in full possession of his faculties, surviving George Sand by twenty-two years. Throughout his life he was never known to refer to his youthful love affair with the French novelist until his ninetieth year, when closely questioned by the French researcher Dr Cabanès. Even then he was reticent. Perhaps it was due to the memory of a humiliation which time had not altogether effaced.

No sooner had George returned to Paris than she and Musset were irresistibly drawn back towards each other. But love at close quarters was not the same sublime emotion professed at eight hundred miles apart. Musset relived the Venetian triangle, tormented George with questions about the sequence of events at the time of his illness, was maddened by her assertion that since he had repudiated her love in Venice she owed him no explanations. He embarked on what was to become an emotional cycle: a masochistic need to be told the worst, jealousy and abuse; then remorse, tears and short-lived tenderness. At one time he moved back into quai Malaquais and talked about challenging Planche to a duel for having made vicious comments about the Venice triangle; another time he flaunted a new mistress all over Paris and accused George of infidelity with Franz Liszt to whom he had recently introduced her. Tearful reconciliations were followed by humiliating rows. George wrote to Musset that they were destroying each other and suggested an amicable parting. He agreed. Immediately George's love flared up with renewed violence. She asked him to make it up; he stayed aloof. She became physically ill, went round Paris talking of suicide. For the first time in her life she was unable to work. In her diary she kept reproaching the indifferent Musset:

21 November 1834

You do not love me any more, you do not love me any more, it is obvious. I was ill last night when you left here, you could see I was, and yet you went away. You were right of course to go back to your mother's house, you looked tired. But what about today? Not a word, you have not even sent round to ask how I was. I was hoping you would come and waited for your call from eleven o'clock in the morning until midnight. What a day! Every ring of the doorbell made me jump! I have such a head-ache. I wish I were dead. . . .

I wrote to you this evening, but you did not answer. They said you were out, yet you did not call on me for even five minutes. You must have got in very late, where have you been? Oh God, it is all over. You do not love me any more.[36]

By that time all their friends were involved willy-nilly; Boucoiran as a go-between; Sainte-Beuve a detached observer;

Liszt as a moral adviser; Buloz as a man of the world; Marie Dorval as a kindred spirit. Even Delacroix, who was painting George Sand for the *Revue des Deux Mondes*, was confided in during the sittings. One day George cut off her beautiful hair and sent it to Musset. Her diary reflected that self-abasement which so often goes with rejected love:

You know very well that I love you, that I cannot love anyone but you. Take me in your arms, do not say anything, do not let us argue, just be kind to me, hold me tight, you know you still find me attractive in spite of my short hair and the two deep wrinkles recently appeared on my cheeks. And when you have satisfied your desire and you feel your impatience return, send me away, taunt me, but never say those terrible words *This is the last time*. I shall suffer as much as you like but please allow me from time to time, even just once a week, to have a tear, a kiss, which would give me courage to live on. But you do not want me, you have had enough of me.[37]

Every now and then she went back to Nohant and her family in a futile attempt to put things out of her mind, then was irresistibly drawn back. By January 1835 they had made it up and the tormented cycle began all over again. George was worried about the difference in their age, humiliated by his bouts of drinking and whoring. Musset fluctuated between adoration and sadism. After one of their reconciliations he sent her a gushing note:

Happiness, happiness, then death, death together. Yes, you forgive me, you love me. Live, O my soul, you shall be happy. Yes, happy through me. Yes, I am 23 years old, why am I 23 and at the prime of my life if not to pour out my life so that you can drink it from my lips? Tonight at ten o'clock, and you may be sure I shall be early. Come as soon as you can, come so that I can go down on my knees before you, ask you to live, love, forgive.

Tonight, tonight.[38]

It was no use. As soon as they were together they began to tear each other to shreds with reproaches and recriminations. By March George knew that the only way to keep her sanity was to run away. Once her mind was made up she set about it in a way worthy of the author who had thought out the complicated plots of *Indiana* and *Lélia*. She asked Boucoiran to book her a seat on the next midday coach to La Châtre, then come and fetch her, giving him explicit instructions what to say should he find Musset with her:

6 March 1835

You will arrive at my place at five o'clock, look pressed and busy, you will tell me that my mother has just arrived in Paris, that she is very tired and fairly seriously ill, that her maid has left her, that she wants me right away and that I must go to her without delay. I shall put on my hat, say I shall be back soon, and you will call a carriage for me. During the day you will come back to fetch my overnight bag and take it to the coach station. It should be easy for you to pick it up without being noticed. I am sending you my travelling cushion which needs seeing to, the clasp has been lost.[39]

As it happened the charade was unnecessary. Musset did not call that day. When he did, the following morning, he was told by the maid that Madame had left for Nohant and that M. Boucoiran had seen her off. Musset accepted the slap without any manifestation of emotion. To Boucoiran he wrote with chilling courtesy:

7 March 1835

Sir,

I have just left Mme Sand's where I was informed that she is at Nohant. I would be most grateful if you could let me know whether this is indeed so. As you saw Mme Sand early this morning you would no doubt be familiar with her plans; and if she is not due to leave until tomorrow perhaps you would be good enough to tell me whether she has any reason to avoid seeing me before her departure. I need hardly add that if this is the case I shall respect her wishes.[40]

That was the end of the affair. On her first night back home George shut herself in her study and covered twenty pages in her calm, confident writing. It was the beginning of *Mauprat*, a cloak-and-dagger story in which she was to re-state her emotional creed: 'Love's ideal is most certainly everlasting fidelity.'[41]

Musset too turned his experience into literature. Six months after the final separation he allowed the *Revue des Deux Mondes* to publish the first chapter of *La Confession d'un enfant du siècle* which was his romanticised version of the Venice triangle. The full novel was published in February 1836, when George was already unhappily in love with Michel de Bourges. Musset's gallant treatment of her part in the drama moved her to tears. Impulsively she wrote him to say that she would love him for ever. It was a theatrical gesture which neither took seriously. No friendship survived between them like the perfume of love. Several years later there was a chance meeting at the theatre, a courteous exchange of notes about the return of the love letters; the rest was silence.

Both Musset and Sand kept drawing on their experience for several years to come. Musset used his in the poems *Souvenir*, *La Nuit d'octobre*, the plays *Lorenzaccio* and *On ne badine pas avec l'amour*. George Sand, with her fluent pen, produced at least ten works inspired by her Venice memories. Apart from three *Lettres d'un voyageur* and *Jacques*, there were novels like *Les Maîtres mosaïstes*, *L'Orco*, *Mattéa*, *L'Uscoque*, *Gabriel*, *La Dernière Aldini*, the first part of *Consuelo*, which owed their inspiration to the knowledge of Italy gained during her association with Musset and Pagello.

In 1839 she brought out a much-altered new edition of *Lélia*, where the character of the young poet had been re-written in a way that made him reminiscent of Musset, while his Lélia had been cured of her emotional impotence. In 1858, a year after Musset's death, she could still draw on a love affair which had taken place twenty-five years earlier and brought out the novel *Elle et Lui*. She little expected that it would result in a new wave of moral ash-raking.

Chapter 9

❦❦❦❦

Everard

Once, in a romantic mood, George Sand claimed that her conversion to socialism was effected one April night of 1835, during a nine-hour harangue from the republican lawyer Michel de Bourges. It was a poetic exaggeration. Neither in 1835 nor at any later date was George prepared to exchange her own abstract notion of socialism for Michel's militant doctrines. She clung with obstinacy to a utopian concept of universal justice which she had derived from a most unlikely source. 'Oddly enough,' she candidly admitted in her autobiography, 'it was perhaps Mme de Genlis, the one-time governess of Louis Philippe, to whom I owe my first socialist and democratic instincts.'[1]

The octogenarian Countess de Genlis, who some fifty years earlier taught the future Louis Philippe English and physical jerks, was an indefatigable writer of pedagogical essays and romantic novels. Sophie Victoire, George Sand's mother, used to read some of her stories to her little daughter. At the age of sixteen or seventeen the then Aurore came across *Les Battuécas*, a novel which the mature George Sand still recalled as 'eminently socialist'.[2] It described the idyllic life of a secluded tribe protected by impassable mountains from the infiltration of corruptive influences. The young girl embraced with enthusiasm the notion of a just society guided by the simple principle of honesty. To her that was socialism in a nutshell. In 1835 she still believed that personal honesty was a sound enough foundation for a viable social order. Michel de Bourges's vehement exposure of the evils of moderate egalitarianism failed to sway her. Not even the evidence of Louis Philippe's first five years made her doubt her utopian view of a just society based on nothing more tangible than the principle of honesty.

When in 1830 Louis Philippe became King of the French by the Will of the People, many believed that a new dawn of liberalism was about to break. The king swore fealty to a charter drawn up by the Assembly, eased franchise qualifications, revoked the law which had made Catholicism a state religion, and provided schools for the villages. He became the Citizen King, preferring a top-hat to a crown, a walking-stick to a sceptre, distributions of free sausages to state ceremonials.

Yet no internal peace followed and economic hardship among the workers fomented discontent. The troubles started in Lyons, where most of the working population were employed in the thriving silk industry. A year or two before Louis Philippe's accession some of the silk-weavers formed mutual-aid societies with the object of offering help to needy members. Soon they began to take up members' grievances against employers. When in 1834 twelve hundred plush-weavers had their wages reduced in order to maintain the manufacturers' margin of profit, fifty thousand silk-weavers agreed to strike, and on 14 February twenty thousand looms came to a standstill.

That first crossing of swords was won by the employers. After eight days of strike the hungry workers returned humbly to their looms, but the new spirit of solidarity had not been crushed. When laws were passed making workers' associations illegal, the silk-weavers published a strong protest in the *Echo de la fabrique*, signed by more than two and a half thousand members. It ended on a clear note of defiance:

> The members of the mutual-aid societies declare that they will never bow their heads under the cruel yoke and their meetings shall not be suspended. Taking their stand on their right to live by their work, they will resist any brutal attempt to violate it with all the energy which free men are capable of; and they will not shrink from any sacrifice for the defence of a right which no human power should deny them.[3]

Shortly after the unsuccessful strike six of its leaders were arrested and committed for trial. The outcry against the laws banning workers' associations was taken up by tailors, hatters, shoemakers. Mass demonstrations were planned to coincide with the opening of the trial in April, and the city authorities called in ten thousand troops. The rest followed inexorably. While the accused were facing their judges in the courtroom, barricades were being built in the streets. The unequal battle between the insurgents and the National Guard raged for several days and was quelled in torrents of blood. Similar insurrections broke out in Paris, Marseilles, Saint-Etienne, Besançon and Epinal. All were put down in equal manner.

After the battle a hundred and twenty-one people were arrested in the various centres of trouble and sent to Paris to be jointly tried by the Chamber of Peers which, by royal ordinance, was constituted a court of justice. The trial was held a year later and came to be known as the April Trial or, because of its magnitude and nature, *Le Procès monstre*. Eminent republican lawyers from Paris and the provinces worked together to prepare the case for the defence in what was obviously going to be a show-trial. Among those retained to defend the Lyons group of prisoners was Louis Chrysostome Michel, the republican lawyer from Bourges in the region of Berry.

Republicanism was Michel's heritage. A few months before he was born his father, a poor woodcutter, was killed by rioting royalists for his republican beliefs. It was 1797. Michel's mother was an illiterate peasant woman who worked in the fields. She was astonished to hear from the village *curé* that her son, by the age of nine, had taught himself reading, writing and Latin from an old prayer-book. From then on the boy's education was taken in hand by wealthy protectors. Michel studied law in Paris, established a practice in Bourges, married a rich widow and adopted her children. He was a brilliant speaker. Contemporary descriptions praised his reasoning and delivery, particularly his gift of sparking off fireworks without stooping to histrionics. It was said that he feared nobody except his wife. Although a native of a small village in Var, he became known to his colleagues and clients as Michel of Bourges. Berry republicans like Dutheil, Planet, Fleury, Papet and Rollinat greatly admired him. When they heard that George was looking for a good lawyer, they unanimously recommended Michel.

In April 1835, just before George was introduced to him, Michel was putting the final touches to his brief for the *Procès monstre* which was due to open the following month. He had been notified by Fleury and Planet that Baroness Dudevant wished to consult him professionally on how to obtain a judicial separation from her husband, and sent word that he would be pleased to advise her.

It was more than four years since George had made her amicable arrangement with Casimir Dudevant about living away from home three months out of six, and more than two since she had last conformed to it. All that time Casimir had acted the compla- cent husband and turned a blind eye to his wife's clandestine meetings with Stéphane de Grandsagne, her cohabitation with Sandeau, her affair with Mérimée, her attachment to Marie Dorval; but he could hardly shrug off a Venetian holiday which kept a mother away from her children for eight months and the much publicised relationship with Musset. He felt ridiculed, and his own copulations with Nohant servant-girls did not seem to redress the marital balance.

There was no question of divorce; divorce went out when the monarchy was restored in 1814. Separation however was possible. Casimir was quite willing to separate from a wife who had flaunted her affairs in his face and who at the same time was impervious to the moral judgment of ordinary society, while his wife welcomed a chance to shake off the last vestiges of depen- dence. In February 1835, while George was still in the throes of her love for Musset, another arrangement was made. Husband and wife were going to split up. George was to keep Nohant and have custody of Solange, while Casimir was to have the revenues from an old investment house in Paris and custody of Maurice.

The arrangement was due to come into effect in November of

that year, but hardly had it been signed when Casimir withdrew his consent. He could not bring himself to do without Nohant, which he had come to regard as his own by virtue of his marriage. George, keener than ever to gain her independence and keep the property which was hers by inheritance, was furious with a law which allowed a husband to cancel a signed undertaking. She wanted legal advice. Planet and Fleury drove her to Bourges, some fifty miles north-east of Nohant, settled her in a hotel and brought Michel to see her.

At first sight he looked sixty, though in reality he was only thirty-nine. He was small, bent, bespectacled and bald, with an old man's habit of protecting himself against head-colds by winding two or three scarves round his skull. Thus crowned he would go about in heavy wooden clogs like a peasant, incongruously sporting fine white shirts freshly laundered every day. George was never to forget the date of their first meeting, 7 April 1835.

It was seven in the evening when they met; it was four o'clock the following morning when they parted. Michel had dismissed the case Dudevant v. Dudevant in a few minutes and devoted the rest of the time to winning George Sand over to his idea of socialism. The four of them – Michel, Planet, Fleury and George – had long left the hotel and carried the discussion into the quiet street of Bourges, walking backwards and forwards, unable to resist a dazzling display of oratory. Michel deployed all his weapons, brought forth his best arguments, gave free rein to his political passions. Planet and Fleury had never seen him so eloquent, so masterful, so bent on making an impact. In the morning he wrote George an ardent letter and a day later followed it up with a ring inscribed with the date 9 April. George was overwhelmed. All thoughts of Musset, abandoned in Paris only four weeks earlier, vanished for ever.

But in spite of her emotional capitulation, George remained unconvinced by Michel's militant ideas. She put her counter-arguments down in the sixth of her *Lettres d'un voyageur*, which since her Venice days had become a regular feature of the *Revue des Deux Mondes*. This latest one was addressed to *Everard*, a name she chose in order to conceal the identity of the person to whom she was writing. It was begun within a week of their meeting and, as usual, ran to a prodigious length. Eventually she came to the fundamental difference between her own idea of socialism and his:

My friend, you seriously reproach me with social atheism; you say that anything which exists outside the utilitarian doctrines can never be truly great or good. You suggest that by remaining uncommitted I set a bad example and that I must either shake off my indifference or commit moral suicide, cut off my right hand and never again speak to fellow men. You are harsh, but I love you for that, for your harshness is beautiful and respectable. You also say that non-involvement is the refuge of the coward and the egotist, since there is no aspect of human behaviour which is not either useful or harmful to humanity. . . . What I am trying to say is this, Everard. Social virtue is not necessary for everybody, only for the few; what is universally necessary is honesty. You be virtuous, I shall try to be honest.[4]

Michel had accused George of frittering away her talent on romantic novels without a social message. In her *Lettre à Everard* she claimed for herself the artist's right to accept social ideas rather than form them. 'I am poetic by nature, not a law-giver,' she wrote, 'a fighter in case of need, but not a parliamentarian. You may demand my possessions and my life, but leave my poor soul to the sylphs and the nymphs of poetry.'[5]

There was a much more tangible point of divergence between George's socialism and Michel's. Militant republicans like him believed in what was known then as 'the equality of property' or 'the sharing of property'.[6] Romantic republicans like George believed in a sharing of happiness which was not dependent on the requisitioning of private land. She could not visualise an egalitarian society which would require her to part with Nohant and share it out among the landless. She ended her *Lettre à Everard* on a facetious note which left no doubt about her attitude. Announcing that she was about to go abroad soon, she concluded the article:

> Listen: should you declare a republic while I am away do take all I have, do not feel embarrassed. I have land, give it to those who have not; I have a garden, let your horses graze in it; I have wine, drink it; I have tobacco, smoke it; I have printed books, use them as wadding for your guns. In my entire patrimony there are only two things I shall grieve for: one is the portrait of my old grandmother, the other is six square feet of grass planted with cypresses and rose bushes. It is there that my grandmother sleeps next to my father. I am putting the grave and the picture under the protection of the republic and demand that on my return I should be compensated for my losses as follows: a pipe, a pen and some ink, which should enable me to earn my living and on receipt of which I shall spend the rest of my days writing that you have acted properly.[7]

In May, barely a month after their meeting, Michel left for Paris to play his part in the *Procès monstre*. George informed Sainte-Beuve that she was about to return to quai Malaquais and was surprised when he wrote back suggesting that it would be better for her if she stayed away from Musset a little longer. She had forgotten about Musset. The little dandified poet had been completely ousted by the masterful peasant from Bourges.

For the first time in her life George had a married man for a lover and appearances had to be kept for his sake if not for hers. Michel took lodgings at a discreet distance from quai Malaquais and soon a domestic pattern was set. During the day Michel conferred with colleagues and clients and attended the stormy court sessions; in the evenings he took George out to dine or cruise on the Seine, for which last purpose she would don one of her trouser suits.

One evening Michel and Planet took her to the theatre. The night was warm and the three of them strolled leisurely back, stopping on the Saints-Pères bridge to admire the river. That night a reception was being held at the Tuileries and strands of music came floating through the clear air. Michel held forth as usual. He was bitter about the progress of the trial and in a militant mood. In her autobiography George described how he stood there on the bridge, turbaned like an oriental potentate, calling fire and brimstone upon the corrupt monarchical society, hitting the balustrade with his walking-stick. 'In order to rejuvenate and renew your corrupt society,' she quoted him as saying, 'this beautiful river must be red with blood, this accursed palace must be reduced to ashes and this vast city you are admiring must be razed to the ground to allow the poor to plough the land and put up cottages.'[8]

The walk continued and so did the harangue. In his ferocity Michel broke his stick against the walls of the Louvre. George, who in April 1834 had been oscillating between Musset and Pagello in Venice while the silk-weavers were being massacred by government troops in Lyons, could not understand his extremism. It alarmed her, made her fear for his safety. Her fears were justified. Some time after the bridge scene Michel asked her to draft a letter to the press denouncing the court proceedings and questioning its competence. Her draft seemed to him too mild and he penned one of his own. In due course he was summoned, found guilty of contempt and sentenced to one month's imprisonment. He was allowed a stay of execution so that the case should proceed without additional complications.

George shaped her entire existence round Michel. When he was in Paris she was in Paris too; when he was in Bourges she returned to Nohant and met him secretly at a La Châtre hotel. Once, during the summer recess, she took lodgings at Bourges where Michel visited her whenever he could escape from his wife's watchful eyes. It was Paris however which gave them their best chance of freedom. Michel was overworked and ill, and George spent much of her time looking after him and nursing him. She felt in her element: needed, authoritative, maternally possessive.

But Michel, like Stéphane de Grandsagne some eight years earlier, did not want to be mothered. He wanted to dominate. The interminable siege of George Sand's soul continued unabated. The more he stormed and raged, the more she withdrew into passive resistance. He called her stupid, she called him an idea-machine. He threatened to leave her if she did not come over to his point of view; she retorted that he had no stable point of view and that he arbitrarily jettisoned one for another. The truth was that in Michel she met her match. It was inevitable that the meeting of two domineering temperaments should result in constant friction.

They were still having fierce arguments when the *Procès monstre* was drawing to its close. In the autumn of 1835 a large number of prisoners escaped through a tunnel and were never recaptured. The rest were found guilty of endangering the state and sentenced to periods of imprisonment ranging from two to twenty years. In October Michel returned to Bourges to serve his own month's sentence and was tolerably lodged in the city jail which had once been a ducal palace. George returned to Nohant to face a husband she was still hoping to dislodge.

In all her dealings with Casimir Dudevant George considered herself fair and above reproach. For years she had regarded him as no more than a business partner and was indignant when he unilaterally cancelled their arrangement for the division of their joint property. The law of the land made a wife's dowry the husband's chattel. Thanks to precautions taken at the signing of the marriage contract in 1822 Aurore Dupin retained a right to her inheritance, but not sole possession. George felt that by offering Casimir the revenue from their investment house in Paris, which was also part of her dowry, she was ceding him more than his fair share. The ownership of Nohant became a bitter bone of contention. Relations at home became extremely strained and on 19 October 1835 a domestic scene occurred which brought things to a head.

It happened at a dinner to which Dutheil, Fleury, Papet and some other Berry friends had been invited. According to their later depositions the storm broke out over nothing. Young Maurice asked for a second helping of cream, his father angrily told him there was none left. Maurice ran to his mother in tears, George shouted at her husband not to bully her son in her own house. Casimir shouted back that he would soon show her whose house it was, rushed out to fetch his gun and threatened to blow everybody's brains out. George ran upstairs with Maurice and locked herself up in her room.

The following morning she drove to Châteauroux to consult Rollinat in his dual capacity of friend and lawyer. He suggested referring the case back to Michel. Without stopping they drove all the way to Bourges, bribed the prison warden to let them into Michel's cell and conferred with him until two in the morning, when they were stealthily conducted out. Both lawyers advised George to make the most of the domestic scene witnessed by so many friends and take her case to court. It was still going to be reasonably friendly. Casimir was approached and given to understand that it would be made worth his while not to contest his wife's demands. He agreed to vacate Nohant, resigned his office as mayor of the village and left for Paris with the children, returning Maurice to his boarding-school and putting Solange in a *pension*. Alone at Nohant George wrote to her mother in Paris to be civil to Casimir when he called on her, so as not to give him an excuse to turn nasty again.

The case came up before the La Châtre jury in January 1836. Under her maiden name of Aurore Dupin Baroness Dudevant accused her husband of cruelty, to wit the slap delivered in the presence of the Duplessis twelve years earlier; adultery, to wit his affairs with servant-girls; and disorderly behaviour about the house, to wit his drinking sessions with neighbouring squires. As the suit was undefended the court granted the mother custody of the children and possession of the estate. Casimir demurred in the hope of being paid the compensation previously hinted at; but when his wife asked him instead for a hundred thousand francs towards the liquidation of their joint assets, he woke up. He demanded a re-trial. This time George moved out of Nohant pending proceedings while Casimir moved back in. George invited herself to stay with the Dutheils at La Châtre and every now and then rode to Nohant for a clandestine meeting with Michel in the same secluded pavilion which had served her well in the spring of her love for Jules Sandeau.

In the meantime Casimir, a former student of law, prepared a list of grievances against his wife. He cited Aurélien de Sèze, Stéphane de Grandsagne, Gustave Planche and Alfred de Musset. He accused her of unfeminine behaviour and subversive ideas. 'Mme Dudevant,' he concluded, 'affects the character of a young man, smokes, swears, dresses in man's clothes. She has lost all the feminine virtues and does not know the value of money. She is the author of *Lélia* and in June 1835 published a political manifesto [*Lettre à Everard*] in the *Revue des Deux Mondes.*'9

Casimir overplayed his hand. In view of his allegations the jury found that the marriage had irretrievably broken down and confirmed the previous verdict. Casimir lodged an appeal before the high court of Bourges, where Michel took over his mistress's defence. On his advice she asked the long-forgotten Aurélien de Sèze to forward the innocent love-diary which she had once sent him, so that it should be read out in court as proof of her chastity. Then she moved to Bourges to the house of a mutual friend, where she could discreetly receive the unchaste visits of her lawyer and lover.

The case was heard on a bright June day. Mme Dudevant turned up in a prim white dress with white lace and listened demurely to Michel's fine rendering of excerpts from her love-diary to Aurélien. The jury dismissed the case. Casimir threatened to lodge another appeal before a higher court and the case might well have dragged on for years but for the sensible intervention of George's half-brother Hippolyte. Hippolyte had sided with Casimir, but after the Bourges appeal he realised that nothing useful could be gained by further litigation. He persuaded Casimir to accept a settlement out of court.

In July 1836 a final binding agreement was reached between the lawyers of the two parties. Mme Dudevant was allowed sole possession of Nohant and custody of Solange, while M. Dudevant was granted the revenue from the investment house in Paris and custody of Maurice. It was exactly the same arrangement that the couple had originally agreed upon eighteen months earlier.

George was triumphant. After fourteen years of sharing,

Nohant was hers alone. At long last she could call her inheritance her own. She could administer it as she pleased, throw the house open to Paris friends or leave it to go away without having to invent excuses. She could resume the role of the charitable lady of the manor and yet keep to the unconventional social existence she had fashioned for herself. At thirty-two she achieved as much independence as the law of the land would stretch to.

But a year of litigation could not have gone by without leaving a mark. 'A lawsuit, and I speak from experience, is like an undertaking to walk across the sea with dry feet,'[10] she wrote to Buloz. It gave her a further insight into the unequal status of women before the law. In her autobiography she translated her personal experience into general terms:

> If a woman wants to separate from her husband she may plead incompatibility without bringing dishonour on the man whose name she bears. She may allege a husband's riotous life, outbursts of temper and adultery under the conjugal roof without obtaining release from her unhappiness, but also without irrevocably branding him in the eyes of society. . . .
>
> A woman however is allowed only one kind of honour. Once she is unfaithful to her husband she is branded, dishonoured, vilified in the eyes of her children. Moreover, she is liable to a shameful penalty, to imprisonment.[11]

She never forgave Casimir for having refused to disgorge Nohant without a struggle. Money mattered little to her, but land meant solidity and roots. When in 1837, shortly after the judicial separation, old Baroness Dudevant died and Casimir became at long last the squire of Guillery, George claimed it as her children's patrimony.

In theory the possession of Nohant should have meant freedom for George to pursue her affair with Michel under her own roof. In practice it made little difference to a relationship which had long ceased to be satisfactory.

With all his sophistication and progressive ideas Michel was at heart a peasant who could not long tolerate a strong-minded woman like George. The intellectual independence which had once presented a fascinating challenge soon became a source of irritation. George for her part could not grasp that Michel's interest in her was as much subject to fluctuations as his socialist ideas. She accused him of wickedness. 'Sometimes you seem to me like the spirit of evil,' she wrote one day. 'You have in you resources of cold cruelty and extraordinary tyranny towards me.'[12]

But she could not tear herself away from her tyrant. That bald, unprepossessing middle-aged married man succeeded where young handsome boys like Sandeau, Musset and Pagello had failed. He made George understand physical passion and respond. For the first time in her life she felt desire. 'The blood rushed into my head a hundred times,' she confessed to him in the autumn of 1836. 'In the heat of the sun, in the midst of beautiful mountains, whenever I heard the birds sing and inhaled the sweet smells of the woods and valleys, I had to sit down by myself with my soul full of love and my knees trembling with desire.'[13] When she learnt that Michel, far from being impressed with her awakening voluptuousness, was taking a marked interest in another woman, she was inescapably trapped.

The new phase in their relations began shortly after the conclusion of the *Procès monstre*. George returned to Nohant and Michel had to serve his four-week sentence in jail. On his release George noticed with incredulity that the roles had changed. She was the pursuer, Michel was the granter of favours. She initiated secret rendez-vous, Michel missed them. When in March 1836, in the midst of her battle for judicial separation, she had to return to Paris on business, Michel showed no regret. She was dejected.

Yet she would not be herself if, even at the height of her misery, she would not try to captivate new admirers. Literary Paris was full of young men who approached the author of *Lélia* with a mixture of intellectual reverence and emotional susceptibility. It was only natural that in her efforts to drive away the pain of Michel's coldness George should seek consolation in another man's arms. It was equally natural that such a step should fail to cure her of her love and only serve to bring unhappiness to the temporary recipient of her favours. It happened to be the writer Charles Didier.

At thirty Swiss-born Didier was heart-throbbingly handsome, with prematurely silver hair lending distinction to a youthful face tanned by a recent visit to Spain. But underneath his good looks there was a streak of unhappiness. As a child in Geneva he was constantly bullied by an elder brother; as an adolescent he discovered that his much-revered mother was not a wife but a housekeeper. His father was a well-connected Huguenot lawyer who was unable to provide comfortably for his numerous children. Young Didier wanted to be a writer. At twenty he published a first volume of verse. At twenty-five he arrived in Paris with a letter of recommendation to Victor Hugo. When a young unknown writer calling herself George Sand published a novel entitled *Indiana*, Charles Didier published a novel called *Rome souterraine.*

Like any other member of the Paris literary community, Didier had heard about the disintegrating association between George and Sandeau. When he first met her, in February 1833, he observed her with curiosity and fascination. In his diary he noted that her manner was stiff; he thought she was incapable of passion.

George did not find him attractive. He was too unassertive, too inclined to step aside in favour of more confident claimants. Once he rushed to quai Malaquais when he heard that George was unwell, but retreated just as quickly when other friends turned up to offer their services. George sensed however that she had made an impact and did not hesitate to ask him for a loan of a hundred francs, a large sum for both of them at the time. Their acquaintance petered out when George became Musset's mistress and left for Italy.

In the spring of 1836, when Michel was being evasive in Bourges under pretext of overwork, George went up to Paris on her own. One day she went to an art exhibition with two of her young admirers, ran into Didier and invited all three to supper at quai Malaquais. 'A fantastic night,' Didier recorded in his diary.

'We did not leave until five in the morning. Arago was drunk. I was not. I rested my head on the sofa cushions while she, sad but not in the least curt, ran her fingers through my hair and called me her philosopher.'[14]

The following day he returned to quai Malaquais with three bottles of champagne. Again there were other visitors, but the intimacy increased. Before he left there was a tender exchange of tokens. George gave him her cashmere scarf, Didier gave her his silk foulard. He became an assiduous visitor. On their own George was tender and affectionate; in company she was aloof. He suffered terribly.

Four weeks passed in this way. One day towards the end of April Didier found George at quai Malaquais on her own. She kept him for supper and allowed him to stay for breakfast. They spent the rest of the day walking in the Jardin des Plantes, then went to Didier's apartment where George in her turn stayed the night. In his diary he wrote: 'She dressed with my help. We had lunch, then I took her to Henri IV College to see Maurice. She talks a great deal about Michel and assures me of the intellectual nature of their friendship. She swears she has not had a lover since Musset.'[15]

A few days later George moved into Didier's lodgings. She explained that in view of the forthcoming lawsuit at La Châtre it was not safe for her to live on her own at quai Malaquais, for her husband was sure to burst in and seize the furniture. Didier wished for nothing better. George settled down to work in a room which Didier had ceded her. When she had done her quota, usually well past midnight, she would emerge and be sociable. Didier would sit at her feet, bury his head in her lap, allow her to ruffle his hair. He was experienced enough to sense that she was not behaving like a woman in love. In his diary he wrote: 'I study her all the time. I do not understand her. Is she true? Is she playing a comedy? Is her heart dead? O siren, what do you want of me?'[16]

She wanted nothing of him. She wanted Michel. In May she returned to Berry and put Didier right out of her mind. She barely found it necessary to let him know that she had won her first legal round; but when he wrote that he would come down to Nohant to see her she did not have the heart to put him off. On his arrival she silently put her arms round him and for the next five days gave him what he later described as the happiest days of his life.

That summer George was preparing the new edition of *Lélia*. The new Lélia was to lose her emotional aridity which had incensed some of the early critics and gain a positive attitude to love. It was not so much revising as rewriting. Didier listened to George's new ideas, made suggestions and had the satisfaction of seeing her accept some of them. When their work was done the lovers walked, rode, admired the Berry valleys and inhaled the scented summer air. The only cloud on the horizon was Michel. George had a compulsive need to bring up his name at every opportunity. In the midst of his bliss Didier was tormented by doubts.

After his return to Paris George hardly wrote to him. He reproached her for her cruelty; she reproached him for reproaching her. She fluctuated between revulsion and remorse. Above all she did not want people to think that they had once been intimate; she did not want Michel to think that she was anything but faithful.

Towards the end of August she took her children for a holiday in Switzerland. She had shaken Didier off, but in her own way she tried to atone for having briefly been his mistress while pining for another man. She dedicated to him her *Lettre d'un voyageur* which described the Swiss tour. She was not unkind. On her return to Paris she invited him to call at the new apartment she was sharing with Franz Liszt and his mistress Marie d'Agoult. Didier was so overcome by the sight of her that he burst into tears in everybody's presence.

She knew how he felt. At Nohant she too was undergoing an emotional crisis with Michel. After several months' silence she wrote to him on an impulse and asked him to come down and join a house party which included Liszt and Marie d'Agoult among others. Didier did not fit in. He roamed about on his own, recalling the five happy days of the year before. George, already regretting her generous impulse, was cold. She became effusive only on the day of his departure. He left as bitter as ever. The following year he married an heiress.

They never met again although they moved in the same literary circles and although Mme Didier sometimes ran into Mme Sand at friends' houses and reported it to her husband. In 1841 George brought out a collected edition of her *Lettres d'un voyageur* and substituted the dedication to Didier with a dedication to a fictitious friend called Herbert. Didier was hurt all over again. He continued to refer to her in his diary, note her movements, appraise her books. Gradually she became Madame Sand. In 1849, some thirteen years after their short affair, he referred to her for the last time.

Throughout the rest of his life he was dogged by misfortune. His books were not a success, his wife left him, he lost his eyesight. He went on living in Paris with little money and no friends. One cold March night of 1864 he shot himself through the heart. His death passed virtually unnoticed. The talk of literary Paris was the dramatised version of George Sand's *Le Marquis de Villemer* which had only just opened at the *Odéon*.

The summer of 1836 was a difficult one for George. She had regained Nohant but was unable to attract Michel to it. After her brief interlude with Didier, she accepted an invitation from Liszt and Marie d'Agoult to join them in Switzerland for a holiday and set out with her children, a maid and a young student of twenty who acted as an escort. Switzerland in September was beautiful and the holiday was a great success. Still she yearned for Michel. Before starting on her way back she asked him to meet her in Lyons and was bitterly disappointed when he did not show up. Instead, on her arrival at Nohant, she received an angry letter accusing her of infidelity.

She had learnt from experience that jealousy did not make Michel more attentive; it only made him unpleasant. Whether his suspicions were justified as in the case of Didier, or unfounded as in the case of her holiday escort, it was essential to allay them. She wrote back indignantly:

Nohant, October 1836

Michel, you are mad . . . I have told you a thousand times that if I ever had the misfortune of being unfaithful to you, out of weariness, momentary weakness or morbid need, I would certainly confess my fault and leave you master to punish me with total oblivion should you feel incapable of retaining even the slightest friendship towards me. Such a punishment would be disproportionate to a fault which is gross but forgivable, and which you yourself have been guilty of with your wife even after we have come together. But I will not beg, not even of you, and I would bear with fortitude the consequence of such a misconduct. The remorse I should feel would be proportionate to the nature of the crime, and I would certainly not go to the desert to seek penitence for a sin which you and many other respectable men have committed a thousand times. I should only weep for the loss of a heart which had been my solace and my joy. I do not think that any other physical or spiritual love would ever console me or take my mind off such a loss.

Having said this much I would like to state that I never committed such a crime, nor any other suchlike thing which might lead to more serious things.[17]

Postal communication was risky, for Mme Michel was no fool. George invented a code to disguise obvious references should her letters fall into the wrong hands. Michel was *Marcel*, Bourges was *Orléans*, Nohant was *Le Chesnay*. To her son Maurice she referred as to a girl called *Marie*; to Eliza Tourangin, the young woman who let them have a room in her house at La Châtre, as *Speranza*. The 7 April, the date of their first meeting, which for George took on a mystical meaning, became *Genril*.

She wrote long humble letters, begging Michel to let her see him, complaining of ill health, trying to rouse his compassion. She was no longer the confident manipulator of emotions who in the midst of her anguish still knew that the final choice was hers. Now she was a suppliant, prepared to accept any crumbs. 'What have I not suffered during the past six months?' she wrote at the beginning of 1837. 'My spirit is broken. Love has overcome pride and become my constant companion.'[18]

After one of their infrequent meetings in Bourges George heard what she had long suspected, that Michel was having an affair with another woman, possibly even with two at the same time. For the first time in her life she was jealous with a primitive, stabbing jealousy. In March 1837 she wrote:

'When we met you only said you loved me, you took me in your arms and I believed all you wanted me to believe, I did not dare ask any questions. Do be kind to me today and deliver me from a torment which keeps gnawing at me and which I cannot overcome in spite of my silence, my efforts, a way of life which is both stoic and Christian, hidden tears which would have roused Christ to compassion if he lived again, and fits of anger which even the divine Epictetus could not have suppressed if his heart was burning with love like mine. Deliver me from my misery, give me back the inspiration for my work, the peace of my nights. Please condescend to justify yourself. I am humbling myself before you, I, who am little humble by nature. . . . Tell me you have never loved this young girl except like a father. Say it, I shall believe you. . . .

'Now I must tell you of something else which has been tormenting me ever since my last visit to Bourges and which so far I have tried to suppress and overcome. You are being accused of something like bestiality. People say you are in love with a certain fat woman I know, who is repulsively obese, vain and insolent. How can I not suffer and not doubt you? You cannot possibly like her, you would have talked to me about her, and you never have. You do not much like her husband, you said so yourself. Why then do you go to her house? I know she is a musician, but her singing is off-pitch and unbearably affected. I know that for a fact, I heard her sing. You have an exquisite sense of beauty and genuineness. You cannot possibly admire or enjoy this affected performance. She is also wicked and I know she hates me from the bottom of her heart. She never misses a chance of maligning me and spreading evil rumours about me. I know this, I have more or less heard her say things about me.

How can you bear to be intimate with a creature who maligns me and hates me? I would never allow anyone to speak ill of you in my presence however much you may have offended me. I would hate anyone who did so and would turn away from them for ever. Tell me then, Michel, what you want with her and why you are spending with her all the hours you can snatch away from work? Does this woman relieve you of pent-up desire in the way prostitutes do? If this is the case I can forgive you. If you are sincere you will admit it without false pride or hypocrisy. Oh how far do I let my love and humiliation carry me? If you could only swear to me that you like me best, that no other woman can give you the physical pleasures you say you have found in my arms. Tell me what you like, for if you are doing that thing just to relieve yourself you too must be suffering.

'I cannot bear to think of that body of yours, so beautiful, so adored, so imprinted with my love, so many times clasped, roused with my kisses, hurt and pressed in moments of delirium, brought back to life with my lips, my hair, my burning breath! Oh how I get carried away by these memories. . . . Oh God, will this body which I idolise be sullied by contact with a disgusting belly, with a vain slug? Would your mouth have sucked the breath of a mouth prostituted to self-adoration and social vanity? No, it is impossible.

'The other rumour worries me more but surprises me less. It is about someone younger, prettier than me and no doubt purer, if purity means the absence of disenchantments and unfortunate attachments. At least this young woman would be a rival I could not and would not despise. But the other would be unworthy of you and me, especially of you. Oh God, no, I must be dreaming all this. It cannot be, it has never happened.

'If I am wrong, if I have been misinformed, do not hesitate to tell me so. Just scribble these two letters: *no*. I am not asking for anything else. I shall blindly accept your word. God forbid that I should ever doubt it. . . . Please answer me, tell me the truth. Do not be afraid to tell me the truth, I can take it, I am braver than you. If you do not love me any more do not make me languish, do not keep me in utter dejection. But if you love me at all do not allow me to beg. Tell me the truth, I shall accept anything you say.'[19]

But George did not want the truth. She wanted to be loved. Within two days she wrote again:

Nohant, 22 March 1837

There is only one thing which can save my life, Michel. Say it. Do you love me? Say it and I shall live. I know you love some-one else, at least I think you do, I am desperate. Never mind, tell me you love me and I shall believe it. Let me see you for a day, for an hour. Lie to me, have the kindness to lie to me. I shall not say anything, I shall not reproach you with anything. There will be no questions, nothing. My last letter was crazy. If my suspicions made you angry please forgive me. If they were justified please do not tell me so. Keep the truth to your-self. And if you are unfaithful to me, you can be just as unfaith-ful to her. Easter is coming. Please give me 24 hours. I shall meet you wherever you wish. . . .[20]

Her letters were interminable. Sometimes Michel did not bother to answer them; perhaps he did not even read them to the end. George found excuses for him and continued to send pages and pages of pleading. From time to time Michel would yield to pressure and grant a rendez-vous. She would gallop by night to La Châtre or Châteauroux and spend a few hours in his arms in a rented room. When on one of these occasions he said he was too overworked to find time in the future for such expeditions, she offered to take a house in Bourges; when he said he was too tired for love-making, she assured him she would be content with his spiritual love.

At growing intervals Michel would grant a rendez-vous at a hotel half-way between Bourges and Nohant and the night of love would make George's suffering vanish like a nightmare. After one such occasion she wrote to him:

Nohant, 7 May 1837

Angel of my life, I am happy if you love me. I cannot say any more tonight. I am too tired. I rode eighteen miles in two hours. I found my son well. Liszt and Marie d'Agoult have come to stay. I am dead tired, but not because of that rushed journey. What sweet weariness and what peaceful sleep weigh heavy on my eyes! Is it true that you love me as you used to? Is it not a dream? Will I not wake up tomorrow as sad and hurt as ever? No, because you do love me. Say it, write it, tell me that you too have a feeling of well-being, that I have made you happy, that the pleasure I give you is greater than the suffering I cause you.... Love me and have the kindness to write and tell me so until we meet again. This is the only thing which will keep me going.[21]

Such moments of hope were rare. Michel had neither the time nor the inclination to ride thirty miles out of Bourges to meet a mistress he no longer needed. It was also difficult to explain his overnight stays to his wife. He tried to win a respite by putting George off, but she only renewed her reproaches. He felt harassed on all fronts. Before May was out he was writing angrily:

Damn it all! At home I have to fight day and night because of you. Fair enough, nothing good is given to a man without a struggle. If at least I could find a haven of peace in your arms, a refuge from harassment. But no, you make demands, you fight me too. I have an enemy at home, an enemy in you. I am telling you this cannot go on. I would turn a Trappist monk if I believed in such things. I must have peace. I will not fight women. It is undignified.[22]

George refused to understand. 'You refuse to come to me,' she wrote, 'because with your ideas of a Pasha you expect me to come to you like a submissive odalisk.'[23] Still she was prepared to travel any distance at any time just to be with him for a few hours. In June he grudgingly suggested a meeting at a Bourges hotel, giving George very short notice. She was hurt, but did not dare pass over the precious summons. She sent him a brief note:

I am unwell. I cannot travel tomorrow in the heat of the day and I am too tired to start tonight. I should arrive dead tired and you would have little pleasure of me when you join me at the hotel. I shall therefore set out tomorrow night and arrive Thursday morning. I shall then go to sleep until you find the time to come and see me. Goodbye for now. I am very ill, I think I have an inflammation of the chest. I do not know what brought this on so suddenly. But I would have to be much iller before I give up the journey tomorrow night.[24]

The meeting was unpleasant. There were a few more letters full of mutual recriminations, then no more. George gave up.

As fate would have it, they did meet again later that year, in circumstances that neither of them could have foreseen.

In the autumn of 1837 Casimir Dudevant suddenly descended on Nohant while George was in Paris, grabbed his daughter Solange and led her to his baronial château at Guillery. George's determined pursuit and successful recovery of the child became the talk of Berry and when mother and daughter returned through Châteauroux Michel drove from Bourges to meet them and offer his congratulations. George was no longer the forlorn mistress of a few months earlier. She was escorted by the young writer Mallefille who had recently become her lover. Michel was curious, George very civil.

At that time Michel was trying to have himself elected as Deputy and when, shortly after Solange's rescue, he found himself canvassing in the neighbourhood, he invited himself to stay at Nohant. George had her Paris friend Mme Marliani with her, and for good measure sent an urgent message to Papet at La Châtre: '*Cher vieux*, Michel is here, come and see him.'[25] Mallefille was away. George was tense and elated at the prospect of a renewed friendship. Michel was courteous and inscrutable. The following month she heard that his canvassing had been successful, he had been elected Deputy for Niort. He did not bother to write to tell her. The old bitterness returned with a vengeance.

It was impossible to live at Nohant and mix with fellow socialists without hearing of Michel's progress. George knew that he had been elected a Deputy for a second time and made himself

Alfred de Musset,
engraving by M. Waltner
after the medallion
by David d'Angers

Pietro Pagello,
from a portrait
by the Venetian
painter, Bevilacqua

Marie d'Agoult (later known as Daniel Stern), drawn by Claire-Christine from the sculpture by Léopold Flameng

Franz Liszt, by Devéria

as many enemies as friends. Later he fell foul of Louis Napoleon and temporarily lived in exile. In 1853 he died in Montpellier, still *persona non grata*, and his coffin was escorted under heavy guard to its final resting place in Berry.

In her autobiography, completed two years after his death, George referred to Michel as Everard, the name she had invented for him in her *Lettre d'un voyageur* of many years earlier. She praised his intellectual prowess and acknowledged his influence over her socialist evolution. She emphasised his virtues and romanticised the fortitude with which he bore ill health. Yet even at that distance in time she could not help being hurt by his insatiable need to impress and conquer. 'When I first met him,' she wrote, 'he had not yet reached that stage in life when he wanted to look young, wear a wig, put on fashionable clothes and go into society. I never saw him like that. That transformation did not occur under my eyes and I am glad it did not.'[26]

All her life George believed that her love letters to Michel had been destroyed and therefore felt free to describe their association as 'a fraternal pact'.[27] Perhaps she was hoping to obliterate the ever-humiliating truth when she wrote:

There was a sweet bond between us, and the purity of our friendship made it all the more precious. I realised of course that the nature of our relations could be misunderstood, but I did not really care. Our friends knew it for what it was, and their constant presence sanctified it all the more.[28]

In her autobiography she gave Everard more space than to any other man in her life. Perhaps she still felt the compulsive need to evoke in words the image of the lover whose evasiveness was the secret of his hold over her.

❧❧❧❧❧❧

Chapter 10

Prophets and friends

Ever since her first political discussion with Michel de Bourges, George felt that his socialist doctrines were based on unacceptable premises. The more he expounded them, the more she sensed the inconsistencies in his line of argument. Their mutual friend Planet, who like George divided his professional life between Berry and Paris, shared her misgivings. In her autobiography she described their perplexity at the time:

> I discussed my doubts with Planet, who could not resolve them any more than I could and who, genuinely tormented as he was, had a way of saying, whether it was relevant or not: *Friends, it is time to put the social question.* Good old Planet, he used to say it in such a funny way that his suggestion was always received with guffaws of laughter until it became a catch phrase. We got into the habit of saying *Let us put the social question* when we meant *Let us sit down to dinner;* and when a tiresome visitor got on our nerves, we would suggest putting the social question to him in order to get rid of him.[1]

George never pretended to be an original political thinker. On the contrary, she consciously sought to be recruited and won over. 'I would give myself up to a cause,' she wrote in 1835, 'provided I am persuaded of its merit. I am not capable of discovering things for myself or resolving things. I can only embrace what seems right.'[2]

What seemed right was a social formula based on human kindness. Michel's socialism struck George as cold and cruel, devoid of the very quality which should have inspired it. Moreover, Michel had no religious faith while she, although far removed from the unquestioning devoutness of her adolescence, had retained a fundamental belief in the humanitarian values of religion. She hankered after a message which would combine the social truth with the religious truth. She kept putting the social question to whoever seemed likely to lead her to an answer. She was a disciple in search of a prophet. In her autobiography she related how in 1835 she found one in the person of the social philosopher Pierre Leroux:

[Both Planet and I] realised that neither of us properly understood the connection between the revolution which had taken place and the one we were still dreaming about. Suddenly I had a bright idea. 'I have heard Sainte-Beuve say,' I told Planet, 'that there are two people whose superior intelligence had pierced the problem and shed light on it in a way which might answer my expectations and resolve my doubts. . . . They agree on the essential points of their creed and have gathered round them a school of sympathisers who encourage them in their hard work. These two are Pierre Leroux and Jean Reynaud. When Sainte-Beuve saw me tormented by doubts like Lélia, he advised me to seek the light through them and offered to introduce me to them. I declined because I was diffident. I felt too ignorant to understand their teachings, too limited to appreciate them, too shy to expose my inner doubts. But it so happens that Leroux too is shy, I have seen him, and I know I could be at ease with him. But how to approach him? How to get hold of him for a few hours? Would he not laugh in our faces like the others if we *put the social question to him*?'
'I'll take care of that,' replied Planet. 'I shall dare put the social question to him. I do not mind if he laughs in my face, as long as he enlightens me. Write to him in the name of a simpleton friend of yours, a miller, or a peasant, and ask him to expound his social catechism to him in two or three hours' conversation. I hope I shall not be shy with him, and you would be able to listen and benefit.'

I then wrote to Pierre Leroux along these lines and he came to dinner with the two of us in my garret.[3]

At forty Pierre Leroux had already published several works on the state of society. Unlike George and most of her other republican friends, he had worked his way up from the very bottom. His father was a Paris lemonade-vendor, and he himself, married with several children, made a meagre living as a compositor and printer. He made an immediate hit with George and Planet. He explained to them that since the most natural way of life was within the framework of society, society had to be maintained. It needed however to be improved, and that could only be done with the aid of religion. God was everywhere, both in the material and spiritual world; and while wealth as such was not ungodly, it had to be curbed when it interfered with progress towards social perfection.

George was particularly charmed with Leroux's theory about marriage. Like her he wanted it based on equality between the sexes and maintained that equal status for husband and wife was a guarantee against marital unhappiness. When he left quai Malaquais George knew that she had found her spiritual master. She began telling her friends that Leroux was the social prophet of the age. 'Have you read Leroux?' she would ask anybody who put the social question in her presence. 'I am sure that one day he will be read in the same way that Rousseau's *The Social Contract* is being read today.'[4] She could not do enough for him. She gave him money to tide him over his financial difficulties and pestered Buloz to commission articles from him; but Buloz, a close-fisted editor at the best of times, refused. 'No, no,' he said. 'God is not a topical subject.'[5]

In her efforts to spread Leroux's social theories, George introduced him to Mme Marliani, wife of the Spanish consul in Paris, whose acquaintance she had recently made. She listened with pride and admiration as he expounded his views to a circle of adoring female aristocrats assembled in Mme Marliani's drawing-room, his small body ensconced in a deep chair, his muddy boots soiling the carpet, his never-laundered shirts filling the air with pungent smell. She adopted his views on class, family and property. For the next ten years she wrote under the inspiration of his philosophy such mystical works as *Spiridion*, *Horace*, *La Comtesse de Rudolstadt*, *Le Péché de M. Antoine*. Buloz did not much like the new trend in her work, but George was unmoved. Leroux's ideas were gospel.

Like so many of his predecessors, Leroux fell in love with his ardent disciple. George however was not tempted and steered him into calmer waters. From time to time she asked him to go through a finished manuscript and check the accuracy of her philosophical ideas based on his teachings. She respectfully acknowledged her debt in *Spiridion*, which she dedicated to him in the following words:

To M. Pierre Leroux,
Friend and brother through the years, father and master through virtue and knowledge, please accept this tale of mine not as something worthy of being dedicated to you, but as a token of friendship and veneration.

Even when no longer preoccupied with religious socialism, George did not deny her prophet. When he died in 1871 after a turbulent political career, an old and ailing George Sand walked sadly behind his coffin.

At about the same time she met Leroux, George was introduced to a fellow-seeker of the social truth who was soon to become her 'sweet child and brother'.[6] It was Franz Liszt.

They met in the autumn of 1834 through Musset who, having effected the introduction, immediately became jealous. On the face of it he had good reason to be, for there was an avowed affinity between the thirty-year-old siren and the twenty-three-year-old musician. Both were tormented by things divine; both had a religious streak; both were seeking a moral philosophy which would remove social injustice; both read avidly; and both combined an aristocratic way of life with democratic ideas. Liszt had read and admired *Indiana* and *Lélia*, George admired

Liszt's genius. Paris had it that they were lovers. Both denied it.

In fact Liszt was in love with Countess Marie d'Agoult and anxious for her to meet George Sand whose novels she too had read and admired. As a rule George had little use for her friends' wives, let alone mistresses; at the most she acknowledged the wives in polite postscripts to letters addressed to the husbands. But in Marie d'Agoult's case George sensed that she would have to make an exception if she were to maintain cordial relations with Liszt.

When they met at George's third-floor apartment at quai Malaquais, the two women eyed each other critically. They were about the same age, but totally contrasting in appearance. George was robust with black hair and sleepy dark eyes; Marie was as slim as a willow in spite of two childbirths, with golden hair and blue eyes. The meeting was not a success. George did her best to make Marie d'Agoult feel uncomfortable, blandly leading the conversation to her deep-rooted aversion of old countesses. Marie, a *grande dame* of the old school, remained gracious. Much later, in a *Lettre d'un voyageur* dedicated to Liszt, George romanticised that first meeting beyond recognition and described Marie as 'that golden-haired fairy in a blue dress who one evening descended from heaven into the poet's attic and sat amongst us like those marvellous princesses who appear to the poor artists in Hoffman's tales'.[7] Instinctively she had turned Marie from a flesh and blood woman into a creature of fantasy; she was more acceptable that way.

Some time after that first meeting Marie d'Agoult left her husband and her one surviving child and set up house with Liszt in Geneva. It was said that her decision to brave social conventions and live for love was partly inspired by George's novels and her way of life. Even then George did not warm up to her. There was an unavowed rivalry between them over Liszt, whom each wanted to hold in her own way. In January 1836, when Marie had already given birth to a daughter by Liszt, George was still negotiating the terms of their friendship-to-be as an extension of her own loving friendship with Liszt. She wrote:

'You must dispose yourself in a way which would make it possible for me to love you as much as I love myself. It should be easy. First of all, because I love Franz, it is part of my system. He told me to love you and says that he can answer for you as for himself. I met you, that 1st time, and thought you were beautiful; but you were cold and so was I. The second time I told you I loathed the aristocracy, I did not know you belonged to it. Instead of slapping me as I deserved, you spoke of your soul as if you had known me for 10 years. That was good and I wanted to love you there and then; but I do not love you yet. It is not because I do not know you well enough. I already know you as much as I am ever likely to even in 20 years' time; it is you who do not yet know me well enough. And as I do not know whether you can love me as I really am, I do not wish to love you yet. This is something more serious and absolute than mere friendship. If you want me to love you, you must love me first. . . .

'I am capable of anything. I shall commit a thousand stupidities, tread on your toes, answer rudely for no reason, reproach you for a fault you do not have. I shall attribute to you an intention you never had, turn my back on you and be altogether insufferable until I am quite sure that I cannot exasperate you or disgust you. Oh then I shall carry you on my back, cook for you, wash up the dishes. Everything you say will seem divine. Should you step into something foul I will say it smells pleasant. I shall see you with the same eyes I see myself when I am in a good mood; that is when I consider myself perfect and heartily despise anybody who does not agree with me. Dispose yourself to be inside my eyes, my ears, my veins, my entire being; you will then know that no one on earth can love better than me because I love with my eyes open, that is, without being ashamed of the reason which makes me love, that reason being the gratitude I feel towards those who adopt me. This is my summing up; it is not modest, but it is very sincere.'[8]

Whatever Marie felt about George's proposition, she joined

Liszt in pressing her to visit them in Switzerland. In the summer of 1836, when George badly needed a respite from her emotional tribulations with Michel and Didier, she accepted the invitation. She set out for Geneva with her two children, a Nohant servant-girl who could not tell the difference between Martigny in Switzerland and Martinique in the Caribbean sea, and a young admirer who constituted himself an escort and protector. As usual, George travelled in man's clothes. When the party arrived at the Swiss rendez-vous there was nobody to meet them. Liszt and Marie had gone on ahead to Chamonix, leaving no instructions behind. In her *Lettre d'un voyageur* published later that year and dedicated to Didier, George described in dialogue form how her stranded party went in search of one of the most famous musicians in Europe:

'Where are you staying, Gentlemen?' the postillion enquired [George always referred to herself in her *Lettres d'un voyageur* as to a male traveller].

'At M. *Listz*'s [sic].'

'And where does the gentleman live?'

'I was going to ask you the same question myself.'

'Well then, what does he do for a living? What is he?'

'He is an artist.'

'A veterinary surgeon?'

'Are you a sick animal?'

'He is a fiddle seller,' intervened a passer-by. 'I'll take you to him.'

We were taken up a steep road. The mistress of the house informed us that *Listz* lived in England.

'That woman does not know what she is talking about,' said another passer-by. 'M. *Listz* is a theatre musician. You had better ask at the theatre.'

'Why not?' said my travelling companion. He managed to get hold of the theatre manager who said that *Listz* was in Paris.

'And has no doubt hired himself out to Musard's ballroom orchestra as a flute,' I said angrily.

'Could be,' said the manager.

'Here is the casino door,' someone said. 'All the young ladies who take music lessons know M. *Listz*.'

'I would like to cross over and ask that young one who is just coming out with music sheets under her arm,' said my companion.

'Do, she is rather pretty.'

My companion bowed three times in the old French style and courteously asked the young lady for M. *Listz*'s address. The young lady blushed, cast down her eyes and said in a choking voice that M. *Listz* was in Italy.

'The devil he is,' I cried. 'I am going to put up at the nearest inn. Let him do the chasing if he wants to see us.'

At the inn I was handed a note from M. *Listz*'s sister [it would not have done to scandalise the readers of the *Revue des Deux Mondes*]. *We have waited and waited*, the note said, *but you were not on time. You are tiresome. Now you look for us. We've gone ahead. Arabella. P.S. See the major. He will take you to us.*

'Who is the major?' I asked.

'What do we care?' answered my companion.

'True enough. Waiter, go find the major.'

The major was found. He looked like Mephistopheles dressed up in a customs officer's cloak. He looked me over from head to foot and asked who I was.

'An ill-dressed traveller, as you can see for yourself, and a friend of Arabella's.'

'Ah,' said the major. 'I'll go and get your passports.'

'Is he mad?' asked my companion.

'Not really; we need them to go to Mont Blanc.'

And so we got to Chamonix. It was a dark, rainy night. I happened to stop by the Union Hotel, which the locals pronounce Onion Hotel. This time I was careful not to ask for an artist with a European reputation by name, but conformed to the local custom of describing him instead: a shrunken jacket, long untidy hair, a battered straw-hat, a tie knotted like a string, a temporary limp, mostly humming pleasantly the *Dies irae*.

'Yes of course, sir,' replied the inn-keeper. 'They have just arrived. The lady is tired but the young girl is very sweet. Go on upstairs. They are in No. 13.'

I rushed up to No. 13 determined to throw my arms round the first spleenish Englishman who should open the door. I was travel-stained enough for the gesture to be taken as a commercial traveller's idea of a joke.

The first thing I bumped into was what the inn-keeper had described as the young girl. It was Puzzi [nickname for Hermann Cohen, a young musician and friend of Liszt's], sitting astride a rucksack; he was so changed, so grown, his brown hair so long, his body encased in such a tight-fitting jacket that, by God, I did not recognise him. Instead I took my hat off to little Hermann and said: 'Tell me, handsome page, where can I find Lara?'

Now Arabella's golden head emerged from under an English hooded cape. While I rushed towards her Franz threw his arms round me, Puzzi screamed with surprise, we became a tangle of arms and embraces. The chambermaid, aghast to see a mud-stained young man whom she had taken to be a jockey kiss a beautiful lady like Arabella, dropped her candle and spread the news round the entire hotel that No. 13 had been invaded by a gang of mysterious long-haired savages, among whom it was impossible to tell men from women, masters from servants.

'Actors,' said the chef contemptuously. After that we were branded, pointed at, avoided with horror. The English ladies we encountered in the corridors prudishly pulled down their veils over their faces while their regal husbands asked us at the dinner table whether we would put up a show for them in return for a reasonable collection they would arrange. . . . That night the silver plate was counted up three times; and I distinctly heard Mistress So-and-So and Milady So-and-So, two young dowagers of fifty or sixty, bolt their doors as if they feared an invasion of Cossacks.[9]

From Chamonix the party made excursions to the surrounding mountains. George held long philosophical discussions with the major, a venerable Swiss, who managed to read even as he was riding his mule. One day they all went to Fribourg cathedral to hear the newly installed organ. Liszt took over and played the *Dies irae* from Mozart's requiem. On their return to Geneva he composed a *Rondo fantastique* which he dedicated to *Monsieur George Sand*. George, to return the compliment, sat up all night and produced a lyrical story which she entitled *Le Contrebandier*, *paraphrase fantastique sur un rondo fantastique de Franz Liszt*. The Swiss tour yielded a whole new set of nicknames. George and her children became *Piffoëls*, because of their long noses; Liszt on his own, *Crétin*; Liszt together with Marie, *The Fellows*, in English; Marie was always *Arabella* or the *Princess*, and her baby-daughter, *the little Princess*.

By the time George was ready to go back to France, *The Fellows* decided that they had exhausted the charms of Switzerland. Marie longed for the mundane life she used to lead before her scandalous breach with convention, while Liszt fretted for the admiration of his sophisticated Paris audiences. When George left them at the end of September, it was with the understanding that they would soon follow her.

Indeed the following month they returned to Paris and took a large house called Hôtel de France in rue Laffitte. As George had left quai Malaquais for good earlier that year, they invited her to take over part of the house and share their salon. George later described the exciting company she met there:

> The living conditions at the Hôtel de France, which Mme d'Agoult invited me to share with her, were most congenial for a short stay. She entertained men of letters, artists and men of the world. It was through her I met Eugène Sue, Baron Eckstein, Chopin, Mickiewicz, Nourrit, Victor Schelcher and others. In the same way that her friends became mine, mine became hers. She invited Lamennais, Leroux, Heinrich Heine etc. Her improvised drawing-room was a meeting place for the élite, over which she presided with exquisite grace.[10]

George's meeting with Chopin at Marie d'Agoult's drawing-room did not lead to an immediate friendship. That was to come two years later. On the other hand her meetings with Lamennais led to another spiritual infatuation which was to leave a mark on her thinking and her work.

The abbé Félicien de Lamennais was a Catholic priest who had fallen out with the Church after he had publicly criticised Pope Gregory XVI for condoning the Russian suppression of the recent Polish Revolution. Deprived of religious support, Lamennais became a secular reformer and sought to bring into the republican camp the democratic ideas he had failed to introduce into the Church. He was admired in republican circles. Liszt was much taken with him and even before he left with Marie d'Agoult for Switzerland often mentioned him to George, telling her of his moral courage, his poverty, his worn frock, peasant-style blue woollen stockings, battered straw hat. George too was impressed with the man who in his mid-fifties had the courage to abandon established religion for socialism.

In Marie d'Agoult's drawing-room she had further occasion to hear him expound his ideas. In him she found another prophet who combined the egalitarian ideals of the revolution with the humanitarian values of religion. Lamennais, possibly even more than Leroux, gave her a sense of vocation. She morally prostrated herself before him.

Again there was nothing she would not do for her prophet. She tried to help him settle down in Paris and find him new disciples. She invited him to Nohant and sat enraptured at his feet. She published an article championing his views in the *Revue des Deux Mondes* and thought nothing of antagonising Sainte-Beuve, who did not agree with them. She persuaded Buloz to give up his theatre box to Lamennais, because the latter had evinced a wish to see the actress Rachel. When the abbé announced that he was founding a journal to propagate his views, she offered to contribute without payment. Her first article in Lamennais's *Le Monde* appeared in February 1837.

It was the first of a series entitled *Lettres à Marcie*, in which George intended to discuss various social questions which were particularly relevant to the status of women. The articles were based on real-life letters which she had written over the past year to a young woman called Eliza Tourangin, otherwise known as *Speranza*. *Speranza*, who had housed George's clandestine meetings with Michel, was a respectable young woman with no dowry, who was wondering whether she should marry the first well-to-do man presented to her by her father. George had been trying to dissuade her from accepting an arranged marriage for the sake of material security. In her *Lettres à Marcie* she reiterated the same plea. She claimed women's right to social equality and went as far as to claim equality in love. Lamennais, deeply entrenched in his Catholic view of marriage in spite of his break with Rome, read George's latest script with horror, re-read one or two previous ones which had not yet gone to press, and suspended publication altogether.

George had put her heart and soul into her *Lettres à Marcie* and was not a little hurt by her prophet's conservatism. Marie d'Agoult watched her with compassion. She was staying at the time at Nohant, while Liszt was giving concerts in Paris in an attempt to demolish the reputation of a rival pianist. She kept him posted:

Nohant, 12 March 1837

George has had a misunderstanding with *Le Monde*. The cuts the abbé has made in her third *Lettre à Marcie* have upset her. She wrote him a perfectly civil letter, very affectionate and reasonable, pointing out that she could not go on writing at random, that she wanted to discuss divorce and many other topics and that she needed to know in advance what latitude the abbé would allow her. His reply was cold. He does not want divorce, he wants those literary flowers which she can turn out at the drop of a hat, those fairy tales and fantasies. Moreover, he has not yet published her fourth *Lettre*. She is very upset. I do not know what is going to happen now.[11]

What happened was that within a few months Lamennais had to give up the editorship of *Le Monde*. That summer Marie d'Agoult lamented in her diary the passing of a spiritual partnership which had not lived up to its promise. She wrote:

Lamennais has not been at all clever with George. He did not understand that she came to him disposed to give herself entirely to his cause, devote herself blindly to his opinions, make herself the mouthpiece of his thinking. He did not realise that he had fired the imagination of the writer most likely to popularise his ideas and present them in a less austere and more attractive form. He approached her with hesitation, responded with guarded politeness to her outbursts of enthusiasm; and last but not least, while objecting to her views, did not take the trouble to convince her of his own. Consequently the alliance which was so much talked about turned out to be more imaginary than real. United, these two forces could have engendered great things and come as near to truth as is given to mankind to do so; separated, they lost most of the influence they might have wielded together over a whole generation.[12]

Lamennais seemed to have an ambivalent attitude towards George. He welcomed her as an ally, yet did not allow her to throw her own resources into the battle; he accepted her hospitality at Nohant, yet wrote to a friend somewhat disparagingly of her material astuteness The truth was that he had a poor opinion of women and was in the habit of saying that even the most intelligent amongst them could not follow a logical argument for more than fifteen minutes. Perhaps he was also put off by some Paris gossip which alleged a lesbian relationship between George and Marie d'Agoult, George and Mme Marliani. He certainly resented Pierre Leroux's popularity with these ladies. 'It is not as if they understand the first thing about those doctrines of his they so much rave about,' Lamennais contemptuously said. 'They just like to inhale that brothel smell which he seems to exude.'[13] George did not disown her prophet even after the suppression of her articles. Although no longer a collaborator, she continued to respect his views and wrote generously of him after his death in 1854.

Nohant in the summer of 1837 took on a new charm for George. Never had the garden seemed more colourful, the lime trees more luxuriant, the nightingales more sweetly in tune. She had given up the pursuit of Michel and channelled what Marie d'Agoult described as her overflowing emotional energies into hospitality. The house was full. Old Berry friends like Fleury, Rollinat, Duvernet and Dutheil called and spent long hours discoursing and strolling in the grounds. A budding young writer called Pelletan came down from Paris and was made Maurice's tutor. Didier too came down for a few days, mistaking George's pitying invitation for a renewal of love. One day the actor Bocage came down, fresh from his Paris success in Alexandre Dumas's *Antony*, and tried to persuade George to write a vehicle play for him. Tall, slim, with deep blue eyes and a throbbing voice, he looked much younger than his thirty-eight years and appeared to be making headway with George. His conversation was a mélange of republican ideas and theatre gossip. Marie d'Agoult noted with relish that he maligned Marie Dorval who had played the female lead in *Antony* and who had apparently failed to acknowledge his dramatic superiority. In her diary she dismissed him briefly: 'I tried to engage Bocage in conversation and mentioned some plays by Mickiewicz. *Miss Who?* asked Bocage, after which I gave up the attempt.'[14]

Marie, in her own gentle gracious way, was just as domineering as George in her forceful way. Her attitude to George remained ambivalent. When earlier on she witnessed her anguish over Michel she described her to Liszt as 'a poor great woman';[15] now, with George's emotional revival, she watched with a tinge of envy how the same poor great woman was confidently presiding over a court of young men. Perhaps alone in the entire Nohant set Marie d'Agoult had not fallen under George's spell. With her cold, feminine perception she kept observing and dissecting. Most of all she observed George's way with Liszt, who had finished his concert season in Paris and come down to Nohant. While outwardly sweet and placid, Marie was inwardly worried by a spiritual communion from which she knew herself excluded.

Liszt fitted admirably into George's unconventional daily routine. Like her he talked and walked during the day, settled down to serious work during the night. Often they worked in the same room. Marie would sometimes flit in, beautiful and expensively dressed, to listen to Liszt's playing, while George would soulfully crouch under the grand piano the better to absorb the music, or so she said. At that time Liszt was transcribing some of Beethoven's symphonies for the piano. George, whose break-up with Michel was only a few weeks behind her, found the music soothing. In her diary she wrote:

When Franz plays the piano, I am comforted. All my sufferings turn into poetry, my instincts become exalted. Above all he vibrates in me the chord of generosity. . . . I love the interrupted phrases he dashes on the piano, which seem to stay one foot in the air dancing in space like fluttering feathers. The leaves of the lime trees softly take up his melody and complete it in a mysterious whisper, as if confiding the secret of creation to one another. Perhaps he is trying to compose at the piano. His pipe is next to him, his ruled paper, his pens; each time he has traced his thoughts on paper he entrusts them to the voice of his instrument, and this voice reveals them to the attentive and observant nature.[16]

In spite of the undercurrents of unhappiness and anxiety, life at Nohant that summer was creative. George was putting the last touches to *Mauprat* and already working on *Les Maîtres mosaïstes*, a novel with a Venetian background which on completion, within two months, she dedicated to her fourteen-year-old son Maurice. Liszt continued to play, transcribe and compose; and Marie d'Agoult, inwardly preparing to be the writer she later became under the pen-name of Daniel Stern, quietly observed. In her diary she wrote:

My stay at Nohant was good for me. George's sprightliness, alien to my nature as it is, has all the same brought out in me what little capacity for gaiety I had. She has also deepened my sense of the poetic and opened up before me new vistas of enjoyment. Moreover, I was able to reassert myself in my own

eyes. From extreme diffidence I progressed towards a more
just evaluation of myself; for while it is unhealthy to hold too
good an opinion of oneself, it is equally harmful to think too
little of oneself. . . . It did me good to see George the woman
side by side with George the great poet, George the untamed
child, feeble even at the moment of audacity, unstable in her
emotions and opinions, illogical in her way of life, always
swayed by circumstances, never guided by reason or experience.
I have realised how childish it was of me to think (and how
painful the thought had been) that she alone could stretch
Franz's life to the full, that I was an unfortunate impediment
between two destinies meant to unite and complement each
other.[17]

Towards the end of July *The Fellows* left for Italy. Nohant was
getting quiet. Didier had long gone back to Paris and so had
Pelletan, having quarrelled with George and relinquished his post
as tutor to another young writer called Mallefille. Bocage had
also departed, prudishly anxious not to have his name linked with
George's, except professionally. George was getting restless. She
arranged for Solange to stay on at Nohant under the care of a
young sister of Rollinat, and for Maurice to spend some weeks
with Gustave Papet and his family near La Châtre. Mallefille
returned to Paris while she herself went on to Fontainebleau and
put up, under an assumed name, at the same hotel where she had
stayed with Musset at the dawn of their love four years earlier.
    This time her companion was Bocage, who had discreetly left
Paris to spend a few days with her alone. The weather was glorious and the countryside, so different from the well-beloved but
familiar Berry, intoxicatingly beautiful. In a letter to Marie
d'Agoult George described Fontainebleau as a 'pocket-sized
Switzerland which Parisians have not heard of and which fortunately does not attract anybody'.[18] It was peaceful and isolated,
yet within easy reach of Paris. George travelled up and down
several times, one of the reasons being her mother's deteriorating
health.

Sophie Victoire, in her mid-sixties, had been ailing for some time. Once or twice she seemed to be at death's door, then she rallied. On 9 July, when still surrounded by her house guests at Nohant, George wrote to her for the last time: 'I am so happy, dear mother, to hear that you are better and on the way to recovery. My uncle has much exaggerated your illness. . . . Live and get well soon, and when you are able to travel again I shall come and fetch you and take you to the country to convalesce.'[19]

It was not to be. Once at Sophie Victoire's stuffy cluttered-up apartment, George knew that the end was near. It was many years since she felt any tenderness for the mother whom as a child she loved so passionately. Now she could only give infinite patience. There were other people to look after the patient: the step-sister Caroline, an old family friend who had once carried little Aurore on his shoulders, a hired help. But Sophie Victoire leaned mostly on George. She was a difficult patient, and the doctor advised the family to let her have her own way. At her insistence they once dressed her up and took her for a ride in a hired carriage as far as the Champs Elysées. When she was too weak to be taken out, she insisted on being dressed up in all her finery and propped up in a chair in the sultry courtyard.

While at her mother's bedside George was flabbergasted to hear that Casimir Dudevant had returned to Berry and abducted Maurice. She jumped into a carriage, located young Mallefille and sent him after her husband. Within a few days Mallefille reported from La Châtre that Maurice was safe and sound at the Papets' and that Casimir had not been seen anywhere near their place. It had been a false alarm.

George resumed her vigil. One afternoon she left her mother peacefully asleep and went to Fontainebleau to meet Maurice whom Mallefille had brought up from La Châtre. The following morning, 19 August, when she returned to the Paris apartment, she found her mother dead. A few days later she wrote to Gustave Papet:

24 August 1837

Dear old friend, I have lost my poor mother. Her death was painless and calm, there was no suffering. She did not realise that the end was near, she thought she was going to sleep as usual and wake up a few minutes later. You know how careful she was of her person and how vain. Her last words were: 'Arrange my hair for me'. Poor little woman. Fine, intelligent, artistic, quick-tempered, generous, somewhat mad, hard about little things, kind about big things. She had caused me much suffering and my worst troubles were due to her. But in her last years she made up for the past and I had the satisfaction of knowing that at long last she understood me and did me justice. In my conscience I know I have done for her all I should.[20]

A few weeks later she wrote to Marie d'Agoult in Italy:

16 September 1837

My poor mother is no more. She rests in the sun, under beautiful flowers, with butterflies fluttering over her without a thought for death. I was so struck by the gaiety of the grave which I visited one beautiful morning at Montmartre cemetery, that I could not understand why the tears rushed into my eyes.[21]

In her autobiography George dedicated a long chapter to her mother's virtues and faults. It was a perceptive analysis, but in essence a literary study rather than an emotional evocation. The moment of grief had been long forgotten. It was perhaps only on that fine autumn day, when visiting her mother's fresh grave at Montmartre, that George felt her loss like a child. She had her prophets, her friends and her lovers; she had her own children. But on that autumn day, for a brief moment, they all receded before the finality of death. The word *mother*, perhaps the most mystical in George's entire vocabulary, was no longer hers to speak. 'All these instinctive emotions which seem to be caused by something outside our reason or our control,' she concluded her letter to Marie d'Agoult, 'no doubt mean something. But what?'[22]

After the funeral George returned to Fontainebleau, as did Bocage who had returned from a month's tour of Belgium. Maurice was there too, enjoying his walks and his rides with his mother. George watched over him with an eagle eye. Casimir had obviously made no attempt to abduct him and had furthermore behaved perfectly correctly when he attended Sophie Victoire's funeral, but George was suspicious. For once her mistrust of Casimir was justified. On 13 September he turned up at Nohant, spoke threateningly to young Mlle Rollinat and the maids, declared that his daughter was being neglected and poorly educated, and took her away. The news took a whole week to reach George at Fontainebleau. She rushed to Paris, invoked the law and was impressed and gratified when the Minister of Justice 'had the telegraph put to work'[23] in order to discover Solange's whereabouts. Weeks later, when Solange had been safely recovered, George gave Dutheil a delightfully vivid account of the events of that harassing period:

I run to Paris. I have the telegraph trained at Dudevant. I appeal to the police. I get a court order. I run to the ministers. I raise hell, I get my legal rights established, I leave for Nérac [near Guillery] where I arrive one morning as fresh as a smoked herring after three days and three nights on the *chaise poste*, accompanied by Mallefille, the man of many adventures; by Bocage's servant, a man of strong fists; and by a clerk sent by my Paris solicitor M. Genestal, a man of many precautions. I descend on the local commissioner, Artaud's brother-in-law, a charming young man. The public prosecutor pulls a face but gives me a requisition order. The police officer, the more humane of the two, agrees to escort me with his quartermaster and two adorable policemen. I insist on taking a bailiff along so that he can break the doors down in case we encounter resistance. At the moment of departure an unforeseen difficulty arises. To break down the doors we need authorisation from the mayor of Pompiey, but the aforesaid mayor will not give us the authorisation because he happens to be a friend of Dudevant's. I cajole the commissioner, and the latter, mollified, gets into my carriage together with the police officer, the bailiff etc. with the others following on horseback. Imagine what an escort! What an exit from Nérac! What amazement!

The entire town and the outlying suburbs are up to watch us. . . . At last we arrive at Guillery. Dudevant has been forewarned, has made ready to run away. But the house is surrounded, the bailiff's clerk makes a note of what he sees, and M. Dudevant becomes gentle and polite. He fetches Solange and leads her by the hand as far as the threshold of his royal residence, having invited me to step inside, which I graciously decline. Solange is handed over to me like a princess on the border of two states. We exchange a few pleasantries, the baron and I. He threatens to reclaim his son by law, and we part charmed with one another. A report was drawn up on the spot and I hope to make him pay the costs of my journey.[24]

It all ended well. When the excitement had died down George took Solange to spend a few days' holiday in the Pyrenees together with Mallefille, the man of many adventures, who had become her lover.

Félicien Mallefille, aged twenty-four as against George's thirty-three, was a brilliant young Creole educated in Paris. At twenty-one he was already the author of a successful play and an *habitué* of Marie d'Agoult's Paris drawing-room. On first sight George judged him repulsive. He sported a handlebar moustache, a beard 'seven feet long'[25] and a disdainful attitude to cleanliness. To all intents and purposes he was another Planche. All the same he was invited to Nohant on Marie d'Agoult's recommendation and offered the post of tutor which had fallen vacant after Pelletan's departure. Predictably young Mallefille fell in love with George; unpredictably George found it possible to put her fastidiousness aside, particularly after the rush to reclaim Solange, and began to speak of him in glowing terms. Bocage had quietly gone out of her emotional life although, perhaps the only one among her lovers, he remained a friend.

The holiday in the Pyrenees, like the stay at Fontainebleau, was another sentimental journey. George took Mallefille round the same beauty spots she had first seen in 1825, with Aurélien de Sèze riding by her side. When the holiday was over she took

Mallefille back to Nohant, where life resumed its customary pattern. She slept in the mornings, talked to her friends and her children in the afternoon, worked her eight-hour quota during the night. Mallefille acted as tutor to Maurice as well as secretary to his mother. There was a great deal of in-coming and out-going mail. One day George read with a shock that her old friend and benefactor, the deputy Duris Dufresne, had been found drowned in the Seine. His death remained a mystery.

She was working on *La Dernière Aldini*, another novel based on her Venetian memories. As always, she did not entrust the manuscript to the post and sent Mallefille up to Paris to deliver it in person. On its publication, the following year, it was dedicated to Mme Marliani.

Autumn was giving way to winter, the year was drawing to a close. George stayed on at Nohant. There was time to work, entertain, visit the poor of the village and start proceedings against Casimir Dudevant with the object of making him renounce the income from the investment house in Paris. George kept in touch with old friends like Papet, Néraud, Dutheil, Marie d'Agoult, Liszt and Leroux, and reached out for new ones like Meyerbeer and Berlioz whom she had met through Liszt. Prophets were rubbing shoulders with musicians; the circle was widening. Soon it was to engulf Chopin.

❦❧❦❧❦❧

Chapter 11

Preludes

'What an unprepossessing woman that Sand is,' remarked the twenty-six-year-old Chopin when he first met the thirty-two-year-old George towards the end of 1836. 'Is she really a woman? I am inclined to doubt it.'[1] Fastidious and reserved, he was wary of the redoubtable novelist who sported her love affairs in public, smoked like a man and addressed many of her male friends in the second person singular. His idea of femininity was based on the image of his childhood sweetheart Maria Wodzinska, daughter of the Polish Count Wodzinsky, to whom he had proposed a year earlier in Marienbad and whom, in spite of her father's opposition and the distance between Paris and Warsaw, he was still hoping to marry.

George on the other hand was intrigued by Chopin even before she met him. She knew by hearsay that he had left his native Poland on the eve of the patriotic insurrection against the Russians and that, like her, he had settled in Paris in 1831. Liszt described him as a musician of outstanding merit; Paris hostesses as a romantic young man in search of a muse. In the course of one evening he was known to fall dreamily in love with three different women, leave each of them with the impression that she was the only one for him, and forget all three by the following morning. George continuously asked to be introduced and one evening, when Chopin was giving a recital in his own exquisite apartment in rue Chaussée d'Antin, Liszt took both her and Marie d'Agoult to hear him. Later they met again at Marie's drawing-room at the Hôtel de France.

Those formal meetings excited George's interest all the more. Everything about Chopin appealed to her: his delicate health which wanted nursing, his nostalgia for his oppressed country, his romantic admiration for beautiful women and, above all, his musical genius. Being musical herself, she may well have wished to have over Chopin the same hold that Marie d'Agoult had over Liszt; or perhaps, worn out by Michel's tyranny, she felt the need to be looked up to by a younger and weaker man, who at the same time was a man of distinction. It was perfectly in keeping with her temperament that at the beginning of 1837, while writing pathetic love letters to the evasive Michel, she was also penning gay little invitations to Chopin via Liszt who was about to join her and Marie d'Agoult at Nohant. 'Tell Chopin,' she wrote on 17 February, 'that I beg of him to come down with you, that Marie cannot live without him, and that I adore him.'[2]

There were more notes in the same vein. Liszt faithfully transmitted the invitations, but Chopin could not make up his mind. By mid-July he was still hesitant. 'I might go and stay a few days at George Sand's,'[3] he scribbled as an afterthought in the margin of a letter to a Polish friend. He did not. Instead he left for London, was introduced to the piano maker James Broadwood and gave a recital at his Bryanston Square house. Marie d'Agoult, observing George's habit of having herself bled whenever she felt over-excited, remarked that she would have done better to have had Chopin instead. But Chopin would not be had and by the time he returned from London George had made other arrangements. Bocage filled the vacuum left by Michel; Mallefille filled the vacuum left by Bocage.

But it was not in George's nature to be content with an easy conquest. Mallefille's total commitment, like Pagello's a few years earlier, robbed her of the element of anxiety which she needed in order to keep her emotional involvement at high temperature. Chopin's reticence, not unlike Michel's evasiveness, made her all the keener. One day Liszt wrote from Italy that Chopin had dedicated his new *Douze Etudes* to Marie d'Agoult and asked George to thank him on her behalf on her next visit to Paris. George asked for nothing better. She wrote back enthusiastically, expressing her exuberance in a mixture of French, English and nonsense-words which *The Fellows* were bound to appreciate:

Nohant, 2 January 1838

Piffoël will heartily shake *Sopin* by the hand for the sake of *Crétin* and also for the sake of *Sopin because Sopin is very zentil.*[4]

But the trip to Paris did not materialise. January was bitterly cold and George had a severe attack of rheumatism. The pain shot through her right arm and side down to her knee. She could hardly walk or hold a pen. Yet she continued to work her usual quota, dictating to Mallefille and sometimes to Maurice who had grown into an intelligent and adoring fifteen-year-old. The rheumatism was followed by tooth-ache. All thoughts of travel had to be abandoned. That winter Honoré de Balzac was staying with friends in the neighbourhood and sent word to George that he would like to renew the cordial relations which they had once maintained. He was graciously asked to spend a few days at Nohant.

'This Balzac is a charming fellow,'[5] George had written to Emile Régnault in May 1831, shortly after she had been introduced to Balzac at the office of *Le Figaro*. At that time she was inclined to regard as charming anybody who was kind to Jules Sandeau with whom she was sharing a garret. Unfortunately Balzac carried kindness too far. When the break-up occurred he invited Sandeau to share his apartment and dropped George altogether. Several years passed until Balzac, in his turn, became disenchanted with Sandeau and gave up seeing him. The road was open to reconciliation with George who in the meantime had become the illustrious George Sand. She, for her part, bore no grudge against a much-admired writer who was obviously asking her to forgive a past misunderstanding.

The woman who welcomed Balzac at Nohant in February 1838 was very different from the boisterous tomboy he had met at *Le Figaro* seven years earlier. George had put on weight, grown a

double chin and become matriarchal rather than tenderly maternal as he remembered her at the heyday of her love for little
Jules. She had also become a perfect châtelaine, looking personally
after her guest's minutest needs, providing him with good food
and wine, an exotic hookah and oriental tobacco. Above all she
turned out to be a willing listener. Balzac was notorious for his
self-centredness and his lack of interest in other people's work.
Yet George was generous enough to discern an endearing quality
under the apparent egotism. Later she wrote of him:

> Everyone knew how he exuded self-complacency, so justified
> as to be forgivable; how he loved to talk about his books, tell
> them in advance, make them up while talking, read them out
> aloud in draft or proof form. Naïve and guileless, he turned to
> children for advice, hardly ever waited for an answer, or refuted
> it with the knowledge of his own superiority. He never
> offered anybody the benefit of his experience, he talked only of
> himself, himself and no one else.[6]

Yet Balzac could also listen when it concerned his own work.
He listened with great interest to George's account of the
relationship between Liszt and Marie d'Agoult as she had observed it during the summer. It gave him an idea for a new book.
Seen through George's eyes they were not the devoted lovers
who had braved convention to live together, but slaves to a
dying passion which neither had the courage to abandon. For six
days Balzac absorbed information and discussed the psychological
intricacies of the case. Borrowing a phrase of George's, he now
referred to the lovers not by their proper names, but as *the Slaves
of the Galley of Love*. It was to be the title of his projected
novel.

After his departure Balzac embarked on one of his financial
ventures which invariably failed to make his fortune. This one
was to take him to Sardinia. To George he wrote: 'Believe me,
my dear, that I shall not easily forget the six days I spent at
Nohant. . . . On my return I shall begin work on *The Slaves of
the Galley of Love*. But the title is offensive. I shall have to find

another.'[7] The one he found was *Béatrix*, which was an equally offensive allusion to Marie's ambition of being to Liszt what Beatrice was to Dante. Its publication in 1839 in *Le Siècle* and shortly afterwards in book form caused ill feeling between the two women, not least because George, disguised as Mlle de Touches, was favourably contrasted with Béatrix.

For the time being however the correspondence between Nohant and Italy continued to flow as courteously as ever. One day Marie wrote that Doctor Pietro Pagello from Venice had recently married a plain and unprepossessing young girl straight from convent. The news brought forth no comment.

In the spring George felt well enough to go to Paris to see to a new lawsuit against Casimir Dudevant concerning the liquidation of their joint assets. As she no longer had a place of her own in the capital, she stayed with the Marlianis at the Spanish consulate. One day Chopin gave a recital there. George scribbled and passed to him a meaningful note, '*On vous adore*', to which Marie Dorval, also present, had added with theatrical ebullience '*et moi aussi, et moi aussi, et moi aussi*'.[8] After Chopin's death it was found tucked in a small notebook of his. It was one of the few of George's letters to him, if it may be classified as one, which survived destruction.

There is no knowing when exactly Chopin's reticence gave way before George's persistence. He had long known himself attracted but he was still on the defensive. 'I saw her again three times,' he wrote in his diary. 'I was playing and she looked deep into my eyes. It was a somewhat sad music, legends of the Danube; my heart danced with hers. Her eyes held mine, dark, unusual. What were they saying? She leaned over the piano and her gaze burnt me and flooded me. . . . My heart was captured. I have seen her twice since. She loves me. Aurore, what a lovely name.'[9]

Even then he still held back. In a letter to the Polish Count Grzymala – each new love brought forth a new confidant – George complained that Chopin's attitude to love was mis-conceived and that he tended to recoil from physical consummation. As always when discussing something close to her heart, she wrote without coyness or prudery:

> Until recently I thought it was beautiful that he should abstain, either out of respect for me, or timidity, or even fidelity to someone else. I thought it was a sacrifice which indicated strength of character and chastity. It charmed me and endeared him to me all the more. But the other day, as we were leaving your house, he said something about resisting temptation; that does not agree with my views on the subject. Like the devout, he seemed to pooh-pooh human coarseness, feel ashamed of temptation and fear to sully our love by one further outburst. This attitude to consummation has always disgusted me. If consummation is not just as holy, pure and pious as the rest, there is no virtue in abstinence. The words physical love which are used to express that which has a name only in heaven displease me and shock me like an impiety and a misconception. Can there be a purely physical love for the high-minded and a purely intellectual love for the sincere? Has there ever been a love without a single kiss, and has there ever been a loving kiss without desire? Despising the flesh is only right and justifiable in the case of those who are nothing but flesh; but when in love it is the word respect, not disgust, which one should use. I do not remember his exact words. I think he said something about certain acts spoiling beautiful memories. This surely is nonsense. He cannot really believe in what he said, can he? Who is that wretched woman who has given him such ideas about physical love? Has he had a mistress unworthy of him? Such women should be hanged who degrade in men's eyes the most respectable and holy thing in creation, the divine mystery, the most serious and most sublime act in the entire life of the universe.[10]

There were other contrasts in their temperaments and attitude to life. Chopin was weak and hesitant, George was forceful and brimming over with vitality; Chopin shrank from controversy, George delighted in championing causes; Chopin was a stickler for social proprieties, George flaunted her indifference to convention whenever it suited her; Chopin was at ease only in the opulent elegance of a society drawing-room, George was known to have jumped fully clothed into a Berry river for an unplanned swim; Chopin was always meticulously dressed and considered himself a connoisseur on ladies' *haute couture*, George still travelled in men's clothes for the sake of convenience. Yet they complemented each other. Chopin needed a prop, George needed to dominate; Chopin was melancholic and tubercular, George was in her element hectoring and nursing. Whatever obstacles she foresaw, were due not to temperamental incompatibility but to outside influences.

Her four-week stay in Paris came to an end before she could reach a final understanding with Chopin. The homecoming was disappointing. May was unusually wet and the rain poured down unremittingly for fifteen days. George had not properly shaken off the colds of the winter and succumbed to another congestion of the chest. The children coughed and spluttered. Even Mallefille went down with a cold although he was still able to write to Buloz on behalf of Mme Dudevant to apologise for a delay in submitting a manuscript. Within a week he was sent to Paris to deliver it by hand. He was still unaware of his having been demoted.

The problem which now faced George was not unlike the one which had faced her a few years earlier when she had got bored with Pagello's uncomplicated devotion and longed for the subtleties of Musset's capricious temperament. Again she visualised an amicable arrangement which would allow her to love Chopin and keep Mallefille as a well-disposed if deposed lover. But Chopin had not yet committed himself. Although in love with George, he still hankered after Maria Wodzinska. It was necessary to cajole him into accepting the new reality without looking back.

George's emotional desires usually gave her eloquence and powers of persuasion which were virtually impossible to resist. In Chopin's case she sensed however that a frontal attack would be a tactical error; he was as timorous as she was direct and was more likely to retreat into his shell than come over to her way of thinking. She required an intermediary who would speak on her behalf and use her own arguments to overcome Chopin's hesitancy. The ideal intermediary and messenger of love in this case was the émigré Count Grzymala who kept a paternal eye over his young compatriot. Gallant and still seductive, he was well-disposed towards George and allowed her to embroider a domestic fantasy which enabled her to refer to him as her spouse, *mon époux*, and to Chopin as the little one, *le petit*, their joint beloved child.

As soon as Mallefille left for Paris on his errands, she wrote Grzymala a five-thousand-word-long letter in which she outlined the difficulties of the case as well as her solutions to them. First she clarified her position vis-à-vis Maria Wodzinska so as not to appear like a scheming woman who was taking a lover away from his childhood sweetheart. The difficulty in this case was purely academic because Maria, on her father's insistence and apparently without much regret, had already written from Warsaw to inform Chopin that their precarious engagement was off. It was essential however to appear to do the right thing and by so doing deal the *coup de grâce* to a romantic delusion. Writing to Grzymala George was really talking to Chopin:

This young person whom he wants to love, or feels duty-bound to love, is she fit to give him happiness or would she only increase his suffering and his sorrows? I am not asking whether he loves her, whether she loves him, whether her love is stronger or lesser than mine etc. I more or less know, judging by what goes on inside me, what goes on inside him. I am asking which of us two he must forget or give up for his own peace of mind, his happiness, his health which is too faltering and frail to withstand much stress. I do not want to play the part of the bad angel. I am not Meyerbeer's *Bertram* and I will not compete against a childhood sweetheart if she is as pure and beautiful as *Alice* [characters from Meyerbeer's *Robert le Diable*]. If I ever thought there was another bond in the life of our child, a feeling in his heart for another woman, I would have never stooped to inhale a perfume reserved for another altar.[11]

But she knew perfectly well that there was no altar in Chopin's heart for Maria Wodzinska, only a psychological knot which had to be undone with delicacy and tact. The real difficulty was Mallefille. The young man had never annoyed her or hurt her. His only fault was that he could not inspire in her that exultation of mind and heart which for her was the only form of sublime love. She felt guilty at having to break up with him, yet her sense of guilt in no way detracted from her determination to do so. She explained the delicacy of the situation to Grzymala so that he would be able to convey to Chopin that though her heart was his, her solicitude for Mallefille held her temporarily chained:

Then there is that excellent person, perfect of heart and honour, whom I shall never leave because he is the only man who, having been with me for nearly a year, has not caused me, not even once, not for a single moment, any grief through his own fault. Also he is the only man who has given himself to me totally and absolutely, with no regret for the past, no reservations about the future. Besides, he is so kind and gentle that in time I can tell him everything and make him understand; he is like soft wax on which I have left my imprint and which, should I so wish, I could mould into a different pattern if I go about it with care and patience. But for the time being this is not possible and his happiness is sacred to me.[12]

George always claimed that she was indifferent to public opinion and indeed her claim was true in the sense that she did not care for the opinion of people with whom she had no intellectual or emotional affinity. But she did care a great deal for the good opinion of the people she liked. It was therefore important for her to persuade Grzymala, and through him Chopin, that she was not a flighty woman who wandered from one lover to another, but a sincere person motivated by the search for the sublime. She continued:

'A great deal has been said about moral behaviour, chastity and social virtue. I am not yet clear about any of these questions and have therefore never come to any firm conclusion about them. All the same I am not indifferent to these issues and may as well tell you that the need to find a theory which would agree with my feelings has been the main preoccupation of my life and a constant source of unhappiness. My emotions have always been stronger than the arguments of reason, and the restrictions I tried to impose on myself were to no avail. I have changed my ideas a dozen times. Above all I believed in fidelity. I preached it, practised it, expected it. Sometimes people failed me, sometimes I failed them. And yet I had no feeling of guilt because I have always felt that my infidelities were caused by fate, by a search for an ideal which impelled me to abandon the imperfect in favour of what appeared to be nearer perfection. I have known many kinds of love. I loved like an artist, a woman, a sister, a mother, a nun, a poet. Some loves died the same day they were born without ever being revealed to the person who had inspired them. Some made a martyr of me and drove me to despair, almost to distraction. Some kept me shut away for years in a sort of excessive sublimation. Every time I was perfectly sincere. I entered on these different phases just as the sun, to quote Sainte-Beuve, enters the signs of the Zodiac. Whoever saw only the superficial facets judged me false or mad; whoever looked more deeply could see me as I really am, an ardent seeker of beauty, starved for truth, sensitive of heart, weak of judgment, often absurd, always of good faith, never petty or vindictive, sometimes short-tempered and, thank God, able to forget bad turns and wicked people.

'Until now I have always been faithful to whomever I was in love with, perfectly faithful, in the sense that I have never deceived anyone and that I never ceased to be faithful without very strong reasons which had killed the love in me through the other's fault. I am not inconstant by nature. On the contrary, I am so used to loving only the one man who loves me well, so undisposed to catch fire, so used to associating with men without thinking that I am a woman, that I was really perplexed and consternated by the effect which this little creature had produced on

Michel de Bourges,
by L. Massard

George Sand in 1839,
engraved from the painting
by Charpentier

Frédéric Chopin

me. I have not yet recovered from my confusion and if I were conceited I would badly fall in my own estimation to see myself stoop to an inconstancy of the heart at the very moment when I believed myself calmed and settled for ever. I think it would have been wrong, even had I foreseen this irruption, to reason and try to combat it, but as it happened I was taken unawares and it is not in my nature to govern myself by logic when love takes hold of me. I therefore do not reproach myself, I only note that I am still impressionable and weaker than I had imagined myself to be. It does not matter, I am not conceited, I shall now know better than to boast about virtue or strength of character. I am only grieved because my beautiful sincerity, which I have practised and been proud of for so long, has now been breached and compromised. I am going to have to lie like everyone else. I assure you this is more humiliating than a bad novel or a hissed play; I am mortified. Perhaps it is vanity; perhaps it is a voice from heaven which warns me to watch more carefully over my eyes and ears, and particularly over my heart. . . .

'No love without fidelity I said only two months ago, but it is true, alas, that when I returned to Nohant I no longer felt for Mallefille the same affection I once had for him. And it is equally true that since he left for Paris – you may have seen him there – I have not missed him or awaited his return with impatience, but suffered less and breathed more freely.'[13]

There was one more point that George wanted Chopin reassured about. She wanted him to know that she was not possessive. 'I shall want to know nothing, absolutely nothing, of his own way of life, or he of mine for that matter,' she told Grzymala to tell Chopin. 'He would be able to follow all his religious, social, poetic or artistic bents without my ever asking him to account for any of his actions, or I for mine.'[14]

Grzymala's answer must have conveyed that his talk with Chopin had been encouraging, for a few days later George informed him that she was returning to Paris. 'Come and see me,' she wrote cheerfully, 'and try to keep it from the little one. We will give him a surprise.'[15]

But the little one had accidentally found out and was torn

between love and alarm. 'I am not surprised,' he wrote hurriedly to Grzymala in Polish, 'because yesterday I saw Mme Marliani who told me of her arrival. I shall stay indoors until five o'clock and carry on with my lessons (I have already given two today). What is going to happen? Only God knows. I am really not well at all. I have tried to see you several times.'[16]

What happened was a complete and perfect understanding between George and Chopin. There began one of the happiest periods of their love. George stayed on at Mme Marliani's and carried on with her work, while Chopin lived in his own apartment and went on giving piano lessons at twenty francs a time. When the lessons were over George called. There was no question of setting up house together; Chopin insisted on discretion. Only a few intimate friends were in the secret: the Marlianis, Grzymala, the young musician Fontana who had studied at the Warsaw Conservatoire, and young Doctor Jean Matuszinsky, who had shared Chopin's apartment for a time. Another loyal and trusted friend was Delacroix, who began to paint a double portrait of George and Chopin. Many years later the canvas was divided in two, the half with Chopin eventually finding its way to the Louvre, the half with George Sand to the Hansen Collection in Copenhagen.

Three months of bliss passed like a dream. Towards the end of the summer George wrote to Delacroix:

Paris, September 1838

I am still in the same state of intoxication as when you last saw me. There is not one single little cloud in our clear sky, not one grain of sand in our lake. I am beginning to believe there are angels who come down to earth disguised as men and who dwell amongst us for a little while in order to comfort and take back to heaven those poor, weary, desolate souls who are about to perish down below. . . . You think this happiness cannot last? If I consult my memory and my reason it certainly cannot last. But if I consult the state of my heart and my elation, it seems to me it can never end. What does it matter anyhow? If God sends Death to take me within the hour, I shall still not complain for I shall have had three months of intoxication without blemish.[17]

The only cloud in the clear sky was Mallefille. Mostly he was at Nohant teaching Maurice, but from time to time he came to Paris and claimed George's company. It was not impossible to establish a state of abstinence on the strength of her being a guest at Mme Marliani's and even persuade Mallefille to write a flattering article about Chopin for publication in the September issue of the *Revue et Gazette musicale*. But Mallefille was not altogether blind. In fact he was only too prone to jealousy. Even at the heyday of his idyll at Nohant he once challenged another young tutor to a duel because he disliked his attentions to George. In Paris his jealousy became an encumbrance and to gain a respite George instructed him, still in his capacity of tutor, to take Maurice on a fortnight's educational trip to Le Havre.

But she had misread Mallefille's character. He was not the soft wax she had imagined him to be but a hot-blooded Creole whose suspicions had been aroused. He cut the trip short and with a lover's unerring instinct made straight for rue Chaussée d'Antin.

There are two extant versions of what happened that August night. According to Marie d'Agoult, Mallefille posted himself outside Chopin's house and waited for George's arrival. When she arrived he rushed in after her, became violent and attempted to kill both her and Chopin. Grzymala threw himself between the rivals, calmed Mallefille as best he could and led him out of the house still muttering threats and revenge.

According to the second version the scene was more farcical than violent. Mallefille, pistol in hand, waited on the other side of the pavement for George to come out of the house. As soon as she did he hurled himself across the street with intent to shoot. Fortunately a large van emerged at that very moment from a side street and blocked the way. George picked up her skirts, ran as fast as she could along her side of the pavement, jumped into a passing *fiacre* and had the coachman whip his horses all the way to the safety of the Spanish consulate.

Whichever the correct version, it was imperative to appease

Mallefille and persuade him to accept the change of circumstances with good grace. Again George appealed to an intermediary, this time to no lesser an authority than Pierre Leroux, her prophet and guide of social conscience. Leroux had settled in Berry, and when George heard that Rollinat and Mallefille were going to call on him for a philosophical discussion, she appealed to him without preamble:

Paris, 26 September 1838

Listen, dear friend, you must do a good deed and also grant me a personal favour. Mallefille is going to call on you tomorrow together with my friend Rollinat, my *Pylade* [a nickname she had invented for Rollinat], that virtuous and perfect friend I have so often talked to you about. Mallefille and I have quarrelled and I no longer love him. He has a noble and splendid nature but now he has taken it into his head to become jealous, quite wrongly I assure you, even if the facts are against me. But even if his suspicions were well founded he would still be wrong to act towards me as he did. It is three months now since I have started telling him every day that the affair was over. I did it with gentleness, tact, caution and patience. I really think I have nothing to reproach myself with. But as often happens with young people of little sense, his love which used to be so placid (in fact too placid for me, who was prepared for anything) flared up at the sight of obstacles, and rejection whipped up his vanity. Now he thinks he has a deep, tragic, unbridled passion for me and by dint of talking so much about it he makes himself feel all the frenzy and agony of a real passion.[18]

George instructed Leroux not to broach the subject directly but lead up to it in a way which would inspire the unsuspecting Mallefille to confide of his own accord. He was then to try to make Mallefille see sense and point out that 'a mistress does not deserve to be made a public scandal of just because she has given him six months of absolute affection and total devotion'.[19]

Mallefille was however a bad loser and it was partly to escape his threats and a possible scandal that George suggested going abroad for a few months. Chopin was tubercular and Maurice had a persistent cough; it seemed a sensible idea for all of them to move to a warmer climate. Manuel Marliani, the Spanish consul in Paris, recommended Spain and thus Majorca was decided upon. The preparations for the move were made in secrecy. Chopin gave out that he was going to spend the winter somewhere in central France, while George kept her own destination vague. Only a few intimates knew what the plans were. Pleyel undertook to ship a piano over to Majorca while Mme Marliani promised to re-address mail.

The autumn sky was grey and overcast when George, Maurice, Solange and a maid set out for Perpignan. A week later they were discreetly joined by Chopin who, in spite of the non-stop jorurney from Paris, arrived 'fresh like a rose and rosy like a turnip',[20] as George reported to Mme Marliani. Count Marliani's diplomatic contacts smoothed the passage into Spain and in November the party reached Palma in Majorca without mishap. The harbour crowd watched with curiosity as *El Mallorquin* disgorged its few passengers. Chopin was dressed up as if for a Paris drawing-room with a coat buttoned up to his chin, elegant trousers and shoes, silk cravat, white gloves and tall hat; Solange, obviously a girl, was dressed in boy's clothes; Maurice, obviously a boy, wore his hair as long as a girl; and George, for once inconspicuously dressed, was making herself conspicuous by demanding with mounting impatience to be taken to a hotel. The crowd listened uncomprehendingly, then melted away. The travellers were alone.

In *Hiver à Majorque*, published three years after her three-month stay on the island, George Sand described the Majorcans as lazy, money-grabbing, irascible and intolerant. By French standards they were certainly primitive, their pace slow, their catering facilities for tourists non-existent; by Majorcan standards however the visitors were overbearing, impatient and contemptuous of local customs. Mutual hostility was inevitable.

The difficulties started the moment the travellers set foot on the island. There were no hotels in Palma, no inns, no lodgings of any description. George, with little Spanish and no experience of the local dialect, knocked on every conceivable door in search of a bed. In a moment of panic she visualised her entire party sleeping in the open 'like Arabs'.[21] At last two inferior rooms were found over a barrel-maker's workshop. The din was infernal.

George and Chopin had planned a long stay away from France and a congenial house where they would both be able to work was of first importance. George had letters of recommendation to the French consul Flury and the banker Canut and through them heard of people who might have rooms to let. But even when going to see a house by appointment she could not break through the barrier of suspicion and hostility which the locals put up against foreigners. There was a whole set of rules she was not familiar with. 'At first they say it is impossible to view the place and advise *mucha calma* [patience],' George wrote to the French consul in Barcelona. 'Then, little by little, if you look honest and your shoes are not worn out, they crack open a window, then a door, then at long last make up their minds to show you the house. And what a house! I think that your Majorcan is an ill-disguised Jew, he has an honest air but he knows how to sniff your pocket without appearing to do so.'[22]

Nobody in Majorca had ever heard of a house being let furnished; nobody had ever heard of shops stocking ready-made furniture. All such notions were outlandish. 'When you arrive,' George wrote to the Bulozes in Paris, 'you buy a plot of land, then you build, then you order furniture. Then you apply for a government permit to live somewhere and finally, some five or six years later, you begin to unpack and change your underwear, still waiting for customs permit to import your shoes and handkerchiefs.'[23]

A few days later she triumphantly reported that for the first time within living memory a furnished house to let had been found in the countryside just outside Palma. It was owned by Señor Gomez, another ill-disguised Jew, who was willing to let it with its entire contents. On inspection the contents consisted of trestle-beds, rough chairs, kitchen tables and sooty braziers. Most of the windows were no more than gaping holes. 'A Palma house consists of four bare walls without doors or window panes,'

George recalled in *Hiver à Majorque*. 'Even the better-off families do not have glass put in the window space. If anyone wishes to provide himself with this comfort, which is quite vital in winter, he must first get the frames made and installed. Consequently when a tenant moves out he removes the frames, the locks, even the door hinges, and takes them away with him. His successor has to replace everything from scratch, unless he has a taste for living in the open, which is quite common in Palma.'[24]

Yet *So'n Vent* [House of the Wind] provided a roof over their heads and George, with her knack for making even a bare room look like home, was looking forward to a period of peace and hard work. So was Chopin. To his friend Fontana he wrote in the first flush of enthusiasm:

15 November 1838

I am in Palma, surrounded by date-palms, cedar trees, cacti, olive trees, orange and lemon trees, aloes, fig trees, pome-granates, all those trees which at the Jardin des Plantes we see only in hot-houses. The sky is turquoise, the sea lapis lazuli, the mountains emerald and the air like the sky. Every one goes round in summer clothes as it is so warm. At night we hear singing and guitar-playing for hours on end . . . an admirable life.[25]

They settled down to work. George had promised Buloz to send him the last two instalments of her mystical novel *Spiridion* which was being published in the *Revue des Deux Mondes*, while Chopin had promised Pleyel the finished score of his *Préludes*. While waiting for the arrival of his piano from Paris, a local upright was hired. Its quality confirmed Chopin in his suspicion that the Majorcans were all savages.

The optimistic mood was swept away by the first gust of winter gale. *So'n Vent* lived up to its name. The wind blew in through the unglazed windows, the thin walls soaked up the rain, the charcoal braziers filled the house with smoke. Chopin's chronic cough became violent, he began to spit blood. Three eminent physicians were called in, solemnly shook their heads and pronounced him incurable. 'One sniffed my spittle,' Chopin wrote to Fontana with a touch of gallows-humour, 'the other tapped my chest to see where the spittle came from, the third felt me while I was coughing it out. The first said I was going to die, the second that I had breathed my last, the third that I was already dead.'[26]

Immediately the word went round that the young man up at *So'n Vent* had a contagious disease and was a danger to the community. Señor Gomez gave George notice to quit, not forgetting to charge her an exorbitant sum for the compulsory purchase of the infected sheets. Three weeks after their arrival the travellers were homeless again. Fortunately George had had her eye on an alternative accommodation even before Chopin was taken ill and the change of residence took place almost straight away.

This time they had three cavernous rooms at what had once been the Carthusiasn monastery at Valldemosa, a few miles south of Palma. The order had been disbanded by the government some two years earlier and the spacious building turned into a state guest-house. In summer it was patronised by middle-class merchants from the mainland, but in winter it was quite deserted. The only permanent resident was a Spanish political refugee. He and his wife decided to move on to a safer place of refuge and offered George the lease of their three rooms and furniture at what seemed a reasonable sum. It was still necessary to buy some essentials which to a Spaniard seemed superfluous, like mattresses and a modern stove to keep the place heated, but those were trifles considering the security of tenure. The Majorcan piano was duly transported from *So'n Vent* and installed in the room allotted to Chopin.

But by then he was too ill to make much use of it. He continued to cough his lungs out and it was as much as George could do to stop the local doctor bleeding him. Relying on her own experience of practical medicine, she undertook to cure the patient with rest and a proper diet. Diet presented unheard of difficulties. 'I have not got the slightest recollection of what I ate in Pisa or Trieste,' she wrote later, 'but even if I live to be a hundred I shall never forget the arrival of the provisions basket at the charterhouse.'[27] The bread arrived soggy with rain, the fish foul-smelling, the chicken scraggy, the milk diluted. In an attempt to cure that last evil George bought a nanny-goat; but even the nanny-goat, a native Majorcan, refused to oblige until given a little ewe for company. After that milk became more plentiful.

The staple diet was pork, which the Majorcan housekeeper served up in a pride of varieties. There was pork roast, pork stew, pork broth, pork pancake and even pork dessert. Chopin was nauseated by the smell. To make him take any food at all George had to do the cooking herself. She also had to do the shopping in Palma, which entailed several hours' travel by waterlogged roads, and haggling with the vendors who showed great solidarity in raising their prices and keeping them unaltered except to raise them higher when George protested. She soon realised that the entire Majorcan adventure was a 'dismal failure'[28] and that it was better to cut it short. But sailing back to the mainland in rough weather was out of the question. Chopin was too ill to be moved. The only thing to do was to look after him as best she could until such time as he should be able to brave the crossing.

As always in times of illness George was a dedicated nurse. Not only did she do the ministering and the cooking, but also the cleaning and the bed-making, as the Majorcan maids seemed to shed vermin wherever they went. A few months later, when on the road to recovery, Chopin humbly recalled: 'She had to nurse me on her own, for God preserve us from Spanish doctors. I saw her make my bed, tidy up my room, prepare beef-tea, deprive herself for my sake, not receiving any mail, and still looking after the children who constantly needed her loving care in that unaccustomed way of life.'[29] George, for her part, wrote to Mme Marliani that Chopin was a sweet and ideal patient.

The devoted nursing together with the warmth engendered by a stove newly installed at great cost eventually arrested the progress of Chopin's illness. In January his spirits rose at the news that his long-awaited Pleyel had arrived in Palma. Even then it took nearly three weeks of solid arguing before it was released from dock. George's letters to Mme Marliani were full of rage.

In *Hiver à Majorque* she condensed the experience into a few hard-hitting sentences:

> For a piano which we had shipped over from France we were asked to pay 700 francs; it was practically as much as the piano had cost to buy in the first place. We decided to send it back, it was not permitted; leave it in dock until further notice, it was forbidden; have it moved out of town and thus avoid storage dues which came on top of customs dues, it was contrary to regulations; leave it in town and thus avoid exit tax which was not the same as entry tax, this was impossible; throw it into the sea, that was the most we could hope to do provided we proved our ownership of the piano. After fifteen days of arguing it was agreed that instead of moving the piano out of town by one gate, we would be allowed to move it out by another, thus getting away with only 400 francs paid.[30]

Life at the charterhouse began to fall into a pattern. With Chopin's improving health George was able to divide her day between her domestic duties, her children and her writing. She spent six or seven hours a day teaching Maurice and Solange grammar, history and such other subjects as she thought necessary. She boasted that in one day with her they made more progress than in a whole month with any of their former tutors. Often she took them on long walks to collect flowers and stones, returning after dark, guided by a dim cloister lamp which beckoned like will-o'-the-wisp. The children thrived on this regime. Solange seemed to have shed much of her contrariness and Maurice, fully recovered from his cough, filled book after book with sketches. At night, after the teaching, the nursing and the daily chores, George settled down to writing, constantly grumbling about the inferior quality of the local ink. She completed the last two instalments of *Spiridion* and picked up her revision of *Lélia* for the scheduled second edition. Chopin too was working well. He completed the *Préludes*, wrote business letters to Pleyel and Fontana, reviled Jewish and Teutonic publishers, started on the *Ballades, Polonaises*, a *Scherzo*, a *Mazurka*.

It was not an altogether isolated life. At Carnival time George and Chopin were visited at the charterhouse by a procession of masquerading peasants and watched their dances. Once a Polish friend from Paris turned up unexpectedly and stayed for a few days. There were also social visits to the French consul Flury in Palma. It was observed that George never smoked on those occasions. Furthermore, she was elegantly but soberly dressed in dark colours or black, her hair, now grown long, held up by a dagger-shaped silver comb.

But nothing would reconcile either George or Chopin to the Majorcans. After less than six weeks they both made up their minds that they hated them beyond redemption. Neither grasped that they were giving offence by constantly criticising the local way of life. The simple, unsophisticated Majorcans resented being goaded by foreigners and made to feel uncivilised. They retaliated by being hostile. Furthermore, they disapproved of a relationship between a married woman and a young musician, with two fully-aware children sharing the love-nest. Worse, the foreigners were not only immoral but irreligious. Not once during their entire stay on the island did any of them attend Mass on Sunday. The whispering campaign became an open condemnation from the mayoral office. George and her family were taken for heathens, Moslems or Jews. Chopin's illness was God's punishment for their impiety. No kindness was due to those who had forsaken the ways of the Lord; and while it was unbusinesslike to deny them what they wished to buy, it was not ungodly to charge them exorbitant prices. George thought the Majorcans were all thieves. It never occurred to her to question her own standards or make some concessions to the mentality of the people who were after all her hosts. Far from placating them, she was planning revenge. 'I am going to write about my journey,' she promised Buloz, 'but I will have nothing published as long as I am still here. They will roast me alive. I am already in bad odour in these parts because I do not go to Mass.'[31]

She could not wait to leave Majorca. In February Chopin felt fit enough to undertake the sea crossing. Everything essential was packed, everything superfluous was left behind. The Pleyel *pianino* which had cost so much to import was carried back to Palma and offered for sale. But none of the wealthy residents, not even the French ones, would buy a piano which had been touched by a consumptive. At the eleventh hour Mme Canut, the wife of the local French banker, decided to risk her life for the sake of a good deed and bought it for twelve hundred francs. Chopin had had the use of it for only three weeks. Months later he was still writing to M. Canut to remind him that the outstanding amount had not been paid into his Paris account. The *pianino* remained a cherished possession of the Canut family for a hundred years, then was allowed to be taken back to Valldemosa, where it is now one of the chief attractions for tourists visiting the charterhouse.

It was *El Mallorquin* again which took the party across. As the tourist season had not yet started, the space on deck was taken up by livestock. Wherever the passengers went they were pushed out by pigs. George thought there were at least a hundred of them; in retrospect, remembering how Chopin was denied a decent berth because of preferential treatment of pigs, she increased their number to two hundred. Chopin took the crossing badly, began to cough blood all over again and arrived in Barcelona more dead than alive. The party put up at the same hotel they had patronised on the way out. George was outraged when the hotel owner, like Señor Gomez two months earlier, forced her to pay for the compulsory purchase of the bedding which he was going to burn after use. She thought it was another trick to extort money and accused him, and all the Spaniards of Spain, of 'Jewish practices'.[32] What she never knew was that the law of the land imposed heavy penalties on anyone who failed to burn bedding used by people afflicted with contagious diseases.

It was still February when they reached Marseilles. The change from Spain was unbelievable. They had a good hotel, warmth, comfort, and the attentions of a French doctor. Nobody wanted to burn Chopin's mattress from under him, nobody recoiled when he offered to shake hands. If anything, they were becoming too popular. 'All the musical and literary riff-raff'[33] who heard of the two celebrities staying in town felt duty-bound to pay their respects. George warned Mme Marliani that should she hear that Sand and Chopin were dead, she was to know it was only a ruse to get rid of unwanted callers. In fact Chopin was on the road to recovery. The climate in Marseilles was mild and suitable for convalescence. They decided to stay on until the beginning of summer. A piano was hired, work was resumed. George began to catch up on Paris gossip. One day she heard that Didier had married an heiress, at a London registry of all places. To Mme Marliani, her informant, she wrote that she had seen it coming.

With the passage of time it became clear to George and Chopin that their relationship had become public knowledge. There seemed no point in continuing to conceal something that Paris society had come to accept. There only remained the practical problem of where to go. As neither had a place of their own in the capital, they decided to go and stay openly at Nohant, where Chopin had never been before. They paid a quick visit to Genoa, for George another pilgrimage to a shrine of a dead love, then started on the return journey. They travelled by easy stages and arrived at Nohant towards the end of May. After seven months of nomadic existence they were home.

But the Spanish experience had left a deep scar. Nearly every letter George wrote during the first few months after her departure from Majorca contained some carping reference to the Spanish people. To Mme Marliani she wrote: 'Oh how I hate Spain. . . . Now that I have shaken the dust of Spain off my feet I swear I shall never speak to a Spaniard as long as I live.' Then, recollecting just in time that although French by birth Mme Marliani was Spanish by marriage, she quickly added: 'Manuel Marliani is not a Spaniard, my dear; his kind heart, honesty, candour, generosity and sympathy give the lie to the paternal prejudice.'[34] To Boucoiran she wrote: 'Spain horrifies me. . . . It is a country abandoned to anarchy, folly and cruelty';[35] to Rollinat: 'Spain is an abominable country';[36] to Bocage: 'It is a country of brigands and vermin';[37] and to Dutheil: 'It is a vile country, good only to look at.' Then she added more soberly: 'Now that we are out of it I am not sorry to have seen it.'[38]

Time did little to mollify her judgment. It only served to turn her impetuous reaction into stylised criticism all the more carping for being offered in a seemingly dispassionate manner. The Majorcan episode remained a case of mutual intolerance. Oddly enough, when summing up her unhappy winter in Majorca George reached the very conclusion which might well have helped to make her stay on the island more tolerable had she but realised that its wisdom applied to herself as much as to the Majorcans:

Man is not meant to live only with trees, rocks, a clear sky, a blue sea, flowers and mountains, but with his fellow creatures. In the agitated days of our youth we sometimes imagine that solitude is a refuge from the assaults of life and may soothe our wounds. This is a grave mistake. Experience shows that if we cannot live in peace with our fellow men no romantic pleasure or aesthetic contemplation will ever fill the abyss in our souls.

I have always dreamed of living in a desert, as every honest dreamer will admit to have done at some stage of his life. But believe me, friends, our tender hearts will not allow us to dispense with human society. It is far better to be tolerant, for we are like children of the same mother who though they might irritate, quarrel and fight, can never do without one another's company.[39]

❦❧❦❧❦❧

Chapter 12

Maturity

Over the years legend and truth have become so intricately woven into the history of George Sand's liaison with Chopin, that it is not often realised that their life together was not a series of highly charged situations. In fact their nine-year-long relationship was predominantly placid. Both had arrived at a stage in their lives when they needed stability rather than excitement. 'I need to lead a more settled life,' George wrote on the way back from Majorca. 'I am no longer a bachelor';[1] while Chopin, temperamentally constant in spite of a wake of ethereal drawing-room romances, longed for a family life. What resulted was a domestic set-up which was as near a family as was possible in the circumstances.

To all intents and purposes it was a family. Maurice and Solange, still young enough to accept without too much questioning, adjusted to Chopin's presence in their lives. The Berry friends were quick to sense that he belonged. From 1839 onwards old faithfuls like Papet, Planet, Rollinat, Fleury, Néraud, Duvernet, Dutheil, the whole Berry phalanx, hardly ever ended a letter to George without courteous regards to 'Chopin, Maurice and Solange'.[2] Even George's half-brother Hippolyte, who had settled with his wife and daughter near Nohant, took Chopin to his drunken bosom and accepted him as a permanent addition to the household. Chopin made it easy for George's entourage to accept him. He avoided all outward familiarity, formally addressed her as *vous* and clung to the myth that he was a houseguest. With his stiff sense of propriety he referred to her, even in his letters to his family, as his hostess or Madame Sand. Without in any way being deceived, Paris and Berry accepted the set-up as a stable arrangement.

After the return from Majorca a pleasant domestic routine was established at Nohant. Chopin was allotted a room with a piano, while George devoted herself to teaching. Every day, Sundays not excepted, she gave Maurice and Solange their lessons from midday to five in the evening, while Chopin practised and composed in his room. After the day's labours the family would assemble for dinner, which was mostly served in the garden as it was summer. In the evening friends would call, chat, puff clouds of smoke. Sometimes Chopin would play to them. He was not allowed to exert himself for although Papet had examined him and found his lungs clear, his larynx was not. The three children, as George referred to her family, retired at the same time, leaving her to her nightly vigil. She spent most of her time either reading or preparing material for the next day's work with Maurice and Solange.

Her reference to Chopin as one of her 'three children'[3] indicated the change in her feelings for him. She was no longer the pursuer who needed to conquer a hesitant lover; she was no longer the ecstatic mistress incredulously counting the days of bliss; she was the seasoned nurse who had virtually snatched her patient from death's door and who would never again be able to whip up that intoxicating feeling of loving desire. The passion had mellowed into tender protectiveness. A calm intimacy succeeded the emotional ardour. The change was not unsuited to Chopin's temperament and he responded with an ever-increasing adoration. In his diary he wrote that autumn:

Aurore's eyes are veiled. They only sparkle when I play; then the world becomes bright and beautiful. My fingers glide gently over the keys, her pen flows over the paper. She writes while I play for her. Music from above, from upstairs, sweet Chopin music, limpid like words of love. For you, Aurore, I shall crawl on the ground, nothing will be too much for me, I shall give you everything. One look from you, one caress, one smile when I am tired. I want to live for you only; to play sweet melodies for you alone. Are you not cruel, my love, to keep your eyes veiled?[4]

As none of the intimate letters exchanged between Chopin and George survived, it is difficult to assess their innermost feelings for each other without a certain degree of conjecture. Those who knew Chopin socially admitted that they never really knew him. He was reticent, distant, even snobbish; he was very attached to his family in Poland and a loyal friend to his two or three Polish intimates in Paris; he was innocently idealistic, but took no interest in social reform. Those who frequented the Chopin–Sand household described him as the feminine partner in the association. Yet with all his alleged femininity he was the only one of George's lovers who imperceptibly made her shed some of her unladylike habits. It was under his influence that she gave up without regret her habit of travelling in men's clothes, and it was in deference to his fastidiousness that she curbed the unbridled jollity in her Nohant drawing-room and accustomed her boisterous Berry friends to be more mindful of social refinements. Chopin, for his part, had long ceased to confuse her need to dominate with masculinity. He no longer doubted that she was tender and feminine. There was no nonsense between them about her being his brother George, as she had been to Musset, and even to Michel de Bourges. Alone among all her previous lovers he called her Aurore, as, oddly enough, did her own husband Casimir; and when she was not Aurore she was *Jutrzenka*, his loving translation of the name into his native Polish.

It was inevitable that some Polish words and phrases should infiltrate into the Nohant household. The children, exposed to some Polish conversation when Grzymala came down to stay, picked up sounds and sometimes amused themselves by calling Chopin *Chopinsky*. When Solange was later sent to a boarding-school she signed herself once or twice with a schoolgirl's sense of humour as *Solangeska Sandska*. George herself picked up a smattering of Polish and under Chopin's guidance once began a letter to Grzymala with the words *Kochany Mezu, lubie cie bardzo* (Dear spouse, I love you well).[5]

193

During the summer months of 1839 much work was done at Nohant. Chopin composed the *Sonata in B Flat Minor*, a *Nocturne in G Minor* and three *Mazurkas* which were published together with the one composed in Valldemosa. He also found time to give Solange piano lessons and ordered from Paris a Weber piece for four hands. Yet in spite of the creativity that Nohant encouraged, it was obvious that he could not long lead a country life. There began a long and agonising search for a Paris apartment, into which Fontana, Grzymala and Mme Marliani were firmly drawn in.

It was not quite clear what their brief was. Chopin, unlike Sandeau, Musset, Pagello or Mallefille, was not prepared to live openly with a married woman, whether officially separated from her husband or not. At Nohant there was the tacit pretence that he was a house-guest; a shared apartment in Paris would have made such pretence impossible. The idea was therefore to find either a large house divisible into two separate units, or two separate apartments in the same neighbourhood. Chopin was much preoccupied with the search and wrote Fontana endless letters with detailed instructions. There were to be no noisy workshops in the vicinity, no evil smells from the sewers, no fumes, smoke or soot. There was to be plenty of light and a view over gardens. Chopin drew a plan of the ideal accommodation, specified colour of wallpaper, curtains, disposition of furniture. He fussed and worried and all but drove himself into a state of nervous collapse. George was much more placid.

In the autumn two separate apartments were rented and the long-awaited return to Paris finally took place. The distance between them was found inconvenient. Fortunately another apartment fell vacant in the same block occupied by George in rue Pigalle, overlooking the same courtyard and inter-connected to hers by an outside staircase. Chopin discreetly moved in with his red couch, Persian carpet and Pleyel grand. He had his windows draped with heavy velvet curtains drawn back to reveal richly gathered muslin ones. There were masses of flowers brightening up the delicate greys of hangings and wallpaper.

George favoured brown. Her dining-room was furnished with carved oak chairs, a large oak dining-table and a portrait of Grzymala in the splendid costume of a Polish nobleman. Her drawing-room was done up in coffee-coloured wallpaper, with green upholstered chairs, pictures by Delacroix, Chinese vases always filled with fresh flowers, a showcase of bric-à-brac and an upright rosewood piano. The bedroom had no bed; instead two mattresses were laid on the floor '*à la turque*'.[6]

For the next few years the two apartments in rue Pigalle were a place of reunion for some of the most illustrious names of the time. George entertained Balzac, Heinrich Heine, Delacroix, Leroux, Lamennais; Chopin entertained Berlioz, Meyerbeer, the cellist Franchomme, Pleyel, James and Betty Rothschild, and a host of Polish aristocrats in exile. He took a naïve pride in being sought out by titled ladies, unlike George who professed disdain for old countesses. She was civil however to Chopin's countesses and princesses, exchanged friendly notes with Countess Potocka, Countess Tchernishev, Princess Tchartoryska and Princess Sapieha, and attended meetings of Polish émigrés.

The most intimate of her female friends at that time was still Mme Marliani. It was she who inadvertently turned the grudging but courteous friendship between George and Marie d'Agoult into an avowed dislike.

When, in the summer of 1837, Liszt and Marie d'Agoult left Nohant to live in Italy, they parted with George on the best of terms and with reciprocal promises of an early reunion. They kept up a regular correspondence and George's only complaint was that some of the letters were slow in reaching their destination. She kept Marie informed of the fluctuations in her personal circumstances, while Marie gave her news of Liszt's concert tours and reported the birth of a baby girl who was named Cosima. All this amiability did not stop George from dissecting Marie and Liszt before Balzac when he came down to Nohant only a few months after their departure. The unsuspecting Marie continued to write as amiably as ever, but distance and the passage of time robbed the correspondence of its charm. To her annoyance Marie found that whatever information she had about George's affair with Chopin, it came not directly from her but via Mme Marliani. No more charitable than George, she too felt the need to dissect a friend's love life and wrote to Mme Marliani with the insight she felt she had gained during her stay at Nohant eighteen months earlier:

Florence, 9 November 1838

The trip to the Balearics amuses me. I am sorry it had not taken place a year earlier. Whenever George had herself bled I used to say to her: 'If I were you I would take Chopin for a lover.' How many lancet strokes would have thus been spared! But then she would not have written her *Lettres à Marcie*, would have not had Bocage, and it might have been better for some good people. Is the establishment in the Balearics going to be of long duration? From my personal knowledge of both of them they are bound to develop a dislike for each other after one month's cohabitation. Temperamentally they are poles apart. But what does it matter? It is the nicest thing that could have happened, and I am delighted for both of them. But what about Mallefille in the midst of all these agitations? Is he going to drown his Castillian pride in the waters of the Manzanares as he said he would? Was George right after all whenever she said that he was outrageously stupid and ridiculous? As for Maurice, I have never been alarmed for his 'state of health'. In any case the Spanish sunshine is an odd cure for heart palpitations. You are quite right to admire Chopin's talent; it expresses so exquisitely the sweetness of his nature. He is the only pianist I can listen to not only without boredom but with profound absorption. Keep me informed about everything.[7]

Mme Marliani was a kind, simple soul who could not allow Marie the natural pleasure of slightly running down a friend behind her back. She little dreamed that George had acted in a similar manner towards Marie and that Balzac was at that very moment working on his devastating *Béatrix*. She showed the letter to Lamennais; and Lamennais, who deep down despised all three women and took a perverse pleasure in setting them up against one another, solemnly advised that the contents should be disclosed to George. Mme Marliani complied.

The result was shattering. George, battling valiantly with the elements in Majorca, considered the letter a betrayal of friendship and Marie a snake in the grass. Unfortunately she could not write to tell her so because Mme Marliani had made her promise not to give her away. All she could do was to stop answering Marie's letters. Marie blamed the post. She continued to write as courteously as ever, informed George of the birth of a baby boy who was named Daniel, reported on Liszt's Italian successes. Both she and Liszt were disappointed with the first instalments of *Spiridion* which they read in the *Revue des Deux Mondes*. To Mme Marliani Marie wrote with a liberty she felt entitled to:

Pisa, 23 January 1839

Since her *Lettres à Marcie*, which hardly count because they were discontinued and did not develop any of the things they promised, George has only written worthless novels. Her emotional phase is clearly over, and what a splendid one it was too, as witnessed by *Lélia* and *Lettres d'un voyageur*. What she now needs is time to collect herself, reflect and crystallise her ideas. Alas neither Bocage nor Mallefille, nor indeed Chopin, will help her or guide her towards this new road.[8]

The zealous Mme Marliani passed on to George the contents of this new letter as well. In the midst of her difficulties at Valldemosa, trying her best to snatch a few hours' work from her nursing and domestic chores, the letter could only add fuel to the fire. Marie however was still in the dark. When she heard from Mme Marliani that George and Chopin had left Majorca and were wintering in Marseilles, she wrote to invite them to join her and Liszt in Italy, adding gaily that she could undertake to provide two splendid pianos in the house. George's silence persisted.

In September 1839 Marie was shattered in her turn when Balzac's *Béatrix*, or *Les Galériens de l'amour*, was published in *Le Siècle*. There was no mistaking the similarity between her and Béatrix and there could be no doubt that he had based his story on information supplied by George. Liszt remained unperturbed, but Marie was deeply hurt to see her love for him recognisably satirised. It so happened that by the end of that year she returned to Paris while Liszt continued his touring. She wrote to Mme Marliani, enclosing a note for George whom she knew to be living in rue Pigalle, asking for an explanation.

There was nothing for it but to tell part of the truth. Mme Marliani wrote to Marie that her past references to George had made her seem like an enemy, and that there was nothing wrong about quoting an enemy's pronouncement to a dear friend. George too wrote a long letter, then put it aside and sent instead a brief note inviting Marie to rue Pigalle for a three-cornered confrontation.

The three women, when they met, extricated themselves from the mess with remarkable dexterity. They agreed to put the entire blame on Lamennais who had advised Mme Marliani to pass on Marie's comments instead of keeping them to herself. The delicate matter of Balzac's novel was not raised; perhaps because it was not a success and had only had a limited circulation. Marie and George shook hands and promised to be friends again; as for Mme Marliani, Marie parted from her with a cold bow. When Liszt was informed of the terms of the truce he professed himself satisfied.

For a while the three women made an attempt to pick up the old threads. George invited Marie to share a box at the theatre, Mme Marliani invited both of them to her dinner parties. But it was impossible to revive a friendship which even in its heyday had more envy than warmth in it. Mutual calumnies began to be voiced and circulated, simple actions were misinterpreted and resented. Within a year of the reconciliation Marie was writing to Liszt: 'Mme Sand hates me.'[9] In spite of the odd meeting or letter the dislike persisted. A few years later George published *Horace* which among its female characters had an unpleasant though erudite countess singularly reminiscent of Marie d'Agoult. Marie did nothing but she never forgave. Many years after her amicable separation from Liszt, when she had already made a name for herself as a chronicler of the times under the pen-name of Daniel

Stern, she let drop that the real cause of George Sand's hatred for her was the novelist's failure to steal Liszt from her at the time of their stay at Nohant. George however persistently denied that she ever had any romantic inclination towards him.

The alienation from Marie d'Agoult was a process which George had half-willed and which she accepted without regret, even though it meant the temporary loss of Liszt. What was of more consequence at that stage in her life was the deterioration in her professional relations with François Buloz, the editor cum proprietor of the *Revue des Deux Mondes*.

George had never been close to Buloz in the way she had been to her first editor Latouche. There was no romantic admiration, no room for coquetry. Buloz was the sober editor who published everything George submitted; George was the indefatigable writer whose name was the glory of the *Revue*. Theirs was a working relationship, close enough to allow for the occasional reference to children's illnesses, lawsuits and domestic difficulties, reserved enough to discourage emotional confidence. Their frequent letters dealt with subject-matter, dates of publication, proofs and, above all, money. Somehow Buloz never shook off the stingy habits acquired during the early days of the *Revue*. By agreement he was required to pay cash for every manuscript accepted; in practice he deferred payment as long as he could and turned a deaf ear to constant reminders. Demands for money became the most recurring theme in George's letters to him. It became a sort of ritual in which both parties knew all the responses by heart. Neither ever lost their sense of humour. In 1836, having addressed to Buloz six reminders without any effect, George sent him a seventh in dialogue form:

Buloz!
Ay?
Buloz!!
Ay?
Damn you Buloz!
Beg your pardon?

Money!

Can't hear you.

500 francs!

What are you talking about?

Damn you! You promised me 6000 francs in a few days. All I'm asking is 500 francs by tomorrow.

Never heard anything about that.

You aren't deaf by any chance are you? I want 500 francs, give me 500 francs, 500 francs.

I can't hear a word you are saying.

Well if you are deaf at least you can read, or so it seems by the excellent quality of the articles you publish in the *Revue*. I've written to you six times, but you seem to be deaf in the eyes. A strange affliction which medical science has not encountered so far. . . .

(500 francs) George (500 francs).[10]

The constant tussle for money became an accepted routine like haggling in a Berry cattle market. Yet the more George earned, the more she needed to earn. She was no spendthrift; on the contrary, she was practical and down to earth in the management of her property. But her style of life at Nohant, where she might have half a dozen house-guests and as many as twelve for dinner any day of the week, was costing her more than she could afford. Moving to rue Pigalle in Paris, where entertainment was on a much smaller scale, involved her in fresh expenses towards furniture, carpeting, hangings and the comforts of everyday life. The children's upbringing was costing more. Solange was being educated at a boarding-school, Maurice was studying art with Delacroix. There was also George's customary generosity which made her subsidise Leroux, offer financial help to some of his disciples, give money to deserving working-class poets. With all her income from investments and her considerable earnings from writing, she never had quite enough. To her friends she always described herself as someone forced to write without respite in order to extract her rightful fees from a close-fisted slave-driver.

She was therefore piqued beyond measure when Buloz, the

editor who could never have enough of her work, took it upon himself to criticise her latest novels and warn her against their unpopular mystical trend.

The source of her new mysticism was Pierre Leroux whose religious socialism she discovered at a time when she badly needed a fresh intellectual and emotional stimulus. She began by weaving his theories into the revised text of *Lélia* and would not allow it to be published without his final checking. The Leroux-inspired *Lélia*, published in 1839, was a success; but the Leroux-inspired *Spiridion*, published later that year, was too far-fetched for most of the *Revue* readers. They had come to regard George Sand as a novelist who wrote unconventionally about love between men and women; not many of them were prepared to accept her thoughts about love between man and God. Her friends were dismayed. Marie d'Agoult professed not to understand *Spiridion*; Liszt thought he discerned in it traces of 'weariness, exhaustion and decadence';[11] and Sainte-Beuve, relying on other people's judgment, decided not to read it.

Yet *Spiridion* was more than a literary elaboration of Leroux's ideas. In a way it reflected George's own religious evolution from the agnosticism of her childhood through the fervent catholicism of her convent days to the final rejection of external piety in favour of some deeper mystical faith. Spiridion, born a Jew, became a catholic, then a protestant and finally a believer in a faith which embraced all existing religions. He founded a Benedictine monastery and on his death left behind his own Book of Revelations. When many years later republican soldiers burst into the monastery and killed his surviving disciple, they little realised that their own ideals of liberty and equality were basically another facet of Spiridion's all-embracing religion.

Although *Spiridion*, like most of George's works, was first published by instalments in the *Revue* and then again in book form, Buloz was not happy with the sales. He felt he was losing money and begged George to go back to such formulas as had made *Indiana* and *Lélia* best-sellers. George refused to cover the same ground twice and retorted that she was not the sort of novelist who would pander to the taste of middle-brow ladies and their chambermaids. She was convinced that by venturing into the world of metaphysics she was reaching out to a higher form of art.

Not content with *Spiridion,* she wrote *Les Sept Cordes de la Lyre* in which she combined her newly found mysticism with a form of art she had not seriously tried her hand at before, that of play-writing. The play centred on the love of an old philosopher for his beautiful young ward, the ward's attachment to a magic lyre, and Mephistopheles' attempts to lure the innocent. When Buloz read the manuscript he promptly offered George five thousand francs not to have it published. She was indignant and held him to their original agreement. The reception was unfavourable. Critics pronounced the work a pastiche on Goethe's *Faust*; readers judged it a dull essay in metaphysics; and Buloz saw his subscribers deserting him and his newspaper falling to rack and ruin. Without mincing his words he wrote to George that with works like *Les Sept Cordes de la Lyre* she was flaying him alive. George had never felt so insulted in her life and wrote back in white heat:

Nohant, 25 June 1839

Really, my dear Buloz, you have become witty, but I find your wit flat. You have also become pretentious, you think you understand what you edit. I'll be hanged if you understand the first thing about the second part of *Faust*, and as for his style, Henri Blaze's is no less metaphysical than mine. [By sheer coincidence Buloz had commissioned an article from Blaze about Goethe's *Faust*.] What is far more serious is that you say you have been 'flayed'. That is an ugly word. Well done, that is how an editor should speak, that is the sort of language I understand. I am therefore going to pay you back, yes, me, everything you have lost on *Les 7 Cordes* and I propose very seriously that we should rescind all our agreements as I am not in the habit of flaying people, I am not a Shylock the Jew and in any case I would not know what to do with your skin. However hard up I may be, I will still not allow offensive remarks about money. Literary criticism, yes, as much as you like, you excel in it and I would only profit by comments such as yours. Restrict yourself to that, but as to criticism about money you will find it can be answered only with money. The day I leave the *Revue* I shall make enough not only to publish *Engelwald* (and I am warning you that this work is going to be ten times more 'metaphysical', 'phantasmagorical' and 'esoteric' than *Les Sept Cordes de la Lyre*), but also to idemnify you for all the losses which have 'flayed' you. Until you make up your mind either to pay me cash for everything I send you or sever an obligation which you find onerous, I shall not send you a single manuscript which might increase your losses. You had better stop complaining, you have a habit of speaking ill of your contributors and treating them more or less like rabble who are out to ruin you.[12]

In her fury George wrote anything that came into her head, paying no attention to punctuation or nicety of style. She ended with a last dig at the editor who was too ignorant to recognise his own ignorance:

Goodbye, dear Buloz, you call me tigress of Armenia, this is no doubt a printer's error because the classical saying is tigress of Hyrcania, and as far as I know Armenia has never been renowned for its tigers, though perhaps for its editors. Give my love to Christine, I pity her for being married to a jackal of Etuvia, there are no more jackals in Etuvia than there are tigresses in Armenia.[13]

The quarrel was patched up, in no small measure thanks to Christine Buloz to whom both husband and novelist took their grievances. Buloz graciously thanked George for correcting his classical misquotation and came up with a new attractive proposition. Since 1838 he had been not only editor of the *Revue des Deux Mondes* but also the Royal Commissioner of the Théâtre Français. He disapproved of *Les Sept Cordes de la Lyre* because of its obscurity, but he still felt that George had it in her to write a good play. He asked her to write one for the Théâtre Français and in due course she sent him *Cosima*, so named in honour of the baby daughter born in Italy to Liszt and Marie d'Agoult. Cosima was a young middle-class wife from Florence who fell in love with a seductive Venetian nobleman. The understanding husband was prepared to step aside and relinquish his place to the lover, but the Venetian turned out to be no better than Casanova. In the end the dishonoured Cosima committed suicide in order to save her kind and loyal husband from a duel with the fickle lover.

Buloz judged the play not without merit and agreed to put it on. There followed an intensive correspondence between Nohant and Paris about who should play the title role, Buloz making his own suggestions, George discarding them one by one in favour of her old friend Marie Dorval. After many delays the rehearsals started. George came up to Paris to supervise and make her intentions clearer. The cast seemed to like the play, but outside the theatre the word went round that Sand was expounding some more of her social heresies. Pillars of society who had disapproved of her message of equality in love revived the old rumours about her and Dorval; and critics who had condemned *Spiridion* and *Les Sept Cordes de la Lyre* for their metaphysical obscurities were getting ready for the kill.

After further delays the first night was finally fixed for 29 April 1840. George haughtily refused the services of the *claque* and relied on the merits of the play to rouse the audience to applause. Buloz had given her a hundred and forty complimentary tickets to be distributed among friends, but the atmosphere in the two-thousand-seat auditorium was palpably hostile. The audience hissed and booed, jeered at every speech. The disconcerted actors fluffed their lines, even the great Marie Dorval could not carry off the part. When the final curtain came down there was no doubt that the play was a fiasco. At the splendid supper-party given by Mme Marliani after the performance every possible topic of conversation was discussed except *Cosima*.

George pretended to be above it. 'The whole thing was like a farce,' she wrote to the engraver Luigi Calamatta. 'If there is a sad side to it, it is to see such coarseness and degeneration of taste. I never thought the play was beautiful; but I shall always believe that it is fundamentally honest, and that the sentiments it expresses are pure and delicate. I bear the misconception philosophically. I was not born yesterday and I know what times we live in and what sort of people we have business with. Let them shout. There would be nothing to write about if such people were not what they are.'[14]

The reviewers, like the first-night audience, were unkind. Even Heinrich Heine, who recognised that the first-night disaster was 'a conspiracy on the part of the aristocracy and the bourgeoisie to turn into a failure the theatrical début of an author who had championed irreligious and immoral doctrines',[15] found nothing pleasant to say about the play. In his review he wrote:

> All women, even the most ardently emancipated amongst them, need a male guide and authority in their life, and thus George Sand has her own literary director of conscience, a philosopher monk called P. Leroux. Unfortunately this excellent man exercises a confusing influence over his penitent's talent, dragging her as he does towards obscure dissertations on half-explored ideas. He encourages her to enter upon sterile abstractions instead of allowing her to abandon herself to the serene joy of creating colourful and living characters, practising art for art's sake.[16]

After seven performances *Cosima* was taken off. George's faith in Leroux's teachings never wavered. 'His is the only philosophy which is as clear as daylight and which speaks to the heart like the gospel,' she declared. 'I immersed myself in it and was transformed by it. It has brought me peace, strength, faith, hope, patience and consistent love of humanity.'[17] The same month that saw the public condemnation of *Cosima* Leroux introduced her to the Avignon carpenter Agricol Perdiguier who was to serve as a model for her next religio-socialist novel, *Le Compagnon du Tour de France.*

Perdiguier was an outstanding example of the new generation of self-taught and articulate proletarians who sought to improve society. Through Leroux, himself a man of the people, George met several working-class poets who sang the cause of equality between the classes. She came to know and admire Charles Poncy the mason, Savinien Lapointe the cobbler, Magu the weaver, Gilland the locksmith, Jasmin the barber, Reboul the baker. They sent her their verses and she told them how great they were. Some, like Poncy and Magu, became lifelong friends. George became familiar with their domestic circumstances, remembered to congratulate them on the weddings of their sons and daughters, introduced them to useful people, lent them money, wrote about them in the press and, inevitably, used nearly every single one of them as a model for a character in her future novels.

Among these new artisan friends, none was so close to her social-religious ideas as Agricol Perdiguier. He was in his mid-thirties when she met him, about her own age; poor, dedicated, married to a dressmaker who bore him several children and shared his ideology. As a carpenter he belonged to a fellowship which combined the characteristics of a medieval guild with those of a masonic lodge. It was divided into chapels, each championing its own selected cause, or task, which might be liberty, or truth, or honesty. Each chapel had its own Mother who ran a hostel where members could stay for unspecified periods and live communally in the manner of their particular cause.

Through his study of social history Perdiguier had come to regard the communal living within the fellowship as the embodiment of the principles of democracy and Christianity. For the better performance of his task, which was the promotion of liberty, he toured the country and gave talks to fellow members. He called on them to abandon the internal differences within the chapels and unite against the exploitation of the working class. He was so hard up that before the tour was over he wrote to George and asked for a loan to help him and his family out. George did not have to be asked twice. She sent him money and made his wife Solange's regular dressmaker.

George was interested in Perdiguier's ideas about democratic

Christianity and studied a fellowship manual which he had published under the title of *Le Livre du Compagnonnage*. She had known him only a few months when she began recreating him in the character of Pierre Huguenin, the hero of her *Le Compagnon du Tour de France*. To Perdiguier she wrote on 20 September 1840:

> I am already halfway through a book which I hope will be read by some members on tour. It was inspired by your book, and if mine has any spark or idealism, all credit is due to you. I count on you to help me with corrections as I may have been inaccurate about the ways of the Fellowship. With your permission I would like to mention my debt to your book in the preface to mine. Those who call themselves men of the world should be made to realise that there are loftier ideas and finer sentiments in the workshops than in the drawing-rooms.[18]

Like Perdiguier, the hero of the novel toured France, talked to members of his fellowship and called for the breakdown of class barriers. But unlike Perdiguier he did not have to wait for years before his ideas met with success. His call fell immediately on receptive ears, and a rich noblewoman was among the first to discard class prejudice and become his disciple and mistress.

As usual, George handed the manuscript to the *Revue des Deux Mondes* for publication in instalments prior to its re-issue in book form, but Buloz was frightened. The call for a complete breakdown of class barriers was too much for him. He suggested so many cuts and alterations that for the first time since the beginning of their association George took the script back and by mutual consent had it published directly in book form. It appeared within seven months of her first meeting with Perdiguier.

As Buloz had predicted, it was a failure. The social message of the book was too uncompromising even for the most progressive. 'Nobody wants to read anything more by George Sand,' stated the owner of a thriving bookshop in Paris. '*Le Compagnon du Tour de France* has killed her in spite of the successful author's privilege of writing at least twenty bad books for every good one.'[19]

The following year George signed an agreement with Buloz for the publication of another novel she was working on. Although Buloz was not aware of it at the time of signing, *Horace* was to be even more iconoclastic than *Le Compagnon du Tour de France*. Again the hero was a working-class man modelled on one of George's newly met proletarian poets. There was an idle and irascible bourgeois and, last but not least, a pretentious countess who was recognisably modelled on Marie d'Agoult and who epitomised the faults of the aristocracy. When Buloz reached the end of the story, which allowed an honest prole to live openly with a fallen woman and adopt her child by a previous lover, he threw his hands up and flatly refused to publish.

This time there was no half-hearted slanging of classical invectives. Both jackal and tigress took their case to court. All attempts to make them see reason were in vain. Buloz insisted on his right to modify, George refused to let him alter a single word. There was nothing for it but to part company. In the autumn of 1841 the nine-year-long association between the *Revue des Deux Mondes* and George Sand came to an end. There followed a period of pretended indifference and half-hearted overtures. Five years later Buloz's eldest son died. George rushed in to offer her condolences and the old friendship triumphed. It took however ten more years before she returned to the *Revue* as a regular contributor.

Whatever the astute Buloz felt about the loss of an illustrious author whose name he had helped to build, George at first felt liberated. She had long been toying with the idea of founding a magazine of her own, and the break-up did not find her unprepared. She had been making plans with Leroux and the writer Louis Viardot, and together they started the *Revue Indépendante*. As usual, everything moved with great speed. George worked tirelessly on the thousand and one things connected with starting a newspaper, made useful contacts, obtained money, persuaded her childhood friend Charles Duvernet to stand guarantor for a vast sum, supervised personally every single detail. The first issue of the new magazine was published within two months of her split-up with Buloz.

George had lofty aspirations for the *Revue Indépendante* which, like the *Revue des Deux Mondes*, was to be published twice monthly. It was to be a literary magazine with a social message. It was to spread the Christian idea of equality, enlighten the masses about their rights and inspire them to establish their own truly democratic institutions.

Not many of George's literary friends were prepared to share her enthusiasm for 'the Christian idea'[20] as a social philosophy. Sainte-Beuve, with whom she had recently renewed a lukewarm friendship, remained aloof; Lamennais was sarcastic; others openly hostile. It was imperative to attract illustrious names to the new *Revue* in order to assure its success. One of the first names which came to mind was that of Henri de Latouche, George Sand's first editor and literary mentor.

Since his withdrawal from *Le Monde* some nine years earlier, Latouche had lived at his country retreat, spasmodically bursting into print and nursing grievances against most of his former associates. Unpredictably he came to regret his past harsh judgment of George and followed her career with a tinge of sadness. In 1840 he published a novel which included a reconciliation scene between a pleasant châtelaine and an estranged old writer. George did not see it, but her old Berry friend Charles Duvernet who was a relative of Latouche assured her that the old man was trying to make amends. Latouche, for his part, must have heard something of the *Revue Indépendante* from Duvernet, who had a financial interest in it. The way for a reconciliation had been paved but George, fearing a rebuff, approached Latouche with the utmost formality. She wrote:

15 November 1841

The editors of the *Revue Indépendante* keenly desire the collaboration of Monsieur de la Touche. I have undertaken to ask him for it, in the hope that he will not refuse the friendly approach which I have volunteered to make on their behalf, thus indicating that I no longer hold against him a certain allegation about a hostile attitude taken by the *Revue des Deux Mondes* through my influence. In everything which concerns M. de la Touche I have nothing but friendship and gratitude, and my sentiments for him are so pure and constant that I come to him with my head high and my hand outstretched.[21]

Latouche was so delighted by the letter that he accepted the outstretched hand without delay, stoically ignoring George's incorrigible habit of misspelling his surname. George was pleased. When they met she rediscovered in him all the qualities which had made him such a discerning editor in the past; but to Charles Duvernet, their successful go-between, she confided that things could be easier if Latouche did not suspect everyone of being against him. As things turned out he proved to be more co-operative than she had hoped. He contributed to the *Revue Indépendante* several times and continued to do so even after George had given up her responsibility for it.

Other contributors were not so reliable. Leroux had a way of leaving proofs uncorrected and on one occasion could not be traced for twenty days. George redoubled her efforts and did the work of five. She had the satisfaction of seeing *Horace* published in her own magazine and later *Consuelo*. She also wrote a series of articles on the new wave of proletarian poetry. But in spite of her Herculean labours and Viardot's staunch support the paper could not pay its way and was eventually wound up. George however had developed a taste for publishing and before long was planning with her old republican mates Planet, Dutheil, Fleury and Duvernet a Berry socialist magazine. *L'Eclaireur de l'Indre* came into being in 1844, after George had manfully pestered all her friends to contribute something towards its foundation fund. Even Chopin, who had no interest whatever in political socialism, was made to fork out fifty francs. Leroux, who had proved unsuitable as editor, was contracted to print the magazine in his Berry printing press.

While George was writing and championing causes, Chopin was

composing and giving piano lessons, sometimes as many as five a day. He took his teaching seriously and was particular about the choice of his pupils. He set much store by sensitivity and intelligence of interpretation and often demonstrated on a second piano what he tried to convey. He was charming to his beautiful pupils, but none the less critical. The story went round that one day a pupil played her piece to him, then looked up expectantly for his comments. 'Was that music?' Chopin nonchalantly asked from behind his own piano. 'I thought it was the dog barking.'[22]

His health continued to fluctuate. Sometimes he coughed daintily into his handkerchief, sometimes he coughed violently and was too ill to go anywhere. George looked after him with untiring solicitude. She never allowed him to start his day's work without making him swallow some drinking chocolate or hot broth. When aristocratic matrons desired him to give piano lessons to their daughters in their own drawing-rooms rather than at rue Pigalle, she made them send their carriages to fetch and return him and furthermore pay thirty francs a lesson instead of the usual twenty. She treated him and spoke of him as her 'regular patient'.[23]

Sometimes patient and nurse changed roles. George had always boasted of her 'iron health',[24] but all the same she was subject to crippling rheumatic pains, congestion of the chest and what she thought was liver trouble. Sometimes it was she who had to keep to her bed. On such occasions Chopin would look after her with exemplary devotion and restore her to health. He also knew how to comfort her in moments of despondency. 'He is as kind as an angel,' George wrote to her brother after the failure of *Cosima*. 'Without his perfect and delicate friendship I would often lose heart.'[25]

Life at rue Pigalle was pleasantly domestic. In the evenings, when Chopin had finished his day's work and George had not yet retired to her study to start writing, they would spend a few hours in the drawing-room like any family. George would hem handkerchiefs or teach Solange, on holiday from her boarding-school, some needlework; Delacroix would drop in for a chat; and Chopin would play games with a mischievous puppy recently added to the household. It was a brown mongrel with white chest and paws who annoyed Solange by showing a marked preference for Chopin. He was baptised Mops, 'which in Polish simply means an inoffensive little dog,'[26] George wrote to Maurice, away on holiday, after having cleaned the mess on the carpet.

She hardly ever wrote to any of her intimates without giving them some news of Chopin. She referred to him affectionately by every possible variation on his name. He was *Chopino, Chopinet, Chop, Chip, Chip-Chop, Chip-Chip*, even *Chippette*; only seldom Chopin, or *Fritz* as he was to some of his old friends. Marie d'Agoult, observing with envy the stable association with Chopin at a time when her own with Liszt was beginning to disintegrate, wrote that there was some talk in Paris about George being pregnant; but she, Marie, was sure that the change in George's waistline was due to no more than middle-age spread.

Marie was one of the first to suggest that Chopin was subject to fits of jealousy and that George would have gladly left him had she not feared that such a step would kill the sick man there and then. In fact Marie was seven years ahead of events, as George had been about Liszt and his princess. The basic rule at rue Pigalle was discretion. When Countess de Musset wrote most deferentially to ask whether Chopin would give piano lessons to her gifted young daughter, he agreed to offer only the occasional professional advice; it would have been *mauvais ton* to give regular lessons to the sister of a former lover of George's. George was equally bland. When at the beginning of 1841 Alfred de Musset published a poem in the *Revue des Deux Mondes* inspired by a chance meeting with her at the theatre, she merely remarked that she did not mind being sung about if it helped an impecunious poet turn an honest *sou*.

For several years Chopin and George helped each other with their work. No matter what subject George was writing on, she would let Chopin read the manuscript page by page as she wrote and wait for his comments. When she was working on *Consuelo*, which had an opera singer for a heroine, Chopin virtually collaborated on the musical background of the book. She dedicated to him *La Mare au Diable*, a romantic love story set against the rustic background of Berry, which was to become one of her most popular novels. Chopin did not dedicate a single work to George Sand, but he relied on her judgment and perception. 'For eight years,' she later recalled, 'I was daily initiated into his musical thinking and inspiration. His piano revealed to me his raptures and conflicts, his triumphs and torments. I understood him as well as he understood himself.'[27] On a more practical plane she was able to create for him the physical conditions which were conducive to inspiration. The winter months in Paris were usually taken up by teaching, discussions with publishers, social calls. It was mostly at Nohant, during the long summer months, that Chopin composed. It was there that he found both peace and stimulation for his work.

It was in no small measure thanks to George's encouragement that he was able to go through with one of his first public recitals for several years. He had played before Louis Philippe in 1838, shortly before his departure for Majorca, and then again in 1839 after his return to Paris. But those were command performances held at the royal palace in front of a small gathering; a public recital at a hired hall was anathema to him. One day however he was caught off guard and agreed to give a recital at the Salle Pleyel. Before he could go back on the agreement most of the tickets, unusually expensive ones at that, had been sold. There began what George spiritedly described as 'the Chopinesque nightmare'.[28] Chopin refused to allow any display of posters, the printing of programmes, the sale of the remaining tickets. When he heard that Pauline Viardot, the adored soprano with whom he had hoped to share the recital, had a previous engagement in London, he became a nervous wreck. George soothed him, arranged for another illustrious soprano to step in, smoothed every imaginary difficulty.

The recital, on 26 April 1841, was a resounding success. Chopin played some of his recently published compositions which had never yet been heard in public. The *France musicale* praised him to the skies and wrote that he had created a new school of music for the piano. George forgot the nightmare and wrote to her brother with maternal pride:

Chopin has been idle throughout the summer, then gave a
recital when in two hours and two strokes of the hand he
pocketed more than 6000 francs, in the midst of *bravos, bis* and
frenzied foot-stamping by the most beautiful women in
Paris.[29]

That same year Chopin gave a third command performance at
the royal palace and the following one another recital at the Salle
Pleyel, which he shared with the cellist Auguste Franchomme
and the soprano Pauline Viardot. It was another resounding
success.

A few months later a search for new accommodation was
initiated. After three years at rue Pigalle it became apparent to
both George and Chopin that their status required a more fashionable address. Mme Marliani found them two vacant apartments
in a modernised block into which she herself had recently moved.
Situated near the present rue Taitboul, it comprised fifty spacious
apartments, several bright studios, mews for residents' coaches
and horses and various other amenities devised by the imaginative
owner, an Englishman who lived in London. Square d'Orléans
as the complex was called, or alternatively place d'Orléans, cité
d'Orléans and even Orleans Court, was a noble edifice built in
the style of an Italian *palazzo*, overlooking a large tree-lined court.
The rent was high and the residents were accordingly persons of
means. Apart from the Marlianis they included the Viardots, the
dancer Taglione, the sculptor Dantan who a year earlier had made
a small bust of Chopin, and many other successful friends. It
became a rich artists' colony. During the day everybody worked
according to their inclination or routine; in the evening they
assembled at Mme Marliani's for a communal dinner at shared
costs. Later other residents would drop in. The informal conviviality reminded George of Nohant. 'In the evenings we drop in
on one another like good country neighbours,'[30] she wrote to
Charles Duvernet in Berry. She hired a billiard table and encouraged further neighbourly calls. Maurice, a promising young
artist of twenty-one, was given a studio of his own in the same
block.

The move agreed with Chopin as much as it did with George, if for different reasons. It suited him to have a splendid drawing-room where he could receive his countesses, accommodate two pianos and display his collection of knick-knacks. It became his retreat and his sanctuary. In theory he intended to work there; in practice he only used it for lessons, spending the rest of his time receiving or returning calls. The serious work was mostly left to the less disruptive summer months at Nohant.

In the spring of 1844 news reached him at square d'Orléans that his father had died in Warsaw at the age of seventy-three. Chopin was much attached to his family and kept up a loving correspondence with them, in Polish to his mother and sisters, in French to his French-born father. The death was a hard blow, and it immediately told on his health. Before rushing him off to Nohant for a rest-cure, George wrote her only known letter to Mme Chopin in Warsaw:

Paris, 29 May 1844

Madam,

I can think of no words to comfort the excellent mother of my dear Frédéric except to assure you of the courage and resignation of that admirable child. You would know how stricken with sorrow his heart is, but he is not ill thank God and in a few hours we are leaving for the country where he will be able to rest after this terrible blow.

His only thought is for you, for his sisters and the rest of the family whom he so much loves and whose grief preoccupies and disturbs him as much as his own.

At least you need not worry about his physical condition. I would not attempt to take away his grief which is so deep, justified and enduring; but I can at least look after his health by surrounding him with as much affection and care as you your-self would give him. This is a pleasant duty the performance of which gives me happiness and in which I shall never fail. That I promise you, Madam, and I hope you have faith in my devotion to him. I will not tell you that your bereavement has struck me as if I had personally known the remarkable man whose passing you are mourning. My sympathy, however sincere, cannot alleviate this terrible pain. But when I tell you that I shall devote my life to his son and that I regard him as my own, I know I can give you some peace of mind on his account. This is why I have taken the liberty of writing and telling you that I am deeply devoted to you as the beloved mother of my dearest friend.

George Sand.[31]

Mme Chopin wrote back most graciously. In the summer Chopin's sister Louise and her husband came to France to see him and at George's insistence accepted an invitation to Nohant. The two women took to each other instantly; George thought that Louise was far less conventional than Chopin. After eighteen days the Jendrzejewiczes had to start on their return journey, due to the limited validity of their Polish exit permits. Before Louise left George gave her the original manuscript of *La Mare au Diable* which had been dedicated to her brother.

❧❧❧❧❧❧❧

Chapter 13

Sublimation

In 1840 George was instrumental in bringing about the marriage of the Spanish-born soprano Pauline Garcia to the writer cum theatre manager Louis Viardot. Since then she had been watching the couple with a proprietary eye. It could not escape her notice that young Pauline felt esteem rather than attraction for her middle-aged husband. 'That child,' George wrote of her in her diary, 'can love her husband only in a certain way. Her love for him is tender, chaste, generous, deep, unagitated. It is love without intoxication, love without suffering; in short, it is love without passion.'[1]

Without realising it, George was describing the state of her own love for Chopin.

Ever since her first few days as Pagello's mistress in Venice several existences earlier, George had known that love without passion was for her like food without salt. She needed that element of suffering to keep her heart aflame; she required that measure of resistance in the loved one to make her soul respond with ecstasy to a sign of tenderness. In 1840 her love for Chopin no longer fitted that formula. Furthermore, it was no longer rejuvenated by reciprocated physical need. The need was Chopin's alone. George's feelings for him had been totally purged of physical desire. She admitted that much to Grzymala in a letter she wrote to him several years later:

12 May 1847

For the last seven years I have lived with him, and with others, like a virgin. I have grown old before my time. It was done without any sacrifice on my part, I was weary of passion, I was incurably disillusioned. If a woman could have ever inspired him with trust it should have been me, but he never understood it. Many people say that I have exhausted him with the violence of my desire; others accuse me of having driven him to distraction by my verbal outbursts. You know what the truth is. He accuses me of having killed him by the imposed privation; I am convinced I would have killed him had I acted differently.[2]

George may well have believed that intercourse would have aggravated Chopin's condition; the fact remains that what was privation for him was a relief for her. But transforming a lover into a platonic friend was no easy task; it was an assignment which defeated its own professed object by making the patient agitated and suspicious. Nor, in spite of the declaration to Grzymala, was it ever fully achieved. That much becomes clear from a letter George wrote to a total stranger, a lady who through a mutual friend knew of the estrangement between Mme Sand and Chopin towards the end of his life and who took it upon herself to bring about a deathbed reconciliation. George's reply, a curiously defensive one, throws further light on the last years of the relationship:

His best doctor in our part of the country, who was also one of his best friends [Gustave Papet], has been advising me for some time to loosen the bond between us until it ceased to be one altogether. I have been working towards that end for a long time and had it depended on me alone it would have been achieved without a jolt. But with a nature like his, so nervous, strange, unhappy (though at the same time noble), it was impossible; and I myself often lost my temper in the face of his unfounded accusations.[3]

There is no proof that George had at any time discussed with Dr Papet the remedial properties of abstinence, or that abstinence had ever been suggested to Chopin on medical grounds. He was left to draw his own conclusions. Since he could not face the fact that his mistress had reached a passionless limbo, he accused her of infidelity. George, who had not been unfaithful, was getting weary of his suspicions and his claims to something which she could no longer give. There were periods of tension. Chopin would either lose his temper or seek refuge behind a mask of icy courtesy; George would try to reason then lose her temper too. In between storms they were tender and devoted, but their friends noticed that 'love was no longer there'.[4] George was becalmed.

Then, suddenly, she came alive again. At near-forty she found a new source of exultation in the person of the eighteen-year-old singer Pauline Garcia-Viardot, whose musical genius and initial reticence rekindled that exquisite heartache which George called passion.

Pauline was the daughter of the Spanish composer Garcia and the much younger sister of La Malibran. Born in 1821, she led a nomadic life with her touring family, spending some time in London, New York and Mexico before arriving with her mother in France. Her Paris début, at the age of sixteen or seventeen, was much aided by Alfred de Musset who pushed his musical patronage so far as to ask for her hand in marriage. George first heard her sing at the Théâtre Italien some time after her return from Majorca and was bowled over in the same way she was when she first saw Marie Dorval on the stage several years earlier. She fell completely under the spell of the voice, the artistry and the personality of the young singer. She invited her to dinner and when Pauline failed to confirm the date, she wrote to her in the same vein of confident adulation which characterised her early correspondence with Marie Dorval:

> Queen of the world, you have not yet told me which day you would be able to give me. Am I to give up the hope of seeing you at my place together with M. Lablache [Pauline's bass partner] who has already agreed to come? I would like to know my fate and not bait my friends with the vain hope of meeting

you again. You know them already and it will be a very informal gathering. There will be no curious window-shoppers to stare at you. I am too jealous of your company to share the happiness of seeing you with any but the élite of your admirers. Tell me whether it is next week or this coming Sunday that I am to brighten up my poet's attic with four candles and display my best two pots of reseda. If I had millions, I would spend them that day on oriental carpets to be spread at your feet.[5]

It was risqué language to address to an eighteen-year-old, but George was impassioned. Pauline Garcia embodied everything she unconsciously sought. She was great enough to be put on a pedestal, dependent enough to be mothered, unforthcoming enough to be pursued. To her diary George confided the following year: 'She is the only woman I have loved so tenderly within the last ten years. . . . Yet she is only a child of nineteen and I doubt that the gap between our ages can ever be bridged.'[6] She was well aware of the interpretation which could be put on her interest in the young girl and fervently stated in her diary that what she felt for Pauline was pure and sacred. Indeed, with the maternal element always prevalent in her emotional involvements, it was not difficult to channel the new passion into a mother–daughter relationship, unembarrassing for Pauline, still intoxicating for George. She called Pauline 'Dear child of my heart',[7] 'Dear daughter',[8] and mostly that untranslatable maternal endearment which endured even when Pauline herself became a mother, '*Ma fifille*'.[9] Pauline first addressed the older woman deferentially as 'Dear Madame Sand',[10] or 'Dear maternal friend',[11] but as time went by she too acknowledged George's place in her heart by signing herself as '*Votre fifille*'.[12] Throughout their entire association, which lasted until George's death, neither ever departed from the formal *vous*.

Pauline was living with her mother, but it was George who brought about the marriage between the nineteen-year-old singer and the forty-year-old Viardot, who subsequently gave up his post as manager of the Théâtre Italien to devote himself entirely to his wife's career. It was not a love-match on Pauline's side, but it endured and yielded several children who were brought up to regard George Sand as a revered grandmother.

One of Pauline Viardot's first engagements after her marriage was to give a series of recitals at Cambrai, in the north of France. George, who at the height of her passion for Marie Dorval dreamed of accompanying her on tour as a dresser or a maid, now accompanied the Viardots. She shared the discomforts of provincial hotels, suffered with Pauline from the coarseness of the audiences, battled with managers of inferior halls. To her 'three children' left in Paris to fend for themselves she wrote: 'Love your old woman as much as she loves you.'[13]

Even though the relationship had become stable, it was not devoid of the occasional hurt. Pauline had learnt to love George as a daughter might, which meant that she often put her out of her mind for longer than a mother would be willing to accept without reproach. When she was on tour, as she frequently was, she was negligent about writing letters. 'This child cannot love me very much because she does not know me,'[14] George noted in her diary. To the child, touring England, she wrote:

18 April 1841

My dear little daughter, I am happy when you write and not annoyed when you do not. I love you very much and even if you did nasty things to me, pushed my nose in or did something like that [George sketched a pair of hands suggesting mischief] I should still love you. I hope you know that. That is why I am not disheartened by your silence, comforting myself with the thought that you cannot forget those by whom you know yourself loved.[15]

In the summer of 1841 George and Chopin left Paris to spend a few months at Nohant, a habit they were to keep for several years to come. The Viardots came down for two weeks. In no time the house was full to capacity. There were Maurice and Solange down for the holidays, Hippolyte with his wife and young daughter Léontine, the Berry regulars and Delacroix, for whom George had fitted out a permanent studio in the house. The very air of Nohant quivered with creativity. Chopin and Pauline Viardot practised little-known songs by eighteenth-century composers; Maurice sketched; Delacroix painted; and Louis Viardot, when not hunting, was writing essays on Spanish literature or going over his translation of Cervantes. George was working on *Consuelo*, the story of a dedicated opera singer who, like Pauline Viardot, was plain but undaunted by such an obvious drawback.

In the evenings there was much social fun. Chopin had a remarkable gift for mime and was fond of displaying it before a choice audience. Without any warning, he would hastily smooth his hair before the wall mirror, then turn round to give a hilarious imitation of the half-wit emperor of Austria, an old Polish Jew, or a sentimental English old maid. Some days the entire house-party went out for walks in the woods, George and the young ones energetically striding ahead, Chopin, with his hair meticulously curled and his hands in white gloves, following daintily on a donkey.

Two summers later the Viardots left their first-born daughter Louise at Nohant while going on an engagement to Vienna. George was as proud of baby Louise as she had been nearly twenty years earlier of her own baby Maurice. 'Your little girl has brought forth four fine teeth this week,' she wrote to Pauline in Vienna. 'If this goes on she will eat you up. She is very well, dances, laughs, chatters away, speaks Polish with Chopin, Berrichon with Françoise [the maid] and Sanscrit with Pistolet [the dog], pees everywhere, eats, sleeps and makes us all very happy.'[16]

A few days later George sent another delighted account which Pauline kept reading over and over again:

Nohant, June 1843.
Dear angel of a daughter, your little love is well and properly looked after. She is as gay as a chaffinch, as fresh as a rose, as chatty as a linnet, as sweet as a lamb. I have never seen a sweeter or brighter child. . . . She babbles in such a funny way, she calls me Mummy if you do not mind and says 'Little

Chopin' in a way which melts all the Chopins in the world. Naturally Chopin adores her and spends his life kissing her hands. It must be admitted that the young lady is not hard on him. As a matter of fact she is an outrageous flirt and compromises him publicly. There are no pouts, funny gestures or monkey tricks which she does not practise on him. When she has had her soup there follows the scene of running round the dinner-table with a leg of chicken in her hand. Pistolet follows her lovingly, keeping an eye on the bone which is his by right. But the little one hands it to me for preference, and I must accept the gift with good grace or else have my sleeves pulled out of shape.[17]

The following years brought more visits to Nohant, more babies and more tours. Though Pauline was too over-wrought during her tours to write as often as George would have wished her to, she tried to make up for her apparent neglect when the tension of the moment was over. From a Russian tour she brought back hand-made peasant slippers for every member of the Nohant family, writing that George's were full of loving kisses. She sent little sketches made from memory, of Maurice, Solange, George, Leroux; sometimes of herself singing, deliberately exaggerating her unattractive nose, or of her 'not too sisterly sisters-in-law'[18] falling asleep to the sound of her singing. When she did write her letters were affectionate and full of vitality.

Yet her love for George, like her love for her husband, was tinged with a sense of guilt born of her inability to be as emotionally gripped by them as they were by her. In Viardot's case it sometimes drove her to put physical distance between them to enable her to think kindly of a husband whose loving presence left her unresponsive. In George's case it made her feel blameworthy. She was often on the defensive. When in 1846, after several years of an unevenly spaced correspondence, George failed to write for an unusually long time, Pauline felt guiltier than ever. Beneath her operatic ejaculations her misery was deepfelt when she wrote:

What have I done, dear adorable *ninounne*, that you no longer write to me, no longer think of your daughter, no longer love her? Have I not obeyed all your counsels, always been frank and loyal towards you as I am towards all those I love? For Heaven's sake, if I have offended you in any way please tell me and I will throw myself at your feet, kiss your hands and ask your forgiveness from the bottom of my heart. Reproach me, crush me, strike me down, but please break this icy silence which hurts and frightens me so, which alone disrupts the calm of my life. For a long time now I have felt you no longer love me as much as you used to and your coolness has been gnawing at my heart. I beg of you, mother, love me as you always did. If I have done something wrong punish me, but then forgive. If your cruel silence is the punishment, I will accept it and wait for forgiveness. Take pity on me, do not let me suffer too long. I so much need your affection in order to live in peace.[19]

George ruefully answered that she had been so much in the habit of pestering Pauline with her frequent letters that once she relaxed the pace it looked, wrongly, as if she did not care any more. Then she added:

You are crazy to be worried about my silence and a goose to think that I no longer love you or that I love you less than I used to. How could it be? Are you not what is best and most perfect in the world, at least the world I know? There is no one I could esteem more than you, or love as much. So you must never have such ideas again. Whether I write or not, whether I see you often or seldom, at no time must you attribute this privation which I impose on myself to anything but passing circumstances. After my children, I would even say with my children as you are one of them, I could not have a more tender and lasting affection for anyone except you and Chip-Chip, who is also my child.[20]

The reference to Chopin in the midst of her loving assurances to Pauline was symptomatic. They were all her children, Maurice,

Solange, Chopin, Pauline. At forty-two, as she was when she wrote that letter, there was only one emotion which could still grip her heart and fill it with agitation. It was that protective, possessive, compulsive hankering which George called maternal love.

Chapter 14

Solange

When Solange Dudevant was born in September 1828, Aurore Dudevant, as George Sand then was, became the proud mother all over again. She adored the plump, fair-haired baby who, if conjecture is right, had been conceived in love. Her letters to Sophie Victoire were full of her. She boasted of her rosy complexion, her appetite, her babyish tricks and wiles. She reported with wonderment that Fatty, as she affectionately called Solange, was markedly different from her brother Maurice when he was a baby. She was robust, vivacious, constantly demanding attention and rapidly developing the knack of getting her own way.

In her maturity George Sand knew herself well enough to observe that her loves for men had a strong maternal element about them. Indeed maternal love for the man of the moment was a driving force which blinded her to all but her own emotional craving. It even made her put aside her instinctive caring for the children of her body. When in January 1831 she felt the urge to join little Jules Sandeau in Paris and carve out a new life for herself, she did not hesitate to delegate the care of Maurice and Solange to a husband she did not respect, a tutor who was not altogether keen, and a couple of peasant-girls who could hardly read or write. And it was conceivably in the hope of winning back Stéphane de Grandsagne through the constant presence of his little daughter in Paris, rather than in answer to Solange's need to be with her mother, that George brought her to quai St Michel the following year, to live in a garret she shared with a lover.

It was a questionable step whatever the motive. Even the bedazzled phalanx of Berry students who had accepted her independent way of life, her love association with Sandeau, her men's outfits and tobacco smoking, were taken aback to see her plunge a three-and-a-half-year-old girl into a den of illicit love. But the mother made light of the possible effect of such a step on an observant child. To Emile Régnault, her confidant and adviser in those days, she explained:

> She will sleep on the couch on a small mattress and as she is only $3\frac{1}{2}$ years old, I assure you she will not notice anything, will ask no questions and make no embarrassing remarks. Even Maurice would not notice anything, he is so innocent, so you need not worry about the moral aspect of this plan. I have no more desire to scandalise my daughter than the most virtuous of mothers. When the time comes I shall take another lodging which will lend itself to more serious precautions.[1]

George wishfully shut her eyes to the dangers of a regime which would allow a child to live six months of the year with a mother's lover, the other six with a mother's husband. She assured Régnault that Solange would adapt. In the event it was little Jules who adapted. He took Solange for walks in the Jardin des Plantes and knew better than to contradict her when, at the sight of a giraffe, she solemnly assured him that she had one of her own back at Nohant. Other young admirers, like Emile Régnault or Emmanuel Arago, were also converted into child-minders and treated the daughter, for the sake of the mother, like a fairy princess.

But tame walks in a public garden were no substitute for the pleasures of Nohant. Solange missed the freedom of country life and the company of some half a dozen peasant children who used to play with her. She also missed her mother who had to go out about her business and often left her with kindly neighbours. She felt neglected as she had not felt in her Nohant environment. She began to throw tantrums. Ordinarily a hearty eater, she would refuse to touch her food for no apparent reason; and when George took her out for a walk, she would squat on the pavement and refuse to budge, attracting much curiosity and embarrassing remarks. One day George instructed young Emmanuel Arago to drive Solange to the Luxembourg Gardens and there let her run around freely. Solange announced that she would not run around, she would be driven inside the park like a lady. When Arago was about to dismiss the *fiacre* and took Solange in his arms to help her down, he noticed that she had no shoes on. She had thrown them into the street when he was not looking. 'Let us see you make me run in the park barefoot,' she said triumphantly.[2]

As soon as she reached school age, George put her in a Paris *pension*. Solange liked it well enough, but the moment she was back in the garret for an afternoon off she became impossible. Feeling wanting, George tried to make up by pandering to her every wish. The harder she tried, the more difficult Solange became. She rejoiced in her power. One day Emmanuel Arago – George was good at delegating chores – returned Solange to her *pension* after an outing and said to her at the gate:

'Solange, what would you like me to bring you next time I come to take you out?'

'Nothing. But you can do me a great favour if you really care for me.'

'What is it? You have only to ask.'

'Well, my boy, don't you ever come to see me again.'[3]

Maurice was the very opposite. When also put in a Paris boarding-school he hated every minute of it. All he wanted was to be with his mother in her garret, never losing sight of her, quietly keeping himself amused by sketching *bonshommes*, funny little people. At school he was often ill, recovering the moment his mother came to fetch him. George and her husband had fierce arguments about Maurice, Casimir maintaining that the boy was shamming, George demanding that he should be taken away from school and continue to be privately educated at Nohant. Casimir insisted that at nine it was high time for Maurice to go to a respectable boarding-school like any other boy or girl of his class; indeed like the boy's own mother and father when they were his age. Maurice stayed on. He became so sick with longing that he could no longer enjoy his mother's company even when he had her all to himself. When taken to see her at the elegant new apartment at quai Malaquais he would refuse to do anything, spend the precious hours watching the clock hands ticking away and burst into tears when the time came to be returned to school.

As usual George discussed the problem with her friends and as usual she accepted the advice that agreed most with her inclination of the moment, which in 1833 was to go to Italy with Alfred de Musset. The suggestion was that the long separation would force Maurice to tear himself away from his mother's apron-strings and give him an uninterrupted chance to settle down to the well-ordained life of a school-boarder.

Maurice did settle down. In fact he settled down so well that he neglected to write to his mother for weeks on end, sometimes for months; unless it was his way of punishing her for leaving him. From Venice George kept urging her Paris minions to go to see Maurice at school and give her some news of him. They failed to oblige. In desperation she wrote to Buloz:

> 30 May 1834
>
> I am terribly anxious about my son from whom I have had no news for two months. Try to find out how he is. I keep asking everybody. Nobody cares.[4]

Why anybody should have cared more than the boy's own mother was a question George did not ask herself. It did not occur to her to cut short her Venetian stay and return to Paris to find out, or, failing that, to rely on Casimir's being at hand in case of need. Instead, she kept urging the dismissed Musset to call at Maurice's school. 'For the love of God,' she wrote to him, 'go and see my son. Tell me how he is, whether he still remembers me, whether he looks human. Every night I dream his body is being brought to me dead or covered in blood. What a life! I really feel like putting an end to it, I really do.'[5]

Was it for the love of God George asked Musset to call on her son, for the love of her son, or for the love of Musset which was reawakening after a passionless existence with Pagello? She could not admit, least of all to herself, that her love tangles, at their height, took precedence over a mother's instinct. She compromised by delegating and compensated by over-worrying. To Musset she wrote again:

> If you see my son tell him he has not written to me for more than two months and that I am much grieved by it. I am sad not to have my daughter with me, and now that I have arranged to stay on and not return until August, I think of her day and night with incredible impatience and longing. What is it, that love which mothers feel for their children? It is still something mysterious for me. It inspires solicitude and anxiety which are a hundred times more heartrending than those felt by a woman in love, yet it offers less joy and rapture in the knowledge of possession; it generates a longing which is hardly noticeable in the first few days of separation but which becomes consuming like a fever the longer it lasts.[6]

While Maurice was at his Paris boarding-school, Solange was at Nohant, looked after by her father and instructed by unsatisfactory governesses. But when Casimir, weary of being his daughter's minder and also genuinely worried about the inadequate tuition, suggested sending her to a *pension*, George wrote all the way from Italy to dissuade him. As it turned out Solange became a late reader and for the best part of her childhood an appalling speller.

On her return from Italy George kept travelling feverishly between Paris and Nohant, following the tormented path of her love for Musset. Maurice reacted to his mother's unsettling visits by becoming morbidly attached to her; Solange, by performing acts of naughtiness which forced her mother to take more notice of her. By then George and her husband could not see eye to eye about anything. There were violent rows in front of the children, sordid accusations and mutual exaggerations. The children were beginning to understand. Solange was packed off to a *pension* and wrote touching little love-letters to her mother. 'I kiss you one thousand five hundred two hundred thousand times,'[7] was her favourite signing-off in those days. George exhorted her to work hard. '*I should be very glad if you write to me in english* [*sic*],' she wrote in English. '*Good night, little dear, I love you.*'[8]

But Solange did not want to work and thought instead of a hundred ways to attract attention by being naughty. She was just over eight when George wrote to her:

My dear child, I hope you will see the error of your ways and make up your mind to behave better in the future towards me and your brother. You have a kind heart, but too violent a temperament. You are an intelligent girl and you are growing up. It is time you took yourself in hand and started to correct yourself.[9]

Solange could not understand why she was being kept away from home while Maurice had been temporarily recalled. She felt the *pension* was an unfair discrimination. All she wanted was to return to Nohant by means fair or foul. George explained that the only way to hasten her return was by completing her educational syllabus; she extolled the rewards of industry, selflessness and loyalty. She tried a humorous approach; she teased Solange about the risk of dislocating her jaws with too much yawning. Sometimes Solange would take her mother's admonitions to heart and promise to try harder. Once or twice she even reported good marks for homework. But mostly she would fall back on mischief, or sham an illness which would require her return home. Again George would rebuke her, Solange would feel contrite and make fresh resolutions, only to break them. It was a vicious circle.

In the summer of 1837, a year after Casimir Dudevant had relinquished Nohant and the children no longer witnessed the telling rows between their parents, Marie d'Agoult had occasion to observe them in their day-to-day life. Maurice was fourteen, Solange nine. In her diary Marie d'Agoult wrote:

Solange is a beautiful girl, extremely well-built, alert and full of animal grace. When the wind ruffles her long golden curls falling over her classic shoulders, and when the light plays on her bright face, she looks like a wood nymph. . . . Her spirit is as forceful as her body, her intelligence destines her for the sciences. She has a loving heart and a passionate untamable temperament. Her life will be full of conflicts. She will not bend to the ordinary rules. Her faults will be on the grand scale, as will her virtues. . . . Maurice is her very opposite. He will become a man of common-sense and good order and will have all the convenient virtues.[10]

That same year, while George was staying partly at Fontaine-bleau with Bocage, partly looking after her dying mother in Paris, Casimir Dudevant arrived unexpectedly at Nohant and took Solange away with him to his estate at Guillery. George later described in dramatic terms how the nine-year-old girl threw herself at her father's feet and begged him not to take her away. What Solange really felt remained unrecorded. She herself gave an account of the event to her brother Maurice in a letter which defeats translation because of its innumerable spelling mistakes and lack of punctuation. It ran something like this:

My dear little darling dont cry they found me dont be sad. to return me to *maman* there were three sweet policemen a little old man Mallefille a police officer another very very very old police officer. You told Mallefille to fetch us and he is keeping his promise because he is taking us back. My father was cross when he saw the policemen I've been to the Pyrenees I've seen the Breach of Roland I rode a horse and I'm coming back on a big coach with three horses to see you and kiss you isnt it lovely my little darling. At Lourdes the bridges and houses are made of marble I saw Marboré and waterfalls of 12 and 6 feet. Goodbye my sweet keep well.[11]

For a while both children were kept at Nohant, educated by a series of tutors of whom Mallefille was the most consistent. At fifteen Maurice was docile, expanding his talents, 'with a real aptitude for art',[12] while Solange, at ten, was more interested in playing the lady of the manor. George jokingly referred to her as *La Baronne*; other friends, pandering to a child's vanity, called her marchioness, princess, queen. Solange wanted to dazzle. She never forgave Sainte-Beuve who, when he saw her in Paris at an age when she was losing her milk teeth, said in his most avuncular manner: 'You will do well, Mademoiselle, to grow up kind, as you will never grow up beautiful.'[13]

George continued to shroud her children in love, constantly telling them that she loved them and exhorting them to love her. The theme recurred in her letters like a magic incantation. During a short business-trip to Paris she wrote to them to Nohant:

Good morning, Maurice, good morning Solange. Love me, think of me and write to me. Tell me your latest leech stories. Poor boy, the cold weather will make you worse, and I am not there to look after you. And my lioness, is she sensible and good? Are the portraits going well? [Auguste Charpentier was down at Nohant to paint George and Solange] Are you being good? Above all, do you think of your little love, your poor Piffoël, who dreams all night long of her little ones and who cannot live without them? Goodbye both of you, I kiss you and kiss you a hundred thousand times.[14]

After her Italian escapade a few years earlier George would no longer consider going abroad for any length of time without her children; nor was there any need to, seeing that they were in her sole charge and Casimir no longer had a say in the matter. As before, she liked to see her lover and her children living like one happy family. The stay in Majorca agreed with the children. Maurice, who had been a delicate child, regained his health and made excellent progress with his sketching, while Solange became more amenable. 'Maurice says it is because she had thrown up all her venom during the sea voyage,'[15] George happily reported to Mme Marliani. The happy phase did not last long.

Instinctively Solange shunned anything which required effort. At eleven she once came across an old diary of her mother's and was surprised to hear that it contained thoughts. Not to fall behind, she offered to write in it some of her own. 'You can't,' said George who later recorded the whole conversation. 'You haven't got any.'

> 'Yes, I have,' said Solange.
> 'Let's hear one then.'
> ' "I love you".'
> 'What about another?'
> ' "I don't like Greek history".'
> 'Let's hear another.'
> ' "I'm hungry".'
> 'And another?'
> ' "Shall I go and play in the garden?" There, that's enough thoughts for one day.'[16]

Solange's career at her various *pensions* continued to be unsatisfactory. At the end of one school year, during which she had made no noticeable progress, the good mistresses awarded her two prizes: one for having kept healthy, the other for growing. Indeed at twelve Solange was a big hefty girl, fully developed and aware of her charms. In the country and Majorca she was dressed in boy's clothes; at the *pension* she demanded a constant supply of beautiful new frocks. 'You will be good enough to change only twice a week like the other girls,'[17] George severely answered.

Solange had obvious intelligence, a talent for music and an ear for languages, yet she was not getting anywhere. George was pained when her brother Hippolyte suggested that the best thing would be to marry her off early. He even went as far as suggesting a bridegroom, none other than Gustave Papet, once George's accomplice during her illicit meetings with Jules Sandeau and latterly Chopin's regular doctor. George had learnt to accept Hippolyte for what he was, an incurable alcoholic, and replied gently:

April 1841

Solange is at boarding-school, she must get down to work because she is only twelve and a half and before carrying out the beautiful matrimonial projects you are making for her, she must learn to read and write properly. Maurice is working hard, he is sensible and already has quite a collection of paints and brushes.[18]

At square d'Orléans, where Maurice was given a studio of his own, Solange had a beautiful room next to her mother's. More than ever she acted the great lady, making frequent allusions to her remote and irregular descent from Augustus the Strong. When Maurice walked into her room she asked him in pained tones to be good enough to leave, as he smelled of cigarettes; but the moment he was gone she chased him up to his studio and made it impossible for him to work. Sometimes George took her out riding and noted with a mixture of pride and anxiety that she rode 'like the devil'.[19] But her outbursts of activity were rare. Mostly, when at home, she would sleep three or four hours at a stretch during the day, or sit in front of her mirror.

The great change in her life occurred at thirteen, when she was accepted into a *pension* run by M. and Mme Bascans. The latter found a way into the girl's heart in the same way that one or two of the good sisters at the *Couvent des Anglaises* had found a way to her mother's in similar circumstances. For three years Solange accepted school discipline and did some work for the love of Mme Bascans. When she grew up and had a baby she asked Mme Bascans to be its godmother.

During that new phase she began to realise that her mother was one of the leading writers of France. She took to reading her novels and discussing with George her preference for one or the other. She was growing up. She was no longer the little child who could be reduced to tears of repentance by a disapproving mother. She was beginning to question and criticise, to analyse and accuse. It was a different Solange who wrote to her mother at the age of fifteen:

I do not deserve your reproaches, my dear. You tell me my style of writing is mannered. If this is the case, which is quite possible, it is not intentional. Not everybody can write like you, so please do not blame me if my style is not natural. Perhaps it does not appear to be so because it is too much so.

You more or less imply that I do not love you. Well, ever since I saw you calmly write a letter to Mme Perdiguier in order to reduce her to tears, I have thought that that is what you are trying to do to me too. Furthermore, in order to hurt me even more you give lessons to Luce [a Nohant maid of Solange's age] while I have to be in Paris. You are not nice when you scold me.[20]

The three years at the *Pension* Bascans completed Solange's formal education. As sixteen she was returned home for good and became a young lady of leisure. Pauline Viardot recalled a telling incident from that period.

She and her husband had just acquired a country mansion and the Sand household was invited over to stay. Pauline, in her proud capacity of châtelaine, took the family for a tour of the gardens; she and George walked ahead while the others followed behind. A curious swishing sound kept puzzling Pauline until she turned round. There was Solange, expressionless, slashing with a whip at the flowers on either side of the garden path. Rows and rows of stems stood headless, the severed crowns lying mutilated on the ground. For a moment Pauline felt murderous. 'What appalled me most,' she later recalled, 'was that viciousness, that gross wickedness, so loathsome because it had no rhyme or reason, no other aim except the displeasure of others. It was always like that. Solange practised evil in the same way some people practised art, just for the love of it.'[21]

Modern psychologists might disagree with Pauline's conclusion and diagnose Solange's behaviour as a desperate call for attention. Whatever it was, it increased the friction and accelerated the process of alienation. Motherly daughterly love kept receding until nothing was left except the deep instinctive tie of the blood.

By contrast, Solange's relations with Casimir Dudevant had become tolerable. In spite of various lawsuits intended to secure the children's stake on Guillery, George did not try to sow hatred in their hearts for the man whose name they bore. As the years went by husband and wife came to a measure of understanding. The kidnapping of Solange was forgotten and the children were allowed to spend part of their summer holidays at Guillery; first Maurice, later Solange as well.

Casimir had become a perfect squire, looking after his estate and peasants, leading a temperate life and winning local esteem. He was still a handsome man and a good catch, and at least one determined lady lay siege to his virtue. He was much relieved when she died. In 1844 he settled down with his housekeeper, Jeanny Dalias de Xaintrailles, and would have married her had the law of the country permitted divorce. As it was he lived with her quietly and respectably, giving his name and a dowry to the daughter she bore him. On Sundays he attended Mass and his one regret was that the irregularity of his union debarred him from receiving the sacraments.

Maurice and Solange may well have been amused by their father's ostrich-like attempts to conceal his domestic situation from the Church by sending Jeanny away from the drawing-room whenever he had visitors; but they did not dislike him. When in 1841 Solange began to sign herself as Solange Sand, she was taking her cue from her mother who had recently taken to addressing her as Mlle Solange Dudevant-Sand. The letters to Maurice were also addressed by this hyphenated appellation until the Dudevant part, the children's legal surname, was left out altogether.

When George referred to Maurice, Solange and Chopin as her three children, she genuinely believed that the children of her body would accept the child of her choice as one of them. For a few years they did; then, as age opened their eyes, they began to resent the place he occupied in their mother's life. Maurice, at nineteen, was jealous and openly hostile; Solange, at fourteen, had an ascendancy over Chopin which troubled her mother. There was already much tension among the three children when George introduced a fourth one into their midst.

Her name was Augustine Brault, a pretty young relative of George's on the bird-vendor's side of the family. Augustine's mother had been a kept woman, her father was a tailor's assistant. George had met the Braults through Sophie Victoire and was charmed with their little girl's sweetness and intelligence. When in 1845 she heard that the parents intended their adolescent child to follow in her mother's footsteps, she offered to take charge of Augustine and bring her up at Nohant like her own. The Braults agreed, though not before they had made George undertake to pay them a regular allowance to make up for the loss of a child. George had hopes of adopting Augustine, but legal complications made it impossible. All the same she referred to her as her adopted daughter, or her fourth child, and set aside a handsome dowry for her.

Augustine was slim, dark-eyed and dark-haired, a striking contrast to the fair, well-built Solange. When they went for walks in the village all eyes turned to admire them. *Titine* repaid George's kindness as Solange never did. She was gentle and affectionate, took to her lessons and showed an aptitude for music. George often set her up as an example to Solange. Solange hated her.

Maurice could no more treat Augustine as a sister than Solange did, if for different reasons. At nineteen or twenty he was a young man on the loose, recovering from a romantic crush on Pauline Viardot. His attentions to the young girl became a source of fierce domestic discord. Solange, always jealous, gave herself airs and treated Augustine as a social inferior; Chopin, suspecting that Maurice was only having fun with the girl, suggested that she should be sent away for her own good; Augustine, putting her trust in Maurice, incensed him further against Chopin. Rumours began to fly around. From Paris the Braults wrote to ask George whether Maurice's intentions towards their daughter were honourable. She replied that her son was too young to marry and must be given time to consider. There followed a painful period of slander and recriminations. Father Brault circulated a pamphlet in Paris claiming that the illustrious George Sand had lured his innocent daughter to Nohant in order to procure a mistress for her son. Chopin, who believed that Maurice had seduced the girl, told him what he thought of him; Maurice denied the accusation and told Chopin he was not wanted at Nohant; servants were called to give evidence and one of them, a loyal old soul to whom George had once dedicated a book, was dismissed.

George was trying her best to protect her son, do the right thing by Augustine, restrain Solange and above all silence Chopin in order to placate Maurice. Chopin could not understand why after so many years as a confidant and adviser on family issues he was being told to mind his own business. He utterly failed to appreciate that at that stage in their relationship a mother was bound to resent any criticism of her son from a man she no longer loved as a lover. In his state of physical frustration his well-meaning arguments often degenerated into scenes of jealousy. George lost her temper with him. To Marie de Rozières, a mutual friend, she wrote:

24 July 1846

I had done well to be a little cross with him; it gave me courage one day to tell him some home truths and warn him that I might get tired of him. Since then he had been sensible, and you know how kind, sweet and wonderful he can be when he is not mad.[22]

The rest of the summer passed amicably enough, at least on the surface. Delacroix came down to stay as usual, Latouche visited, eligible bachelors courted the two young ladies of the house. One fine day Solange announced that she had got herself engaged to a gentleman farmer called Fernand de Préaulx. She was eighteen.

The young man seemed eminently suitable. He was well-born, well-to-do, handsome and much in love with Solange. Both George and Chopin were pleased with the happy choice the wayward girl had made and a measure of goodwill was restored in the family. When Chopin left Nohant in November 1846 he little thought he would never set foot in it again. The understanding was that he would come down the following summer as usual. From Paris he kept up a restrained and respectful correspondence with George in the second person plural, which she answered in the same vein. She continued to show much concern for his health which was rapidly deteriorating. Sometimes she asked him to run little errands for her, such as finding some articles of clothing left in her cupboards at square d'Orléans and sending them down to Nohant. In one of his replies he solemnly reported that he had sent down the sweets and '*coald* [*sic*] *cream*'[23] she had asked him to get for her.

In the new year George took Solange to Paris to buy her trousseau and draw up the marriage contract. In between shopping expeditions they sat for an artist called Clésinger who was sculpting their busts in marble. Chopin frowned at the thought of George and Solange spending long hours with a notorious bohemian who was known to beat his pregnant mistress. Nor did he approve of the artist's gallanteries with the two ladies and his way of bombarding them with verbosity and flowers. His fears were justified. After three or four sittings Solange announced that she was breaking her engagement with de Préaulx and marrying Clésinger instead.

Jean-Baptiste Auguste Clésinger was far from being a mother's dream of a son-in-law. He was uncouth like the cuirassier he had once been, fond of the bottle, and above all, an inveterate spendthrift. Chopin was dead set against Solange marrying a hurricane of a man instead of the nice gentlemanly de Préaulx, and George, again in accord, whisked her off back to Nohant. The cuirassier followed in hot pursuit, stormed the mother, renewed his protestations of immortal love for the daughter, and eventually succeeded in breaking George's resistance. He then dashed off all the way to Guillery to obtain Casimir Dudevant's consent to the marriage of his daughter, a formality required by law. Casimir could no more resist the attack than George. Clésinger returned triumphant and insisted on an instant wedding. George, who at the time of the engagement to de Préaulx suspected that the main motive behind it was Solange's desire to be addressed as *Madame*,

Pauline Viardot, engraving

Alexandre Damien Manceau in 1849, by Lehmann

now noted that for the first time in her life the child was really and truly love-sick.

On closer acquaintance she disapproved of her future son-in-law even more, but Solange was hell-bent on marrying her sculptor. There was even a suggestion that she might elope with him if not allowed to marry without further delay. George was galvanised into action. There was no time to recall Maurice from a touring holiday in Holland, just enough time to notify Casimir who drove non-stop from Guillery and stayed three days at Nohant as his wife's guest. The wedding was held one spring day of 1847, within weeks of Solange's breaking up with de Préaulx. There were few guests and no festivities. Instead George donated a thousand francs to the village poor. The day after the ceremony Casimir left at the crack of dawn. To a friend George wrote that his presence had added to the general gloom as he had brought with him all the old grievances and rancours. He had not provided Solange with a dowry.

After the wedding a formal notification was sent to friends and country neighbours: 'Madame Sand wishes to inform you of the marriage of her daughter Mlle Solange Sand to M. Clésinger.'[24] The wording caused stupefaction and all but revived old rumours. It was unheard of for the bride's mother to be designated by a pen-name, for the bride to be designated by a name not legally hers, and for the father, though present, not to be mentioned at all. The whole procedure suggested an attempt to play down an embarrassing occasion.

Chopin was not among those notified of the wedding. In a letter written to Grzymala shortly before it was to take place, George asked him to keep it a secret from Chopin, explaining that she could no longer put up with his presumptuous meddling in family affairs. In fact Chopin had ceased to voice objections to Solange's choice, and had even written to wish her happiness. In any case the wedding could hardly be a secret after it had been formally announced in the Forthcoming Marriages column of the Paris *La Presse*. The truth was that George was hurt. She had not expected criticism, at any stage, from a man who should have felt nothing but unquestioning gratitude for her constant maternal solicitude. To her way of thinking Chopin was just as ungrateful as Solange. He was therefore bound to be in the wrong when he objected to Clésinger, equally in the wrong when for the sake of Solange he showed him friendship at a time George had come to hate him.

What brought further tension between them was the publication of *Lucrezia Floriani*, which was clearly drawn from recent personal experience. Lucrezia of the novel was a well-to-do unmarried actress with four children. Prince Karol of the story was a sensitive moody person who condemned the actress's morals even before he met her. When they did meet her devoted maternal love for her children so moved him that he fell in love with her himself. She was as devoted to him as she was to her children, and because he was a sick man, nursed him back to health. Unfortunately Prince Karol was as difficult as he was sensitive, and tormented Lucrezia with his insane jealousy. In the end she died of sorrow and disenchantment.

The novel appeared in instalments in *Le Courrier français* in the summer of 1846, then in book form the following year. Artistic Paris immediately identified Lucrezia with George and Chopin with Prince Karol. The later instalments were awaited with mounting suspense and Franz Liszt, still corresponding with Marie d'Agoult, complained that he was not able to get hold of a copy. When, at the end of the story, Lucrezia died, friends concluded it was George's way of telling Chopin to get out of her life. They waited avidly for his reaction. They were disappointed when after a social gathering at a Paris drawing-room, where the book had been read out aloud as part of the evening's entertainment, he had nothing but praise for it. The more they sounded him, the more he praised it. To his sister Louise in Warsaw he mentioned the novel in general terms and blandly added that although George had written some ninety novels up to date, her eyesight remained unimpaired.

Paris friends concluded that Chopin was either obtuse, or too proud to show the hurt. George tried to avoid an open discussion. She spoke to him deprecatingly of the new novel and suggested that it was not worth his while reading it. To others she vehemently denied any similarity between Chopin and Prince Karol. Chopin too preferred to avoid an open discussion. He shut his eyes to the cooling off of the past two years and when his family wrote from Warsaw to ask what he was going to do with himself during the summer of 1847, he replied: 'What I always do, of course. I shall go down to Nohant as soon as it gets warm.'[25]

In July 1847, some two months after the hurried wedding, the Clésingers came down to Nohant to spend the rest of the summer. Solange was pregnant, her husband boisterous. George was horrified to learn that between them they had already gone through a large portion of the money she had settled on them, including the revenues from the Paris investment house she had wrested from Casimir several years earlier. Married life had not made Solange put aside any of her old grievances. She quarrelled with Maurice and brewed mischief against Augustine who was being seriously courted by the artist Théodore Rousseau. She revived the old story about Augustine's seduction by Maurice with the result that Rousseau jilted her, Maurice was mad and Augustine, cheated for the second time of a chance to marry, was bitter against the whole family. George rebuked Solange. To get her own back the daughter dropped some hints about her mother's relationship with the young political journalist Victor Borie who had stayed at Nohant the previous winter. Again Nohant became the scene of vicious quarrels. Clésinger took his wife's side because he had come to hate George for her constant reproaches about his careless way with Solange's money. Words led to violence. Clésinger struck his mother-in-law, Maurice aimed his gun at him, George screamed at Solange and her husband to leave Nohant and never darken its doors again. After they had left she poured out her heart not to Chopin, who might have allowed himself a mild I-told-you-so, but to Marie de Rozières, the family friend who had once been Solange's piano mistress:

What I have suffered at Solange's hands ever since her marriage is impossible to describe. Only you can appreciate my patience, compassion and concealed hurt, because only you know how much she has made me suffer ever since she was born. This cold, ungrateful and bitter child has played the comedy very well until the day of her marriage, and her husband even better. Hardly in possession of money and independence they threw off the mask and thought to dominate me, ruin me and torment me to their heart's content. My resistance exasperated them and during their fifteen days' stay they behaved with unprecedented insolence. You will not believe what frightful scenes have taken place here. In the end I was forced not just to send them away but literally throw them out. Such scenes are impossible to describe, I shall sum them up in a few words. We have nearly cut one another's throats. My son-in-law rushed at Maurice with a hammer and may well have killed him had I not thrown myself between them and struck his face, at which he hit me in the chest. But for a man-servant, the parish priest and some other friends who happened to be present, Maurice would have shot Clésinger dead with his pistol. They threw themselves into the affray and forced everybody apart.

Solange had been fanning the fire with her ferocious hate. She had incited these deplorable outbursts with her vicious gossip, her lies, her unbelievably wicked maligning, without the slightest provocation or wrong-doing on Maurice's part or anybody else's. That fiendish couple left last night, head over heels in debt, jubilant in their insolence, leaving behind a scandal they will never be able to live down. For three days I had been living in my own house in fear of murder. I never want to see them again, they will never soil this place again with their feet. They have gone too far. Oh God, I have done nothing to deserve such a daughter.[26]

Clésinger was not the man to take an insult lying down. On his return to Paris he drank his way through the rest of Solange's dowry and spread malicious gossip about her mother. The writer Arsène Houssaye noted in his diary:

Clésinger is having rows with his mother-in-law who is

threatening him with the thunder of her pen. 'I shall not mention him by name,' she warns, 'but everybody will recognise him.' 'And I,' says Clésinger, 'shall sculpt her naked with her face masked and no fig-leaf, and everybody will recognise her.'[27]

Solange hit even harder. She went straight to Chopin, gave him her own version of the frightful scene at Nohant and touched him on the raw when she hinted that her mother had been having fun with another man. He cancelled his intended visit and stopped answering George's letters. She sent a barrage of anxious enquiries about his health. He took them for hypocrisy and continued to regard Solange as the wronged daughter. When he did eventually write, it was only to tell George that Solange was ill and in urgent need of maternal care. He stressed his impartial affection for both Maurice and Solange but added that in the present circumstances he could not withhold his sympathy from an ailing girl who was expecting her first baby.

George smarted under the reproof which came from the very man whose life she had so many times saved with the same maternal care he was accusing her of denying to her own daughter. She wrote that no friendship was possible between them after he had chosen to side with the perfidious Solange, and concluded:

Do look after her since you feel you have an obligation towards her. I shall not hold it against you, but you will understand I cannot detract from the role of an outraged mother, and that from now on nothing will make me deviate from its authority and dignity. No more shall I be a dupe and a victim. I forgive you and will never again reproach you as your attitude is sincere. It somewhat astonishes me, but if you feel freer and more at ease like that, I shall not grieve over that extraordinary *volte-face* of yours.

Farewell, my friend. I hope you will recover soon from all your ailments, I have reason to hope so; and I shall thank God for this bizarre conclusion of nine years of exclusive friendship. Let me hear from you from time to time.

There is no point in going over the rest.[28]

She never wrote to him again, nor he to her. Each waited for the other to make the next move. Chopin mentioned to Solange that he had had no news from her mother for a long time; George complained to Mme Marliani that Chopin had not written for three whole months. Nothing happened. They began to air their grievances against each other to mutual friends.

George continued to live at Nohant, having given up the lease of her apartment at square d'Orléans. When she had occasion to go up to Paris she put up at Maurice's, who had taken a bachelor apartment of his own. The only one who had no home of her own was Solange, since Clésinger had spent her entire dowry and was chased by creditors. Instead, she went to stay with her father at Guillery. In view of her pregnancy a perfunctory correspondence was resumed between mother and daughter, but it was to Chopin that Solange wrote first to announce the birth of her baby daughter towards the end of February 1848. In his reply he described how he broke the good news to George at a purely accidental meeting:

Paris, 5 March 1848

Yesterday I called on Mme Marliani and when I was about to leave I found myself in the entrance hall face to face with *Madame votre mère* who had just come in with Lambert. I said good morning to *Madame votre mère* and asked if she had had any recent news from you.

'I heard about a week ago,' she said.

'You have not heard anything yesterday, or the day before?'

'No.'

'Then I can tell you that you are a grandmother. Solange has a baby daughter and I am happy to be the first to give you this good news.'

I then bowed and walked downstairs. The Abyssinian [a nickname given to the explorer and diplomat Edmond Combes] walked down with me, but as I had forgotten to mention that you were well, a detail of particular importance to a mother (now you will be able to appreciate this, Mother Solange), I asked him to go up again as I did not have the strength to climb those stairs again, and tell her that both you and the child were doing well.

I waited for the Abyssinian to rejoin me when *Madame votre mère* came down with him and asked many questions about your health. I told her that you were fit enough to have written to me in pencil two days after the baby's birth, that it had been a difficult delivery but that the sight of your little daughter made you forget all the pain. She asked whether your husband was with you and I said that the envelope seemed to have been addressed in his hand.

She asked me how I was and I said I was well, then told the porter to open the door for me. I bowed and the next thing I knew I was at square d'Orléans, having walked all the way with the Abyssinian at my side.[29]

It was their last meeting.

Solange's baby lived only a week. Casimir did all he could to comfort his bereaved daughter but, as she wrote to her old *pension* mistress, 'he is not the one who has brought me up'.[30] She asked Chopin to convey to her mother how much she needed her. 'What I am asking you is probably useless,' she added bitterly. 'She will not budge. Had she cared for me she would have been with me already. How can she be so unloving? I, who have lost a daughter, although only a few days old, cannot understand her. It is terrible and cruel to be a mother no longer. She does not know what it means. May God spare her that knowledge in the near future.'[31]

Chopin was in no position to tell the genuine grief from the self-pity in Solange's letter, let alone convey anything to George. Shortly after their last encounter he left for a tour of England and stayed there for seven months. Pauline Viardot was also touring England at the same time. George wrote to ask her whether she had seen Chopin in London and added: 'I still love him like a son although he has been ungrateful to his mother. I must get resigned to not being happy with some of my children. Only Maurice, you and Augustine are left me.'[32] She persisted in representing her entire relationship with Chopin as a maternal attachment, partly to gratify Maurice who could not tolerate a lover in his mother's recent past, and partly to suppress a feeling of guilt. A mother's displeasure was more dignified than a mistress's cooling off.

In May 1849 Solange gave birth to another daughter at Guillery and for once was not disgruntled. She even overlooked the threat to her patrimony through the presence in her father's house of another baby girl, her own half-sister, whom Jeanny had presented to Casimir the year before. She returned to Paris in the autumn to find Chopin dying. She and Clésinger visited him faithfully and were among the last to see him on his deathbed.

George, informed at Nohant of Chopin's rapid decline, remained immovable. Even in the face of imminent death neither was able to make a gesture of reconciliation. Some friends were too prejudiced to allow it; others, who would have wished it, were unable to break the barrier of mutual bitterness. Chopin died on 17 October 1849 surrounded by grief-stricken friends and relatives. The news reached George at Nohant.

She did not attend the grand funeral service in which Mozart's *Requiem* was sung with Pauline Viardot as one of the soloists, nor the commemoration service a year later, when a sculpture by Clésinger was unveiled in Chopin's honour. She buried the hurt and the grievance. In her autobiography, which she was already working on at the time of Chopin's death, she referred to him as a musical genius whom she had loved and nursed like a mother. Many years later when her intimate letters to him were returned to her by an extraordinary chain of coincidences, she destroyed them. Little remained to suggest the love that she had once borne him as a woman, apart from scant references in early letters to friends, and an impetuous sentence in a brief note written to him in 1845:

Aime-moi, cher ange, mon cher bonheur, je t'aime.[33]

With which she enclosed a lock of her hair.

Chapter 15

❧❧❧❧❧

The dream of the spirit

The winter of 1847–48 found the Nohant household dispersed. Solange was at Guillery expecting the birth of her first baby; Chopin was ill and estranged in Paris; and Maurice, a young artist of twenty-four, was making his début in the capital. At Nohant George was working hard on her autobiography, *Histoire de ma vie*, and was looking for documentary data relative to her father's early life. Nothing was further from her mind than a revolution.

Maurice, a socialist republican like his mother, kept her posted. The relative freedom of speech allowed by the Citizen King and his minister Guizot had found a fresh outlet. Legitimists, radicals and republicans were arranging banquets where for the price of six francs, the equivalent of two days' wage for the average worker, anybody could eat, drink and make rousing speeches against the regime. When Maurice wrote that the banquets were causing political unrest, his mother dismissed them as unimportant manifestations engineered by power-thirsty government ministers.

But the unrest in Paris was growing. When the speeches at the banquets became too provocative Louise Philippe, on Guizot's advice, attempted to forbid them. The attempt backfired. On 24 February 1848 angry Parisians marched through the streets demanding Guizot's dismissal. Louis Philippe yielded to pressure. The masses continued to march. Louis Philippe sent out the National Guard. The National Guard joined forces with the marchers. Other troops were called out, a stray shot led to open defiance, barricades were put up, more shots were fired, forty people were killed. The maddened crowds began to march on the royal palace. Louis Philippe, King of the French by the Will of the People, realised that the people no longer wanted him. He abdicated and together with his queen left for England, crossing the Channel under the assumed name of Mr and Mrs Smith. The Second Republic was born.

As soon as she heard the news George dropped *Histoire de ma vie* and rushed off to Paris to see for herself how the French people, 'the most wonderful people in the universe',[1] were fulfilling the promise of the revolution. She was intoxicated with what she saw. The events of 24 February were for her the realisation of all that was good and noble in the spirit of France. Her own Maurice had been behind the barricades and fought for freedom. She was in an exalted mood when that same week she accidentally ran into Chopin at Mme Marliani's and learnt from him about the birth of Solange's baby. In the circumstances her private sorrows seemed trivial before the greatness of the moment. To Poncy, one of the proletarian poets whose work she had been sponsoring, she wrote with ecstasy:

Paris, 8 March 1848

Long live the republic! What a dream, what enthusiasm, what perfect conduct, what perfect order! I have just arrived in Paris, I rushed here, I saw the last of the barricades open up under my feet. I saw a great people, sublime, naïve, generous, the French people in the heart of France, in the heart of the world, the most wonderful people in the universe. I spent nights without going to bed, days without sitting down. We are mad, intoxicated. One night we went to sleep in a mire, next morning we woke up in heaven. ... The republic has been won, its future is assured, we would rather die than give it up.[2]

The most natural thing for her to do was to offer her services as a writer to the glorious republic. Several members of the provisional government were old friends. One was Emmanuel Arago, Solange's minder during the early days of the garret and in recent years a frequent visitor to Nohant; another was Louis

Blanc whom George had once considered as a possible match for Solange; yet another was Ledru Rollin, met through Michel de Bourges during the April Trial. Lamartine, who headed the provisional government, was a fellow writer. When George went to see them they welcomed her with open arms and offered her a post at the Ministry of Information. She was to write and edit a political column in *La République*, the newly founded government organ which was to be posted for the benefit of the people on every public wall in Paris and the provinces. She asked for nothing better. She was to do in the name of the republic what she had set out to do years earlier in her own *Revue Indépendante* and *L'Eclaireur de l'Indre*. She was to write for the people about the people. She was to guide the people of France towards true socialism.

She attacked her assignment with her usual energy. She contributed to *La République*, founded the short-lived *Cause du Peuple*, produced a ceaseless flow of ideological articles about equality, the noble spirit of the people, political emancipation, and the need to vote for the true socialists in the forthcoming elections promised by the provisional government.

But many people looked askance at her brand of socialism. In her ardour for the right word, George sometimes used the word *communisme* which had been coined a few years earlier and which for her meant a system of utopian sharing. In her own Berry simple people who read her articles posted on the walls of their local town halls concluded that Baroness Dudevant was proposing to deprive them of their land and share it out to beggars who had never done an honest day's work. Once, during her absence, a threatening crowd marched on Nohant and shouted 'Down with Mme Dudevant, down with Maurice Dudevant, down with the communists'.[3] In her next article George explained that communism was 'a desire to see the disappearance of extreme wealth and extreme poverty through all the legitimate means accepted by public conscience in order to pave the way for real equality'.[4] She hastened to add that in practical terms it was not an immediate prospect. She realised however that writing articles was not enough. She conceived the idea of sending Paris-trained agents to the provinces to spread the right social doctrine among the country people. To provincial mayors she issued directives in the name of the government.

Unpaid, she worked without respite, pressed her advice on members of the cabinet, organised meetings in lowly Paris tenement houses, found time to do a hundred and one things. No task was too hard for her, no detail too small. She went to the theatre to hear Rachel sing the *Marseillaise* to enthusiastic audiences and arranged for Pauline Viardot to be commissioned a version of her own. She wrote a short play called *Le Roi attend* and coached Rachel in the lead for a free performance given by the Théâtre Français, renamed Théâtre de la République. She travelled backwards and forwards, revitalised Berry socialists, used her influence to obtain promotion for staunch supporters, arranged for Maurice to become mayor of Nohant. For once she got her own back on Michel de Bourges by hinting in the right quarters that his socialism was of the wrong kind and thus temporarily chequered his ascent to power.

In the midst of her hectic political duties she clinched a marriage between her 'daughter' Augustine and a much older Polish émigré called Charles de Bertholdi. Gossipmongers whispered that the generous dowry was proof, if proof were needed, that the bride had been deflowered. Maurice, in his capacity of mayor, performed the wedding ceremony.

The February Revolution of 1848 gave a tremendous fillip to the feminist movement in France.

As early as 1833 Sainte-Beuve called attention to the growing number of women who were protesting publicly about their status in all walks of life. 'Many women have begun to speak their mind and are now writing articles for the press, short stories and novels,' he wrote. 'They are revealing their suffering, claiming a more equal part in life, appealing against society.'[5]

Even before 1848 many more women took up the call and wielded pen and position to demand equal rights before the law. In Paris women like Flora Tristan, Désirée Gay, Jeanne Deroin and Eugénie Nyobet published books and articles representing the plight of women in a man-made society; in the provinces the torch was carried by Pauline Roland, a disciple of Leroux.

Within days of the February Revolution Eugénie Nyobet started a newspaper called *La Voix des femmes* which became the hothouse of the feminist movement. Old battle-axes were joined by new ones like Suzanne Voilquin, Elise Lemonnier, Adèle Esquiros and Gabrielle Soumet who sometimes signed her articles as G.S. They campaigned on every conceivable front. They infiltrated into the National Workshops set up by the government to ensure full employment and participated in their running. They organised petitions demanding the right to vote like men and collected signatures all over the country. They founded women's clubs and tried to win supporters for their cause among men of influence. The universal suffrage introduced by the provisional government preparatory to general elections gave them fresh scope. They badgered fellow socialists and republicans to recognise their right to be elected to the National Assembly even before they were given the right to vote. Jeanne Deroin offered herself as a test-case candidate and was adopted by hopeful supporters. Sixteen lists sent to the central selection committee of the Left bore her name.

But one woman nominee was not enough and in any case Jeanne Deroin's name was not widely known outside feminist circles. The cause needed someone known all over France. The obvious choice was George Sand whose name was a household word and who since the Revolution had been working closely with members of the provisional government. *La Voix des femmes* regarded her as the most eloquent and consistent champion of women's rights. 'George Sand's word is sacred law to us,'[6] an editorial declared. At a meeting held on 6 April at a women's club, Mme Eugénie Nyobet proposed George Sand as a candidate for the Assembly in the following short speech:

The candidate to whom we give our support is a *he* and a *she* at one and the same time; a man for her vigour, a woman by divine will and poetical nature. We propose George Sand as our nominee. The first woman to be proposed to the Assembly will be accepted by men. Sand is different from them and her genius is not like theirs; but perhaps, because they are men of vision, they will do her the honour of calling it masculine. She has made herself a man by her spirit, yet remained a woman through maternal love. Sand is powerful, yet undaunting. Let all women give her their pledge so that all people may vote for her.[7]

So sure were Eugénie Nyobet and her colleagues of George Sand's cooperation that they had not informed her in advance of the proposed nomination. Then the inconceivable happened. George Sand, the woman who had done more than any of her contemporaries to call attention to women's inequality, publicly dissociated herself from the cause of political emancipation. Two days after the nomination two Paris newspapers carried her reply in the form of a Letter to the Editor:

A newspaper edited by ladies has announced my candidature to the National Assembly. Had it been but a silly joke at my expense, crediting me with a ridiculous presumption, I would have borne it in silence as would anyone who knows that sometimes it is quite impossible to escape practical jokes. But I am afraid that my silence may give the impression that I support the principles which the above-mentioned newspaper claims to uphold. I would be grateful if you would kindly publish the following statement:

1. I hope that no voter will take it into his head to waste his vote by writing my name on his ballot paper.

2. I do not have the honour of being acquainted with one single lady among those who form clubs and edit newspapers.

I apologise to those ladies who have shown such goodwill towards me for taking such precautions against them . . . but I cannot allow my name to be used as a symbol for a feminine movement with which I have never had any relations, cordial or otherwise.[8]

It was too late. Her name was magic. It was adopted by no less than forty lists sent to the central selection committee for approval. The committee members were keen socialists who were prepared to give their serious consideration to the unprecedented nomination of a woman to the National Assembly candidates' list. George had to make her stand clear beyond doubt. In a long letter she outlined her thinking on woman's place in parliamentary life:

Should women take part in politics? One day, yes. But is that day near? No, I do not think so. Before woman's social status can be altered the whole structure of society must be radically transformed.

Some women have put the following question: In order to transform society, should women not begin as from today to take an active part in the political life of the country? I take the liberty to say that they should not, because the structure of our society will prevent them from carrying out their political mandate with honour.

Since marriage makes a woman entirely dependent on her husband, it is absolutely impossible for her to give political guarantees of her own, unless she chooses to break away, individually, from that state of dependence into which our society has plunged her.

I ask forgiveness of those of my sex who believe it their duty to proceed in a political direction. . . . How do those ladies propose to set about women's emancipation? Do they propose to destroy marriage and uphold promiscuity? If that is what they want, good luck to them. That is precisely what they will achieve through their quest of political life. As far as I am concerned, I wish to state that I categorically dissociate myself from their cause which, on this particular plain, is totally alien to me. . . .

What we need is civil equality, equality within the marriage, equality within the family. That is what women can and should demand. But as for those women who presume to start by the exercise of political rights, allow me to tell you again that this is infantile on your part. Your house is on fire, your home is in peril, and you are pleased to make yourselves the laughing-stock of the country.[9]

The letter was left unfinished but the point was taken. For women to aspire to parliamentary participation was like putting the cart before the horse. Never again was George Sand asked to lend her name to any of the feminist groups which continued to pursue the cause of political emancipation for the women of France.

From her office at the Ministry of Information George continued to pour out propaganda material calling on the electorate to vote for the more uncompromising socialist element within the republic. It was becoming apparent that the people, having achieved a republic and the right to vote, were prepared to leave the leadership in the hands of the moderates headed by Lamartine. They needed to be prodded into greater awareness of socialism. An innocent plot was hatched. George was to write an article calling on the people to give their pledge to the socialist leaders, while the socialist leaders, headed by Ledru Rollin, were to organise a *coup* against the bourgeois-dominated government.

George rose to the occasion. In her sixteenth *Lettre au Peuple* which was posted on town-hall walls on 15 April, she appealed to the electorate to use force in case the forthcoming elections should fail to return the socialists to power. 'If the elections fail to bring victory to the social truth,' she warned, 'if they give power to a group divorced from the trust and loyalty of the people, it would be disastrous for the country. In that case there will be only one course open to the people who have already shown that they can put up barricades: show it again, make nul and void the decision of a false national representation. If the National Assembly threatens to destroy the Republic, the Republic should have the right to defend itself against the National Assembly.'[10]

The day after the article was published, a socialist-inspired demonstration took place in Paris. Later George explained to Maurice that it was not a question of one plot but four, each pulling in a slightly different direction. Hundreds of thousands of Parisians marched through the streets calling for the overthrow of the bourgeois republicans who had failed to give employment to the hungry proletariat. The government had no option but to call out the National Guard, as Louis Philippe had done less than two months earlier. This time the National Guard obeyed orders; the demonstrators were ruthlessly dispersed, the spirit of rebellion was crushed beyond resistance. At the end of that long day George knew that her dream of a socialist republic, the only one she considered worthy of the name, had vanished. To Maurice she wrote in the small hours of the night: 'I have an idea that the principle of the republic has been killed, it has no future, at least not a foreseeable future. Today the Republic was soiled by the cries of the dying.'[11]

A week later the general elections were held. The results confirmed George's worst fears. The majority of the electorate turned a deaf ear to the call of socialism and returned to power the bourgeois republicans headed by Lamartine. Ledru Rollin, one of the socialists who did get elected to the new Assembly, began to tread more warily. George was in a state of uncertainty. She still had the *entrée* of the Ministry of Information, but was no longer trusted with official propaganda. Too many people accused her of having fanned the pre-election riots in her last *Lettre au Peuple*. All she could do was to deny any complicity and maintain that her article was no more than a general exhortation to the people of France to defend the principles of republicanism.

The new Assembly did not come up to the expectations of the electorate. Far from finding a solution to unemployment, it was considering the closure of the National Workshops which had been set up to provide work for the unemployed and which had become centres of subversion. In an explosive situation any excuse was enough to spark off a riot. It was provided by Lamartine's decision not to commit France to sending military aid to the revolutionaries in Poland. On 15 May the Parisians marched against the National Assembly they had elected only three weeks earlier. Led by veteran socialists like Barbès, Blanqui, Raspail and many others, they surrounded the Palais Bourbon, declared the

Assembly nul and void, and proclaimed a socialist government. This time George was only a spectator. Engulfed by the crowds, pushed and carried along, she found herself in front of a building where, from a ground-floor window, a woman was urging the demonstrators to storm the Assembly. When George asked a demonstrator who the woman was he answered that it was George Sand.

The May *journée* was no more successful than the April one. Again the National Guard was called to the rescue, again the socialist coup was averted. Some of the ringleaders were arrested, among them Barbès with whom George had been maintaining a close correspondence during the past few months. Friends warned her that she too might be arrested and advised her immediate departure from Paris. She refused to run away. She stayed on for three days, waiting for the banging on the door and burning her diaries and political documents. When no one came for her she left for Nohant. Her homecoming was far from welcoming. When her carriage was within half an hour's distance from Nohant the local people recognised her and shouted after her in their thick country accent: '*A bas les communisques*'.[12]

She sought solace in *Histoire de ma vie*, which was to occupy her for the next seven years. One day her old friend Rollinat came to stay and in the course of a long stroll in the grounds persuaded her to give up novels with a socialist message and return to rustic love stories like *La Mare au Diable* and *François le Champi* which were winning back those readers who had shunned her after the publication of *Le Compagnon du Tour de France* and *Horace*. George took Rollinat's advice and with her usual imagination and speed produced *La Petite Fadette*, another rustic romance based on her intimate knowledge of Berry customs and folklore. The public loved Sand's return to the genre of the *roman champêtre*, with its idyllic blend of virtuous peasants and high-minded aristocrats. Marie Dorval read the book virtually on her deathbed. Neither she, nor any of the other readers, commented on the fact that the book was dedicated to the arch-socialist Armand Barbès, one of 'our prisoner friends', with whom one was no longer allowed 'to talk politics'.[13]

While working on *Histoire de ma vie* and *La Petite Fadette* George was watching woefully for the political developments in Paris. A new name was being mentioned more and more often as the only hope of a frustrated and cheated people. It was Louis Napoleon Bonaparte.

She had made Louis Napoleon's acquaintance in a Paris drawing-room some time in 1838 and felt a certain affinity with the young prince, four years her junior, who combined a strong dislike for Louis Philippe with a modicum of liberalism. He had already made one unsuccessful attempt to proclaim himself Emperor of the French like his illustrious uncle; when he made another in 1840, Louis Philippe had him arrested and condemned to life imprisonment. While in prison he produced a brochure on pauperism which attracted attention in socialist circles. Louis Blanc went to see him and wrote an article about him which George published in *L'Eclaireur de l'Indre*, where her recommendation was law. Louis Napoleon wrote to thank her and asked whether she too would honour him with a visit. She declined the invitation but sent a friendly reply. Louis Napoleon thanked her for her reply.

He had served six years of his life sentence when the prison authorities started some alterations in the old fortress. One day Louis Napoleon heaved a plank of wood on to his shoulder like a mason's mate and boldly walked out. He made straight for England.

After Louis Philippe's abdication he returned to Paris and in due course had himself elected to the National Assembly. The magic of his name together with his adroit manoeuvring made him a Deputy to be reckoned with. When in December 1848 elections were held for the presidency of the Assembly, Louis Napoleon was elected by five million votes against one and a half million for the runner-up. George was momentarily nonplussed, then accepted the result philosophically. To her publisher Jules Hetzel she wrote: 'I have regained my calm. I cannot tell you how, because I do not know myself. It just happened when I saw the vast majority of the people vote for Louis Bonaparte. I am resigned to the will of the people who seem to say: "We do not wish to go faster than that and we shall take the road which pleases us best." I have therefore picked up my work like a good workman who returns to his task and am making good progress with my memoirs.'14

Before the year was out her thoughts turned to a private sorrow. At the end of December her brother died of alcoholism, without having made up a quarrel which had kept them apart for some time. For years Hippolyte Chatiron had been a regular visitor to Nohant, where George made futile attempts to slow down the process of his disintegration by diluting his wine with water. For years she had put up with his noisiness, his boorish manners and the smell of the stables which heralded his approach. Underneath the coarse exterior she always sensed a genuine affection for herself and her family. Unpredictably, Hippolyte took Solange's side over the quarrel with her mother in the summer of 1847 and left in a huff. He never set foot again at Nohant after that date, never wrote, never made any sign of contrition. His death, without a last message of reconciliation, left a hurt.

Other deaths followed. In May 1849 Dorval died in Paris, to be followed in October of that year by Chopin. In August 1850 Mme Marliani died and less than three weeks later Honoré de Balzac. At the beginning of 1851 Latouche died. George buried her grief and worked on. She no longer kept an apartment in Paris. When she went up on business she stayed with friends or put up in simple lodgings. She made a habit of taking her meals, and sometimes even entertaining, at Père Pinson's, the restaurateur who in her young and carefree days never knew whether to address her as Madame or Monsieur.

Her fecundity was such that she could easily diffuse her talent in several directions without feeling the strain. Now she branched out into play writing. Unlike *Cosima*, her new plays were pleasingly romantic, in the same genre as her rustic novels. There was no difficulty in finding theatre managers who would be willing to put them on. Towards the end of 1851 George went up to Paris to attend the first night of her latest play, *Le Mariage de Victorine*. She found that even in theatrical circles the dominant topic of conversation was an imminent *coup d'état*. People were openly weighing Louis Napoleon's chances of giving the moribund republic the *coup de grâce* and proclaiming himself emperor. Most agreed that his chances were good; the bourgeois were monarchists at heart, while the proletarians were not likely to defend a National Assembly which had given orders to shoot at their comrades. 'If the President does not organise a *coup d'état* pretty soon,' Emmanuel Arago said to George during lunch on 1 December, 'he does not know his business, for at the moment nothing should be easier.'[15]

Le Mariage de Victorine opened a week earlier and had excellent reviews. On the night of 1 December George was taken to see a new farce which she found unremittingly dull. Her escorts at the theatre were Solange, with whom she had made up after the birth of a second baby, and the young engraver Manceau, who had become George's *cavalier servant*. After the show the three of them walked back by the Elysée Palace. 'Odd,' said Solange. 'The President is not entertaining tonight after all. I thought there was to be a grand ball. When I drove by earlier this evening I saw the carpet being laid down on the steps of the palace. Is it not tomorrow he is going to be proclaimed emperor?' Having seen Solange home, George and Manceau passed again by the Elysée Palace. It was one o'clock in the morning. The palace was plunged in darkness and only one guard was on duty outside the gate. 'It won't be tomorrow after all,'[16] said George with a chuckle and returned to her lodgings. Later she recorded that conversation in her diary.

At ten o'clock the following morning, 2 December 1851, Manceau woke her up with the news that during the small hours of the night posters had been put up all over Paris proclaiming the dissolution of the National Assembly by Louis Napoleon. George was unmoved. The republic which was about to die was not hers; her own dream republic had died in April 1848. In the evening she went to see how *Le Mariage de Victorine* was faring and was somewhat surprised to see it performed to a virtually empty house. She had seen no evidence of disturbance in the streets.

It was the calm before the storm. The following day there were clashes between republicans and the troops, shots were fired, cannons were used, people lay dying on the pavements. Friends urged George to leave Paris while the going was good; she was too outspoken a republican to be spared at a time when to be a republican was to be a traitor to Louis Napoleon. She packed hurriedly, sent for Solange and the two-year-old Nini, and together with Manceau caught the train back to Châteauroux. Before leaving Paris she jotted down in her diary:

4 December 1851

Oh if I were a man I would not leave. But we must save the children, this is a woman's first duty, a mother's first urge. And in any case what use would I be here? I can do nothing except get myself killed. My hour has not come yet, the hour of the people has not come yet either. But it will. Patience. Farewell, poor Paris where I was born, the head and heart of France, of Europe, of the entire world. One man's ambition has condemned you to the fire and the sword.[17]

At Nohant they found Maurice safe and sound, but many of their friends were in danger. Anybody whose political opinions could be described as subversive was hunted down. Pierre Leroux, Ledru Rollin, Victor Borie and Jules Hetzel left France in a hurry, others were too late. A massive wave of arrests swept across the country. In Berry alone there were dozens of arrests among people whom George had known all her life. The sentences were severe, ranging from long prison terms to deportation to Algeria and Cayenne. George herself was warned that she might be arrested. Even so she refused to believe that Louis Napoleon was a wicked tyrant. She remembered his preoccupation with social iniquity and clung to the hope that the severe sentences meted out in his name were perpetrated without his specific knowledge. She came to the conclusion that the only way to obtain a reprieve was by direct appeal. Her hour had come.

Disregarding personal danger, she wrote to Louis Napoleon and asked for audience. It was barely six weeks after the coup.

While waiting at Nohant for his reply, she composed another
letter, about two thousand words long, in which she begged him
to pardon the condemned. She was careful not to introduce any
ideological argument. Her opinions, she wrote, were her own
'dream of the spirit', not worthy of discussion. 'I have always
regarded you as a socialist at heart,' she boldly stated, then swept
politics aside and used a strong emotional approach. A few sentences may illustrate the general tone of her letter:

> Prince, my family is scattered and flung to the four corners of
> the earth. Friends of my childhood and my old age, brothers
> and adopted children, are in dungeons or in exile. Your wrath
> has descended on all those who take, accept or even tolerate
> the title of socialist republican. . . . I would not presume to
> discuss politics with you, it would be laughable of me to do so;
> but from the depth of my ignorance and fallibility I beg of you
> with tears in my eyes and with blood streaming from my heart:
> Stay your hand, conqueror! Spare the strong as well as the weak,
> have mercy for the women who weep as well as for the men
> who do not. Be merciful and humane. . . . Amnesty, amnesty,
> and soon, my prince.
>
> Nohant, 20 January 1852[18]

Louis Napoleon wrote back in his own hand to say that he
would be honoured to receive Mme Sand at the Elysée Palace any
day of the week after three in the afternoon. She was issued with
a police pass and went straight to Paris. When she was announced
the President of the Republic came towards her, took her hands
in his and promised to do all he could to release the friends she had
been pleading for. Her intercession seemed to have achieved the
impossible.

Then the hitches began. Louis Napoleon passed his instructions to the ministers and heads of the relevant departments. The
lines of communications were imperfect. George submitted lists
of names; chiefs of police were slow to look at them. The deportation date was drawing near. George wrote again to Louis
Napoleon and begged him to issue fresh instructions to the chiefs

concerned. There began a hectic period of pleading, flattering, cajoling, arguing, always with the risk of overstepping her favour with Louis Napoleon or antagonising a petty official jealous of his authority. For months George kept knocking at influential doors, buttonholing ministers, canvassing at the Palace. She recruited young Prince Jerome, Louis Napoleon's nephew, and when she no longer dared importune the President, she appealed to the young prince instead.

Her efforts bore results. Sick prisoners were released; four young soldiers sentenced to death were reprieved; some well-known socialists had their deportation sentences commuted to exile into a country of their own choice. Some of George's protégés felt she could have done more for them, others viewed with suspicion her comings and goings inside the presidential palace and accused her of being a turncoat. But most of those she tried to help knew that they owed her their lives and what liberty they were allowed. She never lost sight of her protégés. She collected money for prisoners' families and sent letters of encouragement and books to the exiled. She never gave up. Grateful families spoke of her as the Saint of Berry or Our Lady of Good Help. An exiled socialist called her 'Dear lady and excellent protectress of political martyrs', and her old Berry friend Gabriel Planet wrote to her:

Your devotion to friends and unfortunate fellow creatures knows no bounds. Let others admire your genius; as for me, I kneel down before your great heart.[19]

In November 1852 Louis Napoleon held a referendum which was to decide whether France was to remain a republic or be reconverted into an empire. Seven millions voted for the restoration of the Bonaparte dynasty, a quarter of a million voted against, and two millions abstained. The Second Empire came into being and Louis Napoleon became Napoleon III.

George was not surprised at the demise of the Second Republic. 'Alas, France is not republican,' she wrote to her publisher even before the referendum was held. 'She never has been and never will be as long as the two classes which constitute the French people, the proletariat and the bourgeoisie, will persist in believing that their interests are not the same.'[20] Her dream republic, the leveller of social inequalities, receded further into the horizon.

Eighteen years passed. In September 1870 France suffered her disastrous defeat at Sedan and Napoleon III surrendered to the Prussians. In Paris the young Léon Gambetta told the Assembly on 4 September that the Empire had ceased to exist and proclaimed France a republic.

An elderly George Sand, smitten like the rest of France by the Prussian victory, saluted the Third Republic as the fulfilment of a dream that would never again be shattered. Two days after the proclamation she published an article which bore her valediction:

6 September 1870

The republic is viable, since it was reborn from its ashes by the unanimous voice of the people, by a noble wish, without bloodshed or civil war.

This is the third awakening; it may even be regarded as the fourth, for 1830 was also republican at the beginning. This latest noble conquest has been achieved without a struggle; the republic was won by a single word: Long Live France.

I salute thee, O republic. You are in good hands, and a great people will march under your banner after a bloody expiation. The task is hard, but even if you succumb you will always be reborn. The right of man is imperishable.[21]

❦❦❦❦❦

Chapter 16

The playwright

In November 1849 the Paris Odéon gave the first performance of George Sand's own dramatisation of her recently published novel *François le Champi*. The author, possibly remembering the traumatic experience of the opening night of *Cosima* nine years earlier, stayed on at Nohant. She came up only when a spate of favourable reviews had made it clear that the play was a success.

George later claimed that but for the fortunate insistence of her old friend the actor Bocage, by then the manager of the Odéon, she would have never thought of turning *François le Champi* into a play. In fact she did not need much persuasion to return to a form of art which had always attracted her. Long before Bocage approached her she wrote to the English actor Macready whose acquaintance she had made during his 1845 Shakespeare season in Paris: 'Written works are so cold and slow. The world should be governed by the art of the spoken word.'[1]

Her flirtation with the spoken word began during her convent days, when she re-wrote from memory a play by Molière and produced it for the nuns. Her *Lettres d'un voyageur* were often livened up by dialogue, while *Les Sept Cordes de la Lyre*, which had so upset Buloz, was largely written in dialogue form. The failure of *Cosima* halted her dramatic activity, but did not put a stop to it. During her brief term at the Ministry of Information she wrote *Le Roi attend*, a curtain-raiser about royal patronage, which in April 1848 was gratuitously performed by the Théâtre Français before a revolution-intoxicated audience. With all that *François le Champi* might not have been the success it was had not George by then gained some practical insight into the play-

wright's craft. For several years, with no other object than entertaining her household, she had been writing and devising plays
which were performed by the family before an intimate circle of
friends. The result was that what had started as a pastime became
a training-ground for the future.

The theatrical activities at Nohant owed their initial inspiration
to the happy accident of Chopin's powers of mimicry. During
his summer stays in the country he used to entertain the household with his excellent character sketches which in turn inspired
other members of the family to do their own party pieces. Both
Solange and Maurice had a natural gift for improvisation, as did
George and her brother Hippolyte. Charades became a favourite
family recreation. Years later George described the occasion
which turned it into a passion:

> Some twelve years ago, round about 1845, the family took a
> fancy to playing charades, but as we had not set any words to
> be guessed the charade became an improvised playlet. We were
> so carried away with whatever subject we had chosen for the
> game that we could not bring ourselves to stop. Perhaps it was
> not so marvellous as we then thought, perhaps it was not mar-
> vellous at all, we can hardly remember anything any more. Our
> sole audience consisted of a large mirror which reflected our
> movements and a little dog who howled pitifully at the sight
> of his masters in strange costumes. . . . There were six of us
> that evening, my brother and myself, my son and daughter, a
> pretty young relative and an artist friend of my son's. Next day
> we started all over again, following the same imaginative and
> unrestricted pattern of the night before, with as much zeal and
> intensity.[2]

That was the turning point. From that day on the family could
think of nothing else but the next day's improvisation. They spent
their mealtimes discussing ideas and plots, and the intervals
between meals rummaging the house for old costumes and props.
Soon George was writing general outlines for the evening's per-

formance, while Maurice was building scenery and Solange practising her parts. From day to day the sessions became more imaginative and ambitious. They were no longer held in the drawing-room; they were transferred into the large billiard room which was better suited to serve as stage cum auditorium. Old friends like the Duvernets were asked to come and take part, others were invited to sit round and watch. There were no set scripts and no lines to memorise. The plays adopted the principle of the *Commedia dell'Arte*, adhering to an agreed story-line but allowing each character to improvise during the actual performance. By the end of the winter the troupe felt so confident that they asked neighbouring squires to their performances.

The theatrical activity fell into abeyance during the bitter summers of 1846 and 1847, when domestic rows brought about the split-up between George and Solange, George and Chopin. The summer of 1848 was no different. George was mourning the passing away of her dream republic and buried herself behind her desk. One evening, as she was sitting in the drawing-room with little to do, Maurice wrapped a handkerchief round each of his hands, hid behind an armchair and gave a fair imitation of a glove puppet show. What happened was a replica of that remote winter evening. Family and house guests were carried away. The following morning Maurice started carving heads from local wood while George made costumes for them. Maurice's artist friends gave a hand and before long they shaped and clothed the whole repertoire of the *Commedia dell'Arte*, adding many characters of their own invention. Twenty-five-year-old Maurice, with his artistic training, took the task seriously and within a short time established a first-class puppet theatre. George wrote little sketches.

While the speaking parts were taken by friends, Maurice manipulated the puppets virtually single-handed. He had beside him a board with pegs on which he hung each glove puppet as it came off the scene and from which he took the next one due to appear. The changes had to be made quickly and without a break. If, as sometimes inevitably happened, Maurice missed the peg, the actor hiding behind a screen would speak his lines without the puppet being in action. Such mishaps became known at Nohant as Missing the Peg. In later years, when actors from the Paris Odéon became frequent guests at Nohant, they picked up the expression and for years to come would refer to colleagues who missed their cues during a professional performance as having missed their pegs.

The foundation of the puppet theatre led to a revival of live theatre performances. This time conventions were observed. George wrote the full script and the actors – any friends who happened to be staying, including a distinguished politician like Emmanuel Arago – learnt their lines off by heart. Sometimes boys from the village school were asked to take on small parts. Maurice surpassed himself. He designed and built sets, painted backcloths, invented sophisticated stage effects. After two years the productions became so ambitious that the billiard room could no longer house them. At the beginning of 1851, while Maurice was away for several weeks, George had builders knock down a wall, divide the space into a proper stage and auditorium, convert an unused bedroom into storage space. When Maurice returned home he was overwhelmed. That year Solange visited Nohant for the first time since 1847. She surveyed the alterations with a critical eye and remarked that it was a heartless mother who could convert a daughter's bridal chamber into a storehouse.

From then on the performances at Nohant reached new heights. Even Odéon professionals sometimes took part. Many of George's plays had their first showing there, after which she would often alter them before sending them off to a Paris theatre manager. Sometimes she acted in her own plays and the experience gave her fresh insight into the psychology of acting. She once complained to her ever-beloved 'daughter' Augustine that because of the dearth of young girls in the household she was sometimes forced to play a young heroine. 'A heavy make-up can disguise the face,' she wrote soberly, 'but I feel too old [she was fortyeight] to project the feelings of a young girl.'[3]

François le Champi was an incontrovertible success. Paris audiences, possibly seeking an escape from the real drama of political upheavals, welcomed the translation of country life on to the stage. They were moved by the love of a pure-minded peasant for a cultured and understanding lady, enchanted with the Berry dialect which George had introduced into the dialogue. They enjoyed the novelty of seeing peasants as leading characters and were captivated by the blend of rustic realism with literary romanticism. The play had more than a hundred performances, a remarkable achievement in the terms of the day. George Sand's name as a playwright was rehabilitated.

Encouraged by the success, she wrote another rustic play and sent it off to Bocage to read. He liked *Claudie* so much that he decided to play the lead. George was driven into a frenzy of activity. From Nohant she wrote Bocage one letter after another discussing scenery, costumes, tricks of local dialect. She even sent him her own sketches of peasant ox-carts. One day she heard a builder who was installing a new heating system at Nohant sing Berry folk tunes. She called him into the drawing-room and together with a musician friend noted down the melodies for Bocage to use in the stage production. When the slightly tipsy builder rejoined his mates he told them that he might be asked to go to Paris to sing at the opera. After that the entire gang took to singing Donizetti arias at the top of their voices and were very disappointed when nobody asked them to perform in the draw-ing-room.

Claudie was the story of a simple peasant girl who progressed from seduction to a virtuous marriage. George was astounded when Bocage informed her that the censor had made some cuts for political reasons. As before, she stayed on at Nohant when the play opened at the Porte-Sainte-Martin in January 1851 and went to Paris only three days later, when she knew it had been well received. It promised to be another long run. The house was sold out every night, the audience shed tears, Bocage, in the unfamiliar role of an elderly peasant, won much praise. Un-accountably *Claudie* was abruptly taken off after eleven perfor-mances. It was allegedly done on the instructions of the censor who felt that the rehabilitation of a fallen woman smacked of socialism.

By this time George was an established playwright and actors of all calibres tried to ingratiate themselves with her in order to win a part in her next play. She promised Bocage to be wary. 'I shall follow the advice you gave me on the occasion of my first play,' she wrote to him. 'I shall not consort with actors and actresses, there will be no supper parties, no familiarity. It is not worth it; and having another play [*Molière*] coming up immediately after this one, this sort of association may lead to demands I should not be able to satisfy. They hope to obtain from me what they cannot get out of M. Bocage, but I want M. Bocage to remain in sole charge. We have been ill paid for our past kindnesses.'[4]

The year 1851 saw two more George Sand plays open in Paris: *Molière* at the Gaîté and *Le Mariage de Victorine* at the Gymnase. The first was a biographical play, the second a love story ending with the happy marriage of the poor adopted daughter to the son of the house. Contrary to her habit, George went up to Paris to be present at the first night of *Le Mariage de Victorine*. A few days after the opening Louis Napoleon staged his *coup d'état* and George returned to Nohant with Solange and the little granddaughter.

There began that long period of intercession for the release of socialist friends. In between visits to various ministries and prisoners' families George worked on *Les Vacances de Pandolphe* which had been commissioned by the Gymnase and wrote another novel. 'She took fifty-two nights to write it,' Elizabeth Barrett-Browning commented with wonderment. 'She writes only at night.'[5]

One of Elizabeth Barrett-Browning's dearest wishes during her stay in Paris in the winter of 1851–52 was to meet the illustrious George Sand, many of whose novels had long been translated into English. The Brownings had a letter of introduction from the Italian Mazzini who had been a guest at Nohant before going to England. 'I would not miss seeing her for a great deal,' Elizabeth Barrett-Browning wrote in November 1851, 'though I have not read any of her late dramas and only by faith understand that her wonderful genius has conquered new kingdoms.'[6] But catching that 'strange, wild, wonderful woman'[7] during one of her brief visits to Paris, either on her missions of mercy or on theatre business, was not easy. After several missed opportunities a meeting was at long last arranged at Maurice's apartment in Paris. In a letter to her friend and relative John Kenyon the forty-six-year-old English poetess gave her first impressions of the forty-eight-year-old French novelist:

Paris, 15 February 1852

She received us kindly, with her hand outstretched, which I, with a natural emotion (I assure you my heart beat), stopped and kissed, when she said quickly, *Mais non, je ne veux pas*, and kissed my lips. She is somewhat large for her height – not tall – and was dressed with great nicety in a sort of grey serge gown and jacket, made after the ruling fashion just now, and fastened up to the throat, plain linen collarette and sleeves. Her hair was uncovered, divided on the forehead in black, glossy bandeaux, and twisted up behind. The eyes and brow are noble, and the nose is of a somewhat Jewish character; the chin a little recedes, and the mouth is not good, though mobile, flashing out a sudden smile with its white projecting teeth. There is no sweetness in the face, but great moral as well as intellectual capacities – only it never *could* have been a beautiful face, which a good deal surprised me. The chief difference in it since it was younger is probably that the cheeks are considerably fuller than they used to be, but this of course does not alter the type. Her complexion is of a deep olive. I observed that her hands were small and well-shaped. We sat with her perhaps three-quarters of an hour or more – in which time she gave advice and various directions to two or three young men who were there, showing her confidence in us by the freest use of names and allusion to facts. She seemed to be, in fact, *the man* in that company, and the profound respect with which she was listened to a good deal impressed me. You are aware from the newspapers that she came to Paris for the purpose of seeing the President in behalf of certain of her friends, and that it was a successful mediation. What is peculiar in her manners and

Gustave Flaubert, photographed by Nadar

George Sand in her later years

conversation is the absolute simplicity of both. Her voice is low and rapid, without emphasis or variety of modulation. Except one brilliant smile, she was grave – indeed, she was speaking of grave matters, and many of her friends are in adversity. But you could not help seeing (both Robert and I saw it) that in all she said, even in her kindness and pity, there was an under-current of scorn. A scorn of pleasing she evidently had; there never could have been a colour of coquetry in that woman. Her very freedom from affectation and consciousness had a touch of disdain. But I liked her. I did not love her, but I felt the burning soul through all that quietness, and was not disappointed in George Sand.

. . . *Nota bene*. We didn't see her smoke.[8]

In fact they never saw her smoke, although they called on her several more times. Elizabeth Barrett-Browning, who was prevented by ill health from calling as often as Robert did, conveyed the latter's further impressions in a letter she wrote to Miss Mitford:

Paris, 7 April 1852

She seems to live in an abomination of desolation, as far as regards society, crowds of ill-bred men who adore her *à genoux bas*, between a puff of smoke and an ejection of saliva. Society of the ragged Red diluted with the lower theatrical. She herself so different, so apart, as alone in her melancholy disdain. I was deeply interested in that poor woman, I felt a profound compassion for her. I did not mind much the Greek in Greek costume who *tutoyéd her*, and kissed her, I believe, so Robert said; or the other vulgar man of the theatre who went down on his knees and called her 'sublime'. '*Caprice d'amitié*,' she said, with her quiet, gentle scorn. A noble woman under the mud, be certain. *I* would kneel down to her too if she would leave it all, throw it off, and be herself as God made her. . . . She wrote one, or two, or three kind notes to me and promised to '*venir m'embrasser*' before she left Paris; but she did not come, and she told a friend of ours that she 'liked us'; only we always felt that we couldn't penetrate, could not really *touch* her, it was all in vain. Her play [*Les Vacances de Pandolphe*] failed, though full of talent. It did not run and was withdrawn immediately. I wish she would keep to her romances, in which her real power lies.[9]

But George continued to write plays. Between 1851 and 1856 twelve new plays by her were put on by leading Paris theatres, including *Le Démon du foyer*, which had a female character modelled on Solange. The year 1856 culminated in her return, sixteen years after *Cosima*, to the Théâtre Français, by now re-named the Comédie Française. The play was *Comme il vous plaira*, her free adaptation of Shakespeare's *As You Like It*.

During those years there was hardly a season without a new George Sand play being put on by one Paris theatre or another. Some years she had as many as three, following each other in quick succession. Not all of them met with critical acclaim. Some were decidedly unsuccessful. 'What can I say about myself and the theatre?' she wrote in 1858. 'One day it is yes, another it is no. Have I got a talent for it? I do not think so. I used to hope it would come one day. Under my greying hair I still keep telling myself it would come one day. But I have so often been told the contrary that I do not know any more.'[10]

What she did know however was that success did not neces-sarily prove quality and that a *succès d'estime* was often a euphemism for failure. She had learnt the realities of the box-office. In the preface to her Collected Plays published in 1860 she came to a conclusion which could have well been written in our own time:

A playwright who does not achieve financial success soon finds all doors leading to the theatre closed to him. An actor who is not a box-office attraction is soon thanked off. A director who does not recover his initial outlay is ruined and often dis-credited. At a time of unprecedented dramatic activity like ours, success is more important than ever. We therefore cease to rely on the literary merit of a work and become used to hearing from theatre managers: 'This is good, but it will not run; that is stupid, but it will be a success.' When a dramatic situation seems unlikely or a conclusion unfeasable, we often hear: 'But the public like this sort of thing.' Or: 'This is too well written, the public does not listen to what is too well written.' Or: 'Do not give us greatness of character, the public does not understand it.' Or: 'Work for effects. The public loves effects. People do not care whether the development is logical as long as it is ingenious. The secret is to give a long-drawn-out situation an unexpected twist. The audience want to be surprised. They no longer want to be convinced or even moved.'[11]

George, for her part, believed that the public was far more discerning than theatre managers were willing to give it credit for. 'The public does not want to be surprised,' she contended. 'They want to be convinced. They do not hate greatness; they listen to what is good. They even love the beautiful.'[12]

Although she herself, to her own admission, never contributed anything revolutionary to the art of the drama, she regretted the conventionalism of contemporary theatre. 'The climate of our society is not favourable to artistic experiments', she wrote in 1857. 'Our great civilisation has the herd instinct. It wants to cling to the past and believes it is destroying itself if it takes a step towards the future.'[13]

At the end of her theatrical activity, as at its beginning, her ideal theatre remained the *Commedia dell'Arte*, with its wide scope for improvisation. Taking it a step further, she hoped for a theatre which would bring about a collaboration between author and actors, each contributing to the creation of a perfect play. What even today is regarded as an experiment was clearly and logically advocated by her as early as 1857:

I am convinced that the theatre of the past holds the seeds of the theatre of the future. I see it as a theatre of free improvisation as far as dialogue is concerned, though firmly based on a well thought-out scenario which should be studied, agreed to and then carefully rehearsed. This would require from the actors a measure of education and intelligence which many of them possess, today as of old, but which the established system of plays written exclusively by playwrights does not allow them to show and develop. . . . There are many actors who can write and express their thoughts remarkably well. Many have that sacred flame which inspires their thoughts on everyday situations, passion, the tragedy and comedy of human life. Often, while listening to such actors speak their heart, I regret that they do not say all that before an audience in the midst of a scene. Such outpourings vindicate their intelligence so often offended by the need to perform a hollow part in an impossible play.

This is not to say that actors are generally superior to the playwrights who write for them; I am only suggesting that some are. In the same way some playwrights are sometimes unlucky and justifiably deplore the fact that they cannot find intelligent interpreters for all their characters. What I am saying above all is that it will be a better theatre when the two professions, the actor's and the playwright's, become one. The time will come when the Shakespeares of the future will come from among the greatest actors of the day.[14]

After 1856 George slackened the pace of her play-writing and threw herself back with renewed vigour into novels. In 1861 she published *Le Marquis de Villemer* which described how a poor but well-bred lady's companion won the heart and hand of a younger son. The popularity of the novel was such that, as in the case of *François le Champi* and later *Mauprat*, George adapted it into a play.

On the day of the first performance, which happened to fall on 29 February of the leap-year 1864, students began to queue up for cheap seats as early as ten in the morning. It was a gala opening, with Napoleon III and the Empress Eugénie in the royal box together with Prince Jerome and the Princesses. The play made an immediate impact. The audience could not stop clapping, Flaubert shed tears, the six hundred students who had got in stamped their feet in a frenzy of admiration and chanted 'Long Live George Sand'. After the last curtain call two hundred people from the Paris cultural élite crowded round George to offer their congratulations. From that night on, for the rest of the season, the Odéon's nightly takings doubled and even trebled. George remarked that for the company she had become God Almighty.

That was the last of her great successes. A few more plays, some written in collaboration with Maurice, aroused little interest. Eventually the flow ceased. In 1876, when George Sand was a venerable lady of seventy-one, *Le Mariage de Victorine* was revived. A new generation of theatre-goers who had not seen the original production of twenty-five years earlier, was charmed and a long run was assured. In 1876 as in 1851 the theme of innocent love triumphing over class prejudice went straight into people's hearts. For George it was a pleasing last chapter in the long and not always happy story of her association with the theatre.

Chapter 17

❧❧❧

Ageing gracefully

In accordance with the traditional hospitality of Nohant, Maurice had long made a habit of asking his friends to stay in the house for long stretches at a time. George loved having young people about her. Her insistent maternalism put them in her debt and enabled her to help, protect, guide and dominate. In her mid-forties, in spite of a double chin, greying hair and growing stoutness, she retained her confidence in her ability to be needed and loved, inspiring in her young friends that romantic attachment which the French call *amitié amoureuse* and which transcends the boundaries of age. 'I nearly always live with artists, with young men,' she wrote to Mazzini in March 1850. 'We are having fun in my house and I am always in a good mood.'[1]

Some young men became particularly attached. Eugène Lambert, who had served his apprenticeship at Delacroix's workshop with Maurice, was brought down to Nohant for a summer and became an inseparable part of the household for the next twelve years. He threw himself into the affray that summer of 1847 when Clésinger struck his mother-in-law and was George's escort on the occasion of her last meeting with Chopin at Mme Marliani's. He continued to be her *cavalier servant* even when he became a fashionable painter of cats and dogs; in 1853 George dedicated to him her successful novel *Les Maîtres sonneurs*.

Another devoted young man was Emile Aucante, accused of political subversion and saved from exile thanks to George's intercession. After a term of imprisonment he returned to Nohant and gradually took over George's business transactions with publishers and theatre managers.

Some friendships developed into love affairs. The journalist Victor Borie, fourteen years younger than George, stayed at Nohant during the winters of 1846–47 and 1847–48 and became her lover after her uncertain parting with Chopin. The relationship was the subject of much gossip in Paris and Heinrich Heine, himself a dying man, thought it disgraceful of George to be unfaithful to a moribund lover. Uncharacteristically, the affair petered out without an emotional upheaval. Later, when Borie was sentenced to prison and exile for his socialist activities, George loyally tried to help. On his return he took up banking and was welcomed back to Nohant as a martyr though no longer as a lover.

By then another political martyr had succeeded him in George's affections. Towards the end of 1849 the German revolutionary Müller-Strübing, sentenced to death in his native Germany but reprieved, found his way to Nohant, having utilised his term of imprisonment to make himself a classical scholar and a musicologist. George relished the novelty of being in love with a disciplined pedant who needed no mothering even though he was eight years younger than her. To her publisher Hetzel, the latest recipient of her confidences, she wrote in December 1849: 'This is the first time I associate with a man who is morally and physically strong. So far my maternal instinct has always made me gravitate towards the weak; it has turned me into a spoiler of children and a *Maman* who is only too easily taken advantage of. The strong are always dominated by the weak. Perhaps someone with a strong character would offer me a chance to be equal.'[2]

The association was extremely brief; and perhaps, because like the one with Borie it had not been deeply felt, it was amicably terminated. Later George regarded the love she had briefly bestowed on the learned doctor as an act of kindness. On her recommendation he was offered the post of resident tutor to the Duvernet children nearby and at the time of *Claudie* was gaily summoned back to help with noting down folk-tunes. She was pleased when a year later he remembered to bring her flowers for her forty-sixth birthday, though she had a pretty shrewd idea that someone had had to remind him to do so. Shortly afterwards he left for London and disappeared for ever in the English fog.

But for George there could never be a vacuum for long. If anything, her compulsive search for an emotional anchor sometimes led to an overlap. 'I do not believe in happiness,' she wrote to Hetzel in 1849. 'I do not seek it. All I know is that I do not want to live without love. I cannot.'[3] At the age of forty-six love, calm, soothing and stable, came to her in the person of the engraver Alexandre Manceau, who was to stay with her until his death fifteen years later.

Alexandre Damien Manceau, the least ostentatious of all George Sand's lovers, was born in 1817 to a poor working-class family. His father was a commissionaire at the Luxembourg palace at the time the son was already the constant companion of the illustrious novelist. Manceau started life as an apprentice and showed talent as well as application. From 1841 he exhibited regularly and made a name for himself as an engraver of merit. At the same time he led the carefree life of a young Bohemian, taking and shedding mistresses like any of his artistic circle. Maurice, a few years younger than him, made his acquaintance in Paris and invited him down to Nohant where he arrived in the autumn of 1849, just as George was preparing for her theatrical comeback with *François le Champi*.

At thirty-two, thirteen years younger than his hostess, Manceau was frail and soulful-looking. He approached the daunting Madame Sand with reverence and was conquered by her graciousness and simplicity. He left for Paris with the understanding that he would come down again as soon as possible. When he did, some time in the new year, he and George became lovers.

Age had taught George discretion. She was no longer the young firebrand who put love before convention. She had a married daughter and wanted to present an image of a dignified mother and grandmother. To the world outside she pretended that Manceau was just another young house guest like Lambert or Aucante who kept company to a middle-aged matron while her son was away in Paris; but to her confidant Hetzel she wrote without reservation: 'I love him, yes, him. . . . He takes very seriously the need to keep the proud secret of being loved by me and is always afraid of betraying what little justification he thinks he has for it.'[4]

That declaration was preceded by a period of mutual adjustment, not devoid of doubts and emotional storms. George was worried about the age difference and Manceau's reputation for fast living. She was also sensitive to her young friends' opinion of him. Manceau was a self-made man and his constant watchfulness, born out of the need to seize his opportunities, was despised by the Nohant habitués, most of whom had been born into material security. There was also an element of jealousy. The young men about the house resented the newcomer's promotion and eagerly repeated and exaggerated any of his social infelicities. George and he had some painful explanations. In the end the emotional storms left her cleansed and reassured. In a long letter to her confidant Hetzel in April 1850 she gave a perceptive analysis of Manceau and her feelings for him. As always when discussing her love, she put her entire soul into her writing:

'He was born to a poor family and has had no formal or spiritual education. He has not made any studies, he was an apprentice. He is a workman who works like one, because he needs to make a living and knows how to go about it. He is incredibly artistic and possesses an extraordinary intelligence, which he uses to further his own interest, and consequently mine as well. He knows nothing but guesses everything. He is always inquisitive and his enquiries show how active his mind is. He cannot spell, but he writes poetry. This detail is characteristic of the man as a whole. He has a penetrating mind, and that blend of ignorance and perception is very endearing as long as he is not too self-conscious to go on enquiring.

'He has his faults. He is impulsive as well as calculating. When he is impulsive he can hurt most cruelly; when he is calculating he tries to impose and have his own way. These two faults, when they fail to be understood, can make him unpopular. Fortunately a high intelligence and a sense of fair play make him offer amends for his outbursts and turn his calculated gestures into a deep, sincere and loyal devotion. Some people wickedly conclude that his devotion is motivated by self-interest. This is not so. Deep down he is so generous as to be prodigal, unless held back. His self-interest is on the moral plane. He wants to be enlightened, loved, improved. He has no ambition to make money or a name for himself. He is in love with his soul. He wants to improve himself before God, in his own eyes and in the eyes of those few for whom he cares. He does not mind crossing or shocking all the others. . . .

'He loves me. He loves as I have never seen anyone love before. All his faults melt away when we are on our own. Then he becomes as caressing as a cat, as faithful as a dog. All his calculated actions have no other object than to gain the approval of the one he loves. Although he has led a fast life, he is chaste when it comes to true love; as chaste and fervent as body, heart and soul can wish love to be. . . . What do I care if he does not please the others as long as he pleases me? And as he has no other thought in his head except to please me, and as he works towards that end with extraordinary application, I do not stop him.

'I like his ways. He is light on his feet and moves about with assurance. He does not break anything on his way and is not like 69 per cent of men who mistake their nose for their feet and are so absent-minded, inattentive or clumsy that they can never do anything right first time. Do not take this as a witticism. Those small irritations caused by clumsiness are the external manifestation of immense mental and spiritual ineptitude. He applies his entire mind to what he is doing, he puts his entire soul into getting me a glass of water or lighting my cigarette. He never makes me lose my temper. He is punctual, he has a watch and he takes the trouble to glance at it. He has never kept me waiting for whatever meeting we have arranged, though I know he keeps other people waiting just to spite them. When he sometimes does do something wrong towards me I never have to wait for the look or word which put everything right again. He has a woman's touch about him, practical, energetic and resourceful. When I am unwell I seem to recover at the mere sight of him propping a pillow or fetching my slippers. I, who have never asked or accepted personal services, accept his as if it were my nature to be coddled. In short, I love him. I love him with all my heart in spite of his faults and the others' mocking, in spite of his mistakes and stupidities. I love him just as he is, and there is an astonishing calm in my love for him. . . . I feel transformed. I am well, calm, happy. I can take anything now, even his being away. That says it all, for never before have I been able to accept anybody's being away from my side.'[5]

She no longer needed that element of self-torment which she called passion. Three months later, after the celebration of her forty-sixth birthday, which was marked among other things by the performance at the Nohant theatre of a sketch of hers called *L'Anglais en voyage*, she wrote to Hetzel in the same blissful mood:

July 1850

Yes, I am well and happy, so very happy. I think it is the first time in my life that I can say so and selfishly abandon myself to my bliss. I do not mean to become selfish, but until now I have put so much devotion into my loves that it never occurred to me to ask myself whether I loved for my own pleasure; or else those fleeting moments when I could say so to myself were only too soon dispelled by painful surprises and unexpected sorrows. So many people have caused me pain that I am sometimes astonished to see that not everybody is mad, peculiar, evil or weak.

I keep asking myself whether it can and will last. I do not want to think about it. . . . It is so good to be loved and know myself able to love completely, it would be wicked to foresee an end to it. I have no premonition that it might end one day, why should I take it for granted that it would? We all accept the inevitability of death, yet we do not think of it with fear, unless we are cowards or asses. I am 46, I have grey hair, it does not matter. Older women are better loved than young ones. I know that now. It is not the person who has to be well preserved, it is the love. May God preserve this one, it is so good.[6]

With the rest of her friends George remained circumspect, keeping the pretence of a young devoted friend who divided his life, like her other young protégés, between working in Paris and helping out at Nohant. She had to be particularly tactful with Maurice. After Chopin's departure Maurice felt he was the only man in his mother's life. He was her confidant, her ally, her adored son. They had shared the dream of the republic, built the theatre at Nohant, collaborated on plays. Maurice had no thoughts of marrying and could not conceive that his mother, the only woman in his life, could possibly need any other man in hers. He liked his young friends to admire her, but like a jealous suitor would not allow her the freedom of her own emotions. George therefore took pains to represent her friendship with Manceau in the same light as her friendship with the other Nohant familiars. A year after the beginning of the liaison, she wrote to Maurice who was spending the winter in Paris:

Nohant, 2 January 1851

Lambert left here this morning and should be with you by now. He has been very kind, devoted and attentive to me in my loneliness. Now it is Manceau's turn and he too does his best to take your place at your mother's side while you are away. He is busying himself with making designs for your own use.[7]

Manceau was the soul of discretion. Like Chopin, he referred to George as *Madame*: in company, in his diary and perhaps even in his thoughts; no correspondence has survived to shed light on their intimate endearments. He continued to treat Maurice as a friend and colleague and made engravings for books the latter was writing. George exaggerated his kindnesses to her son; Maurice accepted them like the services of a valet.

There was nothing he could say against Manceau's stay at Nohant; but when he learnt that George was proposing to put up at Manceau's on her next visit to Paris, he warned her that such a step would set tongues wagging and insisted that she should stay at his place instead. George shammed innocence and wrote back that nobody could possibly find fault with a middle-aged matron staying for a few days with a young friend of the family. Paris society however was not deceived; when Prince Jerome asked George to lunch in order to discuss her latest plea for political prisoners, he tactfully invited Manceau as well.

The stays in Paris were short and infrequent. Nohant was George's only home and she spent enormous sums on improvements. The same year that the billiard room was converted into a theatre, a system of central heating was installed in the house. For weeks Nohant was invaded by workmen digging holes, hacking out air vents, laying pipes and singing folk tunes or opera arias at the top of their voices. The result surpassed all expectations. 'The central stove throws out heat like the devil,' George wrote delightedly in December 1850. 'It is really comfortable and economical. And what we have neither foreseen nor expected is that it warms up the entire house, the hall and the corridors; and together with the bathroom boiler it generates heat like a steam-house.'[8] A month later, in the midst of a severe winter, she remarked with satisfaction that Nohant was enjoying 'an eternal summer'.[9]

The house was nearly always full, summer or winter. The modern railroad service made Nohant easily accessible to Paris friends. George was the perfect hostess, seeing that her guests had every possible comfort in their rooms, attending personally to their particular preferences. But whether the house was full or comparatively quiet, she never deviated from a strict routine. As she always worked from about midnight to the early hours of the morning, her presence at the breakfast table was rare. Her first formal appearance was usually at midday. After lunch house-guests would stroll in the garden or work in their rooms, while George attended to the running of the house. Her staff of eight knew her to be exacting but generous, paying them always more than they would have got anywhere else. They were devoted to her and few, if any, ever left her service. When they grew too old to work she gave them a pension.

She issued instructions about the gardens and the stables, the fields and the crops. She was as careful of her planning as any bourgeois housewife, as alert to progressive ideas on husbandry as any gentleman farmer. She continued to play her part as the lady of the manor, helping the poor and the sick, remembering the name of every new-born baby in the village. With neighbouring squires she exchanged hampers of mushrooms, poultry and home-made jam. She still found time for jam-making and was particularly proud of her own special recipes.

Dinner-time was reunion time. Family and house-guests would sit round the large oval table, made by the local carpenter, enjoy the good food and talk politics, books and perhaps a forthcoming play at the Nohant theatre. George would preside, stimulating conversation by her presence rather than by active participation. As in her youth, large gatherings tended to silence her. She was at her conversational best with an audience of one or two.

After dinner there was some social entertainment; a game of dominoes or, more often, a reading aloud from a chosen text. George would listen, bent over her embroidery, a baby's garment or a puppet's costume. Later she described those convivial evenings in *Autour de la table*. They invariably ended about midnight with Manceau fetching her oil-lamp and escorting her up to her study, where he had already laid out a sheaf of writing paper, her favourite blue ink, a glass of sweetened water for drinking and another of plain water for dropping her cigarette stubs into. George had a phobia about fires.

Solange, who occasionally came down to stay with her little Nini, found the after-dinner readings unutterably boring. One evening, when the chosen text was *Ivanhoe*, she noticed that Victor Borie had dozed off in his armchair and was loudly snoring. To wake him up she tied a length of string to a strand of his hair, fastening the other end round a stag-beetle she had caught. Borie woke up with a scream, tore out the string together with his hair, swore at Solange and chased her round the house telling her what he thought of her.

In *Le Diable aux champs*, the first of four works to be dedicated to Manceau, George gave a faithful description of life at Nohant in those years. Nearly all her familiars were represented under their own names; Lambert was Eugène, Aucante was Emile, Manceau was Damien, Maurice was Maurice. Even the late

Hippolyte was revived under his pet name of Polyte. Other friends were given names from her own early novels; Jules Néraud was Ralph Brown, after the loyal friend in *Indiana*, while Mme Néraud became Indiana herself. The characterisation was drawn from life. Maurice was represented very much as he was, a gifted young man dissipating his talents in many directions; Solange, hardly disguised under the name of Countess Diane de Noirac, as a haughty young woman, heartless and totally selfish. The title of the book however was no personal allusion. It was the role assigned by Maurice of the novel to one of his puppets.

There were other works in which the heroines were modelled on Solange: the play *Le Démon du foyer*, the novel *Mont-Revêche*, the much later novel *Mademoiselle Merquem*. All Solange could do was to pretend, like Chopin before her, like Marie d'Agoult and Liszt, like Jules Sandeau, Gustave Planche, Casimir Dudevant and so many others of her mother's one-time intimates, that any similarity with an unattractive character of fiction was purely coincidental; which in a sense it was.

She could no longer accuse her mother of unmotherly behaviour towards her in her hour of need. The death of a first baby and the birth of a second had brought them together again. But there was no warmth in the relationship. Mother and daughter judged each other severely, concealing their moral disapproval under pet names borrowed from a past long dead.

Solange wanted to impress. At Nohant she behaved like visiting royalty, oscillating between condescension and frostiness to such a degree that George wondered whether her daughter was trying to be a second Queen Elizabeth. In Paris Solange kept open house, entertained fashionable artists and writers, became friendly with the Count d'Orsay and through him with the imperial family. She kept horses, an English coachman for her carriage, dogs, a large staff. She dressed lavishly and was meticulous about marking her eyebrows with a dark pencil, as once advised by Delacroix. Underneath she remained discontent, envious and self-pitying.

Her marriage was crumbling. Artistically Clésinger was highly thought of. He had won several awards and on 17 May 1849, a week after the birth of the second baby, was made a knight of the *Légion d'Honneur*. Financially however he remained insolvent and temperamentally he was impossible. He was given to frequent outbursts of temper which led to violence. From its very beginning the marriage was rocked by passionate quarrels followed by equally passionate reconciliations. Clésinger took mistresses and Solange, not to fall behind, indulged in affairs of her own. Paris wallowed in the lurid details. George was distressed to see a daughter of hers throw herself into amorous adventures without the purifying flame of love. She accused her of depravity and begged her to remember her moral upbringing. To Maurice she wrote that Clésinger was a madman and Solange a woman without a conscience. She seriously advised him not to stay for dinner when visiting them in their Paris house.

Between two such parents little Jeanne Gabrielle, pet-named Nini, was bound to be a pawn. George was moved by the plight of the little mite and wished for nothing better than to offer her the security of Nohant. Solange too felt that Nohant was the only solid homestead the child could ever hope to have. But when she suggested coming down *en famille* for a few months, George put her foot down. 'I told her formally,' she wrote to Augustine in February 1851, 'that I did not wish to set eyes on her husband ever again, nor to put up her servants, friends, horses and dogs, only herself and daughter.'[10]

The occasional visits to Nohant offered a respite but not a cure. In 1852, when George came up to Paris for a few days, she had occasion to observe the domestic set-up more closely and sadly wrote to Aucante, serving a prison sentence but still bound up with the Sand household: 'Nini is a charming little girl. Unfortunately her mother and father do not get on together and lead each other, and me between them, a hell of a life.'[11]

Family history was repeating itself. The Clésingers took their differences to court, accused each other of infidelity, claimed possession of dowry and custody of the child. The court granted custody to the mother, leaving the issue of joint assets unresolved. It also stipulated that the father should be allowed to have his daughter with him for two months a year. Solange was furious. She declared that Clésinger was the sort of father who would deprive a daughter of food and clothing when she was young, expose her virtue to danger when she was older.

The most sensible thing to do during her ten-month custodianship was for Solange to send Nini down to Nohant. George was in her element with a little grand-daughter of her own. She bought her sensible country clothes, had a dolls' house built for her and at four and a half taught her to read. The entire daily routine at Nohant was made to revolve round her. Manceau looked after her in the mornings, George took over from midday until nine in the evening. She informed Solange that the child was not pining and was putting on weight.

The interlude came to an end when the Clésingers decided to make yet another of their attempts to patch up the rift and sent for Nini to complete the happy reconciliation. When it predictably degenerated into another brawl the frightened little girl was returned to Nohant. Again George and Manceau put themselves out to give her love and security. George ruefully said that her grand-daughter ruled her like a queen. In fact she knew exactly how to handle her and succeeded in making her behave no better and no worse than any other little girl of her age. In his diary Manceau noted in the summer of 1853: 'Nini is becoming really sweet, although she will eat her soup with her fingers, which Granny does not allow.'[12]

For Nini's mother he felt nothing but dislike. In the diary which he kept jointly with George he wrote later that summer:

16 June: Mme Solange is due here tomorrow.
17 June: Mme Solange has not arrived, damn her.
18 June: Mme Solange arrived this morning. Before lunch she complained of the cold country air; in the evening she made Nini eat her dinner entirely naked. My God![13]

If Solange's behaviour was irresponsible, Clésinger's was erratic. In the spring of 1854 he burst into his wife's bedroom and after a violent scene during which he all but killed her, seized a bunch of letters from a current lover and despatched them to his lawyer with instructions to proceed against an unworthy mother. Then, like Casimir Dudevant seventeen years earlier, he dashed to Nohant, grabbed his daughter by the hand and disappeared into nowhere. For a whole month George did not know Nini's exact whereabouts; sometimes she was reported with her father, sometimes with her godmother, sometimes at a Paris pension. Lawyers on both sides were preparing for a new court hearing. Solange, unable to curb her lavish style of living, informed her mother that poverty would force her to sell herself to the highest bidder; then, in a fit of religiosity, went into a convent and asked to be allowed to take the veil. In the meantime the domestic rows continued. Mother and father fought over the child and tore her apart with their vindictiveness and selfishness. In December the judges, taking into account both parents' unreliability, granted sole custody of the child to her maternal grandmother. George was deeply thankful. 'This will strengthen your faith,' she wrote to Solange. 'God has come to our aid.'[14]

Still it was not the end. Clésinger appealed and a stay of execution was granted pending a final verdict. One cold December day he called at the pension and dragged his daughter out for a walk, oblivious of the fact that she was wearing nothing but a thin indoor frock. By the time he returned her to her mistresses she was feverish. Three weeks later she died of pneumonia. Solange, Lambert and Aucante brought the coffin down to Nohant for burial in the family cemetery under the trees. She was five and a half.

Solange never had another child. When she died in 1899, aged seventy-one, she too was buried at the family cemetery. By her own wish no other epitaph was inscribed on her tombstone except the three simple words 'Mother of Jeanne'.

Characteristically, Maurice and Manceau were more concerned about the effect of the child's death on her grandmother than on her mother. When a few weeks after the funeral George complained that she was too distressed to work, they decided to take her to Italy for a long holiday.

Maurice went ahead to Paris to see to the travel arrangements, while Manceau was left to do the packing, which he did in his usual methodical way, putting winter things in one trunk, summer things in another. In March the three of them went through Marseilles, where George called on the doctor who sixteen years earlier treated Chopin during their three months' stay on the way back from Majorca. The next port of call was Genoa, which for George held memories of visits with Chopin as well as Musset. Rome left her unenthusiastic. 'It's quaint, beautiful, interesting, astonishing,' she wrote to Lambert, 'but it is too dead.'[15] She appreciated Florence, but was happier in Frascati. She much preferred the countryside to antiquity. As during her early days with Pagello, she took long walks, climbed hills, collected plants and stones, tired out her companions with her inexhaustible energy. Wherever she went she met old friends: the engraver Calamatta, whose thirteen-year-old daughter Lina was being educated at a Genoese boarding-school; Louis Blanc who felt safer away from France; Mme Alexandre Dumas who was living with the Prince de Villafranca; Etienne Arago, brother of Emmanuel; Maurice's friend the young artist Gustave Boulanger. She even met one or two friends whom she had made through Pagello, and who since had gone up in the world.

The tour revived her spirits. In May she wrote Manceau a poem for his thirty-eighth birthday and a few days later, when the Italian sun was beginning to beat down hard, bought herself a monstrous straw hat like any tourist. After two months of energetic sight-seeing she was ready to return to work. The party split up. Maurice stayed on, then went to stay with his father at Guillery. George and Manceau returned to Paris where she had taken a modest *pied à terre* in the same block in which he had his own apartment. She immediately settled down to correcting the proofs of *Histoire de ma vie* which was to appear that summer, after seven years' writing. At the end of May she returned to Nohant and was welcomed with a salvo of cannons.

Her Italian tour inspired her historical novel *Les Beaux Messieurs de Bois-Doré* as well as *Flavie, Constance Verrier* and several others. It may well have decided her to turn her old love affair with Musset into a novel, which she had eschewed until his death in 1857. *Elle et Lui* was published in the *Revue des Deux Mondes*, marking her reconciliation with Buloz after seventeen years' coolness. George little expected that her poetic licence with the past would unleash a literary spate of vindictiveness which would continue for several generations.

Her most controversial Italian novel at the time was however *La Daniella*, in which George gave vent to strong anti-clerical feelings. Ostensibly it was the story of the love between a poor girl from Frascati and a young artist, but in the midst of the most fantastic adventures the message was hard-hitting. George plainly suggested that the papal rule of Rome was the root cause of all the poverty and corruption she had seen during her recent visit.

As usual, the novel was first published in instalments in a literary magazine. The instalment in which Italy was referred to as a beautiful virgin prostituting itself to unscrupulous adventurers without a chance of ever purifying herself, provoked a storm of protest in catholic France. When the second instalment, still attacking the rule of the Italian clergy, suggested that Italy was getting what she deserved, political intervention became inevitable and the magazine, *La Presse*, was suspended. George appealed to the Empress Eugénie, herself a devout catholic, and moved her to pity by pointing out the plight of the magazine staff threatened with unemployment. *La Presse* was reprieved, but the controversy continued. Calamatta wrote from Genoa that she had misrepresented and misinterpreted what she had seen during an all-too-brief tour of Italy. George remained unrepentant. Her dislike of institutionalised religion found yet another expression in the novel *Mademoiselle La Quintinie* which was published a few years later. The young generation loved her unshackled approach to faith. When in 1864 she attended the first night of her play *Le Marquis de Villemer*, a crowd of enthusiastic students mingled their shouts of 'Long Live George Sand' with cries of 'Long Live La Quintinie'.

Other novels written in her fifties were less controversial, their treatment of love, the eternal subject, seeming more conventional. In her youth George Sand claimed for women the right of choice even within a marriage; in her old age she represented marriage as a happy conclusion to a free choice approved by society. Her detractors suggested that her view of marriage had become regressive; in fact it had become idealised. The rebel who had preached civil liberty now wished to perpetuate the rewards of a long struggle. A happy marriage was the romantic outcome of equality between the sexes.

Her heroes and heroines continued to reflect her manifold interests. Now her novels were no longer populated with musicians and actresses but with mineralogists, entomologists and ornithologists. George had always been a countrywoman with a scientific bent. Ever since her youthful friendships with Stéphane de Grandsagne and Jules Néraud she had taken an active interest in natural science. Even Chopin, in the midst of his coughing fits in Majorca, was encouraged to admire stones and plants she had collected with the children during their morning walks. With the years the interest swept the entire household and George's familiars vied with one another to add rare specimens to her collections. Her heroes of fiction, so often modelled on living friends, became knowledgeable about fossils and insects. When a lover arrived at a country rendez-vous before his sweetheart, he busied himself analysing the geological layers of the rocks.

One day, during an excursion in the Creuse valley, George came across the charming village of Gargilesse. She was so taken with its sloping hills, its river and its medieval church that Manceau, to please her, bought a cottage there and put it at her disposal. It became her country refuge from her country manor. Between 1857 and 1862 she wrote there no less than thirteen novels as well as three plays, a biographical study of Garibaldi and a preface to Maurice's history of the *Commedia dell'Arte* entitled *Masques et bouffons*, which won him a decoration from King Victor Emmanuel. Among the novels was the controversial *Elle et Lui*, written in twenty-five days.

Often Manceau was her only company at Gargilesse; she nicknamed him her *tête-à-tête*. When friends came down they were taken for walks in the beautiful Creuse valley, which George later described in *Promenades autour d'un village*. Again she introduced them into the book, and again she called the fictitious characters by their names in real life. The friends accepted it as an accolade: it was their entry ticket into literary history.

Fame had its disadvantages. At Nohant and in Paris there was a constant stream of literary pilgrims who wanted to pay homage to the illustrious novelist. In her younger, high-spirited days, George was known to allow a chamber-maid to impersonate her and shock an unsuspecting admirer with her uncouth behaviour and language. But age, with a growing sensitivity about her public image, ruled out such practical jokes. George barricaded herself behind a wall of inaccessibility. Even the Brownings, armed with a letter of introduction from George's friend Mazzini, had found it difficult to obtain their first interview.

When not besieged by respectful callers George was inundated with letters expressing admiration, asking her opinion on an enclosed manuscript, hoping for a line in her hand. She had to be selective. 'I do not usually answer the mass of idle and useless letters which people write to anybody who becomes slightly known in the world of art,'[16] she wrote as early as 1851 to someone whose letter she did answer. In spite of her selectivity the number of her correspondents became prodigious; yet her letters, even to strangers, retained their quality of personal warmth which made them so precious to their recipients.

People who knew her only from her writings were baffled when they first met her at a formal gathering. She had no small talk, and unless engaged in conversation by one or two people at the most, would withdraw into herself. There were no conversational fireworks to match her written eloquence. Charles Dickens, who was staying in Paris in the winter of 1856, observed her with astonishment at a dinner which Pauline Viardot had expressly arranged in order to introduce the two writers to each other. There were about a dozen guests round the dinner table, including Maurice, a couple of fashionable portrait painters, and an English lady fresh from the Crimea who rather shocked Dickens by turning up in a trouser suit and smoking to boot. To his friend John Forster he wrote the day after the dinner party:

Paris, 11 January 1856

I suppose it to be impossible to imagine anybody more unlike my preconceptions than the illustrious George Sand. Just the kind of woman in appearance whom you might suppose to be the Queen's [Victoria] monthly nurse. Chubby, matronly, swarthy, black-eyed. Nothing of the blue stocking about her, except a little final way of settling all your opinion with hers, which I take to have been acquired in the country, where she lives, and in the domination of a small circle. A singularly ordinary woman in appearance and manner.[17]

He could not get over his astonishment. Nine days after the dinner, when writing to Wilkie Collins, he again suggested that George Sand looked like the Queen's monthly nurse. Then, perspective having somewhat mollified his initial judgment, he added: '*Au reste*, she has nothing of the *bas bleu* about her and is very quiet and agreeable.'[18]

Dickens did not mention Manceau's name among the dinner guests, but whether invited or not, Manceau was always in the background. He had become indispensable. He helped with the management of Nohant, looked after George's voluminous correspondence, designed sets for the Nohant theatre. He was always in attendance; quiet, solid, reliable. At the same time he continued to apply himself to his art and enhanced his reputation as an engraver. His commissions brought him enough money to finance the Italian holiday which George, encumbered with the enormous expense of keeping Nohant on a grand scale and sub-sidising her children, could ill afford.

As George had once described him, he was as faithful as a dog, as delicate as a cat. His ministrations were invaluable when she was unwell, and unwell she often was. For years she had been suffering from intestinal blockage which she regarded as chronic constipation and which often left her doubled up with pain for days on end. She also suffered from bronchial colds, attacks of rheumatism and migraines. '*Madame* woke up with a migraine which became worse as the day wore on until eight in the evening', was a typical entry in the joint diary. '*Madame* dined on tea with some bread and butter. I did all I could to distract her, took her to the garden to plant some flowers. I was witty, silly, gay. Nothing helped.'[19]

In the autumn of 1860 George went down with typhoid. Manceau nursed her back to health and to complete her recovery took her to Tamaris, near Toulon, to spend the winter in a warmer climate. Inevitably Maurice came too. George immersed herself in work and produced several novels, among them the one called *Tamaris*. Manceau continued to fuss around her, but Maurice was bored. He spent much of his time on board Prince Jerome's yacht which had anchored in Toulon harbour and in the spring accepted an invitation to join him on a long sea voyage. They visited Algiers, Spain and Portugal, then sailed all the way to America and back. On his return, seven months later, Maurice recorded the experience in his *Six milles lieues à toute vapeur* to which George wrote a preface.

She and Manceau stayed on at Tamaris until mid-summer, then returned to Nohant. George had fully recovered. The real invalid was Manceau. For some time he had been coughing into his handkerchief in a way that was all too familiar. 'Manceau is having bad pains on the left,' George wrote to her regular house doctor at La Châtre some time after their return from Tamaris. 'Please call *as if by chance* and try to examine him and ease his pain.'[20]

She had to be circumspect for Manceau, as sensitive as he was faithful, would not admit that he was too ill to serve his dame at all times. At the beginning of 1862, after the house doctor had called at Nohant to attend to Maurice who had contracted a cold, George sent him a hurried note: 'Please come back if you can. For some time now Manceau has been running a high temperature for several hours every day. I thought he mentioned it to you while you were here but now he tells me that it had not occurred to him to do so. As you know he is often feverish but does not take any notice of it. Now he is much worse and I would like you to look at him. He sleeps badly, even for someone like him who has never known what it is to have a good night's sleep. At lunch-time he is fairly hungry and eats well, but after the meal he becomes feverish. At dinner he takes only little food and for the rest of the evening his temperature is down to normal, but he is exhausted. I do not think he is coughing more than usual, but with this chronic fever I feel he must be watched so that a right balance may be maintained.'[21]

George made Manceau take the various medicines prescribed by Doctor Darchy and gave a detailed account of their effect. The tranquillisers were too debilitating, the stimulants too exciting, the cough pills too irritating, the expectorants too violent. 'I am distressed to see him utterly spent one moment, over-excited the next,' she wrote to the doctor some time in 1863. 'But whatever you do you must reassure him. *Never tell him* that you find him worse. Tell it only to me.'[22]

She knew it was only a question of time. Writing to Augustine about old age and grey hair, she added sadly: 'I am afraid Manceau will not live to have any. Poor poor boy.'[23]

❦❦❦❦❦

Chapter 18

At last a mother-in-law

A facetious remark of Maurice's about his intention of marrying a young Parisian actress in order to provide Nohant with a resident juvenile lead threw his mother into disarray. For the first time in her life she had to consider realistically the possible disruption of her way of life resulting from her son's bringing home a bride.

It had always been understood that in the event of his marrying, Maurice would not move out but continue to live under his mother's roof together with his wife and children. As a hypothetical proposition it sounded idyllic; but when faced with a possible rival in the person of a young actress with ambitions of her own, George was alarmed. No idyll was conceivable unless the prospective wife was prepared to accept that George had first claim to her son's loyalty. The future mother-in-law made her stand quite clear in a letter to her son:

> Nohant, 17 December 1850
>
> I want you to go on living at Nohant since I have moulded it to suit your tastes and prepared it to be a haven solely for you. But I could not stay on here if I did not feel loved by my daughter-in-law and if I had to suffer under her hands the sort of life which Solange had led me. Of course I would not want to sow disaccord between you and your wife, I would not utter a word of complaint. I would just go away and comfort myself with the thought that I was leaving you with someone who could compensate you for your loss and give you the delights of a new love, with a new companion and children. You will be

sorry to lose me, I know; but the grief will bring its own compensations. It is I who stand to lose most in this case and who would suffer most.[1]

George need not have worried. At twenty-seven Maurice was as mother-possessed as he was at eleven. No other woman could supplant her in his heart. In Paris he followed amorous adventures like any other young man of his artistic circle, but emotionally he remained untouched. He professed himself incapable of a stable relationship and could not visualise himself in the role of a faithful husband. He wrote to tell his mother not to take his little joke to heart. While the matriarch in George was reassured, the romantic in her was outraged. Her entire life had been one long search for the perfect love which, theoretically, should have culminated in a perfect marriage. She could not allow her son to treat with cynicism what she held most precious. 'Love is something unforeseeable,' she rebuked him. 'Some say it is chance; I think it is not. It is a ray of sunshine which comes from heaven and inflames the heart when the moment is right. It is a miracle which conquers the most recalcitrant. But you must wait for it, for marriage without love is slavery for life.'[2]

Having reaffirmed her romantic creed, George became practical. If Maurice was to make the right choice, she was to help him and guide him. She considered all the marriageable young ladies she knew and dismissed them as unsuitable. To Maurice she explained: 'There are no women at Nohant and I doubt that there are any in the neighbourhood. I do not think that any of the local girls could possibly please you. They are so *bourgeois*, so miserly, so vain and stupid.'[3] She advised him to frequent the fashionable drawing-rooms of Paris and urged him to call on Emmanuel Arago, her publisher Hetzel and even on Marie d'Agoult with whom she had recently concluded a half-hearted peace. 'You are not a young damsel,' she went on. 'You can make calls without me. Once you call on one family you will get to know twenty-five more by the next day. It is only a question of effort.'[4]

But Maurice felt no desire to be married and the miracle which his mother had prophesied did not happen. He continued to glower at Manceau and lay claim to his mother's undivided affection. George was not discouraged. Once she had established what kind of daughter-in-law she would be prepared to accept, she saw no reason to put off the day. She wanted to see Maurice well married. She longed to see grandchildren filling Nohant with their happy prattle. She let all her friends know that Maurice was looking for a bride and enlisted their help. But Maurice was not looking hard enough, and the onus of the search fell on his mother's shoulders. As the years went by she eschewed her objections to the young ladies of the neighbourhood and was prepared to consider any young woman who would answer her requirements, whatever her provenance. Maurice was thirty-seven when she wrote to Jules Boucoiran, his one-time tutor, who had since become the editor of *Le Courrier du Gard* in his home town Nîmes:

Nohant, 31 July 1860

You will probably be unable to find a suitable match for him if you look for a wife among the devout and the Legitimists. I would much prefer a protestant family. See what people feel about it and let me know. I would like him to make up his mind to get married and raise a family. If you find someone charming, with a serious bent of mind, a pleasing face, intelligent and of a decent family which would not attempt to bind the young couple to their own ideas and habits except by bonds of affection, we shall lower our expectations of a dowry.[5]

In the end it was George who discovered the ideal bride and in 1862 brought off the marriage between the thirty-nine-year-old Maurice and the twenty-year-old Lina Calamatta whom, to the end of her life, she lovingly called 'the pearl of the house'.[6]

Marceline Claudine Augustine Calamatta was born in Paris in 1842. Her father was the Italian engraver Luigi Calamatta, who was then working in Paris; her mother, a painter in her own right, came from a distinguished French family. The parents did not get on well. The father, although a catholic, was lax in his observance while the mother was fanatically devout. George knew all three but reserved her affection for father and baby. When Calamatta later became the head of the Milan School of Art, Lina was sent to a boarding-school in Genoa and it was there that George and Maurice saw her again, aged thirteen, during their Italian holiday. Lina was the delight of her teachers and when she left school at fourteen she was awarded a prize for modesty, industry and obedience.

For several years she kept house for her father in Milan, having little to do with her mother. She accompanied him on one of his visits to France and went with him to Nohant. She was eighteen by then, an attractive girl with a good contralto voice. Maurice, who had known Lina since her babyhood, was a perfect host, but he was more interested in Calamatta's views on art than in his daughter's singing. The following summer, while Maurice was sailing round the world in Prince Jerome's yacht, the Calamattas came down again and stayed for three days. George observed the nineteen-year-old girl with new eyes. She saw a devoted daughter, a generous and unspoilt nature, an attractive face. As she listened to Lina's singing in the drawing-room after dinner, an idea formed in her mind. When a few months later Maurice returned from his travels, she proposed Lina as a possible bride. Maurice allowed himself to be persuaded.

George lost no time. Within weeks of Maurice's return from America she wrote to Lina and tactfully asked whether she would consider giving her hand in marriage to her son and heir. Lina conveyed her acceptance in a letter:

Milan, 29 March 1862

Dear kind Madame Sand,
I want to be the one to bring you my little person with a sincere and serious *yes*: if my answer has been slow in coming it is because I was so surprised at your proposal and so little prepared for the idea of marriage that I was frightened by the prospect of suddenly having to leave my father and my beautiful Italy where I have found happiness and where I have preserved my childhood to the age of twenty. Now that Papa has promised to come and see me as often as he can and that I

know he will be really pleased with my *yes*, I give it to you without regret and I say to you: Little mother, I already love you so much that I will not miss Italy much when I join you at Nohant, where the two of you had already made me forget it once during my visit two years ago.[7]

Two days later George wrote back:

Paris, 31 March 1862

Lina my dear,

Trust yourself to us, trust yourself to *him* and believe in happiness. There is only one happiness in life, it is loving and being loved. The two of us will have no other thought in mind or object in life except to cherish you and spoil you. We also love your father so much that we shall do all we can to go and see him, or persuade him to come over and stay as long as possible. We have always been like that with him. For thirty years he has been one of our closest friends and now that he is entrusting us with what he holds dearest in the world, he is, with you, what we cherish most. As a child Maurice loved him by instinct; when he grew up he learnt to respect him; and when he saw you, who take so much after your father, he felt for you an affection which was different from anything he has ever felt before.[8]

She still signed herself formally G. Sand. That same day Maurice wrote to Lina for the first time, using the formal *vous*, which George in her own letter had already dropped in favour of the familiar *tu*: 'Now, my dear little fiancée, when you come to Nohant you will be in your own home and your dear Papa whom I love more than ever will be able to stay as long as he likes; but we shall also visit him in Italy.'[9]

Maurice wanted to travel to Milan to fetch his fiancée himself, but Calamatta preferred the first meeting between the betrothed to take place at Nohant. To Lina the disappointed Maurice wrote, still using the formal *vous*: 'The next fifteen or twenty days will seem very slow to me, my dear fiancée, as in my impatience to see you I have not taken the Alps into account.'[10]

When the Calamattas arrived at Nohant in April Lina delighted everybody, including the non-musical Maurice, with her beautiful singing. The two young people took to each other. George noted amusedly in her diary that they were cheating each other in a game of dominoes. All was going well. Lina adored her future mother-in-law and Maurice was thrilled with an attractive young bride who so readily accepted his emotional priorities. George was immensely thankful. To Boucoiran she wrote: 'Maurice is taking the wife of his choice. He is marrying the daughter of my old and worthy friend Calamatta. The dowry he would have expected from an unknown girl will not be required from someone who is worthy in herself.'[11]

Lina and her father, like George and Maurice, were catholics by birth but anti-clerical by conviction. Casimir Dudevant and Madame Calamatta would have preferred a catholic wedding, but their views were not sought. To the main parties involved a civil ceremony seemed preferable and on 17 May 1862 Maurice and Lina were married by the mayor of Nohant. Shortly after the wedding Maurice took his young wife to Guillery to present her to his father. The three of them got on well.

Announcing the event to Prince Jerome, and his wife Princess Clotilde with whom Maurice had spent seven months sailing round the world, George felt the need to explain. 'No priest,' she wrote. 'We feel we have excommunicated ourselves like all those who had wished to see a united Italy and a victorious Victor Emmanuel. We consider ourselves outside the Church. But do not say this to Princess Clotilde. We must not make angels cry. She believes in the catholic Church; we do not. We would be hypocrites if we attended it.'[12]

The disciple of Leroux and the creator of *Spiridion* was reaffirming the non-dependence of faith on any established form of cult. Soon George found another opportunity to make her views heard. The *Revue des Deux Mondes* had been publishing a novel by Octave Feuillet in which established catholicism was represented in glowing terms. George was outraged. Within six months she wrote a counter-novel and sent it to Buloz for publication. It was *Mademoiselle La Quintinie*.

The heroine was clearly modelled on Lina Sand. Lucie La Quintinie was half-Italian half-French, brought up as a catholic and passionately in love with Italy. For a suitor she was given an enlightened young man who tried to wean her from her dependence on an unworthy catholic priest. He used every theological argument in the anti-clerical armoury and eventually liberated his beloved from her spiritual slavery. True faith triumphed over the exterior manifestation of religion.

The work was written in the realistic style which had made George's rustic novels so popular. There was nothing of the mystical *Spiridion* about it. It was readily understandable and the message was uncompromising. It had instant repercussions. Sainte-Beuve took the unprecedented step of reviewing the first few instalments without waiting to see the entire work. Mentioning that *Mademoiselle La Quintinie* was Madame Sand's reply to Feuillet's *Sibylle*, he described George as a powerful hawk swooping down on a white dove. Buloz's appraisal was more down-to-earth. 'Some readers admire it,' he wrote. 'Some curse it. Some catholics trample the *Revue des Deux Mondes* under their feet; others go out of their way to get hold of a copy.'[13] When the novel was published in book form the controversy became even fiercer. Students held it up as the symbol of liberalism, while conservative catholics were shocked to the core. At about that time a literary banquet to commemorate Shakespeare's tercentenary was suddenly banned by the Paris police without a word of explanation. George indignantly suggested that the authorities must have taken the step because Shakespeare was a protestant.

While the controversy caused by *Mademoiselle La Quintinie* was still raging, the Nohant household had to take a stand on yet another aspect of religious affiliation. Lina was expecting a baby. As neither parents nor grandmother wished to prejudice its future because of their own unorthodox views, a difficult problem presented itself. They decided to seek advice. George wrote countless letters to churchmen known for their liberalism and integrity and after much searching of the heart informed Boucoiran that Lina, five months pregnant, was carrying a future protestant in her womb. She added that the decision was Maurice's.

Once the question was settled, Nohant resumed its ordinary routine. Everybody was busy writing, designing, rehearsing and acting. Even Lina took on small parts. In the spring of 1864 a touring company arrived at La Châtre and George, who had helped to secure them a theatre, went down to the village nearly every evening to see them perform. At the beginning of July the Calamattas arrived at Nohant to be at hand during their daughter's confinement and were pleased to see a midwife living in. Mme Calamatta was appalled however to see Madame Sand, in spite of her age, Alexandre Manceau, in spite of his tuberculosis, and Lina Sand, in spite of advanced pregnancy, all take a dip in the river.

One evening, when the entire household, including Mme Calamatta and the midwife, had gone to La Châtre to watch a play, Lina felt the first pangs of labour. The party returned late at night, just in time to help deliver a baby boy whom George, with the help of the midwife, caught in her large apron. He was born on Bastille Day, 14 July 1863. The following May the parents took the decisive step. They underwent a second marriage ceremony performed by a protestant minister and had their boy baptised in the protestant faith as Marc Antoine Dudevant-Sand. A few weeks later parents and baby went to Guillery to spend the summer with grandfather Dudevant.

But Cocoton, as the baby was fondly called, was not destined to live long. A day or two before the departure from Nohant he seemed unwell, and on arrival at Guillery his sickness was diagnosed as dysentery. His parents and grandfather had just celebrated his first birthday. Maurice informed George of the illness and George wrote back that she was coming to help. Casimir was agitated at the prospect of receiving his wife under his roof, where he was living with a mistress and a daughter of sixteen. 'But I cannot very well stop her if she wants to come and see her grandson,' he conceded uncomfortably. 'She is a mother and she feels the anguish of her children.'[14]

He was nervous. On the day George was expected he summoned his doctor and solicitor to his house and when the servants announced that the carriage of Madame la Baronne had been sighted in the drive, he stepped out, reinforced on either side, to receive her on the steps of the manor. George too had brought reinforcement: Manceau, her own doctor and a protestant minister. She and Casimir had not seen each other since he came to Nohant for Solange's wedding seventeen years earlier. When she caught sight of him she called him Casimir as of old; he avoided using her name. 'Madame,' he said stiffly, 'you know your room. Since you have last stayed here it has not been occupied.'[15] Jeanny Dalias, his housekeeper and mother of his daughter, showed the way. At the door of her room George said to her: 'I entrust my old husband to your care.'[16]

The journey had been wasted. The baby had died the night before and there was nothing George could do except wait for the funeral. That night Casimir presided over a sad dinner attended by Manceau, Maurice, Lina, George's doctor and minister, as well as his own doctor and solicitor. Jeanny Dalias was excluded as usual. George sat wordlessly at the dinner table, a stout sixty-year-old matron with sagging cheeks and greying hair, making everybody uncomfortable by her silence. The following morning the baby was given a protestant burial and was put next to the grave of old Baron Dudevant and Solange's first baby girl who had also died at Guillery. In the evening everybody departed; George and her party returned to Paris while Maurice and Lina returned to Nohant. After George's departure Casimir's doctor asked him what he thought of his wife after so many years. 'I could not bear to call her Aurore,' Casimir said unhappily. 'She looked more like the sunset.'[17]

Only a month before the death of her third grandchild, George had taken a long-planned step which baffled all those who knew her. In June 1864 she relinquished Nohant to Maurice and Lina and moved with Manceau to a small house they had acquired in his name in the village of Palaiseau, in the district of Versailles.

The main reason for her voluntary exile from Nohant, the ancestral home which was her roots, her way of life and the very essence of her being, was Maurice's demand that she should choose between him and Manceau. He had never been able to reconcile himself to the part Manceau played in his mother's life and found it insufferable that Old Mancel, in the presence of Lina, should act the indispensable *majordomo* while he, the heir to Nohant, was continuously relegated to a secondary position. Things came to a head when a pretty chamber-maid who played leading roles at the Nohant theatre gave herself airs and refused to carry out her domestic duties. Maurice issued instructions, Manceau countermanded them. At the end of an ugly scene Maurice informed his mother that unless she sent Manceau away he and Lina would leave Nohant. George could not bear the prospect of an estrangement with her own beloved son and gave in. On 23 November 1863 Manceau wrote in the joint diary:

Following some discussion which was held without my participation, I was informed that I was free to leave at any time. Tears were shed, but they soon dried up. That is all the regret I am leaving behind after fifteen years of devotion. I want to say this here and now so that I need never cry again over it, hoping that one day I may perhaps be able to remember it all with a smile. . . .

So I am allowed to regain my liberty. And if I want to offer my love and devotion to someone else, since this sort of thing seems to give me pleasure, I am free to do so. Free indeed![18]

In his bitterness Manceau was in no position to appreciate that George had not made a free choice but yielded to an ultimatum. Nor could he guess that after she had imparted what seemed the final decision, she spent a restless night in her room reviewing the situation in the light of her own emotional needs.

She was nearly sixty. She had lived with Manceau, from choice, longer than she had lived with any of her previous companions. He was totally committed and had made her life at Nohant smooth and worry-free. She had to admit to herself that other people round her, devoted and adoring as they were, made use of her in some way. Maurice, vacillating between writing and painting, leaned on her financially; Solange, who also dabbled in writing, spent everything George was able to put aside for her; Augustine, who had been handsomely endowed, expected George to use her influence with the imperial family to advance her husband's career. There were all the other dependants who through the years had not hesitated to ask for help: Leroux, Perdiguier, Marie Dorval's children, the retired house servants, the village poor. Manceau seemed to be the only one who gave as generously as she did, however little he had.

Suddenly George knew that she no longer wanted to go on shouldering the enormous burden of Nohant with its lavish style of life, its theatre, its actors, its house-guests and its large staff. At fifty-nine she felt that the time had come to relegate her responsibilities to her son and regain some of the freedom which her age entitled her to. It seemed senseless to part with a needed companion only to please a son who had his own wife to look after him. By dawn she had decided to leave Nohant rather than leave Manceau. On 24 November she wrote in the diary: 'Let us go away together, my dear. Let us go without rancour, bitterness or anger, never to part. . . . We shall give them all, we shall leave everything behind except our dignity.'[19]

Maurice was flabbergasted when his mother told him that she was relinquishing Nohant to him and moving out with Manceau as soon as they had found a place of their own. She explained, as she was to explain for months to come to many of her worried friends, that Nohant had become too cumbersome and that she wanted to live within commuting distance of Paris. For a few days there was much tension in the house, then everything began to fall into place. Manceau left for Paris to start looking for a house and George behaved as if nothing unusual was taking place. When Manceau returned from his preliminary search everybody was affable and the New Year was ushered in with general goodwill.

In January George and Manceau left for Paris together. Manceau had written a short verse-play which the Odéon management agreed to put on as a curtain-raiser. George wrote Maurice and Lina enthusiastic reports of the play's success, maintaining the façade of a loving and united family. She wrote that Prince Jerome had attended the first night and paid praise to the budding playwright. Shortly afterwards she reported that a suitable house had been acquired in the village of Palaiseau, within easy reach of Paris. Money was more plentiful as she had just sold most of her Delacroix paintings at a good price. After that she and Manceau returned to Nohant to prepare for the move.

The news that Madame Sand was leaving Nohant for good struck the neighbourhood like a thunder from a clear sky. The villagers who for so many years supplied the rich manor with their goods and services petitioned her to stay. When it became obvious that her decision was irrevocable the entire artisan population of La Châtre, the cobbler, the bootmaker, the clogmaker, the locksmith, the carpenter, the draper and the charcoal burner all put their names to a florid letter of farewell:

La Châtre, 6 June 1864

Madam,
Dear and Illustrious Compatriot,
   The news of your forthcoming departure has filled the workers of La Châtre with emotion and grief. You must believe us when we say that it not only the kind deeds which your hand has sown which makes us feel your loss.
   Your genius is a light which illuminates the entire world, but your heart has known how to make itself understood by the simple souls of the people. Bound to you by the belief in the sacred communion of democracy and progress, they wish to express on this occasion their affection and regret.
   While you stay away from us we shall remember you in our thoughts. Remember us too. Let not this expression of our respect be our farewell; let our sorrow at your departure be mingled with the hope of your return. . . .
   You have made strangers come to know and appreciate our beloved countryside. Who can be more grateful to you than the children of this region? If your name is the eternal glory of Berry, Berry has drawn out of you your most glorious words. Nobody will be able to fully understand George Sand when

she is away from Berry, from Nohant and from us. Let the memory of that intimate bond cling to you like the perfume of your native countryside and bring you back soon to your old friends.[20]

While George and Manceau were going through the nostalgic process of sorting out possessions accumulated during many years of a settled existence, Maurice and Lina were preparing to go to Guillery and spend a few weeks with Papa Dudevant. The staff was reduced, the stables emptied, the furniture covered with dust-sheets. On 11 June Manceau wrote in the diary: 'Last evening at Nohant. I think we shall all remember it. There is nothing much to say about it though. I think that during the fourteen years I have been here I have laughed, cried and lived more than I had in the entire thirty-three years which preceded them. From now on I shall be alone with her. What a responsibility! But what an honour, and what a joy.'[21] Many years later, when the diary came into Maurice's possession together with the rest of his mother's papers, he scribbled over that entry: 'What a prig! What a fool.'[22]

On the surface the parting was amiable. As soon as George arrived at Palaiseau she informed Maurice that all was well and gave him Manceau's regards. Four weeks later, when Maurice sent a telegram saying that his son's condition was critical, George took it as a matter of course that Manceau should accompany her to Guillery, although Maurice would have preferred, particularly at that painful moment in his life, to have her on her own. Tactfully Manceau spent the night in lodgings in the nearby village. There was no suggestion however that George and he should accompany the bereaved parents to Nohant. There was no going back.

George loved Palaiseau. She described it as a patch of green surrounding a diamond-shaped lake, with golden cornfields stretching as far as the eye could see. There were pleasant country walks and unfamiliar plants and bulbs to add to her collection. The village was as quiet as Gargilesse, yet with a frequent train service to Paris. George often commuted, frequented the theatre and the Monday literary dinners at Magny's restaurant. A new generation of admirers made her feel the queen of the roost: Gustave Flaubert, who called her *Chère Maître*; Alexandre Dumas the Younger who called her *Maman*; the painter Charles Marchal who called her *Chère Grande Amie*.

For Manceau it was all too late. His health was visibly failing from day to day. Doctors came and went, he continued to cough atrociously and spit blood. Characteristically he was more distressed about George's anxiety than about his own condition. He still went to Paris from time to time to carry out errands for *Madame*. But *Madame*'s feelings for him were undergoing the same subtle change which had occurred when she was nursing Chopin, Musset and even Sandeau. Devotion and medical ministrations drove away love and attraction.

The change began several years earlier, when the stability of the relationship occasionally resulted in moments of boredom. In 1861 Alexandre Dumas the Younger brought down to Nohant, along with his own mistress, his friend Charles Marchal. George liked the young painter who accepted her teasing about his fatness with good grace and called her impudently 'My Good Woman'. Before he left Nohant she noted in the joint diary that Marchal had become her 'Fat Baby'. A gallant correspondence followed, partly maternal, partly coquettish. Marchal stayed again at Nohant in 1862 and 1863.

Some time after her move to Palaiseau Alexandre Dumas the Younger asked his *Maman* to use her influence with Prince Jerome to obtain for Marchal the Cross of the *Légion d'Honneur*. George was only too willing to oblige and in due course Marchal came down to Palaiseau to thank her for her goodwill. At thirty-nine he looked young and exciting to the sixty-year-old George. As usual her maternal possessiveness was tinged with coquetry and her spirits soared when the indolent Marchal proved susceptible. In the intoxication of the moment she dropped the dull duties of a nurse and took Marchal to spend a few days at the Gargilesse cottage. Manceau noted in the diary that Marchal had been treating him insolently.

It was George's last escapade. On her return she resumed her nursing with untiring devotion, administered frictions, lotions and steam-baths. It was clear to all but Manceau that he was dying. George kept his spirits up by pretending to collaborate with him on a play he was too weak to write on his own. For three whole months she never left his side.

He died on 21 August 1865, after a cruel fit of coughing which lasted for forty-eight hours. George closed his eyes, changed his clothes and covered him with fresh flowers. To Maurice she wrote the same day in neutral terms so as not to antagonise him even further: 'Our poor friend has ceased to suffer.'[23] She added that Manceau had mentioned him in his will and asked him to come to Palaiseau. To a nephew, from whom she saw no need to conceal the extent of her loss, she wrote like a stricken widow: 'I have lost him, that wonderful man who had been my companion for the past fifteen years, the devoted mainstay of my old age.'[24] The night before the funeral she wrote in the joint diary which from then on she was to keep on her own until shortly before her own death: 'Alone, with him lying next door, in that little room. No longer will I listen for his breathing. Tomorrow night there will be nothing, I shall be even more alone. For ever.'[25]

She buried him in the local cemetery, in a pretty little corner of her own choice. Many friends attended the funeral but not Manceau's parents who were incensed against Madame Sand for having allowed their son to return the ghost without the ministrations of a priest. Manceau had left the cottages at Palaiseau and Gargilesse to Maurice. George feared that the parents and sister might contest the will, but all they asked for was a small personal memento.

After the funeral Maurice took his mother back to Nohant, where Lina was expecting another baby. Over a year had passed since she had left it. She found the house tidy, the garden well kept, the estate in good order. Manceau's death had removed the source of friction between her and Maurice, while Lina was as adoring as ever. After a short rest George returned to Paris and Palaiseau, not as a bereaved mistress but as a hopeful bride. She had found a new emotional anchor in Charles Marchal, with whom she had run off to Gargilesse a few months earlier.

At her request he had attended Manceau's funeral. On her return from Nohant the light-hearted flirtation became a frank declaration of intent and the two became lovers. The effect on George was miraculous. She became young, full of stamina and eager for life. 'It seems to me as if my life has started all over again,' she wrote to Marchal. 'It is as if I see everything for the first time.'[26] She called him her springtime, her fat rabbit, her green toad, her blue lizard, her faithful humming-bird.

But he was not faithful. Although he was genuinely fond of the old enchantress he was not prepared to give up his liberty and his pretty young models. George had to do most of the chasing. She came up to Paris so that he would not be able to say that he had no time to go down to Palaiseau, offered him complimentary tickets to plays, humbly asked whether he would have time to dine with her before going on to wherever he was going. She was elated when he invited her to see him in his studio, was mortified when she found the door locked and rightly guessed that he was cloistering behind it with one of his models. Yet she was careful not to show too much of her jealousy and eagerly accepted his excuses and explanations. When they did meet he was kind and loving. He addressed her as *vous* and his only endearment for her was 'Dear great friend'; she addressed him as *tu* and called him 'My very last'.[27]

At the height of her Indian summer she returned to Nohant where on 10 January 1866 she helped deliver Lina of a baby girl who was named Aurore. In a letter to Prince Jerome George reported that the baby was fine but the mother was unwell, as was the father who had rushed out at the head of the local fire brigade to extinguish a fire and come back slightly burnt. When both parents were fully recovered George hurried back to Paris, Palaiseau, and her straying fat rabbit.

She was restless. Twice she went to stay with Flaubert at his country house near Rouen; once she went to Brittany. She frequented the literary dinners at Magny's restaurant in Paris and the theatre. For the first time in forty years she was living entirely on her own. By early 1867 she had had enough. She packed her belongings and returned to Nohant, never to leave it again.

Nohant, without responsibilities, was a new experience for her. For the first time in her life she could sit back and enjoy the privilege of being the grand lady of the manor without the hard work which went with it. To Alexandre Dumas the Younger she wrote with approval: 'The children are well in control of the boat, and I am pleased not to have to control anything myself.'[28]

Lina was good with her. She accepted as an article of faith that George had first call on Maurice's time and attention and did not make demands which might have clashed with his order of priorities. She let him take George for a month's holiday on the French Riviera at a time when she was again near term; and she made no fuss when on 11 March 1868 the baby arrived while father and mother-in-law, together with two or three other close family friends, were still having a gay time in Cannes. She adored George and built a cult around her. Later she used to say that she had consented to marry Maurice largely because she worshipped his mother.

The new baby was also a girl. Neither was baptised at birth but towards the end of 1868, when Gabrielle was eight months old and her sister Aurore nearly three years old, they were baptised together by a protestant minister. Prince Jerome came down to Nohant to stand godfather to Aurore, while a nephew of George's stood godfather to Gabrielle. The following year Luigi Calamatta died, and his widow, always a devout catholic, took the veil. Lina became even more attached to George. George, for her part, loved her as if she was her own flesh and blood. 'My daughter Lina is my true daughter,' she wrote to Flaubert. 'The other one is well and beautiful, which is all I expect of her.'[29]

Visitors to Nohant tended to dismiss the unobtrusive Lina as a dumb housewife. George always came to her defence. 'She could have been an artist,' she said of her, 'but she gave herself wholly to motherhood.'[30]

As the years went by, the idyll continued. In 1867, when Lina had been at Nohant for five years, George wrote to Louis and Pauline Viardot: 'Maurice is happy in his marriage; he has a real treasure of a wife, energetic, well organised, a good mother, a good housewife, and with it artistic by nature and intelligence.'[31]

Eleven years after the marriage, when Maurice was fifty, Lina thirty-one and George near seventy, she gave her final happy verdict: 'Lina is still the pearl of the house. She has all the qualities and all the graces.'[32]

~~~~~~~~~~~~~~~~~~~~~~~

Chapter 19

A military assignment

'I do not write for those sixth-form schoolboys or little dress-makers who read George Sand,'[1] the twenty-three-year-old Gustave Flaubert declared in 1844, at the beginning of his literary career. Little did he dream that a time would come when he would be calling her the Great George Sand and *Chère Maître*, or even, delicately mixing his genders, *Chère bon maître adoré*.[2]

He did not actually meet her until the spring of 1859, when she was a world-famous novelist in her mid-fifties. Flaubert was then, at near-forty, the author of just one published novel, the controversial *Madame Bovary*, which two years earlier had landed him in a lawsuit on a charge of immorality. There was no immediate blossoming of friendship. George lived mostly at Nohant and Palaiseau, Flaubert at his country house near Rouen. They met chiefly on those occasions when both attended the literary dinners at Magny's restaurant in Paris. In 1862 Flaubert sent review copies of his newly published *Salammbô* to those of his colleagues whom he hoped would be sympathetic. George was impressed and wrote a glowing review in *La Presse*. Flaubert wrote to thank her. She wrote back to say he had only his genius to thank. The friendship was sealed. When Manceau had his one-act play put on at the Odéon Flaubert was there to applaud. When Manceau died Flaubert was there to condole.

In his mid-forties he was still a handsome man, tall, fair, with a Viking-like mane and beard. His love life was mainly over after the break up of a long liaison. He lived solely for literature and when he was not writing, laboriously and painstakingly, he was reading or taking notes. In Paris he had a small apartment where his Sunday *habitués* were Turgenev, Emile Zola, Alphonse Daudet and the brothers Goncourt. Most of the year round he lived with his widowed mother in his château at Croisset, which was surrounded by a magnificent garden stretching down to the Seine.

After Manceau's death George accepted his invitation to stay a few days at Croisset. They went sight-seeing in Rouen, discoursed and gently probed each other's souls. A few months later the visit was repeated. While lovingly pursuing her fat Marchal, George instinctively lavished coquettish solicitude on Flaubert. She was quick to point out that he was the same age as her son, which in her terms was a discreet invitation to greater intimacy, yet she never called him by the double-meaning endearment *Mon enfant*. There was a mutual reticence. By the end of a year the probing gave way to an undemanding fondness. George called him her *troubadour*, after an inn sign they had seen together, or her *Bénédictin*, for his recluse habits. He called her *Chère maître* or *Chère bon maître*. George, using the privilege of her age, addressed him familiarly as *tu*; he never deviated from the formal *vous*.

They continued to lead their independent lives in their respective parts of the country, and made up by exchanging frequent letters. They sent each other pressed flowers, bulbs, books. George sent him her entire Collected Works. Flaubert sent her other people's novels. She asked him when he would be able to send her some of his own. He explained that he was a slow worker. 'Your ideas flow grandly and inexhaustibly like a river', he wrote to her. 'Mine are like a thin trickle of water. It needs a large artistic construction to turn it into a cascade.'[3] George was abashed. In the four years it had taken Flaubert to write *Madame Bovary* she had produced no less than a dozen novels and three or four plays. 'When I see the anguish you go through when you are working on a novel,' she humbly wrote in 1867, 'I am disconcerted by my own facility and tell myself that my work is slipshod.'[4]

In the spring of 1868 she paid her third and last visit to Croisset and the following year, at Christmas, Flaubert came down to

Nohant for the first time. The visit was a great success. After his departure Lina took to reading his novels and astounded a gathering of friends by defending them against criticism with panache and perception.

In spite of constant invitations and promises Flaubert did not find time to return to Nohant until four years later. He claimed that the slightest distraction from routine put him off work for weeks. There were the occasional reunions in Paris, when both could arrange to be there without inconvenience to either. The friendship continued to flow steadily and reliably in their correspondence. There was nothing they did not discuss: her novels, his novels, other people's novels, her children and grandchildren, her health, his mother's health, her finances, his finances, politics. It was a serene and much cherished attachment which nothing ever disturbed, not even their differences of opinion at the beginning of the Third Republic. It ended only with George's death, four years before his. Many years later Lina, as an act of homage to both, collected most of their letters in one volume.

One of George's unchanging characteristics was her inability to save money. The more she made the more she gave away, and the more she gave away the more she wanted to continue to do so. At the same time, like a good French bourgeois housewife, she wished to see her children well provided. She could never forgive Casimir for resisting her attempts to make him fork out more than he felt he could. Having failed to win an eight-year-long lawsuit against her husband for Maurice's and Solange's right to inherit Guillery without sharing with the young half-sister, she angrily wrote to Flaubert in 1867: 'Maurice is at Nérac, settling out of court after a case which has robbed him of his patrimony. His charming father is stealing some three hundred thousand francs from his children in order to please his cook. Fortunately while *Monsieur* was leading that edifying life of his, I have been working hard and did not break into my capital. I have nothing of my own, but my children's livelihood will be assured.'[5]

By that time the children had reached an age when both could have been expected to fend for themselves. Maurice was forty-four, Solange thirty-nine. Maurice had inherited from Manceau the cottages at Gargilesse and Palaiseau and was heir to Nohant; Solange, without renouncing the small allowance made to her by her father, had accumulated enough wealth from her aristocratic lovers to build herself a sumptuous villa in Cannes and plant its garden with exotic flowers. True enough, neither child had inherited the mother's self-discipline and staying power. They were dabblers. Maurice, having given up painting, was writing novels, plays and scientific articles. Thanks to his mother's influence he had his work published and actually made a small name for himself, but a close friend described him as a gifted amateur without ambition. Solange too had a novel published and was toying with the idea of writing a scholarly biography of her royal ancestor the Maréchal de Saxe. Nothing much came of her literary aspirations except that once, during an advice-seeking visit to old Sainte-Beuve, she happened to mention that the Nohant household was in financial straits.

Sainte-Beuve was moved. He proposed that the Académie Française, of which he was a member, should vote George Sand a certain literary award worth twenty thousand francs. Unfortunately the other few candidates were all less controversial than the author of the anti-clerical *La Daniella*. When the proposal was put to the vote two members, one a former lover and the other a former enemy, Prosper Mérimée and Alfred de Vigny, gallantly supported it. Another former lover, Jules Sandeau, was so agitated by the need to be fair to a mistress who had rejected him some thirty years earlier, that he stayed away. In the event the supporters were overwhelmingly outvoted and the award went to Adolphe Thiers, later President of the Third Republic.

George was disappointed and so was the Empress Eugénie who was particularly fond of her. She suggested that to make up for the loss of money and loss of face, George Sand should be offered a seat in the Académie Française, as befitted her stature and standing in French literature.

It was a revolutionary idea since, by ancient law, the Académie Française was barred to women. Feminist circles welcomed the chance of breaking into that traditional stronghold of men while progressive men were not averse to allowing equal rights in the sphere of literature. In April 1863 a brochure was published under the title of *Les femmes à l'Académie*, in which a plea was made to repeal the old law and enable the foremost literary institution of France to benefit from women's special brand of intellect and delicacy. The author of the brochure signed himself as *S*. Many readers naturally assumed that the *S* stood for Sand.

Again George disappointed all ardent feminists. Far from taking up the challenge, she publicly dissociated herself from it. Within weeks of the publication of the feminist brochure she published one of her own under the title *Pourquoi les femmes à l'Académie*, in which she argued that women had no business to be in it. 'The place of women is no more at the present-day Academy than it is in the Senate, the Legislature or the Armed Forces,'[6] she stated.

Her reasoning was diffuse and hard to follow. She maintained that by definition the Académie was a purely literary institution, whereas contemporary writing was espoused to social and philosophical ideas. Moreover, as a guardian of tradition it was perforce divorced from progress. Since women were promoters of progress in all spheres, they could not in all sincerity become members of an institution whose aims and ideas were outdated. It was not a case of crying sour grapes, George concluded; it was a case of the grapes having gone off.

Privately she explained that she could not allow people to think that she was so presumptuous as to aspire to the inconceivable. Since few members of the Académie, if any, wished to see her join their number, there was no further attempt to discuss the idea. But the Empress was not prepared to give up her pet project without a fight and continued to broach the subject whenever she could. The Forty Immortals remained impregnable. Even Alexandre Dumas the Younger, with all his adoration for *Maman*, did not feel she ought to be allowed into the sanctuary. Seven years after the idea was first mooted the Empress was still at it. In 1870, only months before the outbreak of the Franco-Prussian war, she was seen having a long intimate talk with

Alexandre Dumas at a Palace reception. A common friend, an erudite American by the name of Henry Harrisse who had a way of knowing everybody and being everywhere, gave George an account of the conversation:

> 'What did the Empress say to you?' I asked Dumas [Harrisse wrote].
> 'She wants Madame Sand to be accepted into the Académie.'
> 'And what did you say to that?'
> 'Well you see, I explained that for a woman to call on so many men was a delicate step which required more thought.'[7]

George was not dismayed. It was not a battle she was prepared to fight. She no longer wished to revolutionise society with her ideas, no longer asked herself where she was going. 'You accustom yourself to regard writing as a military assignment,' she wrote to Flaubert in the autumn of 1868. 'You face the fire without stopping to think that you might be killed or wounded. ... I just carry on, as stupid as a cabbage, as obstinate as only a native of Berry can be.'[8]

Her proficiency remained unimpaired. Every night she went up to her study to write her twenty pages of copy in her firm, round hand, rarely altering a sentence, sending the pages off to be published just as they were. At sixty-four she noted in her diary: 'My brain has not deteriorated. I feel it has accumulated a great deal on the way and is better equipped than it has ever been. It is a mistake to think that old age is a downward slope; on the contrary, it is an upward road which one takes with astonishingly easy strides. Intellectual work gets accomplished as rapidly as the physical progress of a child.'[9]

She still modelled her characters on people she knew, allowing her imagination to embroider complicated adventures and situations. She wrote of love and virtue and later, as her granddaughters were growing up, embarked on children's stories. Some of her books were no longer reviewed, but they never failed to sell. The old name was magic. George chuckled. To Flaubert she ruefully remarked: 'Nobody is happier and more serene than the old retired minstrel who from time to time sings his little romance in the moonlight, without over-worrying whether he sings well or badly, as long as he utters the tune which had been floating in his head.'[10]

Life was as full as ever. Nohant, under Lina and Maurice, remained open to all her friends, though the friends had changed. The old ones were gone, young ones came to replace them. There were the sons and daughters of the childhood friends, young nephews and nieces, new Parisian writers who were captivated by the charm and wisdom of the old lady of Nohant. Juliette Adam, a beautiful young woman and an established writer, became one of George's most adoring new friends. Another was the American Henry Harrisse, an authority on almost everything, particularly on Christopher Columbus and the works of George Sand.

In the summer of 1868 the Adams and Harrisse came to stay. It was a lively house party, with bathing and fishing in the river, walking and talking. In the evenings George played Mozart and Gluck with as much sensitivity as ever; after dinner she cut paper patterns or embroidered, while the others discoursed. The visit coincided with her sixty-fourth birthday. After breakfast family and house-guests went up to the study to offer their good wishes and presents: Maurice, Lina, the Adams and last but not least Henry Harrisse who made a long-winded speech while the others winked behind his back at George who could hardly keep a straight face.

She never got over her weakness for practical jokes. What Marie d'Agoult had called her vulgarity was in fact a schoolgirl's sense of humour. One evening she and Maurice hid a cockerel in the cupboard of the Adams' bedroom. At dawn the cock began to crow. Juliette Adam and her daughter, both in the secret, buried their heads under the sheets while Adam groped about in the dark trying to locate the offensive bird. Eventually he discovered the source of the noise but when he opened the cupboard the cock began to flutter madly about the room, escaping all attempts to capture him. Adam flung the windows open; the cock made for the door. Adam, in nightgown and cap, opened the door to let it out, only to bump right into George and Maurice who were listening behind it, convulsed with laughter.

Most people fell willingly into the spirit of the game. As soon as anyone was asked to go out to fetch something, he could be sure that some dark plot was being hatched against him. There was much laughter and gaiety. Maurice continued to put on puppet shows, devoting weeks of hard work to a single night's performance. The well-trained audience participated as eagerly as the many children who were present. They shouted to the puppets, booed them or encouraged them, made Maurice change his plot and improvise madly to meet the challenge. Flaubert, who had witnessed such a show during his stay, thought it was crazy. George, lovingly teasing, dedicated to him her novel *Pierre qui roule*, in which all the puppets came alive.

In July 1870 Napoleon III was goaded into war against Prussia by Bismarck's inexorable determination to create a unified German empire. Only the year before Empress Eugénie went to Egypt to take part in the opening celebrations of the Suez Canal which French diplomacy and finance had helped to dig. Now diplomacy was forced to make way for strategy.

The news about the outbreak of war reached Nohant one sultry July day, some two weeks after George had celebrated her sixty-sixth birthday. The house was full of guests as usual, the Adams amongst them. Everybody made hasty preparations to return to Paris, and the last afternoon was spent in the garden in an atmosphere of gloom. There was no conversation. Nobody had anything left to say. Suddenly the sound of a military drum pierced the silence. Juliette Adam later recalled:

> The unwonted sound froze the marrow in our bones. Adam, erect, went as white as a sheet. Plauchut stood up. I was glued to my seat. Alice caught my hand in hers.
> 'My heart is pounding,' she said.
> Mine seemed to leap into my throat. I felt sick.
> Then we saw Maurice advancing towards us, a wooden drum dating back to the days of the First Republic slung over

his shoulder. He was as white as Adam. When he came close to us he called out: *Vive la France*. We repeated the words with trembling lips. Madame Sand and I burst into tears.[11]

A wave of patriotism swept across the country, uniting Bonapartists, republicans and socialists under the flag of war. At the Paris opera the leading soprano came down to the footlights with a tricolour in her hand and began singing the *Marseillaise*, the banned battle song of the Revolution. The audience joined in and ended with shouts of *Vive la France* and *Vive l'Empereur*. In the streets people chanted *A Berlin, A Berlin*.

In George's case sentimental patriotism gave way to political indignation. She could see no sense in Napoleon III's decision and maintained that his plunging France into war was an act of personal vanity. 'This war is disgraceful,' she wrote angrily to Flaubert, 'and the authorised singing of the *Marseillaise* in order to glorify it is sacrilege.'[12] As a Frenchwoman, she prayed for victory; as a republican she hoped that the downfall of the Prussians would also bring about the end of the imperial regime in France. With more candour than tact she wrote as much to Prince Jerome who had joined his regiment.

It was a matter of weeks. The French army was no match for the highly disciplined and carefully prepared Prussians. Hastily mobilised troops from distant parts of the country arrived exhausted and were unable to find their units. There were men without tents, horses without harness. In Berry it seemed as if nature itself was siding with the enemy. The summer was unusually dry, the fields parched, the leaves on the trees prematurely yellow. Forest fires broke out, packs of hungry wolves prowled round Nohant, an epidemic ravaged the villages.

The battle of Sedan, on 2 September, ended in the surrender of eighty thousand Frenchmen, the imprisonment of Napoleon III and the flight to England of the Empress and her son. On 4 September Léon Gambetta proclaimed France a Republic and announced that a provisional government would carry on the fight against the enemy. The Germans marched on Paris. 'They come down like a snowstorm,' George wrote in her war diary, 'cold, harsh, implacable and fierce, even though in the ordinary way they are the kindest of people. They do not think; this is not the time for thinking. Thinking, pity and remorse are put off until they return to their homes. On the march they are a war machine, insensitive and awesome.'[13]

Paris held out for four months. Its sole means of communication with the outer world was by carrier pigeon and balloons. Significantly one balloon was named *Armand Barbès*, after the socialist leader banned by Napoleon III; another was named *George Sand*, both flying over the German lines. Henry Harrisse, in Paris, kept George posted by balloon via London, through the good offices of the American ambassador. There was shortage of food and an abortive attempt to overthrow the government for its conduct of the war. In January 1871 King Frederick William of Prussia had himself crowned in the Hall of Mirrors at Versailles as Emperor of all Germany.

In Berry the arrival of the Germans was expected any day. Farm horses were requisitioned for the army, peasants formed home-guard units and drilled with no better weapons than sticks. George, who had acclaimed the Third Republic as the millennium, refrained from publicly criticising the government, although in private she intensely disapproved of Gambetta's efforts to keep the war going at high cost to the nation. She dipped into her pocket and gave generously to the national defence while Maurice, at forty-eight, volunteered for general duties.

One day an officer arrived at Nohant with a message from Auguste Clésinger, Solange's estranged husband. He had armed a small regiment at his own expense and at fifty-seven was fighting in the front line like the dauntless cuirassier he had once been. He had written to Solange in Cannes to ask her forgiveness for the wrongs he had done her and instructed his messenger to help evacuate the Nohant household to a place of safety. His offer was not appreciated. When some time later the family did leave Nohant, it was not for fear of the enemy but because of an outbreak of smallpox in the neighbourhood. They returned as soon as the danger was over, with the two grand-daughters gaily playing at soldiers.

George no longer prayed for victory; she prayed for peace. When after four months of siege a twenty-one-day ceasefire was signed and the starved Parisians spilled into the countryside in search of fresh food, she was thankful. She hoped that the cease-fire would lead to permanent peace, whatever the cost to national pride. 'Misfortune does not defile,' she wrote on 2 February 1871 to a friend who had experienced the siege. 'If France is sunk in blood, she is not sunk in mud. . . . Now we must make peace, get the best terms available and not allow our anger and desire for vengeance to sway us towards the continuation of the war.'14

The terms of the Peace of Frankfurt, signed on 10 May 1871, were harsh. France ceded to Germany Alsace and Lorraine and undertook to pay a war indemnity of five billion francs, allowing a German occupation force to stay in the country as long as the debt remained unpaid. In the National Assembly there were moving scenes when the Deputies from Alsace and Lorraine took their leave. In the place de la Concorde, where eight large statues represented the most important cities of France, that of Stras-bourg was draped in black. Hatred for Germany festered in every French heart.

Throughout the war George had refrained from any public expression of political views. She could only think in terms of human sufferings and claimed that she did not feel called upon to point out the rights and wrongs of the national leadership. But once the war was over she raised her voice in favour of modera-tion. Her patriotism, like her socialism, was a mixture of romantic idealism and common-sense. She wanted to see France reborn from its ashes like a phoenix, but she did not believe that inflicting vengeance on her destroyers could help towards a national renaissance. Behind her eloquent, old-fashioned style there was the characteristic hard core of realism when she wrote in *Le Temps*:

The German people are to be pitied for their victories as much as we are to be pitied for our losses; for their victories mean the first step towards moral disintegration. The drama of their decline has already begun, and as they are working at it with their own hands, it is bound to be rapid. All great material organisations where justice and respect for humanity are ignored, are colossi of clay, as we have learnt to our cost. But the moral decline of Germany does not mean the future salvation of France. We must realise that if we pay back the evil done to us, Germany's destruction will not bring us back to life. It is not by bloodshed that nations renew their strength and become rejuvenated. The corpse of France may still send forth a fresh breath of life; the corpse of Germany will spread pestilence all over Europe.[15]

Her tolerance could be partly explained by the fact that throughout the war she had not seen a single Prussian soldier; Berry had been spared. But in Paris the middle-of-the-road government which had signed the peace treaty came under heavy fire from a socialist group which called itself the Commune. When the government, acquiescing to German demands, gave orders to dismantle the cannon on the heights of Montmartre and disband the National Guard, riots broke out. The Paris Commune formed itself into a socialist government while the elected government sent out troops to suppress it. For ten days, from 18 to 28 May, Frenchmen massacred Frenchmen while the German occupation army stolidly looked on. When the government troops finally overpowered the Commune fighters, twenty thousand people lay dead and half as many were arrested and later deported to the colonies.

Some of George's old socialist friends had sided with the Commune and taken part in the fighting. But George, idealist that she was, saw nothing socialist about the aims and conduct of the *Communards*. She was convinced that they had been motivated by personal ambition of the crudest kind. Nor was she afraid of saying so. The October issue of *Le Temps* carried a political credo which had originally been written as a personal letter to Flaubert but which, because of its length and nature, was sent to the paper instead. Of the Commune she wrote:

It is an orgy of self-styled renovators who have no ideals or principles of any kind, no serious organisation, not the slightest solidarity with the people, no plan for the future. All that has resulted from their pretended social revolution is ignorance, disenchantment and brutality. It released the lowest of instincts, showed the futility of shameless ambition, exposed the infamy of uncheckered usurpation. Small wonder the Commune inspired vehement disgust in politicians who are most dedicated to democracy.[16]

A great controversy was raging about universal suffrage which, under different regimes, had been intermittently granted or withdrawn. Unlike Flaubert, who felt that only the politically enlightened should be allowed to vote, George wanted it restored as a matter of general principle. 'Universal suffrage, that is the expression of popular will, good or bad, is a safety valve without which we are bound to have another civil war,' she argued in *Le Temps*. 'When this marvellous pledge of security is offered to us, when we have found this great social counterpoise, are we to tamper with it and paralyse it?'[17]

Two of her novels had echoes of the Franco-Prussian war, although their setting was not contemporary. In both *Nanon* and *Francia* she described the devastating effect of war on people who had not actually fought in it or directly suffered the humiliating experience of foreign occupation. Her more immediate reactions to a similar situation were expressed however in a diary which she kept throughout the war. When peace was restored, it was published in the *Revue des Deux Mondes* and later in book form under the title of *Journal d'un voyageur pendant la guerre*. It had some harsh things to say about the Germans and had an unexpected sequel. In Mainz one Ferdinand Haas brought out a brochure in German entitled *French Sighs and German Reflections: An Answer to George Sand Aurore Dudevant*, in which he took her to task for her views.

Basically, her views had never changed. In her old age as in her youth she believed in sweet reason and human kindness. Romantic to the last, she trusted the magic power of love to cure personal, social and international conflicts. From the columns of *Le*

Temps she made in 1871 one of her last pleas to her countrymen to usher in the true Republic of Heaven:

Frenchmen, for God's sake let us love one another or else we are lost. Let us kill, denounce and annihilate politics, since it is politics which divide us and turn us against each other. Let us not ask each other what we were and what we claimed yesterday. Yesterday we were all mistaken. Let us decide what we want today. We know now that equality cannot be imposed. It cannot thrive on the barricades for it is immediately trampled down by the victor, whoever he is. Let us instil equality into our way of life and learn to regard it as sacred. And for a start let us bestow on it the gift of patriotism, let us give it love.[18]

Chapter 20

Still loving, still loved

'My generation is going away one by one,'[1] George wrote to Flaubert towards the end of 1866. Indeed many of her old friends, milestones in her emotional and professional development, were long dead: Stéphane de Grandsagne, Chopin, Hippolyte, Marie Dorval, Mme Marliani, Balzac, Latouche. Others followed. Michel de Bourges died in 1853; Musset and Planche, the old rivals, in 1857. The ranks of the Berry phalanx of admirers had thinned with the deaths of Gabriel Planet, Jules Néraud, Emile Régnault, Charles Duvernet. The actor Bocage died in 1862, Delacroix in 1863. Charles Didier, her temporary surrogate for Michel de Bourges, shot himself in 1864; Rollinat, her soul-mate, died in 1867; Mallefille, Chopin's fiery predecessor, in 1868, Sainte-Beuve in 1869, Mérimée and the platonic Aurélian de Sèze in 1870, Leroux in 1871.

That year she became a widow. In March 1871 Baron Casimir Dudevant passed away at the age of seventy-six, having sold Guillery four years earlier and willed half the proceeds to Solange and Maurice, the other half to his legitimised daughter by his housekeeper. Since then he had been living in a village near Guillery, materially comfortable but uprooted and bemused by memories of a wife whose overpowering personality had been the bane of his life. Two years before his death he petitioned the Emperor Napoleon III to grant him the cross of the *Légion d'Honneur* for his services to the country and for his domestic misfortunes 'which had become part of French history', owing to his unhappy marriage to 'Lucile Dupin, known in the world of literature as George Sand'.[2] At Guillery his death was lamented by the villagers who had known and respected him for more than thirty years; at Nohant it was another tomb in the garden of memories.

George never buried herself in the past. The more her old friends died, the more she gave her affection to the living. Gone were the days when an emotional contretemps would make her wish she were dead. 'I was wrong to imagine that there are moments in life when you can give notice without harming anybody, for here I am still needed at an advanced age,'[3] she had written in her diary at sixty-three. With Marchal the painter tugging at her heart, Maurice and Lina worshipping the earth she trod on, Flaubert admiring her and a host of young acolytes anxious to be admitted to the Sand cult, she felt more needed than ever. 'How wonderful it would be to die while I am still as I am', she wrote to Flaubert one day. 'Still loving, still loved, at war with nobody, not dissatisfied with myself and dreaming of marvellous things in other worlds.'[4]

Having arrived at that stage in life when every moment seemed precious, her one fear was that on her sickbed she might be mistaken for dead and buried prematurely. It was not a passing worry; it was a deep gnawing fear which drove her to seek practical ways and means to guarantee herself against such a grim eventuality. She never mentioned her fear to her family, but with her doctor she made no bones about it. In May 1864 Meyerbeer died in Paris and the press published the text of a letter which was found on him. Having carefully studied it George wrote the following month to Dr Darchy:

Palaiseau, 19 June 1864

Have you seen Meyerbeer's letter? He was as frightened as I am of being buried alive and gave instructions to carry out an incision *in the brachial artery as well as in the foot* before being taken away. Is that the best thing to do in order to make sure? ... The other method you indicated seems safer but I fear it is too distressing to carry out. Meyerbeer's method seems more common and is really not much different from an ordinary bleeding.[5]

Her fear of premature burial was not restricted to her own person. When Manceau died she arranged for the funeral to take place a day later than suggested in order to make quite sure that there was no mistake.

But it was not like her to allow an inexplicable fear to affect her way of life. She treated her various ailments as irritating interferences with work and continued to lavish her solicitude on others. During the last stage of Manceau's illness she tripped over the outside steps of their cottage and injured her leg. She was too worried about Manceau to take proper care of herself until infection set in and made it impossible for her to walk. All she could do was to hobble painfully from her room to his. There was even talk of amputation. When the danger was over she wrote briefly to her publisher Hetzel: 'I am going to keep my leg after all. I thought I was going to be forced to part with it. All I needed was to become a cripple, I, who so much love climbing hills.'[6]

At sixty-eight she had an attack of whooping cough. After a course of treatment she was still running a temperature. One summer day she took herself to her bathing cabin in the river Indre and went in. Her doctor was horrified, but the illness cleared up. In her diary she later wrote: 'While immersing myself in the river I often think of those who had bathed with us in the past: Pauline Viardot, her mother, Chopin, Delacroix, my brother. . . . We even bathed at night. We used to walk all the way there and back. They are all dead now, except Mme Viardot and me.'[7]

She was remarkably mobile, going up to Paris for the odd fortnight, touring the countryside *en famille*. She found time and energy to be with her little grand-daughters of whom the eldest, Aurore, was the favourite. She taught them their alphabet, history, botany and sums. She made up stories for them. Between 1872 and 1875 she wrote and published no less than thirteen children's stories, most of them of novel-length.

Life at Nohant, with all its conviviality and practical jokes, conformed to a strict routine of which she was the centre. At nine in the morning, come winter come summer, a Berry chambermaid in immaculate apron and head-dress, would enter her bedroom, pull the curtains, place a cup of coffee on the bedside table and hand her the morning mail which consisted of letters, manuscripts, books and magazines. George would stay in her room until lunchtime, when she would come down to kiss the family and shake hands with the house-guests. After lunch guests and family would be left to their own devices. Théophile Gautier who had been asked down and had the ill-fortune of arriving in the afternoon, was so put out by the non-appearance of his hostess that he was seriously considering catching the next train back to Paris. Later he told inquisitive colleagues at Magny's that Nohant was as dull as a Moravian monastery and that sex was a taboo subject of conversation.

Dinner was at six o'clock sharp, with the grand-daughters on high chairs. There would follow the usual after-dinner occupations like reading chosen texts or a game of dominoes. George, as taciturn as ever, maintained that she needed people round her in order to feel cheerful. One of her sorrows during the Franco-Prussian war was that Nohant was 'deserted'; there was 'nobody' in the house except family and staff.

Age and serenity brought out the *grande dame* in her; she was even more of the lady of the manor than her own aristocratic grandmother Mme Dupin de Francueil had been. The village looked up to her in feudal veneration. Her literary fame was something abstract and mysterious; to the peasants she was the Good Lady of Nohant. The women would call at the kitchen where a large cauldron of soup was always ready for them, ask for jobs, medical advice, used clothes. In the summer they would help with jam-making and fill the house with their chatter and singing. At the end of the summer there would be the harvest feast, with three heavily laden tables set out in the garden for the thirty-odd farm hands. There would be drinking and singing of Berry folk-tunes, with many toasts for the Good Lady of Nohant.

As mayor of Nohant, Maurice sometimes performed civil marriages in the large dining-hall. George attended and wished the newly-weds good luck, without which the ceremony was not considered complete. If one of the house staff got married she would present the young couple with the traditional *treizins,* thirteen coins of the same denomination. Parents who had their babies baptised in the nearby church crossed over to the house, where drink and food would be awaiting them in the kitchen.

Her birthdays, which because of an early clerical error continued to be celebrated on 5 July instead of on the first, were marked with real feudal veneration. On the eve of the fifth the servants would gather round the kitchen log fire and keep a vigil. On the stroke of midnight they would rise and tiptoe upstairs, knock timidly at George's study, then go in one by one to kiss her hand and wish her many happy returns of the day. At dawn, when George would go to bed, they would be up again, feverishly preparing the evening feast to which half the village was invited. When George came down the family would offer their wishes, and Maurice would have the old cannon fired. In the evening the village youth would come for the feast, sing, make music and dance until late into the night. From time to time George would appear on the steps of the house and an excited murmur would swell into a cheer. To the peasants she epitomised the best in the old way of life, presiding over them like the benign and gracious dame of the legends.

In 1873 Flaubert came down for his second and last visit, bringing Turgenev with him. He deplored every minute which was not spent discussing literature and was irritated by the levity of the puppet shows. He wanted George to read Zola and Daudet, young writers whom he admired, and fled from the dining-room in panic when he heard her announce that a fancy-dress evening was to take place. An hour later he returned dressed up as an Andalusian girl-dancer, tambourine in hand, and burst into a mad *fandango*. George joined in and was delighted to see him more puffed out than she was.

She still had a yearning for Marchal. During the war he had written her one or two emotional letters from the battlefield, but when peace was restored he sank back into his old ways. No longer young, rapidly losing his eyesight, he worked little and drank much. 'Wine and women will be the end of him,' George said of him. 'Ten years of maternal love,' she added fretfully, had failed to drive away 'his two evil spirits: laziness and debauch'.[8]

She continued to be friendly with Prince Jerome, whom the republican government allowed to return to Paris after the war. He remained her *Cher grand ami* to the end of her life.

For many years she had been exchanging courteous letters with Victor Hugo. When in 1870 he returned to France after nineteen years of voluntary exile in Guernsey, he and George were firm pen-friends. They lavished compliments on each other's work and used the most florid expressions of admiration. In 1875 George dedicated to him a new edition of her early novel *Valentine*. 'How shall I express my emotion?' Hugo wrote to her. 'As a creator of masterpieces you have that unique distinction of being first among all women. You are the foremost artist whom your sex has produced, not only in our time but at all times, the most powerful mind, as well as the most charming. You are an honour to our century and our country. Allow me to go down on my knees to you and kiss the hand which has written so many exquisite and generous works.'[9]

Oddly enough the two septuagenarians never met, nor did they seem to try to very hard. They exchanged portraits and regarded themselves as great friends, and so they were considered by those who knew them.

The only cloud in George's serene sky was Solange. After the war she sold her Cannes villa at double its price and, together with the money inherited from her father, she bought the château and land of Montgivray, uncle Hippolyte's old place, two miles from Nohant. George did not like the proximity. She and Solange had never learnt to get on and except for a short period during the war, there was little mutual tolerance. Old Hippolyte used to stroll from Montgivray to Nohant at any time of day or night; Solange was discreetly asked not to call without invitation. All the same she used to descend on Nohant without warning, burst into the kitchen and put the fear of God into the servants. Aurore and Gabrielle would rush up to their grandmother's room and inform her in awed tones that the aunt was about. Maurice hardly spoke to his sister; only Lina showed forbearance. There was something about Solange's hungry way of looking at the little girls which touched her heart. But the moments of grace were rare. Indolent, spoilt and malicious, Solange lived selfishly and aimlessly, with no other emotional anchor in life except her mother, whom she loved and hated.

At the beginning of 1876 George finished *La Tour de Percemont* and, true to a lifetime discipline, started immediately on her next book which she called *Albina*. The year before she lost the last of the old guard, Jules Boucoiran, the one-time tutor who remained a friend of the family to the day of his death. Her own state of health was indifferent. For years she had been suffering from what she believed to be acute constipation and from time to time followed a diet of vegetables, eggs, beef tea and lemon juice in the hope of easing it. She accepted physical discomfort as an inevitable companion and willed herself to carry on with her daily routine in spite of fierce attacks of pain. For a day or two she would lie inert on her side and grit her teeth, then relief would come and she would be up and about as if nothing had been the matter with her, fussing about other people's aches and pains. On 19 May 1876 she wrote in her diary:

> Maurice has had an attack of neuralgia from five in the afternoon until half past seven. Aurore [she was ten by then] kept him company and put off her dinner. Later they dined together very gaily and the evening passed without a relapse. . . . As for me, I was in pain again all day. I gave a lesson to Lolo [Aurore], wrote a few letters and read. I have just finished Renan's *Dialogues et fragments philosophiques.*[10]

But the family was worried. Under pretext of his neuralgia, Maurice called in his local doctor and asked him to examine his mother. George gave him a detailed account of recent symptoms in a practical and detached way. Her bowels had not been functioning for two whole weeks, and the pain was atrocious. Still she had no fear and expected the trouble to clear up as it had done before. She was making plans to spend a whole month in Paris, go to the theatre and see friends. To her Paris doctor, whom she liked better than her local one, she wrote on 28 May:

My general state of health has not deteriorated in spite of my great age (I am nearly seventy-two). I do not feel the onset of senility. I am sound of limb, my eyesight is better than it has been for twenty years, I sleep well, my hands are as steady and agile as they were in my youth. When I do not have these cruel pains I notice a phenomenon which must be peculiar to the nature of this localised illness: I feel stronger and more agile than I have ever been. I used to be slightly asthmatic, now I am not. I climb the stairs as nimbly as my dog.

However, since some of the bodily functions have come to a complete standstill, I am wondering where I am going and whether I should not expect a sudden exit one of these days. I would like to know right away rather than be taken unawares. . . . In order to recover I shall do whatever is prescribed, and if I have a day's respite in between attacks, I shall go up to Paris so that you can help me carry on; for I feel my family still need me.[11]

Two days later she could stand the pain no longer. She stopped *Albine* in the middle of the seventh chapter and took to her bed, never to rise again.

For eight days she suffered atrociously and her moans could be heard at the far end of the garden. Her belly was distended, her mouth parched. She could not stay in one position for more than a few moments at a time, she was messy. Doctors came and went. Dr Gustave Papet, little Gustave who had stood guard over her early meetings with Sandeau when they were all young and bursting with life, pronounced her past hope. A surgeon tried to release the intestinal impurities through an abdominal incision. George remained conscious throughout the operation, the sweat streaming down her face. Cancer was mentioned only a generation later.

In the midst of her pains she was distressed by her messiness and insisted on being thoroughly washed and her bedclothes changed in spite of the additional discomfort. She forbade Maurice to come into her bedroom; she could not bear the thought of her adored and adoring son seeing her ugly and vilified. The house filled with friends and relatives. Lina was constantly at her side together with Solange who had been coldly summoned from Paris: 'Come if you wish.'[12] The local priest, hoping to save a lost soul, prowled in the garden in case he should be called upon to offer the last sacrament. The villagers prayed and crossed themselves, France held its breath.

The agony continued with no drugs to relieve it. The night before she died, Lina and Solange heard her cry feebly several times, 'Oh God, let me die, please let me die.'[13] When at three o'clock in the morning Maurice appeared silently on the doorstep she whispered for him to go away. She had been muttering disjointedly, trying to say goodbye to the family, calling each by name. The evening before, she had mumbled something about greenery. At dawn she sank into a coma and in the morning of 8 June she died without regaining consciousness. Solange, Lina, two nephews and a doctor had been kneeling by her bedside. Maurice, woken from a fretful sleep in his own room, kept repeating in a daze: 'My mother, my mother, there is nothing left to live for.'[14]

Even before their mother's demise Solange, less emotional than her brother, raised the delicate question of the manner of the funeral. It had been taken for granted by most friends that George Sand, with her well-known anti-clerical views, would have wished to have a civil burial. After her death it turned out that she had left no instructions on the subject and Solange, calling common-sense to her aid, argued that that in itself was an indication that their mother had not renounced the Church. Maurice was in two minds and when Dr Gustave Papet, in the midst of his grief, announced that neither he nor any of his family would attend a civil burial, the decision was taken. Perhaps Maurice sensed, as Flaubert and some other indignant Paris friends did not, that Papet spoke for the entire Berry peasantry whom George Sand had so much loved.

Since she had died without the ministrations of a priest, there was some difficulty about a church service, but an exchange of telegrams with the appropriate cardinal put things right. Maurice recovered from his stupor and sent out telegrams to old friends: 'My mother is dead.' A formal announcement composed by him described her as George Sand, Baroness Dudevant. In vain did Lina protest that it was a name her mother-in-law would have rather not be remembered by.

The day after her mother's death Solange astounded the household by taking her place at the head of the table and giving instructions to the servants. But it was she, not the domesticated Lina, who washed and covered the corpse with clean sheets and sat beside it for the whole of the first night. The following night only the maid-servants kept vigil, and then only in the adjacent room; the stench had become unbearable. A last-minute hitch was avoided, just in time, with the arrival of a second lead coffin, the first having been found too small to contain the body.

About a dozen old faithfuls came down from Paris for the funeral which was held on 10 June: Flaubert, Dumas, Prince Jerome, Victor Borie, Renan, the publisher Calmann Lévy. Victor Hugo sent a four-page letter of farewell to be read by the open grave, beginning with the words: 'I mourn the dead, I salute an immortal.'[15] On the day the body lay in state for an hour in the hall of Nohant, then was carried to church by local peasants. After the service some two hundred mourners, Berry friends, La Châtre craftsmen, tradesmen and peasants followed the coffin in driving rain to its final resting place in the garden of the manor and shed tears at the passing of the good lady of Nohant.

The world press was full of her death. Turgenev read about it during a return visit to Russia and wrote to Flaubert: 'Poor dead Madame Sand! What a heart of gold she had! What absence of anything petty, mean or insincere! What a good man she was, and what a kind woman.'[16]

In the obituaries George Sand was described as the glory of France and her passing as a loss to civilisation. But it was Flaubert, in his reply to Turgenev, who expressed what her death meant to those who loved her best not for her literary achieve-

ments but for those elemental qualities which made her what she
was:

> The death of poor Madame Sand caused me much distress. At
> her funeral I cried like an ass, and twice: the first time when I
> embraced her grand-daughter Aurore (whose eyes looked so
> much like hers that it was like a resurrection), and the second
> time when her coffin was carried past me. . . . The good country
> folk wept by the grave. It had been raining all day and we were
> up to our ankles in mud in that rural cemetery. It was like a
> chapter out of one of her own novels.[17]

Maurice never got over his mother's death. After a state of
apathy which lasted the best part of four years he dedicated the
rest of his life to collecting her letters to friends and relatives and
bringing them out in book form. Solange, always bitter, with-
held hers. He died in 1889 at the age of sixty-six, surviving his
mother by only thirteen years. Solange died in 1898, aged
seventy-one; Lina in 1901, aged fifty-nine. Gabrielle, the younger
of the two grand-daughters, died in 1909 and Aurore, the eldest,
in 1961, both without issue. The Sand line came to an end. Today
Nohant is a monument and a shrine, from which George Sand
still casts a spell engendered by a forceful personality transcending
the barriers of time and death.

References

Introduction

1. Aurore Sand, *Le Roman d'Aurore Dudevant et d'Aurélien de Sèze*, p. 217.
2. Georges Lubin, *Correspondance de George Sand*, vol. viii, p. 718.
3. Maurice Regard, *Gustave Planche – Correspondance*, p. 308.
4. Juliette Adam, *Mes sentiments et nos idées*, p. 286.
5. L. Evrard, *George Sand et Alfred de Musset, Correspondance*, p. 106.
6. M. L. Pailleron, *George Sand*, vol. ii, p. 83.
7. Aurore Sand, *Le Roman d'Aurore Dudevant et d'Aurélien de Sèze*, p. 212.
8. Casimir Carrère, *George Sand amoureuse*, p. 108.
9. Arsène Houssaye, *Les Confessions*, vol. iv, p. 233.

1 Aurore

1. George Sand, *Histoire de ma vie*, vol. ii, pp. 94–5.
2. Ibid., vol. ii, p. 171.
3. Ibid., vol. ii, p. 154.
4. Ibid., vol. ii, p. 198.
5. Georges Lubin, *Correspondance de George Sand*, vol. i., pp. 14–15.
6. George Sand, *Histoire de ma vie*, vol. iii, p. 69.

2 Heiress of Nohant

1. George Sand, *Histoire de ma vie*, vol. iii, p. 150.
2. W. Karénine, *George Sand*, vol. iii, p. 100.
3. A. Maurois, *Lélia*, p. 53.

3 Madame Dudevant

1. Georges Lubin, *Correspondance de George Sand*, vol. v, p. 43.
2. George Sand, *Histoire de ma vie*, vol. iii, p. 436.
3. Georges Lubin, *Correspondance de George Sand*, vol. i, p. 130.
4. Ibid., p. 136.
5. Ibid., p. 138.
6. M. L. Pailleron, *George Sand*, vol. i, p. 100.
7. George Sand, *Histoire de ma vie*, vol. iv., p. 37.
8. Ibid., p. 306.
9. Ibid., p. 13.
10. Ibid., p. 13.
11. Aurore Sand, *Le Roman d'Aurore Dudevant et d'Aurélien de Sèze*, pp. 155–6.
12. Ibid., pp. 171–2.
13. Ibid., p. 181.
14. Ibid., p. 115
15. George Sand, *Histoire de ma vie*, vol iv, p. 52.
16. Aurore Sand, *Le Roman d'Aurore Dudevant et d'Aurélien de Sèze*, pp. 211–13.
17. Ibid., p. 220.

4 A chance to make a living

1. George Sand, *Histoire de ma vie*, vol. iv, p. 371.
2. Georges Lubin, *Correspondance de George Sand*, vol. i, pp. 383–5.
3. Ibid., p. 438.
4. Ibid., p. 636.
5. Ibid., p. 647.
6. André Maurois, *Lélia*, p. 533.
7. George Sand, *Histoire de ma vie*, vol. ii, p. 167.
8. Ibid., vol. ii, pp. 368–9.
9. Ibid., vol. iv, pp. 60–1.
10. Georges Lubin, *Correspondance de George Sand*, vol. i, p. 308.
11. Juliette Adam, *Mes sentiments et nos idées*, pp. 169–70.
12. Georges Lubin, *Correspondance de George Sand*, vol. i, p. 737.
13. Ibid., vol. i, p. 739.

5 *Do not make books, make children*

1. George Sand, *Histoire de ma vie*, vol. ii, p. 400.
2. Ibid., vol. ii, p. 456.
3. George Sand, *Correspondance*, vol. i, p. 105.
4. Ibid., vol. i, p. 104.
5. Ibid., vol. i, p. 158.
6. Georges Lubin, *Correspondance de George Sand*, vol. i, p. 787.
7. Mabel Silver, *Jules Sandeau*, p. 28.
8. Georges Lubin, *Correspondance de George Sand*, vol. i, p. 784.
9. Ibid., vol. i, p. 818.
10. Ibid., vol. i, p. 818.
11. Ibid., vol. i, p. 813.
12. George Sand, *Histoire de ma vie*, vol. iv, pp. 121–2.
13. Ibid., vol. iv, pp. 106–7.
14. Georges Lubin, *Correspondance de George Sand*, vol. i, p. 817.
15. Ibid., vol. i, p. 875.
16. André Maurois, *Lélia*, p. 139.
17. Georges Lubin, *Correspondance de George Sand*, vol. i, p. 944.
18. Ibid., vol. i, pp. 945–6.
19. George Sand, *Histoire de ma vie*, vol. iv, p. 148.
20. Ibid., vol. iv, p. 148.
21. M. L. Pailleron, *George Sand*, vol. i, p. 177.
22. A. Maurois, *Lélia*, p. 147.
23. Ibid., pp. 150–1.
24. R. Doumic, *George Sand*, pp. 68–9.
25. Ibid., p. 70.
26. M. L. Pailleron, *La Vie littéraire sous Louis Philippe: François Buloz*, p. 378.
27. W. Karénine, *George Sand*, vol. iv, p. 453.

6 *Sappho*

1. Arsène Houssaye, *Les Confessions*, vol. ii, pp. 13–14.
2. Ibid., vol. ii, p. 14.
3. George Sand, *Histoire de ma vie*, vol. iv, p. 212.
4. André Maurois, *Lélia*, p. 154.
5. Simone André-Maurois, *George Sand – Marie Dorval, Correspondance inédite*, pp. 205–6.

6. Maurice Regard, *Gustave Planche – Correspondance*, p. 69.
7. Simone André-Maurois, *George Sand – Marie Dorval, Correspondance inédite*, p. 216.
8. Ibid., p. 206.
9. Ibid., p. 211.
10. Ibid., p. 209–10.
11. Ibid., pp. 206, 212, 208, 211, 217, 216, 206, 207.
12. M. L. Pailleron, *George Sand*, vol. i, p. 200.
13. O. Södergard, *Les Lettres de George Sand à Sainte-Beuve*, pp. 34–7.
14. G. Hanotaux, *Lettres de Prosper Merimée à la Comtesse de Montijo*, vol. i, pp. 318–19.
15. Simone André-Maurois, *George Sand – Marie Dorval, Correspondance inédite*, pp. 219–21.
16. Ibid., p. 222.
17. Ibid., pp. 223–4.
18. Ibid., p. 19.
19. Mabel Silver, *Jules Sandeau*, p. 106.
20. Arsène Houssaye, *Les Confessions*, vol. iv, p. 299.
21. Simone André-Maurois, *George Sand – Marie Dorval, Correspondance inédite*, pp. 247–9.
22. George Sand, *Histoire de ma vie*, vol. iv, p. 235.

7 Lélia

1. Paul Mariéton, *Une Histoire d'amour*, p. 18.
2. O. Södergard, *Les Lettres de George Sand à Sainte-Beuve*, p. 31.
3. George Sand, *Correspondance*, vol. i, p. 220.
4. George Sand, *Lettres d'un voyageur*, xii, p. 339.
5. George Sand, *Lélia, Texte établi, présenté et annoté par Pierre Reboult*, pp. 590–1.
6. Ibid., p. 591.
7. Ibid., p. 163.
8. George Sand, *Lettres d'un voyageur*, p. 107.
9. Jules Bertaut, *Une Amitié romanesque, Lettres inédites de George Sand et François Rollinat*, p. 58.
10. Ibid., pp. 25–6.
11. George Sand, *Correspondance*, vol. i, p. 284.
12. Jules Bertaut, *Une Amitié romanesque, Lettres inédites de George Sand et François Rollinat*, p. 56.

13. Ibid., p. 58.
14. Ibid., p. 37.
15. M. L. Pailleron, *George Sand*, vol. i, p. 206.
16. George Sand, *Lélia, Texte établi, présenté et annoté par Pierre Reboult*, p. 592.
17. Vicomte de Spoelberch de Lovenjoul, *La véritable histoire de 'Elle et Lui', Notes et documents*, p. 264.
18. Ibid., pp. 8–14.
19. L. Evrard, *George Sand et Alfred de Musset, Correspondance*, p. 27.

8 *The love that launched a thousand books*

1. George Sand, *Histoire de ma vie*, vol. iv., p. 207.
2. A. Maurois, *Lélia*, p. 192.
3. Ibid., p. 188.
4. Henri Guillemin, *La Liaison Musset–Sand*, p. 61.
5. O. Södergard, *Les Lettres de George Sand à Sainte-Beuve*, p. 47.
6. Annarosa Poli, *L'Italie dans la vie et dans l'œuvre de George Sand*, p. 58.
7. P. Mariéton, *Une Histoire d'amour*, p. 85.
8. L. Evrard, *George Sand et Alfred de Musset, Correspondance*, p. 111.
9. P. Mariéton, *Une Histoire d'amour*, p. 93.
10. Ibid., pp. 94–7.
11. Ibid., p. 99.
12. Ibid., p. 111.
13. L. Evrard, *George Sand et Alfred de Musset, Correspondance*, pp. 54–7.
14. Ibid., p. 55.
15. Ibid., p. 63.
16. Ibid., p. 63.
17. Ibid., p. 62.
18. Ibid., p. 118.
19. Ibid., p. 145.
20. Ibid., pp. 107–8.
21. P. Mariéton, *Une Histoire d'amour*, p. 143.
22. L. Evrard, *George Sand et Alfred de Musset, Correspondance*, p. 105.
23. Ibid., p. 83.
24. Ibid., p. 85.
25. Ibid., p. 77.

26. Ibid., p. 85.
27. Ibid., p. 91.
28. Ibid., p. 94.
29. Ibid., pp. 106–7.
30. Ibid., p. 120.
31. Ibid., p. 133.
32. Ibid., p. 148.
33. P. Mariéton, *Une Histoire d'amour*, p. 138.
34. Ibid., p. 183.
35. Ibid., pp. 210–11.
36. L. Evrard, *George Sand et Alfred de Musset, Correspondance*, p. 187.
37. Ibid., pp. 192–3.
38. Ibid., p. 221.
39. Ibid., p. 233.
40. Ibid., p. 233.
41. George Sand, *Mauprat*, preface to, p. 29.

9 Everard

1. George Sand, *Histoire de ma vie*, vol. ii, p. 272.
2. Ibid., p. 272.
3. Louis Blanc, *Histoire de dix ans*, vol. iv., p. 262.
4. George Sand, *Lettres d'un voyageur*, pp. 159–65.
5. Ibid., p. 165.
6. George Sand, *Histoire de ma vie*, vol. iv, p. 328.
7. George Sand, *Lettres d'un voyageur*, p. 194.
8. George Sand, *Histoire de ma vie*, vol. iv, p. 329.
9. Georges Lubin, *Correspondance de George Sand*, vol. iii, p. 849.
10. Ibid., vol. iii, p. 422.
11. George Sand, *Histoire de ma vie*, vol. iv, pp. 392–3.
12. Georges Lubin, *Correspondance de George Sand*, vol. iii, p. 660.
13. Ibid., p. 564.
14. John Sellards, *Charles Didier*, p. 56.
15. Ibid., p. 57.
16. Ibid., p. 58.
17. Georges Lubin, *Correspondance de George Sand*, vol. iii, pp. 561–3.
18. Ibid., vol. iii, pp. 672–4.
19. Ibid., vol. iii, pp. 732–8.

20. Ibid., vol. iii, p. 741.
21. Ibid., vol. iv, pp. 32–3.
22. Ibid., vol. iv, pp. 85–6 footnote.
23. Ibid., vol. iii, p. 565.
24. Ibid., vol. iv, p. 112.
25. Ibid., vol. iv, p. 233.
26. George Sand, *Histoire de ma vie*, vol. iv, p. 317.
27. Ibid., vol. iv, p. 371.
28. Ibid., vol. iv, p. 371.

10 Prophets and friends

1. George Sand, *Histoire de ma vie*, vol. iv, p. 328.
2. George Sand, *Lettres d'un voyageur*, p. 165.
3. George Sand, *Histoire de ma vie*, vol. iv, pp. 363–4.
4. Georges Lubin, *Correspondance de George Sand*, vol. v, p. 546.
5. A. Maurois, *Lélia*, p. 268.
6. Georges Lubin, *Correspondance de George Sand*, vol. iii, p. 368.
7. George Sand, *Lettres d'un voyageur*, p. 230.
8. Georges Lubin, *Correspondance de George Sand*, vol. iii, pp. 225–6.
9. George Sand, *Lettres d'un voyageur*, pp. 288–94.
10. George Sand, *Histoire de ma vie*, vol. iv, p. 405.
11. D. Ollivier, *Correspondance de Liszt et de la Comtesse d'Agoult*, vol. i, p. 199.
12. Comtesse d'Agoult (Daniel Stern), *Mémoires*, p. 84.
13. M. L. Pailleron, *George Sand*, vol. ii, p. 267.
14. Comtesse d'Agoult (Daniel Stern), *Mémoires*, p. 81.
15. Ibid., p. 75.
16. George Sand, *Journal intime*, p. 46.
17. Comtesse d'Agoult (Daniel Stern), *Mémoires*, pp. 96–7.
18. Georges Lubin, *Correspondance de George Sand*, vol. iv, p. 177.
19. Ibid., vol. iv, pp. 146–7.
20. Ibid., vol. iv, pp. 174–5.
21. Ibid., vol. iv, p. 190.
22. Ibid., vol. iv, p. 190.
23. George Sand, *Histoire de ma vie*, vol. iv, p. 420.
24. Georges Lubin, *Correspondance de George Sand*, vol. iv, pp. 218–19.
25. Ibid., vol. iv, p. 293.

22 *Preludes*

1. F. Niecks, *Frederick Chopin*, vol. ii, p. 8.
2. Georges Lubin, *Correspondance de George Sand*, vol. iii, p. 699.
3. B. E. Sydow, *Correspondance de Frédéric Chopin*, vol. ii, p. 28.
4. Georges Lubin, *Correspondance de George Sand*, vol. iv, p. 315.
5. Ibid., vol. i, p. 858.
6. George Sand, *Histoire de ma vie*, vol. iv, p. 126.
7. Georges Lubin, *Correspondance de George Sand*, vol. iv, p. 370.
8. Ibid., vol. iv, p. 395.
9. M. L. Pailleron, *George Sand*, vol. ii, p. 131.
10. Georges Lubin, *Correspondance de George Sand*, vol. iv, pp. 437–8.
11. Ibid., vol. iv, p. 429.
12. Ibid., vol. iv, p. 430.
13. Ibid., vol. iv, pp. 434–6.
14. Ibid., vol. iv, p. 431.
15. Ibid., vol. iv, p. 445.
16. B. E. Sydow, *Correspondance de Frédéric Chopin*, vol. ii, p. 254.
17. Georges Lubin, *Correspondance de George Sand*, vol. iv, pp. 482–3.
18. Ibid., vol. iv, pp. 487–8.
19. Ibid., vol. iv., p. 488.
20. Ibid., vol. iv, p. 512.
21. Ibid., vol. iv, p. 519.
22. Ibid., vol. iv, p. 519.
23. Ibid., vol. iv, p. 516.
24. George Sand, *Hiver à Majorque*, p. 34.
25. B. E. Sydow, *Correspondance de Frédéric Chopin*, vol. ii, p. 266.
26. Ibid., vol. ii, p. 274.
27. George Sand, *Hiver à Majorque*, p. 149.
28. Georges Lubin, *Correspondance de George Sand*, vol. iv, p. 534.
29. B. E. Sydow, *Correspondance de Frédéric Chopin*, vol. ii, p. 310.
30. Georges Lubin, *Correspondance de George Sand*, vol. iv, p. 559 footnote, from the original edition of *Hiver à Majorque* vol. i, pp. 308–9.
31. Ibid., vol. iv, p. 540.
32. Ibid., vol. iv, p. 576.
33. A. Maurois, *Lélia*, p. 309.
34. Georges Lubin, *Correspondance de George Sand*, vol. iv, p. 577.
35. Ibid., vol. iv, pp. 393–4.
36. Ibid., vol. iv, p. 586.

37. Ibid., vol. iv, p. 625.
38. Ibid., vol. iv, p. 620.
39. George Sand, *Hiver à Majorque*, p. 183.

12 Maturity

1. Georges Lubin, *Correspondance de George Sand*, vol. iv, p. 655.
2. W. Karénine, *George Sand*, vol. iii, p. 102.
3. Georges Lubin, *Correspondance de George Sand*, vol. iv, p. 615.
4. L. Vincent, *George Sand et le Berry*, vol. i, pp. 309–10.
5. Georges Lubin, *Correspondance de George Sand*, vol. iv, p. 754.
6. Honoré de Balzac, *Lettres à l'étrangère*, vol. i, p. 553.
7. André Maurois, *Lélia*, pp. 311–12.
8. Georges Lubin, *Correspondance de George Sand*, vol. iv, pp. 562–3.
9. André Maurois, *Lélia*, p. 331.
10. Georges Lubin, *Correspondance de George Sand*, vol. iii, p. 597.
11. André Maurois, *Lélia*, p. 312.
12. Georges Lubin *Correspondance de George sand*, vol. iv., p. 689–90.
13. Ibid., vol. iv, p. 691.
14. Ibid., vol. v, p. 47.
15. Ibid., vol. v, p. 36.
16. D. O. Evans, *Pierre Leroux et ses contemporains*, p. 115.
17. George Sand, *Correspondance*, vol. ii, p. 259.
18. Jean Briquet, *Agricol Perdiguier, Correspondance inédite avec George Sand et ses amis*, p. 52.
19. Honoré de Balzac, *Lettres à l'étrangère*, vol. ii, p. 125.
20. Georges Lubin, *Correspondance de George Sand*, vol. v, p. 539.
21. Ibid., vol. v, p. 498.
22. M. L. Pailleron, *George Sand*, vol. ii, p. 264.
23. George Sand, *Histoire de ma vie*, vol. ii, pp. 457 and 464.
24. Georges Lubin, *Œuvres autobiographiques*, vol. ii, p. 626.
25. Georges Lubin, *Correspondance de George Sand*, vol. v, p. 88.
26. Ibid., vol. v, p. 133.
27. George Sand, *Histoire de ma vie*, vol. iv, p. 442.
28. Georges Lubin, *Correspondance de George Sand*, vol. v, p. 282.
29. Ibid., vol. v, p. 290–1.
30. W. Karénine, *George Sand*, vol. iii, pp. 419–20.
31. B. E. Sydow, *Correspondance de Frédéric Chopin*, vol. iii, pp. 150–1.

13 Sublimation

1. George Sand, *Journal intime*, p. 105.
2. B. E. Sydow, *Correspondance de Frédéric Chopin*, vol. iii, pp. 278–9.
3. Ibid., vol. iii, p. 426.
4. André Maurois, *Lélia*, p. 343.
5. Georges Lubin, *Correspondance de George Sand*, vol. iv, pp. 828–9.
6. George Sand, *Journal intime*, p. 104.
7. Georges Lubin, *Correspondance de George Sand*, vol. v, p. 182.
8. Ibid., vol. v, p. 183.
9. Ibid., vol. v, p. 232.
10. Thérèse Marix-Spire, *Lettres inédites de George Sand et Pauline Viardot*, p. 100.
11. Ibid., p. 108.
12. Ibid., p. 120.
13. Georges Lubin, *Correspondance de George Sand*, vol. v, p. 96.
14. George Sand, *Journal intime*, p. 105.
15. Georges Lubin, *Correspondance de George Sand*, vol. v, p. 281.
16. Thérèse Marix-Spire, *Lettres inédites de George Sand et Pauline Viardot*, p. 174.
17. Ibid., p. 174.
18. Ibid., p. 218.
19. Ibid., pp. 223–4.
20. Ibid., pp. 225–6.

14 Solange

1. Georges Lubin, *Correspondance de George Sand*, vol. ii, p. 43.
2. George Sand, *Histoire de ma vie*, vol. iv, p. 310.
3. Ibid., vol. iv, p. 309.
4. L. Evrard, *George Sand et Alfred de Musset, Correspondance*, p. 114.
5. G. Lubin, *Correspondance de George Sand*, vol. ii, p. 604.
6. Ibid., vol. ii, p. 590.
7. S. Rocheblave, *George Sand et sa fille*, p. 30.
8. Georges Lubin, *Correspondance de George Sand*, vol. iii, p. 412.
9. Ibid., vol. iii, p. 584.
10. Comtesse d'Agoult (Daniel Stern), *Mémoires*, p. 82.
11. S. Rocheblave, *George Sand et sa fille*, p. 43.
12. Georges Lubin, *Correspondance de George Sand*, vol. iv, p. 372.

13. S. Rocheblave, *George Sand et sa fille*, p. 45.
14. Georges Lubin, *Correspondance de George Sand*, vol. iv, pp. 391–2.
15. Ibid., vol. iv, p. 534.
16. George Sand, *Journal intime*, pp. 89–90.
17. S. Rocheblave, *George Sand et sa fille*, p. 60.
18. Georges Lubin, *Correspondance de George Sand*, vol. v, p. 290.
19. Ibid., vol. v, p. 88.
20. S. Rocheblave, *George Sand et sa fille*, p. 77.
21. W. Karénine, *George Sand*, vol. iii, p. 453.
22. Georges Lubin, *Correspondance de George Sand*, vol. vii, p. 430.
23. B. E. Sydow, *Correspondance de Frédéric Chopin*, vol. iii, p. 258.
24. M. L. Pailleron, *George Sand*, vol. ii, p. 328.
25. B. E. Sydow, *Correspondance de Frédéric Chopin*, vol. iii, p. 265.
26. Ibid., vol. iii, pp. 292–3.
27. Arsène Houssaye, *Les Confessions*, vol. i, p. 259.
28. B. E. Sydow, *Correspondance de Frédéric Chopin*, vol. iii, p. 297.
29. Ibid., vol. iii, p. 331.
30. M. L. Pailleron, *George Sand*, vol. ii, p. 339.
31. B. E. Sydow, *Correspondance de Frédéric Chopin*, vol. iii, p. 333.
32. Thérèse Marix-Spire, *Lettres inédites de George Sand et Pauline Viardot*, p. 262.
33. B. E. Sydow, *Correspondance de Frédéric Chopin*, vol. iii, p. 217.

15 The dream of the spirit

1. Georges Lubin, *Correspondance de George Sand*, vol. viii, p. 329.
2. Ibid., vol. viii, p. 329.
3. Ibid., vol. viii, p. 450.
4. E. Dolléans, *Féminisme et le Mouvement Ouvrier*, pp. 95–6.
5. George Sand, *Lélia*, Texte établi, presenté et annoté par Pierre Reboult, pp. 590–1.
6. Georges Lubin, *Correspondance de George Sand*, vol. viii, p. 391.
7. E. Dolléans, *Féminisme et le Mouvement Ouvrier*, p. 14.
8. Georges Lubin, *Correspondance de George Sand*, vol. viii, pp. 391–2.
9. Ibid., vol. viii, pp. 401–7.
10. M. L. Pailleron, *George Sand et les hommes de '48*, pp. 106–7.
11. Georges Lubin, *Correspondance de George Sand*, vol. viii, p. 411.
12. Ibid., vol. viii, p. 545.
13. W. Karénine, *George Sand*, vol. iv, p. 129.

References

14. Georges Lubin, *Correspondance de George Sand*, vol. viii, p. 757.
15. George Sand, *Souvenirs et idées*, p. 80.
16. Ibid., p. 80–1.
17. Ibid., p. 99.
18. Georges Lubin, *Correspondance de George Sand*, vol. x, pp. 659–64.
19. W. Karénine, *George Sand*, vol. iv, pp. 221–2.
20. Georges Lubin, *Correspondance de George Sand*, vol. x, p. 613.
21. George Sand, *Questions politiques et sociales*, pp. 355–6.

16 The playwright

1. Georges Lubin, *Correspondance de George Sand*, vol. vii, p. 602.
2. George Sand, *Souvenirs et idées*, pp. 156–64.
3. W. Karénine, *George Sand*, vol. iv, p. 272.
4. Georges Lubin, *Correspondance de George Sand*, vol. x, p. 862.
5. F. G. Kenyon, *The Letters of Elizabeth Browning*, vol. ii, p. 40.
6. Ibid., vol. ii, p. 29.
7. Ibid., vol. ii, p. 40.
8. Ibid., vol. ii, pp. 55–7.
9. Ibid., vol. ii, pp. 63–4.
10. George Sand, *Correspondance*, vol. iv, p. 177.
11. George Sand, *Théâtre*, 1860 edition, vol. i, pp. 4–5.
12. Ibid., vol. i, p. 5.
13. George Sand, *Souvenirs et idées*, p. 160.
14. Ibid., pp. 161–3.

17 Ageing gracefully

1. George Sand, *Correspondance*, vol. iii, p. 186.
2. Georges Lubin, *Correspondance de George Sand*, vol. ix, p. 389.
3. Ibid., vol. ix, p. 389.
4. Ibid., vol. ix, p. 543.
5. Ibid., vol. ix, pp. 543–5.
6. Ibid., vol. ix, p. 608.
7. Ibid., vol. x, p. 17.
8. Ibid., vol. ix, p. 878.
9. Ibid., vol. x, p. 18.
10. Ibid., vol. x, p. 97.

11. Ibid., vol. x, p. 743.
12. A. Maurois, *Lélia*, p. 432.
13. Ibid., p. 432.
14. S. Rocheblave, *George Sand et sa fille*, p. 190.
15. George Sand, *Correspondance*, vol. iv, p. 47.
16. Ibid., vol. iii, p. 244.
17. Walter Dexter, *The Letters of Charles Dickens*, vol. ii, p. 728.
18. Ibid., vol, ii, p. 733.
19. A. Maurois, *Lélia*, p. 419.
20. F. Letessier, *Correspondance inédite de George Sand avec le docteur Pierre Paul Darchy*, p. 527.
21. Ibid., p. 528.
22. Ibid., p. 532.
23. A. Maurois, *Lélia*, p. 441.

18 At last a mother-in-law

1. Georges Lubin, *Correspondance de George Sand*, vol. ix, p. 852.
2. Ibid., vol. ix, pl 855.
3. Ibid., vol. ix, p. 871.
4. Ibid., vol. ix, p. 871.
5. George Sand, *Correspondance*, vol. iv, p. 214.
6. Ibid., vol. vi, p. 272.
7. Annarosa Poli, *L'Italie dans la vie et dans l'œuvre de George Sand*, p. 346.
8. George Sand, *Correspondance*, vol. iv, pp. 324–5.
9. Annarosa Poli, *L'Italie dans la vie et dans l'œuvre de George Sand*, p. 347.
10. Ibid., p. 347.
11. W. Karénine, *George Sand*, vol. iv, p. 411.
12. George Sand, *Correspondance*, vol. iv, p. 329.
13. Annarosa Poli, *L'Italie dans la vie et dans l'œuvre de George Sand*, p. 353.
14. L. Vincent, *George Sand et le Berry*, vol. i, p. 622.
15. Ibid., p. 622.
16. Ibid., p. 622.
17. Ibid., p. 623.
18. A. Maurois, *Lélia*, p. 464.
19. Ibid., p. 464.

20. W. Karénine, *George Sand*, vol. iv, pp. 475–6.
21. A. Maurois, *Lélia*, p. 466.
22. Ibid., p. 466.
23. W. Karénine, *George Sand*, vol. iv, p. 490.
24. Ibid., vol. iv, p. 490.
25. A. Maurois, *Lélia*, p. 472.
26. C. Carrère, *George Sand amoureuse*, p. 425.
27. Ibid., p. 422.
28. George Sand, *Correspondance*, vol. v, p. 120.
29. W. Karénine, *George Sand*, vol. iv, p. 418.
30. George Sand, *Correspondance*, vol. v, p. 252.
31. Ibid., vol. v, p. 186.
32. Ibid., vol. vi, p. 272.

19 A military assignment

1. L. Conard, *Œuvres de jeunesse inédite*, vol. iii, p. 61.
2. Lina Sand, *Correspondance entre George Sand et Gustave Flaubert*, p. 178.
3. André Maurois, *Lélia*, p. 485.
4. Lina Sand, *Correspondance entre George Sand et Gustave Flaubert*, p. 94.
5. Ibid., p. 93.
6. George Sand, *Pourquoi les femmes à l'Académie*, p. 12.
7. George Sand, *Souvenirs et idées*, p. 126.
8. George Sand, *Correspondance*, vol. v, p. 277.
9. Georges Lubin, *Œuvres autobiographiques*, vol. ii, p. 632.
10. George Sand, *Correspondance*, vol. v, p. 299.
11. Juliette Adam, *Mes sentiments et nos idées*, pp. 463–4.
12. Lina Sand, *Correspondance entre George Sand et Gustave Flaubert*, p. 224.
13. George Sand, in *Revue des Deux Mondes*, March 1871.
14. George Sand, *Correspondance*, vol. vi, p. 74.
15. Lina Sand, *Correspondance entre George Sand et Gustave Flaubert*, pp. 275–6.
16. Ibid., pp. 279–80.
17. George Sand, in *Le Temps*, October 1871.
18. Lina Sand, *Correspondance entre George Sand et Gustave Flaubert*, p. 277.

20 *Still loving, still loved*

1. Lina Sand, *Correpsondance entre George Sand et Gustave Flaubert*, p. 27.
2. A. Maurois, *Lélia*, p. 503.
3. Georges Lubin, *Œuvres autobiographiques*, vol. ii, p. 632.
4. Lina Sand, *Correspondance entre George Sand et Gustave Flaubert*, p. 72.
5. F. Letessier, *Correspondance inédite de George Sand avec le docteur Darchy*, pp. 533–4.
6. Ibid., p. 550.
7. A. Maurois, *Lélia*, p. 519.
8. Ibid., p. 522.
9. Victor Hugo, *Correspondance*, vol. iv, p. 22.
10. A. Maurois, *Lélia*, p. 523.
11. George Sand, *Correspondance*, vol. vi, pp. 403–4.
12. W. Karénine, *George Sand*, vol. iv, pp. 614–15.
13. H. Harrisse, *Derniers Moments et obsèques de George Sand*, p. 14.
14. Ibid., p. 14.
15. Victor Hugo, *Actes et paroles depuis l'exil*, p. 242.
16. G. Gailly, *Lettres inédites à Tourgueneff*, p. 104.
17. Ibid., p. 105.

Sources

ADAM, A., *Le Secret de l'aventure vénitienne*, Paris 1938.

ADAM, JULIETTE LAMBER, *Mes Premières Armes littéraires et politiques*, Paris 1904; *Mes Sentiments et nos idées*, Paris 1905.

AMIC, HENRI, *George Sand, Mes souvenirs*, Paris 1893; *Renée, Une Préface à George Sand*, Paris 1879.

BARBIERA, R., *Il Dramma Alfredo de Musset et Giorgio Sand*, Milan 1923.

BARINE, ARVÈDE, *Alfred de Musset*, Paris 1893.

BLANC, LOUIS, *Histoire de dix ans: 1830–1840*, 5 vols., Paris 1841.

BALZAC, HONORÉ, *Lettres à l'étrangère*, 4 vols, Paris 1899–1950; *Béatrix*, Introduction by Maurice Regard, Paris 1962.

BERTAUT, JULES, *Une Amitié romanesque – Lettres inédites de George Sand et de François Rollinat*, Paris 1921.

BOUTERON, MARCEL, *Muses Romantiques*, Paris 1934.

BRIQUET, JEAN, *Agricol Perdiguier, Correspondance inédite avec George Sand et ses amis*, Paris 1966.

CARRÈRE, CASIMIR, *George Sand amoureuse*, Paris–Genève 1967.

CELLIER, LÉON, *George Sand et Victor Hugo*, Paris 1962; *Hommage à George Sand*, Paris 1969.

COLET, LOUSIE, *Lui*, Paris 1860.

CONARD, L., *Gustave Flaubert, Correspondance*, vol. vii, Paris 1926–33.

CONARD, T., *Gustave Flaubert, Œuvres de jeunesse inédites*, vol. iii, Paris 1910.

CORDROC'H, MARIE, *Repertoire des Lettres publiées de George Sand*, Paris 1962.

DÉCORI, F., *Correspondance de George Sand et d'Alfred de Musset*, Bruxelles 1904.

DERRÉ, J. R., *Lamennais*, Paris 1962.

DEXTER, W., *The Letters of Charles Dickens*, vol. ii, London 1938.

DOLLÉANS, E., *Féminisme et le Mouvement Ouvrier*, Paris 1951.

Sources

DOUMIC, R., *George Sand sa vie et ses œuvres*, Paris 1909.

DUSSAULT, L., *George Sand, Etude d'une éducation*, Montréal 1970.

EVANS, D. O., *Le Socialisme romantique: Pierre Leroux et ses contemporains*, Paris 1948.

EVRARD, L., *George Sand et Alfred de Musset, Correspondance, Journal intime etc.*, Monaco 1956.

FAHMY, DORRYA, *George Sand Auteur Dramatique*, Paris 1935.

FLAUBERT, GUSTAVE, *Correspondance*, vol. vii, Paris 1925–33.

GAILLY, G., *Gustave Flaubert, Lettres inédites à Tourgueneff*, Monaco 1946.

GENLIS, MME DE, *Les Battuécas*, 2 vols., Paris 1817.

GODEAU, M., *Le Voyage à Majorque*, Paris 1959.

GONCOURT, E. & J., *Journal*, 2 vols., Paris, 1935–36.

GUILLEMIN, H., *La Liaison Musset–Sand*, Paris 1972.

HANOTAUX, G., *Lettres de Prosper Mérimée à la Comtesse de Montijo*, 2 vols., Paris 1930.

HARRISSE, HENRY, *Derniers Moments et obsèques de George Sand*, Paris 1904.

HEMMINGS, F. W. J., *Culture and Society in France 1848–1898*, London 1971.

HOUSSAYE, ARSÈNE, *Les Confessions*, 6 vols, Paris 1885.

HUGO, VICTOR, *Correspondance*, 4 vols, Paris 1947–1952; *Actes et paroles depuis l'exil*, 3 vols., Paris 1940.

JUDEN, B. & RICHTER, J., 'Macready et George Sand', *La Revue de Lettres Modernes*, Nos. 74–5, Paris 1962–63.

KARÉNINE, W., *George Sand sa vie et ses œuvres*, 4 vols, Paris 1899.

KARLOWICZ, M., *Souvenirs inédits de Frédéric Chopin*, Paris and Leipzig 1904.

KENYON, F. G., *The Letters of Elizabeth Barrett Browning*, 2 vols., London 1897.

KERBY, W. M., *The Educational Ideas and Activities of Mme la Comtesse de Genlis*, Paris 1926.

LAPAIRE, H. & ROZ, F., *La Bonne Dame de Nohant*, Paris 1898.

LEHMAN, H., *Une Correspondance romantique: Mme d'Agoult et Liszt*, Paris 1947.

LETESSIER, F., *Correspondance inédite de George Sand avec le docteur Pierre Paul Darchy*, Bulletin de l'Association Guillaume Budé No. 4, Paris 1961.

LOFTS, N., & WEINER, M., *Eternal France, A History of France 1789–1944*, London 1969.

Sources

LUBIN, GEORGES, *Correspondance de George Sand*, 10 vols, Paris 1964–72; *Œuvres autobiographiques de George Sand*, 2 vols., Paris 1970. *George Sand en Berry*, Paris 1967; *George Sand en Brenne*, Paris 1967.

LOVENJOUL, DE SPOELBERCH DE, *La véritable histoire de 'Elle et Lui'*, *Notes et documents*, Paris 1897; *Mérimée*, Paris 1909; *Les Lundis d'un chercheur*, Paris 1894.

MAGON BARBAROUX, A., *Michel de Bourges*, Marseilles 1897.

MAILLOUX, A., *Une fille d'Alfred de Musset et de George Sand*, Paris 1903.

MARIÉTON, PAUL, *Une Histoire d'amour*, Paris 1903.

MARIX–SPIRE, THÉRÈSE, *Lettres inédites de George Sand et de Pauline Viardot*, Paris 1959; *Les Romantiques et la musique: Le cas George Sand*, Paris 1954.

MAUPASSANT, G., *Lettres de Gustave Flaubert à George Sand*, Paris 1889.

MAUROIS, ANDRÉ, *Lélia ou la vie de George Sand*, Paris 1953.

MAUROIS, SIMONE–ANDRÉ, *George Sand–Marie Dorval, Correspondance inédite*, Paris 1953.

MUSSET, ALFRED, *La Confession d'un enfant du siècle*, Paris 1947.

MUSSET, PAUL, *Lui et Elle*, Paris 1860.

NIECKS, F., *Frederick Chopin as a Man and Musician*, 2 vols, London and New York 1888.

OLLIVIER, D., *Correspondance de Liszt et de la Comtesse d'Agoult*, 2 vols., Paris 1933–34; *Mémoires*, Paris 1927.

PAILLERON, M. L., *François Buloz et ses amis*, 4 vols., Paris 1919–24: vol. i, *La Vie litteraire sous Louis Philippe*; vol. ii, *Le Revue des Deux Mondes*; vol. iii, *Les derniers romantiques*; vol. iv, *Les Ecrivains du Second Empire*; *L'Esprit chez les Romantiques, La Vie parisienne à l'Epoque romantique*, Paris 1931; *George Sand, Histoire de sa vie*, 2 vols., Paris 1938; *George Sand et les hommes de '48*, Paris 1953.

PICTET, ADOPOHE, *Une Course à Chamonix*, Paris 1838.

PLAUCHUT, E., *Autour de Nohant*, Paris 1897; *Lettres de Barbès à George Sand*, Paris 1897.

POLI, ANNAROSA, *L'Italie dans la vie et dans l'œuvre de George Sand*, Paris 1960.

POMMIER, J., *George Sand et le rêve monastique*, Paris 1966; *Autour du Drame de Venise*, Paris 1958.

REGARD, M., *Gustave Planche, l'Adversaire des romantiques*, Paris 1955; *Gustave Planche, Correspondance*, Paris 1955; *Sainte-Beuve*, Paris 1960.

Sources

ROCHEBLAVE, S., *George Sand, Lettres à Alfred de Musset et à Sainte-Beuve*, Paris 1897; *George Sand et sa fille, d'après leur correspondance inédite*, Paris 1905.

ROUGET, M. J., *Sand Socialiste*, Paris 1931.

ROYA, M., see Toesca.

SALOMON, P., *George Sand*, Paris 1953.

SAND, AURORE LAUTH, *Le Roman d'Aurore Dudevant et d'Aurélien de Sèze*, Paris 1928; *Le Berry de George Sand*, Paris 1927.

SAND, GEORGE, *Œuvres complètes*, Paris 1873; *Correspondance*, 6 vols., Paris 1882–92; *Histoire de ma vie*, 4 vols., Paris 1902–04; *Théâtre*, 3 vols., Paris 1860; *Théâtre complet*, 3 vols., Paris 1879; *Lettres à Marcia*, Paris 1869; *Questions d'Art et de littérature*, Paris 1878; *Questions politiques et sociales*, Paris 1879; *Lettres d'un voyageur*, Paris 1857; *Nouvelles Lettres d'un voyageur*, Paris 1877; *Journal d'un voyageur pendant la guerre*, Paris 1871; *Pourquoi les Femmes à l'Académie*, Paris 1863; *Souvenirs et idées*, Paris 1904; *Impressions et souvenirs*, Paris 1873; *Lettres au Peuple*, Paris 1848; *Journal intime*, Paris 1926; *Hiver à Majorque*, Paris 1855; *Mauprat*, Preface by Claude Sicard, Paris 1969; *Lélia, Texte établie, présenté et annoté par Pierre Reboult*, Paris 1960; *Les Femmes de Shakespeare*, Paris 1860.

SAND, LINA, *Correspondance entre George Sand et Gustave Flaubert*, Paris 1904.

SÉGU, FRÉDÉRIC, *Un Romantique républicain: H. de Latouche*, Paris 1931.

SELLARDS, JOHN, *Dans le Sillage de Charles Didier*, Paris 1933.

SILVER, MABEL, *Jules Sandeau*, Paris 1936.

SMEETS-SAND, GEORGE & CHRISTINE, *George Sand à Gargilesse*, Paris 1967.

SÖDEGARD, O., *Les Lettres de George Sand à Sainte-Beuve*, Paris 1964.

STERN, DANIEL (Comtesse d'Agoult), *Mémoires*, Paris 1927.

SYDOW, B. E., *Correspondance de Frédéric Chopin*, 3 vols, Paris 1953–60.

THOMAS, EDITH, *Pauline Roland*, Paris 1956; *George Sand*, Paris 1959.

TOESCA, M. (ROYA), *Le Plus Grand Amour de George Sand*, Paris 1965.

VIENS, C. P., *George Sand and Gustave Planche*, Unpublished Correspondence, Providence, Rhode Island, 1941.

VIGNY, ALFRED, *Journal d'un Poète*, London 1928.

VINCENT, L., *George Sand et le Berry*, 2 vols, Paris 1919.

WRIGHT, G., *France in Modern Times*, London 1962.

Index

Index